ROYAL HISTORICAL SOCIETY

GUIDES AND HANDBOOKS

No. 15

MEDIEVAL LIBRARIES OF GREAT BRITAIN

A LIST OF SURVIVING BOOKS

*

SUPPLEMENT TO THE SECOND EDITION

ROYAL HISTORICAL SOCIETY

GUIDES AND HANDBOOKS
ISSN 0080–4398

MAIN SERIES

1. *Guide to English commercial statistics 1696–1782*. By G. N. Clark and Barbara M. Franks. 1938.
2. *Handbook of British chronology*. Edited by F. M. Powicke, Charles Johnson and W. J. Harte. 1939. 2nd edition, edited by F. M. Powicke and E. B. Fryde, 1961. 3rd edition, edited by E. B. Fryde, D. E. Greenway, S. Porter and I. Roy, 1986.
3. *Medieval libraries of Great Britain. A list of surviving books*. Edited by N. R. Ker. 1941. 2nd edition, 1964.
4. *Handbook of dates for students of English history*. Edited by C. R. Cheney. 1945. Reprinted, 1982.
5. *Guide to the national and provincial directories of England and Wales, excluding London, published before 1856*. By Jane E. Norton. 1950.
6. *Handbook of oriental history*. Edited by C. H. Philips. 1951.
7. *Texts and Calendars. An analytical guide to serial publications*. By E. L. C. Mullins. 1958. Reprinted (with corrections), 1978.
8. *Anglo-Saxon Charters. An annotated list and bibliography*. By P. H. Sawyer. 1968.
9. *A Centenary Guide to the publications of the Royal Historical Society 1868–1968 and of the former Camden Society 1838–1897*. By Alexander Taylor Milne. 1968.
10. *Guide to the local administrative units of England*. Volume I. *Southern England*. By Frederic A. Youngs, Jr. 1979. 2nd edition, 1981.
11. *Guide to bishops' registers of England and Wales. A survey from the middle ages to the abolition of episcopacy in 1646*. By David M. Smith. 1981.
12. *Texts and Calendars II. An analytical guide to serial publications 1957–1982*. By E. L. C. Mullins. 1983.
13. *Handbook of Medieval Exchange*. By Peter Spufford, with the assistance of Wendy Wilkinson and Sarah Tolley. 1986.
14. *Scottish Texts and Calendars. An analytical guide to serial publications*. By David and Wendy Stevenson. 1987.

SUPPLEMENTARY SERIES

1. *A Guide to the papers of British Cabinet Ministers, 1900–1951*. Compiled by Cameron Hazlehurst and Christine Woodland. 1974.
2. *A Guide to the reports of the U.S. Strategic Bombing Survey*. I *Europe*. II *The Pacific*. Edited by Gordon Daniels. 1981.

MEDIEVAL LIBRARIES
OF GREAT BRITAIN
A LIST OF SURVIVING BOOKS

EDITED BY
N. R. KER

SUPPLEMENT
TO THE SECOND EDITION

EDITED BY
ANDREW G. WATSON

LONDON
OFFICES OF THE ROYAL HISTORICAL SOCIETY
UNIVERSITY COLLEGE LONDON, GOWER STREET
LONDON WC1E 6BT
1987

© Royal Historical Society 1987

First published 1987

Distributed for the Royal Historical Society
by Boydell & Brewer Ltd
PO Box 9   Woodbridge   Suffolk IP12 3DF
and Wolfeboro   New Hampshire 03894-2069   USA

ISBN 0 86193 114 9

British Library Cataloguing in Publication Data

Medieval libraries of Great Britain: a list
of surviving books.—(Royal Historical
Society guides and handbooks; no. 15).
Supplement to the second edition
1. Manuscripts—Catalogs
2. Incunabula—Catalogs
I. Ker, N.R.   II. Watson, Andrew G.
III. Royal Historical Society   IV. Series
011′.31   Z240

ISBN 0-86193-114-9

Printed in Great Britain by St Edmundsbury Press
Bury St Edmunds, Suffolk

CONTENTS

PREFACE

Neil Ker began work on this supplement to *Medieval Libraries of Great Britain* in April 1974 and continued intermittently while working on many other tasks, notably the second and third volumes of his *Medieval Manuscripts in British Libraries*. When he died as the result of an accident in 1982 the typescript addenda and corrigenda were on his desk and a text would probably have been ready for the printer within a few months. It is in some ways regrettable that various commitments, including others that he acquired as Ker's literary executor, have kept the present editor from completing the text before now, but in one respect the delay has been beneficial: considerable numbers of manuscripts have come to light or have changed hands since 1982, and although the certainty that these processes will continue could be used as an absurd argument for infinitely delaying completion, it is gratifying that many books can be recorded here which would otherwise have had to wait for listing in a far distant future.

As Ker noted in the Introduction to the second edition of *Medieval Libraries of Great Britain* some 930 manuscripts and printed books were recorded there in addition to those listed in the 1941 edition. (Some of these were not, however, newly 'discovered' or assigned books but were the contents of great medieval collections still *in situ* which had been excluded from the first edition – the cathedrals of Durham, Hereford, Lincoln, Salisbury and Worcester, and Eton and Winchester Colleges.) The present supplement adds, or occasionally reassigns, 451 manuscripts and 82 printed books, the largest single group being one of 34 manuscripts owned by the Cambridge friars, the outcome of Ker's researches in the Vatican Library in the 1970s. A few of the manuscripts and books which have been added were completely unknown, mostly through having been in private hands for generations and never having passed through a sale room. The most conspicuous example is probably the Winchester Anthology, now British Library, MS Add. 60577. A few others are books which have reappeared after having been lost to sight for many years. A good example is the twelfth-century Bede from Kirkham recorded in 1964 as having been sold in 1921 but not subsequently traced. It is now in private hands in California. On the negative side, some books have disappeared from view, probably to reappear in due course; worse, some have been destroyed and are now extant only as detached leaves. Books that have vanished, at least at the moment of writing, include a Crowland Bible formerly owned by Bristol Baptist College, a printed Durandus from Fountains formerly owned by Sir John Ingilby and a twelfth-century Cassiodorus from Guisborough formerly in the Chester Beatty Library in Dublin. Destroyed books include a Shere Church Missal later at Helmingham Hall and a Whitby Abbey Psalter, once the property of Lt.-Col. W. E. Moss. A St Augustine's Abbey Canterbury fragment formerly at Elmstone Rectory has eluded discovery and may have been inadvertently destroyed.

The vast majority of additions to the 1964 lists is the result of the vigilance of scholars and librarians who have recognized and reported evidence of provenance, and also of concentrated study devoted to individual monastic houses and scriptoria. Dr R. M. Thomson's work on Bury St Edmunds, St Albans, Malmesbury and Lincoln Cathedral,[1] Mr A. J. Piper's researches on Durham Cathedral Priory manuscripts,[2] Mrs Tessa Webber's work on Salisbury Cathedral[3] and Professor James Carley's on Glastonbury and Wells[4] have been particularly productive. If it is true that their work would have been much more difficult without the second edition of *Medieval Libraries of Great Britain* it is equally true that this Supplement would have been infinitely poorer without their contributions.

It is impossible to emphasize too strongly that except in one respect this Supplement cannot be used without reference to the 1964 edition. It is true that addenda in the Supplement are self-contained and that once the principles of entry and the use of the *sigla* are understood these new entries can be readily understood, but little or no sense will be made of corrigenda without reference to the 1964 edition. The exception is Durham, the longest single section in the main part of *Medieval Libraries*, including its cell, Durham College, Oxford: apart from the heading (which has not been repeated) this has been entirely revised by Mr Piper, working from the manuscripts and other sources, and it entirely supersedes the 1964 lists. This new Durham section has been re-indexed and the 'Donors, Scribes and other Persons' section on pp. 84–100 has also been completely revised by Mr Piper. Where it seems appropriate, sections of the Supplement are preceded by an explanation of their scope and arrangement.

In one respect users of both the 1964 edition and of the Supplement should be aware that they may have to go behind the printed texts, as it were, and consult the record cards on which these are based. It was never the intention of the original editors of *Medieval Libraries* that it should be self-contained: the first edition was indeed more elaborate than had been envisaged and although the *sigla* devised by Ker convey a great deal of information it was always intended that users should go from *Medieval Libraries* to the catalogues of the collections concerned. This intention becomes impossible, of course, when a manuscript is in a collection like the Cottonian or Harleian, the catalogues of which are almost completely uninformative about provenance and often misleading about dates. The editor of this Supplement has often been tempted—and in some places has succumbed to the temptation—to provide if not a footnote summary of the evidence for provenance at least a reference to a publication where that can be found. Users who want to know the reasons for a decision to

---

[1] R. M. Thomson, 'The library of Bury St Edmunds Abbey in the eleventh and twelfth centuries', *Speculum*, xlvii (1972), 617–45; *Manuscripts from St Albans Abbey 1066–1235*, 2 vols. (Woodbridge, 1982); various papers, with additional material in a single volume, *William of Malmesbury* (Woodbridge, 1987); and his forthcoming catalogue of Lincoln Cathedral manuscripts.

[2] A. J. Piper, 'The Libraries of the Monks of Durham', *Medieval Scribes, Manuscripts & Libraries: Essays Presented to N. R. Ker*, ed. M. B. Parkes and A. G. Watson (1978), pp. 213–49.

[3] In a forthcoming Oxford doctoral thesis.

[4] See under **GLASTONBURY** below, also his forthcoming series of studies of John Leland.

include or exclude a book or to assign it to an institution should therefore, if they can, consult the record cards, kept in the Department of Western Manuscripts of the Bodleian Library and accessible to readers.[1] Many of the cards bear all the facts necessary for making an assessment of the evidence, for on them one can see the doubts, hesitations and changes of mind from which the editors suffered and one can weigh the pros and cons.

A very large proportion of the books listed in *Medieval Libraries* can be ascribed to an institution on the basis of unambiguous internal evidence or, less often, on equally good external evidence. A single question mark against an entry covers, however, several degrees of doubt: in this case consultation of the cards can be useful. The inclusion of a book as *Rejected* is usually for the purpose of correcting a published statement or a traditional ascription, less often to anticipate a false ascription: again, the reason may be found on the card. To Ker and his collaborators there was, however, another category of imperfectly attested books of which no trace appears in the published lists or among the filed cards—books that were omitted without comment although a temporary card had been written and inclusion had in some cases been a possibility. Since some of these cards were reused or discarded one can never know how many there were and the construction of a partial list would not be useful. A few examples may indicate what kinds of evidence earned consideration, only to lead to ultimate omission.

(1) Oxford, Corpus Christi College, 58, a Statius of s.xii/xiii, has an *ex libris* which is admirable as far as it goes—'Iste liber est conuentus Iernemute', but as there were Dominican, Franciscan and Carmelite convents in Yarmouth, from none of which any books have been identified for comparison, this cannot qualify for entry unless one creates a new category for towns without a precise institution. The same lack of precision disqualifies printed books at Merton College, Oxford, and in Cambridge University Library, from Bristol and Newcastle-upon-Tyne respectively.

(2) Cambridge, Trinity College, B.15.31 (366), a Thomas de Chabham of s.xv, has an inscription 'Liber Giraldi Menevensis Archidiaconi . . . habita ex mutuo de Ricardo Moris Vicario omnium sanctorum civitatis Herefordien. Anno 1541.' Perhaps it did come from All Saints Hereford, but the evidence is not good enough and the book is omitted. Likewise Durham, University Library, Bamburgh Sel.24 and Glasgow University, Hunterian 7 (S.1.7) have eighteenth-century inscriptions which assign them to Fountains and Bury St Edmunds respectively. But the value of these is uncertain and the books are omitted.[2]

(3) London, British Library, Sloane 1619, Vita Alexandri Magni, etc., s.xiii, has an inscription recording that 'audita sunt prima tonitrua in domo sancti oswaldi' in 1271. The evidence for or against its inclusion as a St Oswald's, Gloucester, book is too weak to earn it a place.

(4) London, British Library, Cotton Domitian ii, fos. 2–7 contains a chronicle of which John Somer may be the author (*BRUO*). It bears the inscription 'Cronica quodam brevis' and, in another hand, 'Fratris Johannis

---

[1] It would be appreciated if additions and corrections to the 1964 edition and to this Supplement were sent to the Keeper of Western Manuscripts.

[2] Nevertheless, the 1964 edition includes Cambridge, University Library, Add. 2823 under the York Austin Friars, apparently solely on the basis of an inscription dated 1781.

Somour ordinis sancti Francisci de conuentu ville Briggewatter' but whatever the exact meaning of the latter there can be no certainty that the book was ever at Bridgwater.

There are also many examples of books which can be connected with Oxford or Cambridge through having been deposited in one of the loan chests in these universities. Users of *Medieval Libraries* may need to be reminded that although the possession of a book by a member of a religious order entitles that book to be listed under the religious house to which the man belonged, personal ownership of books by members of universities or secular colleges does not qualify them for admission: see Revised Preface to the First Edition, on p. viii of the 1964 edition, which deals with the scope of *Medieval Libraries* in general.

If Neil Ker found himself unable to recollect the names of all those who helped him with the 1964 edition, the editor of this Supplement finds himself even more at a loss, especially for the names of those who helped Ker between 1974 and 1982. Certain long-standing debts of gratitude are at once recognizable, however, the greatest probably being to Dr Ian Doyle, who contributed addenda, corrigenda and comments to Ker from the 1940s onwards and whose advice has been of the greatest possible help to the present editor. Mr Alan Piper's labours (too weak a word) with the revised Durham section make his contribution stand out from all others. Dr Christopher de Hamel, Head of the Western Manuscripts Department at Sotheby's, helped Ker and has helped the present editor even more with tracing the movement of books through the sale rooms (without his assistance a hopeless task) and has also contributed in other ways from his own wide knowledge of manuscripts. Dr David Howlett, Editor of the *Dictionary of Medieval Latin from British Sources*, very kindly checked the Glossary and made a number of improvements. Dr Andrew Wathey contributed references to many additional inventories and lists, especially in the Public Records, and was responsible for the inclusion of several liturgical and music manuscripts. Mr Daniel Huws, Keeper of Manuscripts and Records at the National Library of Wales, Mr Ian Cunningham and Miss Elspeth Yeo of the National Library of Scotland, Miss Janet Backhouse, Mr Michael Borrie and Mrs Ann Payne of the Department of Manuscripts of the British Library, Mr A. E. B. Owen and Miss Jayne Ringrose of the Department of Manuscripts of Cambridge University Library, Mr David McKitterick then also of that Library, and Dr Albinia de la Mare and Dr Bruce Barker-Benfield of the Department of Western Manuscripts of the Bodleian Library have all, because of the importance of the collections in which they work, been called on for help many times and their generous response is acknowledged with gratitude. Too many other curators, librarians and private owners have provided information about books in their care to be individually thanked but users will readily guess at their identity from the locations of the books. Mr James Lawson, Librarian of Shrewsbury School, must, however, be singled out for mention, for his interest and vigilance led to the addition of several items. All the scholars mentioned on p. viii above were generous with their help, not only in their own areas but over the whole range of the subject. To all these and to the many others unnamed who have helped Neil Ker and himself, the editor expresses his warmest thanks.

Special thanks are due to Dr Diana Greenway, whose final act as one of the Royal Historical Society's Literary Directors before she retired was to subject the whole text to careful scrutiny. The result was a great improvement in presentation and the removal of errors and inconsistencies and the editor is deeply grateful. For such faults as remain he is, of course, wholly responsible.

University College London   A.G.W.
February 1987

PRINCIPAL ABBREVIATIONS
AND CONVENTIONAL SIGNS

For most of the abbreviations and signs used, see 1964 edition, pages x, xxx–xxxi. The following are additional to those used in 1964.

acol.	acolyte
adm.	admitted
als.	alias
app.	appointed
b.	born
B.L.	British Library
bp.	bishop
bs.	bookseller
cath.	cathedral
d.	deacon
frag.	fragment
inc.	incepted
lic.	licensed
Mus.	Museum
ord.	ordained
P.C.C.	Prerogative Court of Canterbury
pr.	priest
preb.	prebendary
reg(s).	register(s), registrum
subd.	subdeacon
trans.	translated
vac.	vacant
+	marks an addition to the 1964 lists, i.e. a newly identified book, an *Untraced* book now found, or a book appearing under a particular institutional heading for the first time although previously listed under another heading.
¶	(used in the Durham and Oxford, Durham College, sections only) marks a corrected entry.
***	for the use of this symbol, analogous to * and ** in the 1964 edition, see below, pp. 75–6.
§	for the use of this symbol, in the Glossary only, see below, p. 115.

ABBREVIATED TITLES

(Here and throughout, the absence of a place of publication before the date indicates that publication was in London. For a further explanation of *TC* and *TCS* see p. 75 below.)

AC	J. & J. A. Venn, *Alumni Cantabrigienses*, pt. 1, 4 vols. (Cambridge, 1922–7)
ASE	*Anglo-Saxon England*
BLJ	*The British Library Journal*
Blomefield	F. Blomefield & C. Parkin, *An Essay towards a Topographical History of the County of Norfolk*, 10 vols. (1805–10)
BLR	*The Bodleian Library Record*
BRUC	A. B. Emden, *A Biographical Register of the University of Cambridge to 1500* (Cambridge, 1963)
BRUO	A. B. Emden, *A Biographical Register of the University of Oxford to A.D. 1500*, 3 vols. (Oxford, 1957–9)
Chambers	D. S. Chambers, *Faculty Office Registers 1534–1549* (Oxford, 1966)
C. Pap. L.	*Calendar of Entries in the Papal Registers Relating to Great Britain and Ireland: Papal Letters (1198–1492)*, ed. W. H. Bliss & others, 15 vols. (1892–1978)
de Hamel	C. de Hamel, *Glossed Books of the Bible and the Origins of the Paris Booktrade* (Woodbridge, 1984)
DK Rep.8	*Eighth Report of the Deputy Keeper of the Public Records* (1847), Appendix II
EHR	*The English Historical Review*
Emden, *Dominicans*	A. B. Emden, *A Survey of Dominicans in England based on the Ordination Lists in Episcopal Registers, 1268–1538* (Dissertationes Historicae xviii, Rome, 1967)
Fasti I	J. le Neve, *Fasti Ecclesiae Anglicanae 1066–1300* (Institute of Historical Research, London) i *St Paul's, London*. Compiled by D. E. Greenway (1968) ii *Monastic Cathedrals*. Compiled by D. E. Greenway (1971) iii *Lincoln Diocese*. Compiled by D. E. Greenway (1977)

Fasti II	J. le Neve, *Fasti Ecclesiae Anglicanae 1300–1541* (Institute of Historical Research, London) i *Lincoln Diocese.* Compiled by H. P. F. King (1962) iii *Salisbury Diocese.* Compiled by J. M. Horn (1962) v *St Paul's London.* Compiled by J. M. Horn (1963)
James, *Anc. Libs.*	M. R. James, *The Ancient Libraries of Canterbury and Dover* (Cambridge, 1903)
Ker, *Books, Collectors and Libraries*	N. R. Ker, *Books, Collectors and Libraries: Studies in the Medieval Heritage*, ed. A. G. Watson (1985)
Ker, *Cat. Anglo-Saxon MSS*	N. R. Ker, *A Catalogue of Manuscripts Containing Anglo-Saxon* (Oxford, 1957)
Ker, *Essays*	*Medieval Scribes, Manuscripts and Libraries: Essays Presented to N. R. Ker*, ed. M. B. Parkes & A. G. Watson (1978)
LP	*Letters and Papers, Foreign and Domestic, of the Reign of Henry VIII*, ed. J. S. Brewer and others, 21 vols. (1862–1910)
MMBL	N. R. Ker, *Medieval Manuscripts in British Libraries* (Oxford, 1969–)
Moorman	J. R. H. Moorman, *The Grey Friars in Cambridge* (Cambridge, 1952)
Roth, 'Sources'	F. Roth, 'Sources for a history of the English Austin Friars', *Augustiniana*, viii (1958), 1*–108*, ix (1959), 109*–294*, x (1960), 295*–464*, xi (1961), 465*–572*
Saunders	H. W. Saunders, *An Introduction to the Obedientiary and Manor Rolls of Norwich Cathedral Priory* (Norwich, 1930)
STC	*A Short-Title Catalogue of Books Printed in England, Scotland, & Ireland . . . 1475–1640 first compiled by A. W. Pollard and G. R. Redgrave*, 2nd edn., 2 vols. (1986, 1976)
TC 14.8	*Reg. Johannis de Trillek* (Canterbury and York Soc., 1912)
TC 14.26	*Reg. Thome Myllyng* (Canterbury and York Soc., 1920)
TC 14.27	*Reg. Ricardi Mayew* (Canterbury and York Soc., 1921)
TC 14.28	*Reg. Caroli Bothe* (Canterbury and York Soc., 1921)
TC 14.38	*Reg. Simonis de Sudbiria*, ii (Canterbury and York Soc., 1938)
TC 14.42	*The Reg. of Henry Chichele*, ii (Canterbury and York Soc., 1937)
TC 14.44	*Reg. Henrici Woodlock*, ii (Canterbury and York Soc., 1941)
TC 14.47	*The Reg. of Henry Chichele*, iv (Canterbury and York Soc., 1947)

TC 69.39	*The Reg. of Walter Reynolds* (Worcestershire Historical Soc., 1927)
TC 69.40	*The Reg. of Thomas de Cobham* (Worcestershire Historical Soc., 1930)
TCBS	*Transactions of the Cambridge Bibliographical Soc.*
TCS 14.54	*Reg. Thome Bourgchier* (Canterbury and York Soc., 1957)
TCS 14.55	*The Regs. of Roger Martival*, i (Canterbury and York Soc., 1959)
TCS 14.60	*The Reg. of Edmund Lacy*, i (Canterbury and York Soc., 1963)
TCS 14.62	*The Reg. of Edmund Lacy*, iii (Canterbury and York Soc., 1967)
TCS 14.63	*The Reg. of Edmund Lacy*, iv (Canterbury and York Soc., 1971)
TCS 14.66	*The Reg. of Edmund Lacy*, v (Canterbury and York Soc., 1972)
TCS 14.69	*The Reg. of Thomas Rotherham*, i (Canterbury and York Soc., 1976)
TCS 54.41	*The Early Communar and Pitancer Rolls of Norwich Cathedral Priory* (Norfolk Record Soc., 1972)
TCS 62.78	*Bishop Geoffrey Blythe's Visitations* (Staffordshire Record Soc., 1973)
TCS 69.47	*A Calendar of the Reg. of Wolstan de Bransford* (Worcestershire Historical Soc., 1966)
TCS 69.50	*A Calendar of the Register of Henry Wakefield* (Worcestershire Historical Soc., 1972)
VCH	*The Victoria History of the Counties of England*

LIST OF SURVIVING BOOKS

ABERDEEN. *King's College.*
+ Edinburgh, N.L., Adv. 18.3.10   *s*Eutropius, etc. A.D. 1481.[1]
                     18.3.11   *For* Historia trium regum etc. *read*
                              Suetonius.

ABINGDON, Berkshire.   *Ben. abbey of B.V.M.*
List of books, s.xvi[1], in Rome, Vatican, Reg. lat. 2099, fo. 306[r–v].
+ Cambridge, Corpus Christi Coll., 92.   Florentius Wigorn. s.xii ex–xiv.[2]
+ Charlecote Park, Sir E. Cameron-Fairfax-Lucy (pr. bk). *i*Aristophanes
     (in Greek). Basel, A.D. 1532.
London, B.L., Add. 42555. *For* Apocalypsis glo. *read* Apocalypsis.
+   Cotton Titus D.xx.   *c*Julianus of Toledo, Prognosticon.
                             s.xii[1].[3]   ?
+ Shrewsbury, Shrewsbury School. F.vi.5 (pr. bk).   *e*Sallustius. Brescia,
     A.D. 1495.

AMESBURY, Wiltshire.   *Priory (cell of Fontevrault) and later abbey of
     B.V.M. and St Meilor, of Ben. nuns.*
Windsor Castle. *Add* Jackson Collection, 3. *Cancel query.*
+ London, Dr C. F. R. de Hamel. */*Breviarium (4 fos.). s.xiv.

ANGLESEY, Cambridgeshire.   *Aug. priory of B.V.M. and St Nicholas.*
Heading: *after* monks *add* and a few kept 'in communi', *and for* Ancient Deeds
A.14502 *read* E.40/14502. *After* ii. 231 *add* and *Notes and Queries*, i (1849), 21.

ARBROATH, Angus.   *Ben. (originally Tironensian) abbey of St Thomas
     the Martyr.*
Wolfenbüttel.   *For* Ducal Libr. *read* Herzog August Bibl.
                 Helmst. 499. *Alter date to* s.xiii in. *Add pressmark* [b].

ARBUTHNOTT, Kincardineshire.   *Collegiate church of St Tiernan.*
Heading: the printed book, recorded by Durkan and Ross as untraced, is in the
Reed Collection in Dunedin Public Library.
Paisley.   *For* Free Library and Museum *read* Museum and Art Gallery.

---

[1] Adv. 18.3.10 and Adv. 18.3.11 formed one volume.
[2] Later at **PETERBOROUGH** (1964 edn.) but written at Abingdon after 1174.
See M. Brett in *The Writing of History in the Middle Ages: Essays Presented to
Richard William Southern*, ed. R. H. C. Davis and others (Oxford, 1981), p. 108.
[3] 'Abyndonia' (s.xii) is on a preliminary leaf probably once the cover.

1

ARUNDEL, Sussex. *Collegiate church of Holy Trinity.*

Heading: *add that* books are listed in an inventory of 1505, Arundel Castle Archives, CA60, *and that* the inventory of 1517 cited in 1964 edn. is CA61.

+London, B.L., Royal 7 B.xiv. Speculum spiritualium. s.xv in. [*Cat. 1517* 114].

+*Untraced and rejected:* A. Rosenthal Ltd. (Oxford), Cat. 4 (1943), no. 994 (pr. bk). *i*J. de Voragine. Cologne A.D. 1490.[1]

ASHRIDGE, Buckinghamshire. *House of Bonshommes of B.V.M. (and of the Holy Blood).*

+London, Dulwich College, A.3.f.13 (pr. bk). *e*Decretales Gregorii IX. Paris, A.D. 1519.
Stonyhurst College, 44. *For l*Breviarium *read c*Breviarium.

AXHOLME, Lincolnshire. *Charterhouse of the Visitation of B.V.M.*

Alter footnote to read: . . . who was at Axholme at surrender, 1538, and apparently at Hinton at surrender, 1539: see p. 76 below.

AYLESFORD, Kent. *Carmelite friary.*

Heading: the extracts from the cartulary, formerly owned by Mr F. T. Allen of Ramsey, are now Cambridge, U.L., Add. 7934.

BABWELL, Suffolk. *Franciscan convent.*

+London, B.L., Add. 9830, flyleaf. *e*Alexander de Hales, Summa theologica (?).[2]

+New Haven, Yale U.L., Beinecke Mellon 37, fos. i–iii and pastedowns. *e*.[3]

BANGOR, Gwynedd. *Cathedral church of St Daniel.*

Philadelphia, Pennsylvania U.L. *Add pressmark* Lea 23. *Cancel query.*

BARDNEY, Lincolnshire. *Ben. abbey of St Peter, St Paul and St Oswald.*

Lincoln, Lincolnshire Archives Committee. *Read* Lincoln, Lincolnshire Archives Office, Monson 7/52.

BARKING, Essex. *Abbey of B.V.M. and St Ethelburga, of Ben. nuns.*

+London, Lambeth Palace, 1495.4 (pr. bk). *i*Vitas patrum (in English). Westminster, A.D. 1495.

+Nijmegen, U.L., 194, fos. 41–104. *l*Preces, etc. (in Latin and English). s.xv. ?

[1] Bears the name of William Forster, 'subprior of the College of Arundel, 1531, in the second year of his office'. No prior or subprior was, however, on the establishment of Arundel College (*VCH Sussex*, ii, 108) and although there was a submaster, the holder of that office in 1531 was Christopher Ellys (Arundel Castle MS. CA30).
[2] The *ex libris*, preceded by the title 'pars primi libri de Hales et pars secundi', is in a hand of s.xiii/xiv on a slip of parchment pasted to a modern binding leaf. Presumably the slip was in the previous binding of Add. 9830, P. de Alvernia on the Meteora of Aristotle, s.xiv.
[3] Binding leaves inside a medieval binding used as the cover of a manuscript written in 1556.

BARLINGS, Lincolnshire. *Prem. abbey of B.V.M.*

Wentworth Woodhouse MS.: now deposited in Magdalene College, Cambridge.

BARNWELL, Cambridgeshire. *Aug. priory of St Giles.*

Cambridge, U.L., Add. 6865. *Cancel query.*
+   Mm.2.9. *l*Antiphonale. s.xiii[2].
+ London, B.L., Lansdowne 431. *l*Psalterium. s.xiii[1]. ?

BASINGWERK, Clwyd. *Savigniac and (1147) Cist. abbey of B.V.M.*
+ Aberystwyth, N.L., Peniarth 356. *c*Grammatica, etc. s.xv ex.[1] ?

BATH, Somerset. *Corporation.*
+ Longleat, Marquess of Bath, 55. *e*Statuta Angliae. s.xv in.

BATTLE, Sussex. *Ben. abbey of St Martin.*

Berlin, Staatsbibl. Now Berlin, Stiftung Preussischer Kulturbesitz.
Chicago, Univ. of Chicago Libr., 254. *Add pressmark* [IN].
Hereford, Cathedral, P.v.l. *Add pressmark* [EV].
London, The Robinson Trust, Phillipps 8517: *see* San Marino below.
+ Oxford, Bodleian, Rawl. B.150 *c*Annales, etc. s.xiii.
San Marino, Huntington Libr., HM30319: formerly London, The Robinson Trust.

BEAUCHIEF (de Bello Capite), Derbyshire. *Prem. abbey of B.V.M. and St Thomas the Martyr.*

Sheffield, Central Libr. MD3500. *c*Explanatio verborum, etc. s.xvi in. ?

BEAUVALE, Nottinghamshire. *Charterhouse of Holy Trinity.*

For Cambridge, Trinity Coll. *read* Cambridge, Trinity Hall.

BEDFORD. *Franciscan convent.*
+ Cambridge, Emmanuel Coll., MSS. 4.1.14 (pr. bk). *i*Boetius, De consolatione philosophiae, etc. Lyon, not after 1489.
+ London, Mr N. J. Barker (pr. bk). *i*Albertus de Eyb. Paris, A.D. 1477.

BELVOIR, Lincolnshire. *Ben. priory of B.V.M.*

Cambridge, Trinity Coll., 317. *For* s.xiii *in read* s.xii ex.
+   U.L., Mm.2.8. *e*Hannibaldus de Hannibaldis. s.xiv.
Eton College, 48.ii. *For* ii *read* fos. 107–240 (and fos. 97–106?).

BERMONDSEY, Surrey. *Cluniac priory and (1399) abbey of St Saviour.*
+ New Haven, Yale U.L., Beinecke 426. *m*Flores historiarum. s.xiv[1]. ?
Oxford, Bodleian, Bodley 751. *For* s.xiii *in read* s.xii ex.
+   Rawl. A.371. *c*Martyrologium. s.xv med.[2] ?

---

[1] Compiled and written by Thomas Pennant, perhaps identifiable as the man of that name who was abbot of Basingwerk 1481–1522 (see p. 76 below).
[2] Cf. R. W. Pfaff, *New Liturgical Feasts in Later Medieval England* (Oxford, 1970), pp. 121–2.

3

BEVERLEY, Yorkshire. *Minster (collegiate church) of St John of Beverley.*

+ Aberystwyth, N.L., 9852c. *lc*Kalendarium. s.xv.
+ Leeds, U.L., Brotherton Collection, 16. *l*Preces, etc. s.xv.
London, B.L., Add. 61901: formerly Ripon, Mr H. L. Bradfer-Lawrence.
Manchester, John Rylands U.L., Lat. 186. *Cancel entry and list as Rejected.*
Ripon, Mr H. L. Bradfer-Lawrence: *see* London, B.L., *above.*

BODMIN, Cornwall. *Franciscan convent.*

Winchester, The Presbytery (pr. bk.). Now sold and untraced.

+ **BOSHAM,** Sussex. *Royal Free Chapel.*

H. M. Whitley, 'Visitations and inventories of the King's Free Chapel of Bosham', *Sussex Archaeological Collections* liv (1911), 77–84, Appx. 2, printed from Bp. Brantyngham's Register vol. 1 (Devon Record Office), lists 29 service books and one other, second folios given.

BOURNE, Lincolnshire. *Aug. (Arrouaisian) abbey of St Peter and St Paul.*

London, B.L., Add. 38819. *Cancel entry and add to Rejected.*
+ Oxford, Bodleian, Junius 1. Orrmulum. s.xii$^{\frac{4}{4}}$.[1]   ?

BRECON, Powys. *Ben. priory of St John the Evangelist.*

+ Oxford, Bodleian, Laud Misc. 667. Ordinale Sarisburiense. s.xv.[2]

BRECON, Powys. *Dominican convent.*

Footnote 5: *for* part of Sloane 441 *read* Sloane 441, fos. 1–61^{v}.

BRIDLINGTON, Yorkshire. *Aug. priory of B.V.M.*

Oxford, Bodleian, Fairfax 15 (= Auct. D. inf. 2. 7). *For* s.xii *read* s.xii$^{\frac{3}{4}}$.
for Ripon, Cathedral, xvii.D.2 *read* Ripon, Cathedral, 3.
                xvii.D.3 *read* Ripon, Cathedral, 4.

BRISTOL, Gloucestershire. *Dominican convent.*

+ Oxford, Bodleian, Digby 72. *i*Tabulae astronomicae, etc. s.xv.   ?

BRISTOL. *Corporation.*

+ Bristol, Bristol Record Office. *c*R. Ricart, The maire of Bristowe is kalendar. A.D. 1479.

---

[1] See M. B. Parkes, 'On the presumed date and possible origin of the manuscript of the "Orrmulum" . . .', *Five Hundred Years of Words and Sounds: a Festschrift for Eric Dobson*, ed. E. G. Stanley and D. Gray (Woodbridge, 1983), pp. 115–27. Bourne is suggested on the basis of Orm's statement that he was an Augustinian canon, and on linguistic grounds.
[2] Kalendar contains dedication of church. Previously entered as of Brecon church.

BUILDWAS, Shropshire. *Savigniac and (1147) Cist. abbey of B.V.M. and St Chad.*

+Cambridge, U.L., Ii.2.3. *e*W. Malmesburiensis. s.xii med. ?
+Edinburgh, N.L., 6121. *mb*Augustinus, etc. s.xii ex.
+London, B.L., Add. 11881. *s*Vite sanctorum. s.xii$^{\frac{3}{4}}$.[1]
          Lambeth Palace, 456. *For* fos. 1–106 *read* fos. 1–126.
                    488. *For* fos. 89–117 *read* fos. 89–126.
Footnote 8. *For* 106 *read* 126 *and for* 117 *read* 126.

BURTON-UPON-TRENT, Staffordshire. *Ben. abbey of B.V.M. and St Modwenna.*

Heading: *after* 201 *add* and by F. A. Hibbert, *The Dissolution of the Monasteries as illustrated by the Suppression of the Religious Houses of Staffordshire* (1910), pp. 281–5.

+London, B.L., C.77.d.17 (pr. bk). *e*W. Durandus. Lyon, A.D. 1506.
+Oxford, Lincoln Coll., lat. 113. *e*G. Ebroicensis. s.xiv.
Rejected: Prof. F. Wormald. Now London, B.L., Add. 57533.

BURY ST EDMUNDS, Suffolk. *Ben. abbey of St Edmund, King and Martyr.*

Heading: *Ex libris* inscriptions and pressmarks in Cambridge, Corpus Christi Coll., 404; Pembroke Coll., 18, 29; St John's Coll., 170; in London, B.L., Royal 8 B.iv, 8 F.xiv, 12 C.vi; and in Bodleian, e Mus. 9 are reproduced by R. H. Rouse in *Speculum*, xli (1966), pls. 1, 4–8, 12, 13. Cambridge, Pembroke Coll., 313 contains fragments of old covers and endleaves of MSS 5, 7, 9, 10, 17, 20, 23, 24, 25, 26, 29, 30, 39, 40, 54, 62, 63, 65, 66, 68, 75, 77, 80, 83, 84, 88, 91, 94, 95, 96, 99, 108.

Bury St Edmunds, Cathedral, 4: *see* London, Wellcome Historical Medical Libr., *below.*
          Grammar School: MS. now deposited in Bury St Edmunds, West Suffolk Record Office (E 5/9/408.7).
+   West Suffolk Record Office, A 8/1. *c*Chronica. s.xiii ex.[2] ?
+Cambridge, U.L., Add. 4406, pt. 1. *sm*Cassiodorus, In psalmos (2 fos.). s.xii. [cf. *cat.* xx].[3]
          Ff.1.27. *For* 249 *read* 253, *and footnote* 2 *for* 249 *read* 253.
          For Add. Ff.3.5 *read* Ff.3.5.
          Norton. c.18. Formerly Cambridge, Mr F. J. Norton.
+   Clare Coll., s.n. *s*Orosius (binding frags.). s.xi[2].
          Pembroke Coll., 44. *for* xii *read* xiii in.
                   47. *for* xii *read* xii$^{\frac{2}{4}}$.
                 101, fos. 1–93.[4]
+   St John's Coll., 73. *s*Evangelia. s.xi ex.

[1] One of the missing leaves at the front probably bore evidence of Buildwas provenance reported by Sir Thos. Phillipps in his catalogue of Samuel Butler's MSS., of which this was one. Buildwas provenance is, however, certain. If not by the same scribe the MS. is certainly from the same scriptorium as Oxford, Christ Church, lat.88: see A. G. Watson, *Catalogue of Dated and Datable Manuscripts c. 435–1600 in Oxford Libraries* (Oxford, 1984), ii, pl. 75.
[2] Deposited in Moyses' Hall Museum, Bury St Edmunds.
[3] The Cambridge and Columbia leaves are fragments of one volume.
[4] The Cambridge and Ipswich leaves were originally one volume, and were separated in s.xv.

Cambridge (*contd*)

+   Trinity Coll., 770, pp. 1–73. *cs*Chronicon fani S. Neoti. s.xii in.
        Mr F. J. Norton: *see* Cambridge, U.L., *above.*
+ Columbia, Missouri, Univ. of Missouri Libr., Rare-L/PA/3381.A1/F7,
        no. 14. *s*Cassiodorus, In psalmos (1 fo.). s.xii.[1]
      Dublin, Chester Beatty Libr., W.26: *see* San Marino, Huntington Libr.,
        below.
      Ipswich, Central Libr., 6 fos., 1–176.[2]
      Laon, Bibl. Mun., 238. *For l*Missale *read ls*Missale.
+ London, B.L., Cotton Julius A.i, fos. 3–43, 73. chronicon. s.xiii ex. ?
                Egerton 3776: formerly London, Dr E. G. Millar.
+   Harley 1206. *e*Bernardus Cassinensis. s.xv in. [S(?). 23].
+   4025. *e*Liber thesauri occulti, etc. s.xiv. [S.97].
+   5388 *i*Bernardus Cassinensis. s.xv.
+   5442. *i*J. de Burgo. s.xv. [P.22].
              Royal 8 C.iv. *For* 1–156 *read* 2–156 *and for* 157–210
                               read 157–211 *and add footnote* Royal 8
                               C.iv fos. (iv),1 were added when the two
                             parts were put together in s.xv.
             Lambeth Palace, 105. *Add footnote* The binding leaves, six
                               bifolia of Digestum vetus, s.xiii, are
                               kept separately as MS. 1229, nos. 1–6.
                  218. *For* 89–114 *read* 90–114 *and add to*
                               footnote 6 The flyleaves and pastedown
                             which preceded fo. 90 are kept separ-
                             ately as MS. 1229, nos. 12, 13.
            Sion College, Arc. L.40.2/L.9: *see* San Marino, Huntington
                               Libr., *below.*
      Wellcome Historical Medical Libr., 801[A]:   formerly Bury St
                               Edmunds, Cathedral, 4.
      The Robinson Trust (Helmingham 58); now London, Mr P. L.
                               Robinson.
+   Mr H. C. Pratt: formerly *Untraced.*
      Mr P. L. Robinson: formerly The Robinson Trust (Helming-
          ham 58).
Norwich, Castle Museum, 158.926.4g(4): *read* Norwich, Norfolk and
      Norwich Record Office, St Peter Hungate Museum, 158.926.4g(4).
Oswestry, Lord Harlech. Now Talsarnau, Lord Harlech.
Oxford, Bodleian, Digby 109. *Reject and add footnote* The office and
      mass for St Edmund are for secular, not monastic, use and there is
      no other evidence of Bury ownership.
+   Lat. hist. d. 4. *e*Martinus Polonus, etc. s.xiii ex–xiv
                             in. [C.59].
                    For Lat. misc. c. 26 *read* Lat. th. c.26.
+   Laud Misc. 85. J. Peccham, Collationes dominicales;
                             etc. s.xiv in. [J 13].[3] ?

---

[1] The Cambridge, U.L., Add. 4406 and Columbia leaves are fragments of one volume.

[2] The Cambridge, Pembroke Coll., 101 and Ipswich leaves were originally one volume, and were separated in s.xv.

[3] 'J.12' altered to 'J.13' top right of fo. 1. '175' in upper margin of fo. 1 shows that this is the copy listed by T. James, *Ecloga* (1600) at Pembroke Coll., Cambridge, no. 175.

Oxford (*contd*)
   Bodleian, Laud Or. 174. *Add footnote* The binding leaves, eight fos. of Priscian, s.xiii, are kept separately as MS Laud Misc. 758.
San Marino, Huntington Libr., HM31151: formerly Dublin, Chester Beatty Libr., W.26.
        HM45717: formerly London, Sion Coll., Arc. L.40.2/L.9.
Talsarnau, Lord Harlech. Formerly Oswestry, Lord Harlech.
Untraced: now London, Mr H. C. Pratt, above.
Rejected: Bury St Edmunds Cath., 3, is now Brussels, Bibl. Roy., IV.1008. *Add to rejects* Cambridge, Pembroke Coll., 265; Gonville and Caius Coll., 439 (437); Douai, Bibl. de la Ville, 171; Glasgow, Hunter 7; Hereford, Cath., 0.vi.8, fos. 1–58; London, B.L., Harley 2255, 4349; Oxford, Bodleian, Digby 109.

BYLAND, Yorkshire. *Cistercian abbey of B.V.M.*

London, B.L., Add. 62452: formerly Ripon, Mr H. L. Bradfer-Lawrence.
+   Cotton Tib. D.vi, fos. 149^v–50. De dedicatione altarum. s.xii ex.[1]
+   Cotton Vesp. E.iv, fos. 100–3, 211. Gregorius, etc. s.xii.[2]
+   Lambeth Palace, 1510, nos. 20, 21. *c*Antiphonale (1 fo.). s.xiv.
Ripon, Mr H. L. Bradfer-Lawrence: *see* London, B.L., *above.*

For **CAERLEON,** Monmouthshire, *read* **LLANTARNAM,** Gwent.

Mostyn Hall MS. Post-Dissolution, therefore omit.

CAMBRIDGE. *Franciscan convent.*

  N. R. Ker, 'Cardinal Cervini's manuscripts from the Cambridge friars', *Xenia medii aevi historiam illustrantia oblata Thomae Kaeppeli O.P.* (1978), pp. 51–71, reprinted in Ker, *Books, Collectors and Libraries,* pp. 437–58; J. P. Carley, 'John Leland and the contents of English pre-Dissolution libraries: the Cambridge friars', *TCBS* ix, pt. 1 (1986), 90–100.

+London, B.L., Add. 9831 fos. 2–12 (6 fos.). *i*N. de Lyra.[3]
Rome, Vatican, Ottob. lat. 69. *Add date* s.xiv in. *Cancel query.*
        71. *Add pressmark* [a].
        96. *Add date* s.xiii *and pressmark* [A].
       101. *For date read* s.xiii/xiv.
       611. *Add date* s.xiii.
+   1276. *i*De universalibus, etc. s.xv med.
      2088. *Add date* s.xiv med. *Cancel query.*

 [1] Two leaves, now at the end of a cartulary of Christchurch Priory, Hampshire, which are items *b* and *c* in the catalogue of Henry Savile of Banke's MSS. That MS. has not been identified but item *a* may have been a destroyed Westminster Abbey MS.: see A. G. Watson, *The Manuscripts of Henry Savile of Banke* (1969), p. 24.
 [2] Cott. Faust. B.iv fos. 180–2 and Vesp. E.iv fos. 100–3, 211 are fragments of one volume.
 [3] Add. 9831 fos. 2–12 are endleaves of a now missing MS. of N. de Lyra on Joshua, Judges, Ruth, 1–4 Kings, 1, 2 Chronicles, Ezra, Nehemiah and Esther.

CAMBRIDGE. *Dominican convent.*

N. R. Ker, 'Cardinal Cervini's manuscripts . . .'; J. P. Carley, 'John Leland . . .' (*see above*, **CAMBRIDGE**, Franciscan convent).

London, B.L., royal 10 B.vii. *Cancel query.*

+Rome, Vatican, Ottob. lat.	5.	2eJ. de Friburgo, O.P., s.xiii/xiv.
	99.	*Add date* s.xiii in–s.xiii med.
+	104.	*e*Hugo de S. Victore. s.xiii ex. ?
	159.	*For date read* s.xii/xiii. *Cancel* fos. 1–120.
+	187.	*m*T. Aquinas. s.xiii/xiv.[1]
+	208 fos. 87–324.	*m*T. Aquinas. s.xiii ex.
+	271.	*e*N. Gorran. s.xiv in.
	758.	*Add date* s.xiv ex.
	2055.	*Add date* s.xiv med *and cancel query.*
+	Vat. lat. 3056.	*i*R. Stoneham, Abstractiones Heytesbury. s.xiv/xv ?
+	7095.	*m*T. Aquinas. s.xiii/xiv.[1]

CAMBRIDGE. *Convent of Austin friars.*

N. R. Ker, 'Cardinal Cervini's manuscripts . . .'; J. P. Carley, 'John Leland . . .' (*see above*, **CAMBRIDGE**, Franciscan convent).

Most of the manuscripts in the following list are associated with other manuscripts through the writing of titles and pressmarks or the names of owners and donors or through binding leaves: the titles and pressmarks of Ottob. lat. 193, 200, 2071 are probably in the same hand; the name of owner or donor is in large capitals at the foot of the first leaf of the text in Ottob. lat. 116, 200, 202, 211, 229, 326, 342, 427, 468; a Digestum vetus in 2 cols. of 59 lines was used as flyleaves in Pembroke Coll., Cambridge, 121 and Ottob. lat. 342; a Digestum novum in 2 cols. of 39 lines was used as flyleaves in Pembroke Coll., Cambridge, 127, Ottob. lat. 188 and Ottob. lat. 202; a Digestum novum in 2 cols. of 48 lines was used as flyleaves in Ottob. lat. 196, 323, 427, 612, 1603, 1764; uniform labels bearing title and pressmark, no doubt once on the old covers, have been preserved inside Ottob. lat. 1603 and Ottob. lat. 1764 after rebinding.

+Cambridge, Pembroke Coll.,	121.	*b*Aegidius Romanus. s.xiv. ?
+	127.	*b*T. Aquinas. s.xiii/xiv. ?
+Rome, Bibl. Angelica,	1084.	Augustinus. s.xiii ex. [A.K.]. ?
+	Vatican, Ottob. lat. 73.	*i*H. Suso, etc. s.xiv.
+	116.	*i*Augustinus. s.xiv ex.
+	181.	T. Bradwardinus. A.D. 1244. [D.D.]. ?
+	182.	*ei*H. de Hannibaldis. s.xiii ex. [I N].
+	186.	*m*T. Aquinas. s.xiii ex. [B I].
+	188.	*b*T. Aquinas. s.xiii ex. ?
+	193.	A. de Hales. s.xiii med. [A.B.].
+	194.	Aegidius Romanus. s.xiii ex. [B.O.]. ?
+	196.	*b*T. Aquinas, etc. s.xiii/xiv.
+	200.	*i*T. Aquinas, etc. [B.S.].
+	202.	*i*T. Aquinas. s.xiii ex.
+	211.	*i*T. Aquinas. s.xiii ex [C.9].
+	214.	*i*T. Aquinas. s.xiii/xiv. [D.G.]. ?
+	229.	*i*Gregorius. s.xiii ex.

[1] Vatican, Ottob. lat. 187 and Vat. lat. 7095 formed one volume.

Rome (*contd*)

+	Vatican, Ottob. lat.	235.	T. de Chabham. s.xiii med. [G.F.]. ?
+		323.	Augustinus. s.xiii med. [R.S.]. ?
+		326.	Pseudo-Chrysostomus. s.xiv/xv. ?
+		331.	J. de Voragine. s.xiv [G.D.]. ?
+		342.	*i*W. Brito, etc. s.xiv in.
+		357.	R. Holcot. s.xiv. [M].
+		426.	*m*T. Ringstead. s.xiv ex. [L].
+		427.	*i*Isidorus. s.xiii/xiv.
+		468.	Aegidius Romanus. s.xiii ex. [B.Q.].
+		612.	*b*Aegidius Romanus, etc. s.xiv. [FR].
+		630.	Summa Monaldi. s.xiii. [D.T.]. ?
		746.	*Add date* s.xiv.
+		1407.	Priscianus. s.xii. [HA]. ?
+		1603.	*b*Johannes Monachus, etc. s.xiv [G.P.].
+		1757.	Papias. s.xiii. [FD]. ?
+		1764.	P. de Abano. A.D. 1318. [F].
+		2071.	W. de Ockham, etc. s.xiii–xiv. [G.Q.].
	Vat. lat. 4954.		*Add date* s.xii.

CAMBRIDGE. *University.*

+ Cambridge, Gonville and Caius Coll., 364 (619). Fasciculus morum. s.xiv/xv. [*Cat. 1424*, 25].

+ 414 (631). *e*Albertus Magnus, De natura rerum. s.xiii.

+ Inc.49 (pr. bk). *e*J. Balbus, Catholicon. Venice, A.D. 1487.

CAMBRIDGE. *Clare College.*

List of *c*. 30 books bequeathed by Thomas Lexham, fellow †1383, 'ut perpetue in dicto collegio in libraria eiusdem permaneant', in *BRUC*, p. 366, from Lambeth Palace, Reg. Courtenay (Canterbury), fos. 203ᵛ–4ᵛ.

London, The Robinson Trust (Helmingham 15). Now London, Mr P. L. Robinson.

CAMBRIDGE. *King's College.*

The 1452 catalogue printed also by A. Sammut, *Unfredo duca di Gloucester e gli umanisti italiani* (Medioevo e Umanesimo xli, 1980), pp. 85–94.

+ London, B.L., Harley 1705. Plato (in Latin). A.D. 1438. [*Cat.* D.(10)].

CAMBRIDGE. *King's Hall.*

Heading: *for* Exch. K. R. Acc. Var. *read* E.101, *and add that* E.101/335/17 is a list of A.D. 1440. A further King's Hall list is printed in K. B. McFarlane, *Lancastrian Kings and Lollard Knights* (Oxford, 1972), pp. 234–8.

+ Chicago, Newberry Libr., 33.1. *e*R. Higden. s.xv ex.

CAMBRIDGE. *Michaelhouse.*

Ampleforth Abbey (pr. bk). The number is C.V.21.
+Cambridge, Trinity Coll., VI.15.35 (pr. bk). *e*Barth. Anglicus. Nurem-
berg, A.D. 1492.
+ D.8.122 (pr. bk). *e*Epp. Pauli cum comm.
J. Fabri Stapulensis. Paris, A.D. 1512.
+London, Dulwich College, A.3.f.12 (pr. bk). *e*Theologia Damasceni.
Paris, 1519.

CAMBUSKENNETH, Stirlingshire. *Aug. abbey of B.V.M.*

Glasgow, U.L. *For* B.8.y.7 *read* Gen. 1126.

CANTERBURY. *Ben. cathedral priory of Holy Trinity or Christ
Church.*

Heading: *The words* (extracts given by J. Leland, *Collectanea*, iv, 120) *should
follow* Galba E.iv. *For* Canterbury, Ch. Ch. MS. 27 *read* Canterbury, Ch. Ch., MS.
Lit. 27. A new edition of the catalogues and lists by M. T. Gibson is in preparation
for the British Academy's Corpus of British Medieval Library Catalogues.

Ampleforth Abbey (pr. bk). The number is C.V.220.
+Cambridge, U.L., Ff.3.10. J. Chrysostomus. s.xv ex. [*Ingram* 68].
Ff.4.43. *Add date* s.x.
Corpus Christi Coll., 173. *Read* Sedulius.
S.P.71. *Read m*Jeronimus, Epistolae
(binding leaf).
Pembroke Coll., 148. *Cancel query.*
149. *Cancel query.*
Trinity Coll., 93. *Read* [(D.v.G.)ix; *cat.* 226, Ingram 84].
108. *Read* [*Ingram* 41].
123. *For* s.xii *read* s.xii in.
144. *Read* [*Ingram* 34].
164 (flyleaf). *Cancel* [*Ingram* 131].
391. *Read* [D. G.v.; *cat.* 833].
+ 1135. *s*Prosper, etc. s.x. ex.
Cambridge (U.S.A.), Harvard University. *For pressmark read* [IO;
D.iii G.iiii; *cat.* 99].
Canterbury, Cathedral, 17. *For* 17 *read* Lit.D.11 (17)[1] *and for* 628
read 628–9.
46. *For* 46 *read* Lit.E.42 (46),[1] fos. 1–68, 75–
81 *and for* 360 *read* 361. Footnote 1 *should
read* Fragments (75 fos.) recovered from
bindings: see *MMBL* ii, 289–96.
+ Lit.B.1 (73). *i*Duns Scotus. s.xiii. ?
Lit.A.13 (74). *Add* [*Ingram* 27].

[1] All Canterbury Cathedral MSS. between 1 and 104 on p. 34 of the 1964 edn.
are now referred to as MSS. 'Lit.' plus a letter and number, e.g. Lit.D.11. For the
relevant letters and numbers see 1964 edn., index, p. 346, each entry to be
preceded by 'Lit.'

Canterbury (*contd*)
> Cathedral, Box ABC. Now Add. 128.
> > Box CCC, no. 19a. Now Add. 20.
> > Box CCC, no. 23. Now Add. 127/15.

+ Durham, U.L., Bamburgh Sel. 40. II Esdras, Esther, Tobit glo. (2 frags.). s.xii ex, in Driedo, De captivitate. Louvain, A.D. 1534. [cf. *cat.* 865].[1]

+ Lincoln, Cathedral, 139. Sermones et sententiae. s.xii ex. [*Cat.* 950].

> London, B.L., Add. 37472(1). See 1964 edn., p. 33, footnote 6.

+ 57337. cPontificale. s.x/xi. ?

+ 59616. cLives of St Thomas the Martyr (in French), etc. s.xiii ex–xv[1].

> > Cotton Calig. A.xv, fos. 120–53, and Egerton 3314 formed one volume.

> > > Vesp. D.xix. *Read* D.xix, fos. 1–52.

> > Egerton 3314. *See under* Cotton Calig. A.xv *above.*

+ Harley 603. Psalterium. s.xi in.[2]

> > Lambeth Palace, 62. *Read* [*cat.* 225, *Ingram* 83].

> > Victoria and Albert Museum, 661. See 1964 edn., p. 33, footnote 6.

+ Dr C. F. R. de Hamel. mH. de Bosham. Liber melorum (1 fo.). s.xii ex. [Cf. *cat.* 858].[3]

+ Maidstone, Kent Archives Office, S/Rm.Fae.2. Passionale (2 fos.). s.xii.[4]

> Manchester, Northern Congregational Coll., 1. Now Manchester, John Rylands U.L., Lat. 474.

> New York, Pierpont Morgan Libr., 521 and 724. See 1964 edn., p. 33, footnote 6.

+ Oxford, Bodleian, Add. C.284. csTertullian. s.xi ex. ?

> > Auct. E. inf. 7. *Read* [.to.; *cat.* 784, Ingram 32].

> > Bodley 385. *Add date* s.xi/xii.

+ Lat. misc. b.19 B.47–9. mJob glosatus (fragm.). s.xii ex. [Cf. *cat.* 866].[3]

> > Merton Coll. *The entry should read* Merton Coll., 297B. eStatuta Angliae, etc. s.xv[1]–xv med.

+ New College, Ω.13.2 (pr. bk). iBernardus. Paris, A.D. 1494.

> > Pembroke Coll., fragments. *For 32 read* 16.

> Stockholm. *After* Kungl. Bibl. *add* A.135.

+ Tokyo, Prof. T. Takamiya, 55. sAugustinus (frag.). s.xii in. [*cat.* 325, *Ingram* 77].

+ Wellington (N.Z.), Turnbull Library, MS. Papers 2 (P. Watts Rule). mT. Aquinas, De malo (1 fo.). s.xiii/xiv.[3]

---

[1] See de Hamel, *Glossed Books*, p. 42.

[2] A convincing case for transferring this MS. from St Augustine's Abbey, Canterbury, to Christ Church, is made by Janet Backhouse, *BLJ*, x (1984), 97–113.

[3] Assigned on the evidence of marks in the margin: see 1964 edn., p. 31, footnote 6, and cf. de Hamel, *Glossed Books*, p. 42.

[4] Two leaves from the same volume of the Passionale (*cat.* 361) as Canterbury Cathedral, 46, fos. 31–42.

+ *Untraced:* Sotheby sale 12 Dec. 1967, no. 19, Christie, cat. 9 Dec. 1981, no. 231. *i*Biblia, s.xiii.

Rejected: cancel Cambridge, Trinity Coll., 1135. *Add* London, B.L., Cotton Claud. B.ii.[1]

CANTERBURY. *Ben. abbey of St Augustine.*

+ Aberystwyth, N.L., Peniarth 28. *i*Leges Howeli Da (in Latin and Welsh). s.xiii in. [D.xvi G.iii; unprinted index to cat., fo. 19ᵛ].

+ Brussels, Bibl. Royale, 1103. *s*Augustinus. s.xi/xii. [*cat.* 373].

+ Cambridge, Trinity Coll., 903. Misc. medica. s.xiii–xiv. [Part of *cat.* 1599].[2]

Canterbury, Cathedral, s.n.: formerly Redlynch, Major J. R. Abbey.

> *For* 4 *read* Lit.B.6(4).
> *For* 34 *read* Lit.D.6(34).
> *For* 49 *read* Lit.D.5(49).
> *For* 58 *read* Lit.D.16(58).
> *For* 68 *read* Lit.A.8(68).

+ Cologny-Genève, Fondation Martin Bodmer, Bibl. Bodmeriana, 11. Chanson d'Aspremont (in French). s.xiii. [*cat.* 1520].

Dublin, Chester Beatty Libr., W.27. Now sold and in a private collection.

Durham, U.L., Cosin V.ii.9. *For* Kilwardy *read* Kilwardby, etc.

+ Edinburgh, New Coll., Med.3. *c*Bonaventura, etc. s.xiii ex.[3] ?

Elmstone, Rectory. See *Untraced*, below.

+ Eton Coll., 160. W. de Conchis. s.xiii. [*cat.* 1222].[4]

+   161. Adelardus Bathon. s.xii. [*cat.* 1222].[4]

+ London, B.L., Add. 53710. *c*W. Thorn. s.xiv ex–s.xv.

        54229:   formerly London, Dr E. G. Millar. Date s.xii.

+   Cotton Vesp. A.xviii, fos. 3–86. H. Huntingdonensis, Chronica. s.xiii. [*cat.* 924].

+   Cleop. A.v. L. d'Orleans, Somme le Roy (in French). s.xiii/xiv. [*cat.* 1504].

      Cleop. E.i. *For* fos. 16–55 *read* fos. 17–56.

+   Appx. 56, fos. 91–111. *l*Kalendarium, etc. s.xii.

      Egerton 823. *Cancel query.*[2]

      840A. *Cancel query.*[2]

      Harley 603. *Cancel entry and add to Rejected.* Probably from Christ Church, Canterbury, *q.v.* above.

      Royal 1 A.vii. *Add query.*

      13 A.xxiii. *For* s.xii *read* s.xi.

      Lambeth Palace, 116. *Read* fos. i, 1–131.

      114. *Read* fos. i, ii, 1–163.

      Dr E. G. Millar: *see* London, B.L., *above.*

Maidstone Museum. *For* 1 *read* All Saints P.5.

---

[1] On Claud. B.ii, included in the index to the 1964 edn. as from **CANTERBURY** but by an oversight omitted from the text, see under **CIRENCESTER**.

[2] Cambridge, Trinity Coll., 903 and London, B.L., Egerton 823 and 840A formed one volume: cf. 1964 edn. p. 43 and footnote 4, and A. G. Watson, *TCBS*, vi (1976), 211–17.

[3] See *MMBL* ii, 533, under arts. 6a, b, 7p, 8.

[4] Bodleian e Mus. 223 and Eton Coll., 160 and 161 formed one volume.

+New York, Academy of Medicine. Chirurgica et gynaecologica. s.xiii. [*cat.* 1274].

    Pierpont Morgan Libr., G.18 and 53: formerly New York, Mr W. S. Glazier.

    Public Libr., 8. *Read* [D.viii G.1; *cat.* 665].

    Mr W. S. Glazier: *see* New York, Pierpont Morgan Libr., *above.*

Oxford, Bodleian, Ashmole 341. *Read* Ashmole 341, fos. 1–144 *and correct date to* s.xiii$^{\frac{3}{4}}$.

+   Fr.e.32. Aliscans, etc. (in French). s.xiii. [*cat.* 1533].

    Laud Misc. 125. *Read* 225.

+   Corpus Christi Coll., 232. R. Grosseteste (in French), etc. s.xiii ex. [*cat.*1512].[1]

+   260, pp. 84b,c. Tabulae decennovenales. [D.ix G iii(iiii)].[1]

+   261, fos. 70–115. *s*Collectanea Clementis Cantuariensis. s.xv[2].

Redlynch, Major J. R. Abbey: *see* Canterbury Cathedral, *above.*

+Rouen, Bibl. Mun. 231 (A.44). *l*Psalterium, etc. s.xii[1].

Wolfenbüttel. *For* Ducal Libr. *read* Herzog August Bibl. *Add date* s.xiv.

Untraced: Elmstone Rectory. Augustinus, In psalmos (2 fos.).[2]

+*Rejected:* London, B.L., Harley 603 (see p. 11, footnote 2 above).

CANTERBURY. *Dominican convent.*

+Oxford, Bodleian, Digby 203. *l*P. de Tarentasia, In libros i–ii sententiarum. s.xiii ex.[3] ?

CARISBROOKE, Isle of Wight. *Ben. alien priory of B.V.M.; cell of Lyre.*

A list of 22 books, A.D. 1260, printed in *Annales de Normandie*, iii (1953), 87–90, from a register in the Archives de l'Eure.

CARLISLE, Cumberland. *Aug. cath. priory of B.V.M.*

+London, Mr N. J. Barker. *s*Eusebius. s.xii.

CARMARTHEN, Dyfed. *Aug. priory of St John the Evangelist.*

Aberystwyth, N.L., Peniarth 1. *Cancel query.*

CARROW, Norfolk. *Priory of B.V.M. and St John, of Ben. nuns.*

+Reykjavik, Nat. Museum., 4678 + Nat. Libr., IB 363 8vo + Nat. Libr., Lbs. frag. 51. *e*Psalterium. s.xiv.

---

[1] Corpus Christi Coll., 260, pp. 84b,c, were flyleaves of Corpus 232.

[2] At one time the wrapper of an Elmstone parish register. Listed in 1964 edn. but not now to be traced. It may have been lost when Elmstone Rectory was sold. It is not in the Cathedral, City and Diocesan Record Office at Canterbury or the Kent Archives Office at Maidstone.

[3] The MS. was 'concessus fratri Anselmo de Valoynes ad terminum vite'. One of this name, O.P., S.T.P., was licensed to hear confessions in the diocese and city of Canterbury in 1349 (Lambeth Palace, Reg. Islip (Canterbury), fo. 12).

CASTLE ACRE, Norfolk. *Cluniac priory of B.V.M.*
A list of 10 canon law books bequeathed by Thomas Lexham, †1383, in *BRUC*, p. 366, from Lambeth Palace, Reg. Courtenay (Canterbury), fo. 204.

CHERTSEY, Surrey. *Ben. abbey of St Peter.*
2 books listed in Rome, Vatican, Reg. lat. 2099, fo. 305 (s.xvi[1]).
+ Cambridge, Emmanuel Coll., 252.   *l*Psalterium (frag.). s.xiii in.
+ Oxford, Bodleian, Lat. liturg. d. 42.   *l*Breviarium. s.xiv in.[1]
+   e. 39: formerly *Untraced.*[1]
Untraced: see now Oxford, Bodleian, Lat. liturg. e. 39, above.

CHESTER. *Ben. abbey of St Werburg.*
+ London, B.L., Sloane 285.   Euclides (in Latin). s.xiii ex. [xiii° loco].
Mostyn Hall MS.   Post-Dissolution, therefore omit.

CHESTER. *Priory of B.V.M. of Ben. nuns.*
San Marino, Huntingdon Libr.   *Add date* s.xv/xvi.

CHICHESTER, Sussex.   *Cathedral church of Holy Trinity.*
+ London, B.L., Lansdowne 431.   *i*Psalterium. s.xiii[1].

CLARE, Suffolk.   *Convent of Austin friars.*
5 books mentioned in cartulary, London, B.L., Harley 4835, fos. 41, 43, 49.

CIRENCESTER, Gloucestershire.   *Aug. abbey of B.V.M.*
+ London, B.L., Cotton Claud. B.ii.   *s*Epistolae T. Becket. s.xii ex.[2]
Oxford, Jesus Coll., 3.   *Cancel query.*

COLCHESTER, Essex.   *Ben. abbey of St John the Baptist.*
In title cancel Cf. cell at Snape.
+ Cambridge, Trinity Coll., 1369.   *m*Marianus Scotus. s.xi ex.
+ *Untraced:* H. P. Kraus, cat. 90 (1959), no. 5 (pr. bk).   *i*A. Barclay, Ship of Fools. London, A.D. 1509.
Rejected: Ambrosius, Exameron, etc.   Sotheby, 14 June 1965, lot 2 (Helmingham 2, listed under **COLCHESTER** in 1964 edn.). *See now* **STOKE-BY-CLARE.**

COLDINGHAM, Berwickshire.   *Ben. priory of B.V.M.*
Durham, Cathedral, A.II.8.   *Reject.*

---

[1] Bodleian, Lat. liturg. d. 42 and Lat. liturg. e. 6, 7 and 39 are portions of one manuscript: cf. *BLR*, ix (1974), 72–4, 78–80.
[2] Widely accepted as a **CANTERBURY** book, this must now be ascribed to **CIRENCESTER** because of Mr Michael Gullick's discovery (communicated by letter) that the principal scribe is the Cirencester scribe Walter, who wrote London, B.L., MS. Royal 7 B.vi, and that it bears annotations by Alexander Nequam, canon of Cirencester (*BRUO*).

COUPAR ANGUS, Perthshire.   *Cist. abbey of B.V.M.*

+ Karlsruhe, Badische Landesbibl., 345, fos. 1–12.   *c*Chronicon. ss.xii ex–xiv med.   ?
Rome, Vatican, Pal. lat. 65.   *Add pressmark* [Gra. G.C.].

COVENTRY, Warwickshire.   *Ben. cathedral priory of B.V.M.*

+ Oxford, Bodleian, 4° V.16(2) Th. (pr. bk).   *i*M. Vegius. Paris, A.D. 1511.

COVERHAM, Yorkshire.   *Prem. abbey of B.V.M.*

New York, Mr W. A. Glazier, 39.   Now New York, Pierpont Morgan Libr., G.39.

CROWLAND, Lincolnshire.   *Ben. abbey of B.V.M., St Bartholomew and St Guthlac.*

Bristol, Baptist College, Z.e.38.   Now sold and untraced.
+ London, B.L., Harley Roll Y.6.   *c*Vita S. Guthlaci. s.xiii in.   ?
Lambeth Palace, 145.   *For fos. 138–255 read fos. 138–256.*
+ *Untraced:* A. Wilson, Ltd. (London), cat. 12 (1950), no. 322 (pr. bk).   *i*D. Erasmus, Moriae Encomium. Basel, A.D. 1521; Bristol, Baptist Coll. Z.e.38 above.

CROXDEN, Staffordshire.   *Cist. abbey of B.V.M.*

+ London, Dr C. F. R. de Hamel.   *e*P. Lombardus. s.xii ex.
+ Paris, B.N., lat. 17620.   *c*Martyrologium. s.xiv in.

DARLEY, Derbyshire.   *Aug. abbey of B.V.M.*

+ Cashel, Diocesan Libr., 2.   *c*Psalterium, etc. s.xii/xiii.[1]   ?

DARLINGTON, co. Durham.   *Collegiate church of St Cuthbert.*

Leicester, Mr H. F. Smith.   *Add* [*List*, 1].

DARTFORD, Kent.   *Priory of B.V.M. and St Margaret, of Dom. nuns.*

+ Oxford, Bodleian, Bodl. 255, fos. 1–44.   Rule of St Augustine (in English). s.xv/xvi.[2]   ?
+   Rawl. G.59.   *i*Disticha Catonis (in Latin and French). s.xv   ?

DEER, Aberdeenshire.   *Cist. abbey of B.V.M.*

Edinburgh, Scottish Record Office: now Edinburgh, N.L., 21182. *Add date* s.xv.

DENNY, Cambridgeshire.   *Abbey of St James and St Leonard, of Franciscan nuns.*

+ Cambridge, U.L., Add. 8335.   *e*Northern Homilies (in English). s.xv.

---

[1] Or possibly owned by the mother house, St Helen, Derby. See W. Hawkes in *Reportorium novum: Dublin Diocesan Historical Record*, iii (1962), 83–93.
[2] Bears the arms of Cressener on fo. 44: Elizabeth Cressener was prioress, 1485–1536: see p. 84 below.

DERBY. *Aug. priory of St Helen.*
See **DARLEY** above.

DEREHAM, WEST, Norfolk. *Prem. abbey of B.V.M.*
+ Dublin, Trinity Coll., 223. *i*Augustinus, Enarrationes in psalmos 1–50. s.xiii.
+ El Escorial, Q.ii.6. *c*Psalterium, etc. s.xiv in.
+ San Marino, Huntington Libr., HM55. *c*J. Capgrave, Life of St Norbert (in English). s.xv med.[1] ?
+ *Untraced:* A Rosenthal, Ltd. (Oxford), cat. 16 (1949), no. 146 (pr. bk). *i*W. Lyndwode. Paris, A.D. 1501.

DIEULACRES, Staffordshire. *Cist. abbey of B.V.M. and St Benedict.*
Read London, Gray's Inn, 9, fos. 32–154. *c*Misc. historica, etc. s.xiv–xv. ?

DORE, Herefordshire. *Cist. abbey of B.V.M.*
+ London, B.L., Harley 218 (partly pr. bk). *i*J. Lichtenberger, etc. (partly in English). s.xiii in–xv ex and (Strasbourg), s.a.
+   Westminster Abbey, F.4.21 (pr. bk). *i*Athanasius (in Latin). Paris, A.D. 1520.

DOVER, Kent. *Ben. priory of B.V.M. and St Martin, cell of Canterbury.*
Canterbury, Cathedral, 71. *For* 71 *read* Lit. E.3.(71).
+ London, B.L., Harley 997. J. de Rupella. s.xiii ex. [C.VII.2; *cat.* 118].

DROITWICH, Worcestershire. *Convent of Austin friars.*
+ London, St Paul's Cathedral, 8, fos. 1–133ᵛ, 150–65ᵛ. Sermones. s.xv in ?

DUNFERMLINE, Fife. *Ben. abbey of Holy Trinity.*
Glasgow, U.L. *For* BE.7.b.8 *read* Gen. 333.
+ Madrid, Palacio Nacional, II.2097. *e*Turgotus, etc. s.xiv in.
+ Oxford, Bodleian, Fairfax 8. *b*J. Fordun. A.D. 1489. *Delete from Rejected.*

DURHAM. *Ben. cathedral priory of St Cuthbert.*
   In this completely revised section a plus sign (+) indicates an item added to the list in the 1964 edition and a paraph (¶) indicates a corrected item. The absence of these symbols indicates that the 1964 entry is repeated without change. To the heading in the 1964 edn., pp. 60–1, add A. J. Piper's article (see p. viii footnote 2, above).

+ Aberdeen, U.L., Forbes of Boyndlie. Durandus. s.xiv. [*cat.*, p. 76 A].
+ Aberystwyth, N.L., bo5 P3 (5F) (pr. bk). *i*W. Lyndwode. London, A.D. 1505.
   Ampleforth Abbey, C.V.72 (pr. bk). *i*Hadrianus Sextus. Paris, A.D. 1527.
¶ Birdsall House, Lord Middleton. *see* Nottingham, U.L., *below.*
¶ Bristol, Central Public Libr. EPB 353 (pr. bks; 5 vols.). *i*Duns Scotus. Venice, A.D. 1506.

---

[1] Author's holograph, with presentation picture to abbot John Wygenhale of West Dereham.

Cambridge,
    U.L., Add. 3303 (6). *l*Kalendarium. s.xii. ?
        Ff.4.41. *i*Ivo Carnotensis. s.xii/xiii.
        Gg.3.28. Aelfric (in English). s.x/xi. [1ª.8ⁱ.L; *cat.*, p. 5].

¶   Gg.4.33. *e*Epp. Pauli, etc. s.xii. [H (*erased*); C; *cat.*, pp. 18 H, 93 H].
        Kk.5.10. *e*Biblia, etc. s.xiii.

¶   Mm.3.14. *e*J. de Voragine. s.xiv. [G; *cat.*, pp. 43 G (?). 75 G].
+   Inc 264+778 (pr. bk). *i*G. de Monte Rocherii, etc. Strasbourg, A.D. 1493, etc.
        Inc 1049 (pr. bk). *i*L. Pruthenus. Nuremberg, A.D. 1498.
+   Inc 1953 (pr. bk). *m*P. Lombardus. Venice, A.D. 1489. [30].
+   Inc 4163 (pr. bk). *m*J. Lathbury. Oxford, A.D. 1482.
        Rel.b.51.3 (pr. bk). *i*Postille majores. Lyon, A.D. 1519.
        Rel.c.50.8 (pr. bk). *i*Epistole ex registro beatissimi Gregorii. Paris, A.D. 1508.[1]
  Corpus Christi College, 183. *c*Beda, etc. s.x in. [*Athelstan*].
                      EP.S.3 (pr. bk). *i*J. F. de Pavinis, etc. Paris, A.D. 1503.

¶ Fitzwilliam Mus., McClean 169. *i*Miscellanea. s.xv. [P, P/11].
¶ Jesus Coll.,   1. *e*Decretales glo. s.xiii. [E; *cat.*, p. 47 E].
¶   6. *e*Decretales glo. s.xiii–xiv. [M, M (*altered to* A)/76].
           13. *e*Sermones. s.xiv–xv. [N/ii].
           14. *e*Beda. s.xii. [A].
¶   15. P. Lombardus. s.xiv. [P (*erased*), E; *cat.*, pp. 22 P, 99 P].[2]
¶   20. Summa de vitiis. s.xiii. [*Cat.*, pp. 24 C, 100 C].
           22. *l*Graduale. s.xiii–xiv. ?
¶   23. *e*Psalterium. s.xii–xv. [P (?); *cat.*, pp. 39 P, 116 P].
           24. *cl*Theologica. s.xiv.
           25. Astronomica, etc. s.xii. [A, a/22; *cat.*, p. 75 A].
¶   28. *e*Priscianus. s.xi ex. [N; *cat.*, p. 49 N].
¶   29. Constit. Clementine. s.xv in. [H; *cat.*, p. 47 H].
           41. *c*Speculum religiosorum, etc. s.xiii–xv.
¶   44. *e*Medica. s.xii. [O, 2ª.7ⁱ.Fe; *cat.*, pp. 8, 33 O, 111 O].
           45. *e*Repertorium super Speculum hist. s.xv. [L].
           48. Boethius. s.xiii–xv. [O/ii].
¶   50. Esaias, etc., glo. s.xii. [E; *cat.*, pp. 15 E, 90 E].
           52. *s*Sermones, etc. s.xii in.[3]
           53. *s*Ivo Carnotensis. s.xii in.[3]
¶   54. *e*T. Aquinas, etc. s.xiii–xv. [H].
¶   57. T. Aquinas, etc. s.xiii/xiv. [N, N/32; *cat.*, p. 73 N].
           59. *e*W. de Alvernia, etc. s.xiv. [C; *cat.*, p. 72 C].
           61. *e*Reg. S. Benedicti, etc. s.xiv–xv.
           64. *e*Boetius, etc. s.xii. [B; *cat.*, p. 71 B].
¶   65. Expo misse, etc. s.xii–xiii. [D; *cat.*, pp. 25 D, 101 D].
¶   67. J. Wallensis. s.xiv. [G; *cat.*, pp. 77 G, 79 G].

---

[1] Two binding leaves of Rel. c.50.8 are kept separately as MS. Add. 2751 (7).
[2] The binding leaves (20) contain English sermons, s.xi.
[3] Jesus Coll. 52, 53, and Bodleian, Laud Misc. 52, formed one volume.

Cambridge (*contd*)

¶ Jesus Coll., 69. *e*Summa Raymundi. s.xiii–xiv. [T].

70. *i*W. de Conchis, etc. s.xv.

¶ 71. *e*Ric. de S. Victore, etc. s.xii/xiii. [B; *cat.*, pp. 75 B, 81 B].

¶ 76. Jeronimus, etc. s.xii. [D; *cat.*, pp. 19 D, 94 D].

¶ King's Coll., 22. *e*H. de S. Victore. s.xii. [F (*erased*), C; *cat.*, pp. 21 [F], 37, 41 F, 97 H].

Magdalene Coll., Pepys 1662. *l*Kalendarium. s.xv.

Pepys 2981 no. 18. Evangelia. s.viii.[1]

Pepys 2981 no. 19. Evangelia. s.vii/viii.[1]

¶ Pembr. Coll., 241. *e*Isidorus. s.xiv. [G (*erased*)].

¶ Peterhouse, 74. *e*Pseudo-Isidorus. s.xi ex. [G (*altered to* E), E, 2ª.8ⁱ.S; *cat.*, pp. 35 E, 112 E].

St John's Coll., 112. *e*T. Aquinas, etc. s.xiii ex.–xv. [G; *cat.*, p. 68 G].

¶ 172. *e*Antidotarium. s.xii ex. [C, 2ª.7ⁱ.Ce; *cat.*, pp. 33 C, 110 C].

¶ Sid. Sussex Coll., 32. Florus. s.xii ex. [C; *cat.*, p. 64 A *recte* B].[2]

¶ 51. Hildebertus, etc. s.xii. [P; *cat.*, pp. 24 P, 101 P].

56. *e*Galfridus Vinsauf, etc. s.xv. [K].

100, ii. *e*Pontificale. s.xi.

¶ 101. *e*Decreta non glo. s.xii. [F, 1ª.8ⁱ.F; *cat.*, pp. 35 F, 112 F].

Trinity Coll., 8. *e*Tract. de vitiis, etc. s.xiii. [F; *cat.*, p. 72 F].

¶ 216. Epp. Pauli glo. s.viii. [L; *cat.*, pp. 18 L, 93 L].

365. *bs*T. de Chabham, etc. s.xiii/xiv–xv. ?

¶ 1194. *e*Claudianus. s.xii ex. [A, 2ª.7ⁱ.C; *cat.*, pp. 32 A, 109 A, 119].

¶ 1227. *e*Beda, etc. s.xii. [B; *cat.*, pp. 30 B, 107 B].

¶ Deene Park, Trustees of the late Mr G. Brudenell, XVIII.B.3. Now Durham Cathedral, C.III.22 below.

Downside Abbey, 960 (pr. bk). *i*Augustinus, Epistole. Basel, A.D. 1493.

970 (pr. bk). *i*Jeronimus. Venice, A.D. 1497.

18274 (pr. bk). *i*Bernardus, etc. Paris, A.D. 1508.

Dublin, Trinity Coll., 349, fos. 67–102. *e*Augustinus, etc. s.xii/xiii. [G].

440. *i*N. Wireker. s.xiv/xv.

Ff.dd.4–5 (pr. bks). *i*Biblia cum expo. N. de Lyra (ii–iii). Basel, A.D. 1498.

Durham,

Cathedral, A.I.1. W. de Nottingham. s.xiv/xv. [D].

A.I.2. *e*Concordancie Bibl. s.xiv. [C; *cat.*, p. 53 C].

A.I.3. *e*Nicholaus de Lyra. A.D. 1386. [K, 1ª.2ⁱ.M; *cat.*, p. 51 K].

A.I.4. *e*Nicholaus de Lyra. s.xiv ex. [M, 1ª.2ⁱ.N; *cat.*, p. 51 M].

A.I.5. *e*Nicholaus de Lyra. s.xiv ex. [1ª.2ⁱ.O; *cat.*, p. 119].

¶ A.I.6. *i*Nicholaus de Gorran. s.xv. [S].

---

[1] Two slips cut from Durham, Cath., A.II.16 and A.II.17 respectively.

[2] The second volume of this work is Durham, Cathedral, B.II.34.

Durham (*contd*)

Cathedral, A.I.7.   *e*S. Langton. s.xiii in. [B, 1ª.2ⁱ.Q; *cat.*, p. 50 B].

A.I.8.   *e*H. de S. Caro. s.xiii. [I, [1ª].2ⁱ.F; *cat.*, pp. 44 I, 51 I].

¶ A.I.9.   Postille super Bibliam. s.xiv. [E, 1ª.2ⁱ.S; *cat.*, p. 52 E].

¶ A.I.10.   *e*Berengaudus, etc. s.xii in. [D; *cat.*, pp. 2(?), 76 D, 81 D].

¶ A.I.11.   *e*T. Aquinas. s.xiv. [Q, 1 (*altered to* 2)ª.2ⁱ.A; *cat.*, p. 73 Q].

¶ A.I.12.   *e*H. de S. Caro. s.xiii. [H, 1ª.2ⁱ.B; *cat.*, pp. 11 H, 40 H, 86 H; cf. *cat.*, pp. 124–5].

A.I.13.   H. de S. Caro. s.xiii ex. [Q, 1ª.2ⁱ.I; *cat.*, pp. 44 Q, 51 Q].

A.I.14.   *e*H. de S. Caro. s.xiii. [L; *cat.*, p. 41 L].

A.I.15.   *e*H. de S. Caro. s.xiii. [F, 1ª.2ⁱ.D; *cat.*, pp. 44 F, 52 F].

¶ A.I.16.   *e*H. de S. Caro. s.xiii. [E, 1ª.2ⁱ.E; *cat.*, p. 45 E, 53 E].

¶ A.II.1.   *e*Biblia (4 vols.). s.xii ex. [*Cat.*, pp. 10, 85, 118].

A.II.2.   Biblia, pars ii. s.xii ex. [K].

A.II.3.   Biblia. s.xiii ex. [E; *cat.*, p. 50 E].

A.II.4.   *e*Biblia, pars ii. s.xi ex. [H; *cat.*, pp. 1, 50 H, 80 H, 117].

A.II.5.   Pentateuchus glo. s.xiii. [A, 1ª.A; *cat.*, p. 50 A].

¶ A.II.6.   *e*Libri Regum, etc., glo. s.xiii. [B, 1ª.B; *cat.*, pp. 12 A, 87 A].

¶ A.II.7.   *e*Libri Regum, etc., glo. s.xiii in. [E; *cat.*, p. 50–51 C (*altered from* E ?: E on Misc. Ch. 7125N)].

A.II.8.   *e*Epp. Cath., etc., glo. s.xiii in. [A; *cat.*, p. 53 A].

A.II.9.   *e*P. Lombardus. s.xii ex. [H, 1ⁱ.E; *cat.*, p. 51 H].

A.II.10.   *e*P. Lombardus. s.xiii in. [A; *cat.*, pp. 13 A, 88 A.].

A.II.11–13.   *e*Comment. on Psalms (in French; 3 vols.). s.xiii in. (vols. 1, 2); s.xiii med. (vol. 3). [N, 1ª.5ⁱ.S (vol. 1); R, 1ª.5ⁱ.T (vol. 3); *cat.*, pp. 13 N O R, 88 N O R].

A.II.14.   *e*Isaias, etc., glo. s.xiii. [1ⁱ.F; *cat.*, p. 51 O].

A.II.15.   *e*Evangelia glo. s.xii/xiii. [A; *cat.*, p. 52 A].

¶ A.II.16.   *c*Evangelia. s.viii. [D; *cat.*, pp. 16 D, 92 D].

A.II.17.   *e*Evangelia. s.vii/viii. [C].

A.II.18.   *e*Matheus et Marcus glo. s.xiii in. [F; *cat.*, p. 52 F].

A.II.19.   *e*P. Lombardus. s.xii ex. [B; *cat.*, pp. 17 B, 93 B, 118].

¶ A.II.20.   W. Brito. s.xiii/xiv. [G, 1ª.1ᵉ.G; *cat.*, p. 49 G].

¶ A.II.21.   Comment. in Psalterium, etc. s.xiii. [C, c/22; *cat.*, pp. 27 C, 103 C].

¶ A.II.22.   *e*Alex. de Hales. s.xiii. [G, 1ª.3ⁱ.D, 1ª.2ⁱ.D *altered to* 2ª.2ⁱ.D; *cat.*, p. 52 G].

Durham (*contd*)
Cathedral, A.III.1.　*e*Genesis glo. s.xii. [D; *cat.*, pp. 11 D, 86 D].
　　　　A.III.2.　*e*Leviticus, etc., glo. s.xii. [C; *cat.*, pp. 11 C, 86 C].
　　　　A.III.3, fos. 1–62.　*e*Deuteronom. glo. s.xii ex. [C; *cat.*, pp. 12 C, 87 C].
　　　　A.III.3, fos. 63–173.　*e*Job glo. s.xii ex. [A; *cat.*, pp. 12 A, 88 A].
　　　　A.III.4.　*e*Libri Regum glo., etc. s.xii ex. [D; *cat.*, pp. 12 D, 87 D].
　　　　A.III.5.　*e*Paralipom., etc., glo. s.xii ex. [A; *cat.*, pp. 12 A, 88 A].
　　　　A.III.7.　*e*P. Lombardus. s.xii ex. [K; *cat.*, p. 51 K].
¶　　　　A.III.8.　Psalterium glo. s.xiii in. [B; cf. *cat.*, pp. 13 B, 88 B].
　　　　A.III.9.　*e*Psalterium glo. s.xii ex. [AA; *cat.*, pp. 13 AA, 89 AA].
¶　　　　A.III.10.　*e*G. Porretanus. s.xii med. [L, 1^i.K (*altered (?) to* L); *cat.*, pp. 3, 13 L, 88 L].
　　　　A.III.11.　*e*Misc. theol. s.xiii–xiv.
　　　　A.III.12.　*e*Misc. theol. s.xiii. [G, 2^a.6^i.F; *cat.*, pp. 26 G, 103 G].
¶　　　　A.III.13.　*e*N. de Gorran. s.xiii ex. [A, 2.2.N.2; *cat.*, p. 68 A].
　　　　A.III.14.　*e*Parabole, etc., glo. s.xiii. [L, 1^a.1^e.C.1; *cat.*, p. 51 L].
　　　　A.III.15.　*e*Parabole, etc., glo. s.xiii in. [M; *cat.*, p. 51 M].
　　　　A.III.16.　*e*Ecclesiasticus, etc., glo. s.xii ex. [B; *cat.*, pp. 14 B, 90 B].
　　　　A.III.17.　*e*Isaias glo. s.xii ex. [F; *cat.*, pp. 2(?), 15 F, 90 F].
¶　　　　A.III.18.　*e*Isaias, etc., glo. s.xiii in. [B, A; *cat.*, pp. 15 A, 90 A].
¶　　　　A.III.19.　*e*Jeremias, etc., glo. s.xii ex. [D (*altered to* B), 1^a.1^e.F (*altered to* G); *cat.*, pp. 15 B, 91 B].
+　　　　A.III.20 + A.III.21, fos. 91–137. Jeremias, etc., glo. s.xiii in. [*Cat.*, pp. 15 A, 91 A].
¶　　　　A.III.21, fos. 1–90.　*e*H. de S. Caro. s.xiii. [[1]^a.2^i.C; cf. *cat.*, pp. 44 A, 51 A].
　　　　A.III.22.　*e*Ezechiel et Daniel glo. s.xiii. [B; *cat.*, pp. 15 B, 91 B].
　　　　A.III.23.　*e*Daniel et Esdras glo. s.xii ex. [A; *cat.*, pp. 15 A, 91 A].
　　　　A.III.24.　Proph. Minores glo. s.xii ex. [E. 1^a.1^i.G; *cat.*, pp. 16 E, 91 E].
　　　　A.III.25.　*m*Matheus et Johannes glo. s.xiii in.
¶　　　　A.III.26.　*s*Postille in Exodum, etc. s.xiii in. [V, C; *cat.*, pp. 11 C, 86 C].
　　　　A.III.27.　*e*R. Holcot. s.xiv ex. [1^a.5^i.A].
　　　　A.III.28.　*e*S. Langton. s.xiii. [A, F; *cat.*, pp. 15 F, 90 F].
　　　　A.III.29.　*e*Omeliarium. s.xi.

Durham (*contd*)
Cathedral, A.III.30. *e*Postille super Matheum. s.xiv. [D; *cat.*, pp. 16 D, 92 D].

  A.III.31. *e*N. Gorham. s.xiv. [C, 2ᵃ.2ⁱ.O; *cat.*, p. 68 C].

¶ A.III.35. *e*Tabula super Bibliam. s.xiv. [P; *cat.*, pp. 51 P, 83 P, *cf.* p. 42 D (*recte* P)].

  A.IV.1. *e*Leviticus glo. s.xii ex. [D; *cat.*, pp. 11 D, 87 D, 118].

  A.IV.2. *e*Psalterium glo., etc. s.xii ex. [X; *cat.*, pp. 13 X, 89 X].

¶ A.IV.3. *e*Glose super Psalterium. s.xiii in. [II; *cat.*, pp. 14 II, 89 II].

¶ A.IV.4. *e*P. Pictaviensis. s.xii ex. [FF, 1ᵃ.5ⁱ.X; *cat.*, pp. 13 FF, 89 FF].

¶ A.IV.5. *i*P. de Herenthals, etc. s.xiv.

¶ A.IV.7. *e*Isaias glo. s.xii ex. [G; *cat.*, pp. 15 G, 90 G].

¶ A.IV.8. *e*Evangelia, etc. s.xiii–xiv. [*Cat.*, pp. 16 B, 92 B].

  A.IV.10. *e*Matheus glo. s.xii ex. [B; *cat.*, pp. 16 B, 92 B, 118].

  A.IV.11. *e*Marcus glo. s.xii ex. [D; *cat.*, pp. 16 D, 92 D].

  A.IV.12. *e*Marcus glo. s.xii ex. [C; *cat.*, pp. 16 C, 92 C].

  A.IV.13. *e*Lucas glo. s.xii ex. [D; *cat.*, pp. 17 D, 92 D].

  A.IV.14. *e*Lucas glo. s.xii/xiii. [B; *cat.*, pp. 16 B, 92 B].

  A.IV.15. *e*Johannes glo., etc. s.xii in.-med. [D (*altered to* A); *cat.*, pp. 17 D. 93 D].

  A.IV.16. *e*Johannes glo., etc. s.xii in.-xiii. [G; *cat.*, pp. 17 G, 93 G].

  A.IV.17. Misc. theol. s.xii ex. [*Cat.*, p. 62 AD].

  A.IV.19. *c*'Rituale Dunelmense'. s.x in.

  A.IV.23. Summa Biblie. s.xiv. [1ᵃ.5ⁱ.Q].

  A.IV.28. *e*Beda. s.xii. [A; *cat.*, pp. 18 A, 94 A].

¶ A.IV.34. *e*Notule in Cantica Canticorum. s.xii in. [C; *cat.*, pp. 14 C, 90 C].

  A.IV.35. Beda, etc. s.xii ex. [*Cat..*, pp. 30 A, 107 A].

  A.IV.36. *e*Simeon Dunelmensis, etc. s.xiii in. [*Cat.*, p. 56 M].

  B.I.1. *e*P. Lombardus. s.xiii ex. [B/25; *cat.*, p. 54 B].

¶ B.I.2. *e*P. Lombardus. s.xiii ex. [D, 1ᵃ.6ⁱ.X; *cat.*, p. 54 D].

  B.I.3. *e*P. Lombardus. s.xiii ex. [A, 1ᵃ.6ⁱ.M; *cat.*, p. 54 A].

  B.I.4. P. Lombardus. s.xiii. [2ᵃ.6ⁱ.M].

  B.I.5. *e*T. Aquinas. s.xiv in. [R; *cat.*, p. 73 R].

  B.I.6. *e*T. Aquinas. s.xiv in. [N, 1ᵃ.6ⁱ.S; *cat.*, p. 74 N].

¶ B.I.7. *e*T. Aquinas. s.xiii/xiv. [A; *cat.*, pp. 23 C, 99 C].

¶ B.I.8. *e*T. Aquinas. s.xiii/xiv. [G, C; *cat.*, p. 72 C].

  B.I.9. *e*T. Aquinas. s.xiv in. [T; *cat.*, p. 73 T].

  B.I.10. *e*T. Aquinas. s.xiii/xiv. [B; *cat.*, p. 72 B].

¶ B.I.11. *e*T. Aquinas. s.xiii ex. [E (*altered to* S), 1ᵃ.6ⁱ.T; *cat.*, p. 72 E].

Durham (*contd*)

Cathedral, B.I.12. T. Aquinas. s.xiii/xiv. [E; *cat.*, pp. 23 E, 99 E].

B.I.13. *e*T. Aquinas. s.xiii ex. [O; *cat.*, p. 73 O].

¶ B.I.14. *e*T. Aquinas. s.xiv. [A (*erased*), 1ª.6ⁱ.R; *cat.*, p. 74 A].

¶ B.I.15. *e*T. Aquinas. s.xiii/xiv. [*Cat.*, pp. 23, 37, 100].

¶ B.I.16. *e*T. Aquinas. s.xiv in. [D, 1ª.vⁱⁱ.F; *cat.*, p. 72 D].

B.I.17. *e*T. Aquinas. s.xiii/xiv. [L, 1ª.6ⁱ.E; *cat.*, p. 73 L].

¶ B.I.18. *i*Summa de viciis, etc. s.xiv. [G].

B.I.19. *e*T. Aquinas. s.xiv. [K, 1ª.6ⁱ.G; *cat.*, p. 73 K].

B.I.20. *e*T. Aquinas. s.xiv in. [I; *cat.*, pp. 23 I, 99 I].

¶ B.I.21. *e*T. Aquinas. s.xiv. [I, I/36; *cat.*, p. 73 I].

B.I.22. *e*T. Aquinas. s.xiv in. [H, 1ª.6ⁱ.H; *cat.*, p. 73 H].

¶ B.I.23. T. Aquinas. s.xiii/xiv. [F (*erased*); *cat.*, p. 78 F].

B.I.24. *e*Bonaventura. s.xiv. [D; *cat.*, p. 74 D].

B.I.25. *e*Bonaventura. s.xiii/xiv. [E; *cat.*, p. 74 E].

¶ B.I.26. *e*H. de Gandavo. s.xiv. [A, 2ª.6ⁱ.R; *cat.*, pp. 24 A, 74 A, 100 A].

¶ B.I.27 (originally 2 vols.). P. Tarentasius. s.xiii. ex. [[.]. K; *cat.*, pp. 22 F K, 98 F K].

B.I.28. *e*P. Pictaviensis, etc. s.xiii in. [N, V, T; *cat.*, pp. 22 N, 98 N].

B.I.29. *e*R. de Peniaforte, etc. s.xiv. [P; *cat.*, p. 47 P].

B.I.30. *e*J. de Friburgo. s.xiv. [P, 2ª.8ⁱ.Q; *cat.*, p. 48 P].

B.I.31. J. de Balbis. s.xiv. [B; *cat.*, p. 49 B].

B.I.32. *e*V. Bellovacensis. A.D. 1448. [N].

B.I.33. *e*P. Comestor. s.xiii in. [A; *cat.*, p. 53 A].

B.I.34. *e*P. Comestor. s.xii/xiii. [B; *cat.*, p. 53 B].

B.II.1. *e*Josephus. s.xii med. [A; *cat.*, p. 56 A].

¶ B.II.2. Omelie. s.xi ex. ?

¶ B.II.3. Opus imperfectum in Matheum, etc. s.xiv. [1ª.3ⁱ.X].

B.II.4. *e*J. Chrysostomus, etc. s.xiv in. [A, 1ª.3ⁱ.Y; *cat.*, p. 68 A].

B.II.5. *e*J. Chrysostomus. s.xiv in. [1ª.3ⁱ.V].

B.II.6. *e*Ambrosius. s.xi ex. [E, 2ª.2ⁱ.Q; *cat.*, pp. 3, 57 E, 118].

B.II.7. *e*Jeronimus. s.xii med. [F, 1ⁱ.V; *cat.*, p. 58 F].

B.II.8. *e*Jeronimus. s.xii in. [A, 1ⁱ.R; *cat.*, p. 57 A].

B.II.9. *e*Jeronimus. s.xi ex. [G (*altered to* T), 1ⁱ.T; *cat.*, p. 58 G].

B.II.10. *e*Jeronimus. s.xi ex. [C, 1ⁱ.X; *cat.*, pp. 1, 57 C, 117]

B.II.11. *e*Jeronimus. s.xi ex. [E, 1ⁱ.Y; *cat.*, pp. 1, 58 E, 117].

¶ B.II.12. *e*Augustinus. s.xiv in. [AB (*in red*), 2ª.2ⁱ.G; *cat.*, p. 62 AB].

¶ B.II.13. *e*Augustinus. s.xi ex. [K, 1ⁱ, 2ª.2ⁱ.X; *cat.*, pp. 1, 60 K, 117].

¶ B.II.14. *e*Augustinus. s.xi ex. [L, (1ⁱ.N *canc.*), 2ª.2ⁱ.X (*altered to* Y); *cat.*, pp. 1, 60 L, 117].

B.II.15. *e*Augustinus. s.xiv. [M; *cat.*, p. 60 M].

22

Durham (*contd*)
Cathedral, B.II.16. *e*Augustinus. s.xi med. [G; *cat.*, pp. 59 G, 117].
¶   B.II.17. *e*Augustinus. s.xi ex. [F, 1ª.3ⁱ (*altered to* 2ª.2ⁱ).E; *cat.*, pp. 59 F, 117].
    B.II.18. *e*Augustinus. s.xii in. [AA, 2ª.2ⁱ.F; *cat.*, p. 63 AA].
    B.II.19. *e*Augustinus. s.xiv in. [H, 1ª.3ⁱ.I; *cat.*, p. 60 H].
    B.II.20. *e*Augustinus, etc. s.xiv in. [X; *cat.*, p. 61 X].
    B.II.21. *e*Augustinus. s.xi ex. [N, 1ª.3ⁱ.H; *cat.*, pp. 2, 60 N, 117].
    B.II.22. *e*Augustinus. s.xi ex. [D, 1ª.3ⁱ.A; *cat.*, pp. 1, 59 D, 117].
¶   B.II.23. *e*Augustinus. s.xiv in. [AD, AD (*in red*), 1ª.3ⁱ.B(?)].
    B.II.24. *e*Augustinus. s.xiv ex. [C; *cat.*, p. 59 C].
¶   B.II.25. *e*Augustinus. s.xiii ex. [E, 17; *cat.*, p. 59 E].
    B.II.26. *e*Augustinus. s.xii in. [A; *cat.*, p. 59 A].
¶   B.II.27. *e*Augustinus. s.xiv. [AC (*in red*); *cat.*, p. 63 AC].
¶   B.II.28. *e*Augustinus. s.xiv in. [B; *cat.*, p. 59 A (*recte* B)].
    B.II.29. *e*Augustinus. s.xiv. [2ª.2ⁱ.K; cf. *cat.*, p. 63 AD].
¶   B.II.30. Cassiodorus. s.viii. [E, 1ª.2ⁱ.K(?); *cat.*, pp. 3, 13 E, 88 E].
¶   B.II.31. *e*Omelie. s.xiv. [C, 4ᵗⁱ.C; *cat.*, p. 76 C].
    B.II.32. Gregorius. s.xiii in. [A, 1ª.3ⁱ.M; *cat.*, p. 63 A].[1]
    B.II.33. *e*Isidorus, etc. s.xiii in. [A; *cat.*, p. 65 A].
    B.II.34. *e*Florus. s.xii ex. [B, 2ª.3ⁱ.N; *cat.*, p. 64 C].
¶   B.II.35 (four sections, bound together by *c.* 1500). *e*Beda, etc. s.xi ex.–xv. [G; *Cat.*, pp. 3, 56 G, 65 G].
¶   B.II.36. *e*P. Comestor. s.xiii ex. [A].[2]
    B.III.1. *e*Origenes. s.xi ex. [1ⁱ.Q; *cat.*, pp. 2, 72 A, 118].
    B.III.2. *e*Didymus, etc. s.xii ex. [K, 1ⁱ.Z; *cat.*, p. 59K].
    B.III.3, fos. 1–56. *e*Augustinus. s.xii in. [S; *cat.*, p. 61 S].
    B.III.4, fos. 1–162. *e*Augustinus, etc. s.xiii ex. [2ª.2ⁱ.I; *cat.*, p. 63 AE].
¶   B.III.4, fos. 163–253. *e*Tabula Martiniana. s.xiv. [K; *cat.*, p. 46 K].
    B.III.5. *e*Augustinus. s.xii. [P, 1ª.3ⁱ.K; *cat.*, p. 60 P].
    B.III.6. *e*Augustinus. s.xiv ex. [Ab, 1ª.3ⁱ.E; *cat.*, p. 63 Ab].
    B.III.7. *e*Eugippius, etc. s.xiii/xiv. [V, 1ª.3ⁱ.F; *cat.*, p. 61 V].
    B.III.8. *e*Cassianus, etc. s.xiv in. [D; *cat.*, p. 69 D].
    B.III.9. *e*Gregorius. s.xi ex. [D, 1ª.3ⁱ.O; *cat.*, pp. 2, 63 D, 117].
    B.III.10. *e*Gregorius. s.xi ex. [C; *cat.*, pp. 2, 63 C, 117].
    B.III.11. *e*Gregorius, etc. s.xi ex. [F; *cat.*, pp. 63 F, 117].

[1] B.II.32 was earlier at **COLDINGHAM**.
[2] B.II.36 was earlier at the Franciscan convent at **YORK**.

Durham (*contd*)

Cathedral, B.III.12.   *e*Gregorius. s.xiv in. [F].

¶   B.III.13.   *e*Warnerius. s.xii ex. [G, 1ª.3ⁱ.R; *cat.*, p. 63 G].

B.III.14.   *e*Isidorus, etc. s.xii in. [E; *cat.*, p. 66 E].

B.III.15.   *e*Isidorus. s.xiii in. [D; *cat.*, p. 66 D].

¶   B.III.16 + B.III.10 flyleaves.   *e*Rabanus Maurus. s.xi ex. [A; *cat.*, pp. 3, 67 A, 117].

B.III.17.   *e*Jeronimus. s.xiii in. [A, 2ª.3ⁱ.B; *cat.*, p. 70 A].

B.III.18.   *e*Bernardus, etc. s.xiv ex. [G/8].

B.III.19.   *e*R. Grosseteste, etc. s.xiv ex. [2ª.5ⁱ.C].

B.III.20.   *i*P. Comestor. s.xiii.

¶   B.III.21.   *e*W. Peraldus, Summa de vitiis. s.xiii ex. [B, 4ⁱ.E; *cat.*, p. 71 B].

¶   B.III.22.   *e*Bonaventura, etc. s.xiv. [I, 2ª.6ⁱ.Q; *cat.*, p. 71 I].

B.III.23.   *e*Johannes Lector. s.xiv. [O; *cat.*, p. 47 O].

¶   B.III.24 (originally 2 vols.).   *e*Aegidius Romanus, etc. s.xiv ex. [S, 1ª.7ⁱ.R; *cat.*, p. 43 S].

B.III.25.   *e*J. de Abbatisvilla. s.xiii ex. [M; *cat.*, pp. 27 M, 104 M].

¶   B.III.26.   *e*Anselmus, etc. s.xiii ex. [F/8].

B.III.27.   *e*Tabule. s.xiv in. [Z; *cat.*, p. 83 Z].

B.III.28.   *b*Tabule. s.xiv. [1ª.3ⁱ.S(?)].

B.III.29.   *i*Tabule. A.D. 1438. [A].

B.III.30.   *i*Vitas Patrum, etc. s.xiii–xiv ex. [B].

¶   B.III.31.   *e*Tabule. s.xiv. [F, 2ª.2ⁱ.[.]; *cat.*, pp. 42 AF, 84 F].

B.IV.1.   Gregorius Nazianzenus. s.xii in. [C; *cat.*, pp. 2, 20 C, 96 C].

B.IV.2.   *e*J. Chrysostomus. s.xii ex. [B; *cat.*, pp. 3, 69 B].

B.IV.3.   *e*J. Chrysostomus. s.xiv. [1ª.3ⁱ.Z].

B.IV.4.   *e*Ambrosius. s.xii in. [C, C/15; *cat.*, p. 57 C].

B.IV.5.   *e*Ambrosius. s.xii in. [B, 2ª.2ⁱ.T; *cat.*, p. 57 B].

¶   B.IV.6.   *e*Augustinus, etc. s.xii in. [B (?), Q; *cat.*, pp. 1, 61 R (*recte* Q)].

B.IV.7.   *e*Augustinus, etc. s.xii in. [R, 2ª.2ⁱ.D; *cat.*, p. 61 R].

¶   B.IV.8.   Augustinus, etc. s.xii in. [B; *cat.*, pp. 19 B, 95 B].

B.IV.9.   *e*Prudentius. s.x. [A, 1ª.7ⁱ; *cat.*, pp. 2, 32 A, 109 A].

B.IV.10.   Cassianus, etc. s.xii ex. [G, G/4; *cat.*, pp. 24 G, 101 G].

¶   B.IV.11.   *e*Cassianus, etc. s.xii ex. [C, C/4; *cat.*, p. 69 C].

¶   B.IV.12.   *e*Augustinus, etc. s.xii in. [O, 2ª.2ⁱ.[ ]; *cat.*, pp. 2, 60 O].

B.IV.13.   *e*Gregorius. s.xi ex. [I; *cat.*, pp. 2, 64 I, 118].

¶   B.IV.14.   *e*Vite sanctorum. s.xii in. [L; *cat.*, pp. 54 L, 80 L, 118].

B.IV.15.   *e*Isidorus. s.xii in. [C; *cat.*, p. 65 C].

B.IV.16.   *e*Beda, etc. s.xii in. [G; *cat.*, p. 65 G].

¶   B.IV.17.   Decretum Burchardi, etc. s.xii. [H; *cat.*, pp. 35 H, 112 H].

Durham (*contd*)

¶   Cathedral, B.IV.18.   *e*Collectanea Juris Canonici. s.xii in. [T, 2ª.8ⁱ.K; *cat.*, pp. 35 T, 112 T].

          B.IV.19.   Anselmus, etc. s.xiv. [H, H/15].

          B.IV.20.   Bernardus, etc. s.xii/xiii. [F; *cat.*, pp. 21 F, 97 F].

          B.IV.21.   Bernardus. s.xiii. [B].

          B.IV.22.   *e*Bernardus, etc. s.xii ex. [B; *cat.*, p. 66 B].

          B.IV.23.   *e*Bernardus, etc. s.xiii in. [A; *cat.*, p. 66 A].

          B.IV.24.   *e*Martyrologium, etc. s.xi ex.–xii. [A; *cat.*, pp. 30 A, 107 A].

          B.IV.25.   *e*Aelredus, etc. s.xii ex.–xii/xiii. [B, B/2; *cat.*, pp. 25 B, 101 B].

          B.IV.26.   *e*Regula S. Benedicti, etc. s.xiv ex.

          B.IV.27.   H. de S. Victore, etc. s.xii/xiii. [P].

          B.IV.28.   *e*P. Riga, etc. s.xiii. [R, 4ⁱ.Q.2; *cat.*, pp. 11 R, 85 R].

          B.IV.29.   *e*P. Aureolus. s.xiv. [2ª.5ⁱ.I].

          B.IV.30.   *e*N. de Hanapis, etc. s.xiv. [T/12].

          B.IV.31.   *e*Aegidius Romanus. s.xiv. [T, T/57].

¶   B.IV.32 (originally 2 vols.) + B.IV.39B, fos. 2–4/1–3. *e*R. Armachanus, etc. s.xiv in.–xv in. [S, 2ª.6ⁱ.G; G].

          B.IV.34.   *i*Uthredus Boldon, etc. s.xiv. [T].

          B.IV.36.   *e*R. Higden, Speculum curatorum. s.xiv/xv. [H].

¶   B.IV.37.   Excerpta patrum, etc. s.xii in. [M, 2ª.9ⁱ.K *deleted*, 2ª.9ⁱ.I, 1ª.9ⁱ.I; *cat.*, pp. 35 M, 112 M].

          B.IV.39A.   *e*J. de Voragine, etc. s.xiv [Q, Q/4].[1]

          B.IV.39B.   Vita S. Oswaldi, etc. s.xiii in. [D; *cat.*, pp. 29 D, 106 D].[1]

          B.IV.40.   *e*Mariale. s.xv. [P].

          B.IV.41.   *i*Constit. Clementine, etc. s.xiv in.–xv in.

          B.IV.42.   *e*Tabule, etc. s.xiv/xv.

          B.IV.43.   *e*Tabule, etc. s.xiv. [AH; *cat.*, p. 83 AH].

+   B.IV.45.   *ic*Constitutiones Benedict., etc. s.xiv/xv.

+   C.I.1.   Digestum vetus. s.xiii/xiv. [F].   ?

¶   C.I.2.   Digestum inforciatum. s.xiii in. [F, 2a.9ⁱ.C].

¶   C.I.3.   *e*Digestum novum. s.xiii ex. [A, 2ª.9ⁱ.K; *cat.*, pp. 36 A, 37 A, 114 A].[2]

¶   C.I.4.   *e*Parvum volumen. s.xiii ex. [A, B, 2ª.9ⁱ.I; *cat.*, pp. 36 B, 37 B, 114 B].[2]

¶   C.I.5.   *m*Parvum volumen. s.xiv.

          C.I.6.   *e*Codex Justiniani. s.xiii ex. [A; *cat.*, pp. 36 A, 114 A].

          C.I.7.   *e*Decretum Gratiani. s.xii/xiii. [B, 2ª.8ⁱ.P; *cat.*, pp. 34 B, 112 B].

¶   C.I.8.   Decretum Gratiani. s.xii/xiii. [N; *cat.*, p. 46 N].

          C.I.9.   *m*Decretales Gregorii noni. s.xiii ex.[2]

---

[1] B.IV.39A and B were 2 vols. until after s.xv in, as at present, but were bound in one vol. by s.xvi in.

[2] C.I.3, C.I.4, C.I.6 and C.I.9 are companion volumes.

Durham (*contd*)

Cathedral, C.I.11. *i*Bernardus Compostellanus, etc. s.xiv.

C.I.12. *e*Odofredus. s.xiv in. [C, 2ª.9ⁱ.A; *cat.*, pp. 36 C, 37 C, 114 C].

C.I.13. *e*H. de Segusio. s.xiii ex. [T; *cat.*, p. 48 T].

C.I.14. *e*Sextus liber decretalium, etc. s.xiv in. [1ª.9ⁱ.M; *cat.*, p. 47 I].

C.I.16. *e*Logica vetus et nova. s.xiv in. [Q, 2ª.10ⁱ.A].

¶ C.I.17 (now 2 vols.). Aristoteles. s.xiv. [Cf. *cat.*, p. 77 B]. ?

C.I.18. *e*Aristoteles. s.xiv in. [D, 1ª.10ⁱ.O; *cat.*, p. 77 D].

¶ C.I.19, fos. 1–233 (originally 2 vols.). Constantinus; Bernardus de Gordonio. s.xiii. [K, 2ª.7ⁱ.K; *cat.*, p. 79 K].

C.I.19, fos. 234–324. *e*Avicenna. s.xiv. [B, 2ª.7ⁱ.X; *cat.*, p. 78 B].

C.I.20. *e*Hugutio, etc. s.xiii ex.–xiv. [4ⁱ.M].

C.II.1. *e*Decretum Gratiani. s.xii ex. [C; *cat.*, p. 46 C].

C.II.2. *e*Decretales Gregorii noni, etc. s.xiii ex. [A; *cat.*, p. 47 A].

C.II.3. *e*Decretales Gregorii noni, etc. s.xiii. [D; *cat.*, p. 47 D].

C.II.4. Decretales Gregorii noni, etc. s.xiii ex. [2ª.8ⁱ.P (*altered to* O)].

¶ C.II.5. *e*Decretales Gregorii noni, etc. s.xiii ex. [E; *cat.*, p. 47 C].

C.II.6. *e*P. de Salinis. s.xiv in. [H, 1ª.9ⁱ.D; *cat.*, p. 46 H].

C.II.7. *e*H. de Segusio. s.xiv. [2ª.8ⁱ.N].

¶ C.II.8. *e*H. de Segusio. s.xiv. [2ª.8ⁱ.N.2].

¶ C.II.9. *s*J. Andree. s.xiv in. [X].

¶ C.II.10. *e*Summa Goffredi, etc. s.xiv in. [Y; *cat.*, pp. 36 X, 113 X].

C.II.11. *e*W. Durandus, etc. s.xiv in. [AD; *cat.*, p. 48 AD].

C.II.12. W. Durandus. s.xiii/xiv. [Cat., p. 48 AC].

C.II.13. *e*W. de Pagula, etc. s.xiv. [L; *cat.*, p. 47 L].

¶ C.III.1, fos. 1–18. *e*Excerpta decretorum. s.xii/xiii. [K, 2ª.8ⁱ.T; *cat.*, pp. 35 K, 112 K].

¶ C.III.1, fos. 19–311. *e*Decretum Gratiani. s.xii/xiii. [*Cat.*, p. 46 F].

¶ C.III.2. *e*Decretales Gregorii noni. s.xiii. [N, 1ª.8ⁱ.B; *cat.*, pp. 35 D, 113 D].

¶ C.III.3. 'Decretales antique'. s.xiii in. [H, 1ª.8ⁱ.H; *cat.*, pp. 35 H, 113 H].

¶ C.III.4. 'Decretales antique', s.xiii. [E, 1ª.8ⁱ.I; *cat.*, pp. 35 E, 113 E].

¶ C.III.5. *e*Bartholomeus Brixiensis. s.xiv in. [R, 1ª.9ⁱ.E; *cat.*, pp. 35 R, 112 R].

C.III.6. *e*N. de Tudeschis, etc. s.xiii/xiv. [P, 1ª.9ⁱ.G].

¶ C.III.7. J. Faventinus. s.xiii in. [F, E, Q, 2ª.8ⁱ.D; *cat.*, pp. 35 Q, 112 Q].

Durham (*contd*)

Cathedral, C.III.8.   Glossa Palatina super Decreta. s.xiii in. [V, 2ª.8ⁱ.C; *cat.*, p. 112 V].

¶   C.III.9.   *e*Innocentius IV. s.xiii/xiv. [o D].

¶   C.III.10.   *e*Summa Goffredi. s.xiv in. [O].

C.III.11.   *e*Bartholomeus de S. Concordio, etc. s.xv in. [Q, 1ª.9ⁱ.P].

C.III.12.   Summa Goffredi, etc. s.xiii ex. [2ª.9ⁱ.G].

C.III.13.   *e*Tabule. s.xiii–xiv. [1ª.9ⁱ.O].

¶   C.III.14.   Aristoteles, etc. s.xiii. [S, 2ª.10ⁱ.M; *cat.*, pp. 32 S, 110 S].

C.III.15.   *e*Averroes, etc. s.xiii. [C, 1ª.10ⁱ.P; *cat.*, p. 77 C].

C.III.16.   *e*Averroes. s.xiv in. [K, 1ª.10ⁱ.E].

C.III.17.   *i*Aristoteles. s.xiii ex. [2ª.10ⁱ.K].

C.III.18.   *e*Suetonius. s.xi ex. [AG/9].

¶   C.III.20 (2 fos.) + A.II.10, fos. 2–5, 338–9, and C.III.13, fos. 192–5.   Evangelia (2 fos.). s.vii/viii.

+   C.III.22.   *e*Biblia. s.xiii.

¶   C.IV.1.   Decreta non glosata. s.xii/xiii. [G; *cat.*, pp. 35 G, 112 G].

C.IV.4.   *e*Medica quedam. s.xiii in. [V, 2ª.7ⁱ.Be].

C.IV.5.   Cicero. s.xii. [C, 2ª.7ⁱ.P; *cat.*, pp. 31 C, 108 C, 119].

C.IV.7.   Glose in Ciceronem, etc. s.xii in. [*Cat.*, pp. 31 F, 108 F].

C.IV.10.   Comment. in Boetium. s.xii in. [F; *cat.*, pp. 4, 30 F, 108 F].

¶   C.IV.11.   Alexander Trallianus. s.xii ex. [L; *cat.*, pp. 33 L, 111 L].

C.IV.12.   *e*Constantinus Africanus. s.xii. [H, h/95; *cat.*, p. 78 H].

¶   C.IV.13.   *e*Isaac Judeus. s.xiii in. [2ª.7ⁱ.E4; *cat.*, p. 111 K].

C.IV.15.   Chronica, etc. s.xii in. [1ª.7ⁱ.E(?); *cat.*, pp. 30 O, 107 O].

C.IV.16, fos. 1–166.   Aristoteles. s.xiii ex. [2ª.10ⁱ.F].

¶   C.IV.16, fos. 167–304.   *e*Aristoteles. s.xiii ex. [E (*altered to* G), 1ª.10ⁱ.G; *cat.*, p. 77 E].

C.IV.17.   *e*Aristoteles. s.xiii ex. [2ª.10ⁱ.C].

C.IV.19.   Aristoteles. s.xiii ex. [G, 2ª.10ⁱ.D; *cat.*, pp. 32 G, 109 G].

¶   C.IV.20A.   J. de Ditneshale. s.xiii ex. [M, 1ª.10ⁱ.[.]; *cat.*, pp. 32 M, 110 M].

C.IV.20B.   *e*Tabula in Aristotelem. s.xiv ex. [N, 1ª.10ⁱ.H].

C.IV.21.   *e*Tabule. s.xv in. [EM].

¶   C.IV.22.   *e*N. Bonetus, etc. s.xv. [K/ii].

¶   C.IV.23, fos. 57–128.   *i*G. de Vinosalvo. s.xv.

¶   C.IV.24.   *e*P. de Vineis, etc. s.xiii/xiv. [I, AG; *cat.*, p. 48 AG].

Durham (*contd*)

¶ Cathedral, C.IV.25. *i*Registrum litterarum. s.xv in. [L; *cat.*, p. 124 L].

+   C.IV.26. *i*Grammatica. s.xiii ex.

¶   C.IV.29. *e*Note super Priscianum et super Rethoricam Tullii. s.xii in. [F; *cat.*, pp. 33 P (*recte* F), 111 F].

+   Hunter 58. Excerpta patristica. s.xiv. [F]. ?

¶   100. Medica quedam. s.xii in. [C4; *cat.*, pp. 33 A, 110 A].

          101. *c*Reginaldus Dunelm. s.xii ex.

¶   Inc. 1a–d (pr. bks). *i*N. de Lyra (i–iv). (Strasbourg, *c.* A.D. 1474–77).

¶   1f (pr. bk). *e*N. de Lyra (ii). (Nuremberg, A.D. 1481). [Q].

          2 (pr. bk). *i*P. Comestor. Strasbourg, A.D. 1483.

¶   3 (pr. bk). *i*Bartholomeus Anglicus. Strasbourg, A.D. 1491. [A 8].

¶   4a (pr. bk). *e*J. Duns Scotus. (Strasbourg), A.D. 1474.

+   6 (pr. bk). Boethius. Cologne, A.D. 1481. [33].

¶   11a (pr. bk). *e*Gregorius, Moralia. (Cologne, *c.* A.D. 1479). [H].

+   12 (pr. bk). *m*Alexander Carpenter. Cologne, A.D. 1480. [K].

¶   13a, b (pr. bk). *e*Omeliarium (2 vols). (Cologne, *c.* 1475).

¶   14c (pr. bk). *e*J. Duns Scotus. Nuremberg, A.D. 1481. [LA].

¶   15a (pr. bk). *i*Repertorium in postillam N. de Lyra. Nuremberg, A.D. 1494.

¶   20a (pr. bk). *e*N. de Tudeschis. Venice, (A.D. 1477). [S].

¶   20b (pr. bk). *e*N. de Tudeschis. Venice, (A.D. 1478). [T].

¶   21b (pr. bk). *i*J. Duns Scotus. Venice, A.D. 1481. [A 29].

¶   22 (pr. bk). *e*P. de Abano. (Venice, A.D. 1483). [SA].

          25 (pr. bk). *i*A. de Rampengolis. Venice, A.D. 1496.

          32–34 (pr. bks). *e*Bartholus de Saxoferrato (3 vols). Venice, A.D. 1483.

          35 (pr. bk). *e*J. M. Parthenopeus. Treviso, A.D. 1480.

¶   43 (pr. bk). *e*N. de Tudeschis. Basel, A.D. 1488.

          44 (pr. bk). *i*Augustinus, In Psalmos. Basel, A.D. 1489.

¶   45 (pr. bk). *i*Augustinus, Super Johannem. (Basel, ante A.D. 1492).

          47a (pr. bk). *e*H. Bohic. Lyon, A.D. 1498.

          47b (pr. bk). *i*W. Lyndwode. Paris, A.D. 1501.

¶   48 (pr. bk). *i*J. de Turrecremata. Deventer, A.D. 1484. [31].

          53 (pr. bk). *e*A. de Montalvo. Louvain, A.D. 1486.

+   61 (pr. bk). *i*Alexander de Hales. Oxford, A.D. 1481. [34].

Durham (*contd*)
¶   Cathedral, Inc. 62 (pr. bk). *e*W. Lyndwode. (Oxford, A.D. 1483).
            B.V.58 (pr. bk). *e*J. Dytenbergius. Cologne, A.D. 1524.
¶   D.VI.37 (pr. bk). *i*Hieronymus,   Epistole.   Basel,
            A.D. 1524.
            D.VII.23–24 (pr. bks). *e*Ambrosius (2 vols.). Basel,
               A.D. 1527.
            P.V.16, 17 (pr. bks). *i*Origenes (2 vols.). Paris, A.D. 1512.
+   P.X.40 (pr. bk). *i*G. Reisch. Basel, A.D. 1517.
+   Muniments, Endpapers & Bindings, no. 17. *l*Kalendarium.
                     s.xiii in.   ?
¶   U.L., Cosin V.i.4. P. Lombardus. s.xii ex. [*Cat.*, pp. 13 BB, 89 BB].
            V.i.8. *e*Anselmus, etc. s.xiv in. [D; *cat.*, p. 71 D].
¶   V.ii.1. Numeri glo. s.xii ex. [A; *cat.*, pp. 12 A, 87 A].
            V.ii.2. *e*Ruth, etc., glo., etc. s.xii ex. [D; *cat.*, p. 50 D].
            V.ii.5. *i*Speculum amicitie, etc. s.xiv.
¶   V.ii.6. *e*Simeon Dunelm. s.xii in. [R, O; *cat.*, pp. 4,
                124 O].
            V.ii.8. Odo Cantuar. s.xiii in. [O; *cat.*, p. 75 O].
¶   V.iii.1. *e*Laurent. Dunelm. s.xii ex. [1ᵃ.7ⁱ.Z; *cat.*, pp.
                26 F, 102 F; Leland, *De Script. Brit.*, p. 205].
+   V.iii.3. *m*Constitutiones Clement., etc. s.xiii ex.–xv.
+   V.iii.4. *m*Liber sextus decretalium. s.xiv in.
¶   V.v.6. *l*Graduale. s.xi/xii.
¶   Mickleton & Spearman, 89. *e*P. Limovicensis. s.xiv in. [9.v., g].
¶   GSAD A92K, formerly S.R.2.B.12 (pr. bk). *i*J. Sprenger.
                        (Speier, A.D. 1492).
    Edinburgh,
¶   N.L., Adv. 18.4.3. *e*Paradysus, etc. s.xii. [C (*altered to* T), 1ᵃ.7ⁱ.T;
              cat., p. 67 C].
¶   18.6.11. *e*Medica. s.xii. [D; *cat.*, pp. 7, 33 H, 110 H].
+   U.L., 106. Tabule. s.xiv/xv. [*Cat.*, p. 83 AI].
    Glasgow, U.L., Hunterian 85. Kalendarium, etc. s.xii. [F, 2ᵃ.3ⁱ.T;
      Cat., p. 64 F].
¶ Gouda, Messrs Koch & Knuttel. Now Hilversum, below.
+ Gredington, Lord Kenyon (pr. bk). *i*G. Tornacensis. Lyon, A.D. 1511.
    Hawkesyard Priory (pr. bk). *i*R. Holcot. (Paris), A.D. 1489.[1]
    Hereford, Cathedral, A.ix.2, 3 (pr. bks). *e*V. T. polyglot. Complutens.
    (Alcala), A.D. 1517.
¶ Hilversum, Messrs C. de Boer (pr. bk). *i*Sermones sensati. Gouda,
    A.D. 1482.
¶ Lincoln, Cathedral, 162. *e*Hugucio, etc. s.xv. [M *deleted*, V; *cat.*, p.
               49 M].
+   240. *m*Aelredus. s.xii.
            F.1.14 (pr. bk). *e*Biblia Complutens.,   vol. v.
                (Alcala), A.D. 1517.
+ Liverpool, Merseyside County Museums, 12036. *m*Eugippius, etc. s.xiii/
    xiv. [A3].

---

[1] In 1986 at St Dominic's Priory, Newport, Isle of Wight, pending a decision about its final destination.

London,

B.L., Add. 6162. *c*Laurent. Dunelm., etc. s.xv. ?

¶   16616.   Marcus glo. s.xii ex. [A; *cat.*, pp. 16 A, 92 A, 118].

¶   24059.   *see above under* **COLDINGHAM**.

               28805.   *i*Opusculum rhetorice preceptionis, etc. s.xv/xvi.

¶   38666, fo. 4.   *e*Prosper (flyleaf only). [A].

¶   39943.   *see* Yates Thompson 26, *below*.

        Arundel 332.   *e*R. Grosseteste, etc. s.xiii.

¶   507.   *c*Theologica (partly in English). s.xiii–xiv.

¶   Burney 310.   *e*Eusebius, etc. A.D. 1381. [N, 1ª.7ⁱ.Q; *cat.*, pp. 56 N, 65 N].

¶   Cotton Jul.A.vi.   Hymnarium (gloss in English). s.xi in. [A; *cat.*, pp. 33 A, 111 A].

¶   D.iv.   *e*Chronicon Anglie. s.xiv. [K; *cat.*, p. 124 K].

¶   D.vi.   *c*Chronicon Anglie, etc. s.xiii ex.

¶   Claud.D.iv.   *e*Historia Dunelm. s.xv in.

¶   Nero D.iv.   *e*Evangelia ('Lindisfarne Gospels'). s.vii/viii.

          Otho B.ix.   *e*Evangelia. s.ix. [*Athelstan*].

          Vit.A.ix.   *c*Collectiones J. Washington. s.xv. ?

¶   C.viii, fos. 85–90.   Epp. Pauli. s.viii. [L; *cat.*, pp. 18 L, 93 L].[1]

            D.xx.   *c*Misc. de S. Cuthberto. s.xii. ?

            E.xii, fos. 55–113.   *c*Miscellanea. s.xv med.

          Vesp.A.vi, fos. 61–89.   *c*Chronicon Dunelm., etc. s.xiv. ?

            B.x, fos. 1–23.   Vita S. Brendani (partly in French), etc. s.xiv in.[2]

          Titus A.ii.   *c*Misc. Dunelm. s.xiv. ?

            A.xviii.   *e*G. Monemutensis, etc. s.xiv. [Q].[2]

            D.xix, fo. 170.   *i*(flyleaf only).

          Domit.vii.   *c*Liber vite. s.ix–xvi.

¶   Fragments xxix, fos. 36–39.   *e*(endleaves to Titus A.xviii + Vesp.B.x).

        Harley 491.   *e*W. Gemmeticensis. s.xii. [L; *cat.*, p. 56 L].

            1804.   *cl*Horae, etc. s.xv ex.

¶   1924.   *c*Beda. s.xii. [D; *cat.*, p. 116].[3]

            3049.   *e*Ambrosius, etc. s.xv med. [2ª.2ⁱ.Q].

¶   3858.   *e*Opus vii custodiarum. s.xv in. [I, 2ª.5ᵗⁱ.G; *cat.*, pp. 79 I, 83].

            3864.   *e*Beda. s.xii. [D; *cat.*, p. 64 D].

+   3946.   Gregorius, etc. s.xiii. [D, 1.3ⁱ.T2; *cat.*, pp. 20 D, 96 D].

            4657.   *c*Poemata (partly in French). s.xiv.

            4664.   *i*Breviarium. s.xiii/xiv.

¶   4688.   *e*Beda. s.xii in. [D (*erased*), F; *cat.*, pp. 20 D, 96 D].

¶   4703.   *e*Sermones. s.xiv. [H; *cat.*, pp. 27 H, 104 H].

---

[1] Cotton Vit. C.viii, fos. 85–90, was part of Cambridge, Trinity Coll., 216.

[2] Cotton Vesp. B.x (fos. 1–23) and Cotton Titus A.xviii formed one volume, of which Cotton fragments xxix (fos. 36–39) were the endleaves.

[3] Bodleian, Digby 41, fos. 91, 91*, 92, 101, was part of Harley 1924.

London (*contd*)

B.L., Harley 4725. *i*Bonaventura, etc. s.xii–xiv.

¶ 4747. *see above under* **COLDINGHAM**.

4843. *i*Miscellanea. s.xvi in.

4894. Sermones R. Ripon. s.xiv. [M; *cat.*, p. 76 R].

5234. *e*Isidorus, etc. s.xiii.

¶ 5289. *e*Missale. s.xiv.

Lansdowne 397. *i*Ric. de Pophis, etc. s.xiv. [P; *cat.*, p. 124 P].

Loan 74. *See* Stonyhurst College, *below.*

¶ Royal 6 A.v. Fulgentius. s.xi med. [A, 2ª.3ⁱ.H; *cat.*, pp. 24 A, 101 A].

7 A.vi. *b*Mariale, etc. s.xiv.

+ Stowe 930. *c*Constit. synodales Dunelm. etc. s.xiii–xv.

¶ Yates Thompson 26 (formerly Add. 39943). *e*Beda. s.xii ex. [*Cat.*, pp. 29 O, 107 O].

College of Arms, Arundel 25. *c*Hist. Dunelm., etc. s.xiv. ?

¶ Dulwich College, 23. *e*W. Brito. s.xiv. [H; *cat.*, p. 49 H].

¶ Lambeth Palace, 10–12. Historia aurea (3 vols.). s.xiv. [D E F; *cat.*, p. 56 D E F].

¶ 23. Alex. Nequam, etc. s.xiv/xv. [T, 2ª.5ᵗⁱ.M].

¶ 325. Ennodius. s.x in. [A, 1ª.7ⁱ.O.i; *cat.*, pp. 32 A, 109 A].

483. *e*Pseudo-Grosseteste, etc. s.xiv.

Law Society, 107.d (pr. bk). *e*W. Durandus, Strasbourg, A.D. 1493.[1]

¶ Lincoln's Inn, Hale 114. *i*Misc. Dunelm. ('Liber rubeus'). s.xv–xvi.

¶ Soc. of Antiquaries, 7. *e*Anselmus, etc. s.xii in. [Y; *cat.*, p. 63 Y].

¶ Longleat, Marquess of Bath, 13. 'De officiis divinis que pertinent ad episcopum'. s.xiii. [A *altered to* T, de cancellaria T; *cat.*, pp. 34 A, 111 A].

+ Los Angeles, Univ. of California, Biomedical Libr. (pr. bk). *i*Rhazes. Venice, A.D. 1493.

¶ Nottingham, U.L., Middleton deposit L.M.5. *e*Biblia. s.xiii.

Oxford,

Bodleian, Auct. 1. Q.5.1 (pr. bk). *i*Joannes Franciscus, Brixianus. Venice, A.D. 1500.

Bodley 819. *s*Beda. s.viii.

¶ Digby 41, fos. 91, 91*, 92, 101. *m*Reliquie Dunelm., etc. s.xii.[2]

¶ 81, fos. 133–140. *e*Misc. computistica. s.xi in. [C].

Douce 129. *i*J. de Sacro Bosco, etc. s.xv.

¶ Fairfax 6. *e*Vita S. Cuthberti, etc. s.xiv. [P; *cat.*, p. 55 P].[3]

Lat.liturg.f.5. Evangelistarium. s.xi. ?[4]

¶ Lat.misc.b.13, fo. 51. *i*(flyleaf only) *formerly* London, British Records Assn., 481.

¶ Laud Lat. 12. *e*Biblia. s.xiii. [B *corr. from* C; *cat.*, pp. 10 C. 85 C].

---

[1] Deposited in Canterbury Cathedral Library.
[2] See p. 30, n. 3.
[3] Laud Misc. 700 is probably copied from Fairfax 6, whence also passages were copied in B.L., Harley 4843.
[4] Cf. H. H. E. Craster in *Bodleian Quarterly Record*, iv. 202–3.

Oxford (*contd*)

Bodleian, Laud Lat. 36. *e*Psalterium glo. s.xiii. [I, 1ª.[..]F; *cat.*, p. 51 I].

¶ Laud Misc. 52. Ivo Carnotensis, etc. s.xii in. [E; *cat.*, pp. 24 E, 101 E].[1]

262. *e*Sermones. s.xiv. [K; *cat.*, p. 75 K].

277. H. de S. Victore, etc. s.xii. [1ª.5ᵗⁱ.F; *cat.*, p. 67 D].

¶ 344. *e*H. de S. Victore, etc. s.xii ex.–xiii in. [C (*altered to* D), 2ª.3ⁱ.D; *cat.*, pp. 16 C, 91 C].

345. Miscellanea. s.xiii–xiv. [R].

359. *e*Jeronimus, etc. s.xii. [D; *cat.*, p. 57 D].

¶ 368. *e*P. Blesensis, etc. s.xiii–xv. [E].

389. *e*Pera peregrini abbrev. s.xiv. [*Cat.*, p. 71 G].

¶ 392. *e*H. de S. Victore, etc. s.xii. [A; *cat.*, pp. 21 A, 97 A].

402. Dictamina, etc. s.xiii–xv. [2ª.5ᵗⁱ.P].

¶ 413. *e*Vita S. Godrici. s.xii. [L, 1ª.7ⁱ.V; *cat.*, pp. 29 L, 106 L].

489. *e*J. de Voragine. s.xiii ex. [F].

491. *s*Beda, etc. s.xii. ?

546. *e*Julianus Tolet. s.xi ex. [A; ?*cat.*, pp. 3, 118].

603. *e*Martinus Polonus, etc. s.xiv. [I, 1ª.7ᵐⁱ.F, 2ª.7ⁱ.F; *cat.*, p. 56 I].

¶ 641. *e*P. Chrysologus. s.xiii. [F, 2ª.5ᵗⁱ.T; *cat.*, pp. 75 F, 118].

700. Chronica Dunelm. s.xiv.[2] ?

748. *i*Hist. Dunelm. s.xv.

Lyell 16. *i*'Petrus Ruffensis in summula viciorum'. s.xiv.

¶ Rawl. C.4. *e*Enchiridion penitentiale. s.xiv. [AH; *cat.*, p. 72 AH].

D.338. *e*Jeronimus, etc. s.xii. [L, 1ⁱ.M; *cat.*, p. 59 L].

+ Tanner 4. *i*Augustinus, etc. s.xiii–xiv in. [F].

¶ Wood empt. 24. Augustinus, etc. s.xii. [K; *cat.*, pp. 20 K, 95 K].

Brasenose Coll., 4. *e*Biblia. s.xiii. [A].

Magdalen Coll., lat. 162. *i*W. Milverley, etc. s.xv.

Oriel Coll., C.e.20 (pr. bk). *i*Lactantius, etc. Venice, A.D. 1509, and Paris, A.D. 1515.

¶ St John's Coll., 14. *e*P. de Herentals. s.xiv/xv. [G].

¶ 97. *e*Historia post Bedam. s.xiii in. [K; *cat.*, p. 56 K].

¶ 154. *e*Aelfric (Lat. and Eng.). s.xi in. [E, 2ª.7ⁱ.N; *cat.*, pp. 33 E, 111 E].

---

[1] Cambridge, Jesus Coll. 52, 53 and Bodleian, Laud Misc. 52 formed one volume.

[2] See p. 31, n. 3.

Oxford (*contd*)
    St John's Coll., P.4.46 (pr. bk). *i*N. Dorbellus. Basel, A.D. 1494.
    University Coll., 86. *e*Gratianus. s.xiii. [Q].
+Plymouth, City Museum, C1/S37/11. W. Peraldus. s.xiii [KK, C; *cat.*,
    pp. 28 KK, 105 KK].
+Shrewsbury, Shrewsbury School, XXI. *s*Gregorius, Liber pastoralis. s.xi
    ex. [*Cat.*, pp. 2, 117]. ?
¶ Stonyhurst College, 55. *e*Evangelium Johannis. s.vii.[1]
¶ Tollerton, St Hugh's Coll. Now Durham Cathedral, Inc. 15A, and
    D.VI.37.
+Toronto, Pontifical Institute, A.I.10 (pr. bk). *i*Duns Scotus. Venice,
    A.D. 1481.
Ushaw, St Cuthbert's College,
    XVII.E.4.1 (pr. bk).[2] *i*T. Aquinas. Basel, A.D. 1495.
        E.4.2 (pr. bk).[2] *i*Bonaventura. Strasbourg, A.D. 1495.
¶   E.4.6–10 (pr. bks).[2] *mi*Nich. de Lyra (5 vols.). Lyon, A.D. 1520.
+   E.4.11 (pr. bk). *m*Pseudo-Beda. Paris, s.a.
¶   E.5.4 (pr. bk). *i*J. Sarisburiensis. Paris, A.D. 1513.
+   E.5.6 (pr. bk). *i*D. Erasmus. Basel, A.D. 1534.
¶   E.5.9 (pr. bk).[2] *i*J. Damascenus (in Latin). Paris, A.D. 1512.
        F.4.1 (pr. bk).[2] *i*T. Aquinas, etc. Venice, A.D. 1500, etc.
        F.4.3 (pr. bk).[2] *i*P. Lombardus. Basel, A.D. 1516.
        F.4.4 (pr. bk).[2] *i*L. de Saxonia. Paris, A.D. 1517.
        F.4.5 (pr. bk).[2] *i*Destructorium viciorum. Paris, A.D. 1521.
        F.4.12 (pr. bk).[3] *i*Augustinus. Basel, A.D. 1489.
¶   F.4.13. Now E.5.9 above.
¶   G.4.1–2 (pr. bks).[2] *e*Origenes (in Latin; 2 vols.). Paris,
        A.D. 1512.
        G.4.3 (pr. bk).[3] *i*M. Vigerius. Fano, A.D. 1507.
        G.4.5 (pr. bk).[2] *i*F. de Puteo. Paris, A.D. 1530.
    XVIII.A.3.4–5 (pr. bk). *i*V. Ferrerius (2 vols.). Strasbourg,
        A.D. 1493–94.
        A.3.11 (pr. bk). *m*R. Higden, Polychronicon (in Eng.). West-
        minster, A.D. 1495.
        A.3.12 (pr. bk). *i*Augustinus. Basel, A.D. 1495.
¶   A.3.15 (pr. bk). *i*Dictionarius pauperum. Paris, A.D. 1498.
        [A 41].
+   A.4.1 (pr. bk). *see below under* **OXFORD**, Durham College.
¶   B.1.2 (pr. bk). *m*A. de Spina, Fortalicium fidei. (Nuremberg,
        A.D. 1485).
¶   B.3.5–11 (pr. bks). *mi*H. de S. Caro (7 vols.). Basel,
        A.D. 1502.
+   B.4.3(1) (pr. bk). *m*Ambrosius. Cologne, A.D. 1520.
¶   B.4.4 (pr. bk). *i*Gesta Romanorum. (? Nuremberg, A.D. 1497).
        B.4.24 (pr. bk). *m*B. de Bustis. Lyon, A.D. 1502.

[1] Deposited in London, B.L., Loan 74.
[2] On permanent loan to Ushaw Coll. from St Mary's Roman Catholic Church, Yealand Conyers, Lancs.: cf. *Ushaw Magazine*, no. 184 (1952), pp. 41–47.
[3] Deposited at Ushaw Coll. in 1952 by the trustees of the Silvertop heirlooms, from the library at Minsteracres, Shotley Bridge, Co. Durham.

Ushaw (*contd*)
+   XVIII.B.5.2 (pr. bk). *m*Duns Scotus. (Venice, A.D. 1497).
         B.5.15 (pr. bk). *i*Augustinus. Paris, A.D. 1515.
         B.6.7 (pr. bk). *i*J. Major. Paris, A.D. 1529.
+   B.6.10 (pr. bk). *m*Dionysius Carthusianus. Cologne, A.D. 1532.
         B.7.6 (pr. bk). *i*B. de Bustis. Lyon, A.D. 1513.
         C.2.9 (pr. bk). *i*P. Comestor. Basel, A.D. 1486.
+   C.3.5 (pr. bk). *m*Augustinus, In Johannem. (Basel, not after A.D. 1491).
¶   C.3.13(ii) (pr. bk). *i*Aegidius Romanus, etc. Venice, A.D. 1502, etc.
         C.4.11 (pr. bk). *m*H. de S. Victore, etc. Paris, A.D. 1507.
         C.5.2 (pr. bk). *i*P. Berchorius. Basel, A.D. 1515.
¶   C.5.10–11 (pr. bks). *mi*J. Chrysostomus (2 vols.). Basel, A.D. 1517.
         C.5.15 (pr. bk). *i*P. Tateretus. Paris, A.D. 1520.
¶   G.3.10–11 (pr. bks).[1] *i*Ambrosius (2 vols.). Basel, A.D. 1516.
+   G.4.13 (pr. bk). *m*De quatuor novissimis, etc. (Paris, A.D. 1498 or 1499).
Winchester, Cathedral, 10. *ic*Vita S. Godrici. s.xv in.
York,
¶   Minster, VII.G.4 (pr. bk). *i*W. Burley, etc. Venice, A.D. 1485, etc. [34 (?)].
¶   X.A.7 (pr. bk). *i*Duns Scotus, Nuremberg, A.D. 1481. [29].
         X.G.13 (pr. bk). *i*J. Trithemius. Strasbourg, A.D. 1516.
         XI.G.4 (pr. bk). *i*Psalterium quincuplex. Paris, A.D. 1509.
         XII.J.22 (pr. bk). *i*P. Comestor. Basel, A.D. 1486.
         XIV.B.22 (pr. bk). *e*Panormitanus. Basel, A.D. 1488.
         XV.A.12 (pr. bk). *i*G. de Baysio. Venice, A.D. 1495.
         XVI.D.9 (pr. bk). *e*W. de Alvernia. s.xv. [a/12].
         XVI.I.1. *i*Theologica. s.xv ex.
¶   XVI.I.12. *e*Misc. Dunelm. s.xiii ex.–xv.
¶   XVI.K.4. Augustinus, etc. s.xiv. [H, 1 2; *cat.*, pp. 19 H, 95 H].
         XVI.N.8. *e*Psalterium, etc. s.xiv. [H].
¶   XVI.Q.5. *e*Ezechiel glo. s.xii ex. [A; *cat.*, pp. 15 A, 91 A].
¶   XIX.C.5 (pr. bk). *e*J. Balbus, Catholicon. Strasbourg, A.D. 1482 or 1485. [T].
Untraced: Phillipps sale (Sotheby, 21–26 March 1895), lot 136 to Quaritch, who sold to Harrassowitz. *e*Cassiodorus, etc. s.xiii.
    Messrs Quaritch in 1961 (sold then to E. Rossignol, bookseller, Paris, who sold to an unknown customer). *i*Biblia. s.xiii.
Rejected: Cambridge, Gonv. & Caius Coll. 159 (209); Jesus Coll. 35, 66, 68; Sid. Sussex Coll. 30, 50, 55; ¶ London, B.L., Harley 3100; Oxford, Bodleian, Douce ¶ 270, 293, Laud Misc. 720; Vienna, Nazionalbibl., 1274; York, Minster, xiv.K.3 (pr. bk).

---

[1] On permanent loan to Ushaw Coll. from Hexham Catholic Church.

ELY, Cambridgeshire. *Ben. abbey and (1109) cathedral priory of St Peter and St Etheldreda.*

An all-figure pressmark occurs in the Ely Cathedral copy of Historia Eliensis, Bodley 762, Laud Misc. 647 and Balliol Coll. 49.[1]

Cambridge, U.L., Kk.1.24. *Cancel the entry and add to Rejected.*[2]

Ely Cathedral, s.n. Now deposited in Cambridge, U.L., EDC1. *For* [G (or C) 60] *read* [6.60].

London, B.L., Cotton Tib. B.v, fo. 76 and Sloane 1044, fo. 2. *Cancel entries and footnote 9* Cotton Tib. B.v, fo. 76 . . . Kk.1.24.[2] *Add* Tib. B.v, fo. 76 *and* Sloane 1044, fo. 2 to *Rejected.*

Cotton Calig. A.viii. *Read* fos. 59–209. *i*Vite sanctorum, etc. s.xii–xiv in.

+   Titus A.i, fos. 57–140.   Cronica abbatum et episcoporum Eliensium. s.xv ex.[3]

+   Titus A.i, fos. 141–5.   Vitae episcoporum Eliensium. s.xv.[4]

+ New York, Pierpont Morgan Libr., G.43.   *l*Psalterium. s.xii ex.[5]   ?

Oxford, Bodleian, Bodl. 762. *For* [G.32] *read* [6.32] *and cancel query.*

Laud Misc. 647. *Add pressmark* [10.45].

New College, 98. *Cancel the entry and add to Rejected.*

Rejected: +London, B.L., Cotton Tib. B.v, fo. 76, Sloane 1044, fo. 2; +Oxford, New College, 98.

ETON, Buckinghamshire. *Royal College of B.V.M.*[6]

+ Eton College   13.   *m*Gregorius. s.xiii med.
+   17.   *m*Hugo de S. Caro. s.xiii ex.
+   18.   *m*R. Holcot. s.xiii/xiv.
+   36.   *m*Martinus Polonus, etc. s.xiii/xiv.
+   41.   *m*Haymo Autisiodorensis. s.xi/xii.
+   76, fos. 1–40.   *m*Ieronimus. s.xii.[7]
+   76, fos. 41–132.   *e*Berengaudus. s.xiv ex.
+   81.   *m*Gregorius, etc. s.xii med.
+   82.   W. de Monte. s.xiii in.[7]
               99.   *For* P. de Nathalibus *read* P. Calo.
+   117.   *m*R. Grosseteste, etc. s.xiv–xiv/xv.
+   125.   *m*P. Comestor. s.xii/xiii.
               132.   *For* Galienus *read* Galenus.
+   219, pp. 91–118.   *m*1, 2 Paralipom., glosat. s.xiii.

---

[1] Manuscripts of unknown provenance with a pressmark like this are Aberystwyth, N.L. 735C (7.3); Cambridge, U.L., Ii.4.22 (6.41), Corpus Christi Coll., 131 (6.21) and 397 (12.20); Oxford, Magdalen Coll., 17 + London, Westminster Abbey 34/3 (19.20 in both parts).

[2] CUL, Kk.1.24 contains Ramsey Abbey, not Ely, documents.

[3] Cotton Titus A.i, fos. 57–140 originally preceded Lambeth Palace, 448, fo. 78.

[4] Cotton Titus A.i, fos. 141–5 and Bodleian, Laud Misc. 698 formed one volume.

[5] Suffrages for Etheldreda (only) are added in hand of s.xiii. A leaf of this MS is Quaritch cat. 1036 (1984), no. 63.

[6] For the ten entries here marked *m* see N. R. Ker, *The Library*, 5th series, xxx (1975), 233–7.

[7] Eton Coll., 76, fos. 1–40, and Eton Coll., 82 formed one volume.

Eton College (*contd*)
219. Footnote 6, p. 80 of 1964 edn. *For* 27–46 *read* 27–50.
+ DDg.6.2 (pr. bk). *e*Tertullianus. Basel. A.D. 1521.
+ Oxford, University Coll., 62+63. *b*G. Porretanus, etc. s.xiii–xv. ?

EVESHAM, Worcestershire. *Ben. abbey of B.V.M. and St Egwin.*
+ Aberystwyth, N.L., Peniarth 339. *li*Secretum secretorum, etc. s.xiii.
+ Cambridge, U.L., Mm.6.17. *c*Misc. theol. s.xv.
London, B.L., Cotton Vesp. A.vi, art. 10. *Cancel the entry.*
Mr Philip Robinson. Now Evesham, Almonery Museum, s.n.

EXETER, Devon. *Cathedral Church of St Peter.*
Heading: line 2, *for* 2501 *read* 3501. *Add that* reduced facsimiles of the 1327 inventory in MS. 3671 are in Oliver (nos. 25–57) and F. Barlow and others, *Leofric of Exeter* (Exeter, 1972), pl. viii. What appears to be a fair copy is in MS. 3720.
+ Cambridge, U.L., Hh.1.10. *s*Aelfric. s.xi$^{\frac{3}{4}}$–xii.
Corpus Christi Coll. *For* 201, fos. 179–272^2 *read* fos. 179–272^1.
+ London, B.L., Add. 62104. *s*Missale (fragm.). s.xi med.[1]
+ Cotton Vit. A.vii, fos. 1–112. *s*Pontificale. s.xi$^{\frac{3}{4}}$.
Lambeth Palace, 104. *Read* fos. i, 1–208.
+ Oxford, Bodleian, Lat. bib. d. 10. *s*Lucas et Johannes glo. s.xi ex [*cf. cat.* p. 350].[2]
+ Paris, B.N., lat. 14782. Evangelia. s.xi ex.[3]
Rejected: for Wells, Cathedral, s.n. *read* Wells, Cathedral, 3.

EXETER. *Cathedral of St Peter, Vicars Choral.*
+ London, B.L., Harley 1003. *e*Compendium theologicae veritatis. s.xv in.

EYNSHAM, Oxfordshire. *Ben. abbey of B.V.M., St Benedict and All Saints.*
+ London, B.L., Harley 4887. *c*Historia Britonum, etc. s.xiv. [MXVI]. ?

FAVERSHAM, Kent. *Ben. abbey of St Saviour.*
+ Cambridge, Corpus Christi Coll., 161. *c*Vitae sanctorum. *c.* A.D. 1200. ?
+ *Untraced:* R. Sparrow of Worlingham, Norfolk, in 1816 (pr. bk). *e*H. Schedel, Nuremberg, A.D. 1493.

FEARN, Ross and Cromarty. *Prem. abbey of St Ninian.*
Dunrobin, Duke of Sutherland. Now Edinburgh, N.L., Dep. 314/18.

---

[1] Other fragments are London, B.L., Harley 5977, no. 59; Oxford, Bodleian, Lat. liturg. e.38; London, Westminster Abbey, 36/17–19; and two flyleaves at the front and back of Lincoln, Cath., V.5.11 (pr. bk).
[2] Oliver records the second folio as *ad prudentiam iustorum*. The second leaf of the manuscript begins *prudentiam iustorum* (Luke 1:17: *cf. BLR,* xi (1985), 79–88).
[3] See J. J. G. Alexander, *Burlington Magazine,* cviii (1966), 6–16.

FELIXSTOWE, Suffolk. *Ben. priory of St Felix.*

London, B.L., Royal 7 A.vii. *For* Blesensis *read* de Waltham.

FERRIBY, NORTH, Yorkshire. *Aug. priory of B.V.M.*

+London, B.L., Cotton Faustina A.ii, fos. 99–175. cParadisus Heraclidis. s.xii med.

FINCHALE, co. Durham. *Ben. priory of St John the Baptist and St Godric.*

Inventory, A.D. 1481, printed by J. T. Fowler, *Trans. Architectural and Archaeological Soc. of Durham and Northumberland*, iv (1896), 134–47, from a copy by Thomas Swalwell, now with Finchale Repertory in Prior's Kitchen, Durham, includes a few books other than service books: second folios given.

London, B.L., Add. 35283. *Cancel entry and add to Rejected.*

FLAXLEY, Gloucestershire. *Cist. abbey of B.V.M.*

Heading: Phillipps MS. 1310 (= 19745) is now Oxford, Bodleian, Phillipps-Robinson e.122.

FOTHERINGHAY, Northamptonshire. *Collegiate church of B.V.M. and All Saints.*

90 books 'in libraria' and service books listed in an inventory of 29 Sept. 1445, P.R.O., E.154/1/44. An attached schedule lists a further 15 books.

FOUNTAINS, Yorkshire. *Cist. abbey of B.V.M.*

Cambridge, Trinity Coll., 1054. *For* Divisio scientiarum *read* Divisio sententiarum.

Union Soc. Now Prof. T. Takamiya, Tokyo. *For* s.l. et a. *read* Basel, A.D. 1498.

+London, B.L., Add. 46203. bMissale. s.xii ex.

62129–32, 62132A: formerly Studley Royal, Mr H. Vyner, the second, first, third and fifth manuscripts respectively as listed in 1964 edn. Fragments of a missal formerly with Add. 62129 were identified as pastedowns from Add. 62132A and are now Add. 62132B. The fourth Vyner MS. was stolen in 1964 and is at present untraced.

Henry Davis Gift, M.49: formerly London, Mr H. Davis.

Studley Royal, Mr H. Vyner: see London, B.L., above.

+Private collection. P. Lombardus, Sententiae. s.xiii[2].

+*Untraced:* Sotheby sale 2 March 1970, lot 40 (property of Sir J. Ingilby, Ripley Castle) to Francis Edwards (pr. bk). iW. Durandus, Strasbourg, A.D. 1493.

FRIESTON (Frestuna), Lincolnshire. *Ben. priory of St James; cell of Crowland.*

Read Ripon, Cathedral, 6. eBonaventura. A.D. 1400.

FURNESS, Lancashire. *Savigniac and (1147) Cist. abbey of B.V.M.*

+Urbana, Univ. of Illinois Libr., 132. cR. Higden. s.xiv ex.

GARENDON, Leicestershire.   *Cist. abbey of B.V.M.*

Wells. *Read* Cathedral, VC/II.   *e*Hugo Floriacensis, etc. s.xii.

GLASTONBURY, Somerset.   *Ben. abbey of B.V.M.*

Heading: line 7, after 711 *add* pp. 227–9, 246–50 are printed by J. P. Carley and J. F. R. Coughlan in *Mediaeval Studies,* xliii (1981), 502–14. A new edition of the other catalogues and lists by J. P. Carley is in preparation for the British Academy's Corpus of British Medieval Library Catalogues.

Brinkley, Sir G. Keynes: now Cambridge, Dr S. Keynes.
+ Cambridge, U.L., Dd.1.17.   H. Huntendonensis. s.xiv/xv.[1]   ?
+   Kk.5.34.   Patristica, Ausonius, etc. s.x. [cf. *Cat.* fo. 102v].[2]   ?
   Trinity Coll., 1460.   *Read* [*Monyton list,* 25].
   Dr S. Keynes: formerly Brinkley, Sir G. Keynes.
London, B.L., Add. 21614.   *Read* [*Monyton list,* 53].
     Harley 1918.   *For* Clemens Lanthoniensis *read* Omeliarium.
+   Royal 12 C.xxiii.   J. Toletanus, Prognostica; etc. s.xi in. [Leland].[3]
+ Oxford, Bodleian, Douce 140.   *s*Primasius. s.vii.   ?
     Wood empt. 1.   *Read* [*Monyton list,* 55].
Rejected: Phillipps 9328: now London, B.L., Add. 59839.

GLOUCESTER.   *Franciscan convent.*

London, Lambeth Palace, 151.   *Read* fos. i–v, 1–209.

GUISBOROUGH, Yorkshire.   *Aug. priory of B.V.M.*

+ Cambridge, Sidney Sussex Coll., 62.   *l*Breviarium. s.xiii/xiv.   ?
+ London, B.L., Loans 29/333, fo. 69.[4]
Dublin, Chester Beatty Libr., W.45.   Now sold and untraced: see below.
+ *Untraced:* Sotheby sale 3 Dec. 1968, lot 10, to Traylen.

HAGNABY, Lincolnshire.   *Prem. abbey of St Thomas the Martyr.*

Add footnote Cotton Vesp. B.xi, fos. 1–61 and Royal 13 A.xxi, fos. 13–150 probably formed one volume.

HAILES, Gloucestershire.   *Cist. abbey of B.V.M.*

Edinburgh, Theological Coll.   Now deposited in St Andrews U.L.
Insch.   Now Edinburgh, Miss J. Gordon.
Wells, Cathedral, Chrysostomus.   *For* s.n. *e*Chrysostomus, A.D. 1514
          read 6. *e*Chrysostomus, A.D. 1517.
     Psalterium.   *For* s.n. *read* 5.
Rejected: *for* Bible at Wells Cathedral *read* Wells, Cathedral, 4.

---

[1] For arguments see Carley's forthcoming edn. of catalogues.
[2] For arguments that the MS. migrated from Hyde Abbey to Glastonbury before 1247, see J. P. Carley, *ASE,* xvi (1987), forthcoming.
[3] See J. P. Carley, *ASE,* xvi (1987), forthcoming.
[4] A leaf from an unidentifiable book bearing a note that on Jan. 31 1535/6 the monastic visitors 'visitaverunt monasterium nostrum de Giseburn . . .'.

HALTEMPRICE (or **COTTINGHAM**), Yorkshire. *Aug. priory of B.V.M. and Holy Cross.*

Leicester, Bernard Halliday. Now sold and untraced.

HARROLD, Bedfordshire. *Priory of St Peter, of Aug. nuns.*

Bristol, Baptist College, Z.c.23. Now London, Private Collection 1.

HAUGHMOND, Shropshire. *Aug. abbey of St John the Evangelist.*

+ Oxford, Bodleian, Lat. th. d. 40. *e*Aelredus. s.xii/xiii.
+ Shrewsbury, Shrewsbury School, XXX. *l*Graduale. s.xii$^{\frac{1}{4}}$.

HEREFORD. *Cathedral church of St Ethelbert.*

Heading: *after* former also *add* by A. B. Emden in *BRUC*, pp. 671–2.

HEREFORD. *Franciscan convent.*

Hereford, Cathedral. O.ii.11. *For* Adalberti speculum *read* Engelberti speculum virtutum.

                P.iii.12. *For* Blesensis *read* de Waltham.

+ London, B.L., Harley 3901. *e*Martinus Polonus. s.xiii.
Oxford, New Coll., 285. *Read* fos. 194–251.

HERTFORD. *Ben. priory of B.V.M.*

Heading: *after* 580 *add* and by R. W. Hunt in *Ker Essays*, p. 277.

HINTON (domus loci Dei de Hentone), Somerset. *Charterhouse of B.V.M., St John the Baptist and All Saints.*

Heading: *for* Exch. K.R. Eccl. Docs. 2/45 *read* E.135/2/45.

HOLME CULTRAM, Cumberland. *Cist. abbey of B.V.M.*

Cambridge (U.S.A.), Harvard Coll. *Add pressmark* [liber cxcix].
+ Wellington (N.Z.), Turnbull Libr.[1] Formerly *Untraced*, Yarmouth (Isle of Wight), Mr F. Rowley.

HORSHAM ST FAITH, Norfolk. *Ben. alien priory of St Faith.*

In title read cell of Conques.

+ Cambridge, Trinity Coll., 884, fos. 1–10, 82–8.[2]

HOUNSLOW, Middlesex. *Trinitarian convent.*

*Read i*M. Franciscus de Insulis. Gouda, before A.D. 1485. In J. L. Beijers' auction, Utrecht, 21 April 1959, lot 487.

HYDE, Hampshire. *Ben. abbey of Holy Trinity, B.V.M. and St Peter.*

List of 8 books, s.xvi[1], in Rome, Vatican, Reg. lat. 2099, fo. 306.

+ Aberystwyth, N.L., Llanstephan 176. *c*Registrum brevium, etc. s.xiii[2]. ?
+ Cambridge, U.L., Kk.5.34. *m*Patristica, Ausonius, etc. s.x.[3]

[1] On permanent loan from Bible Society of New Zealand.
[2] See footnote to this MS. under **NORWICH**.
[3] For arguments that the MS. was written at Hyde Abbey see M. Lapidge, *ASE*, i (1972), 85–137. On its possible later migration to Glastonbury in s.xiii see J. P. Carley, *ASE*, xvi (1987), forthcoming.

+Chichester, Cathedral (pr. bk). *i*T. More. London, A.D. 1523.
+Le Havre, Bibl. Mun., 330. *l*Missale. s.xi med.
  Madrid, V.3.28. Now Vitr. 23–8.
+Naworth Castle, Earl of Carlisle (pr. bk). *i*Marcus Marula. Basel, A.D. 1513.
  New York, Mr W. S. Glazier, 19. Now New York, Pierpont Morgan Libr., G.19.
+Oxford, Bodleian, Lat. misc. e. 118. *c*B. Facius, s.xv ex.
+   Brasenose Coll., Latham B.4.6 (pr. bk). *i*S. Grynaeus, Novus orbis. Basel, A.D. 1532.
+   Oriel Coll., 2F.f.14 (pr. bk). *i*J. Cochlaeus. Leipzig, A.D. 1529.
+York Minster, II.N.1 (pr. bk). *i*Gemma Frisius, etc. Antwerp, A.D. 1530, etc.

INCHMAHOME, Stirlingshire. *Aug. priory of St Culmoc.*

Insch, Mr C. A. Gordon. Now Edinburgh, Miss J. Gordon, on deposit in Edinburgh, N.L., Dep. 273.

+**IONA,** Argyllshire. *Ben. abbey.*

Edinburgh, N.L., 10000. *l*Psalterium. s.xiii in.

JARROW and MONKWEARMOUTH, co. Durham. *Ben. abbey of St Paul.*

+Kingston Lacey, Devon, The National Trust ('Bankes Leaf'). *s*Biblia (1 fo.). s.vii/viii.[1]

JERVAULX, Yorkshire. *Cist. abbey of B.V.M.*

+Dublin, Trinity Coll., 516, fos. 208–19. *c*Chronica. s.xiii/xiv.

KING'S LANGLEY, Hertfordshire. *Dominican convent.*

Oxford, Blackfriars. Now Cambridge, Fitzwilliam Museum, 3–1967 (205).
+San Marino, Huntington Libr., HM 27187. R. Holcot, etc. s.xiv ex–xv in.[2] ?

KINGSTON-UPON-HULL, Yorkshire. *Charterhouse of B.V.M., St Michael and St Thomas the Martyr.*

Heading: *for* Exch. K.R. Eccl. Docs. *read* E.135/2/58.

+Lincoln, Cathedral, 209. *e*R. Rolle. s.xiv ex.
Oakham Church. Now deposited in Nottingham, U.L.
+*Untraced:* 'a fine St. Cyprianus; and a Collection of Poems with Miniatures to the Memory of the Earl of Pembroke their Founder fol.'[3]

---

[1] Deposited in London, B.L., Loan 81. Footnote 7, p. 105, of 1964 edn. also applies to this fragment: it is part of the same volume as B.L., Add. 37777 and Add. 45025. On these and other MSS. from this scriptorium see now M. B. Parkes, *The Scriptorium of Wearmouth-Jarrow* (Jarrow Lecture, 1982).
[2] One of the numerous books bequeathed by bp. Robert Rede of Chichester, 1415: see *TC* 14.42, p. 38. Later at St Albans: see 1964 edn.
[3] Record of Kingston-upon-Hull Charterhouse MSS. seen in Cologne(?) by George Suttie: see *The Diary of Humfrey Wanley 1715–1726*, ed. C. E. & R. C. Wright (1966), i, p. xlviii, n. 7.

KIRBY BELLARS, Leicestershire. *Aug. priory of St Peter.*

D. Britton, 'Manuscripts associated with Kirby Bellars Priory', *TCBS*, vi (1976), 267–84.

+ *Untraced:* A MS. containing the Adversaria of Henry Morley, canon of Kirby Bellars, was seen at Abingdon in 1665, bearing Morley's *ex libris* (Oxford, Bodleian, Tanner 88, fo. 250: cf. Britton, pp. 276–7).

KIRKHAM, Yorkshire. *Aug. priory of Holy Trinity or Christ Church.*

Cambridge, Sidney Sussex Coll., 62. *Cancel the entry and list as Rejected.*

+ London, B.L., Cotton Vesp. B.xi, fos. 84–125, 125.*   Aelredus, s.xii ex.[1]

+   Royal 13 A.xxi, fos. 151–92.   Jeronimus, etc. s.xii/xiii.[1]

+ *Untraced:* Brooke sale: now Los Angeles, Dr P. F. Slawson.

+ *Rejected:* Cambridge, U.L., Dd.9.5.

KIRKSTALL, Yorkshire. *Cist. abbey of B.V.M.*

+ *Rejected:* London, B.L., Cott. Tit. A.xix.

KIRKSTEAD, Lincolnshire. *Cist. abbey of B.V.M.*

Beaumont College, VI.   Now Loughlinstone (Ireland), Sir J. Galvin.

LANCASTER. *Dominican convent.*

+ Oxford, Bodleian, Vet. F1 c.90 (pr. bk).   *e*B. Platina. Venice, A.D. 1504.

LANGLEY, Norfolk. *Prem. abbey of B.V.M.*

+ Cambridge, Mrs A. Pedley (pr. bk).   Vitas patrum. Lyon, A.D. 1512.

Oxton Hall.   *Read* Oxton Lodge, Mrs R. Sherbrooke. Now deposited in Nottinghamshire County Record Office.

LANTHONY (secunda), Gloucestershire. *Aug. priory of B.V.M. and St John the Baptist.*

Heading: *for* C.115/A.2, fo. 281 *read* C.115/K.1/6681, fo. 281.

Bristol, Baptist Coll., Z.d.5.   Now sold and in a private collection.

+ Cambridge, Corpus Christi Coll., 390.   Giraldus Cambrensis. s.xii ex.[2]

+ Durham, Cathedral, Inc. 58 (pr. bk).   *i*Jeronimus, Vitas patrum. London, A.D. 1495.

London, B.L., Royal 5 B.i.   *Read em*Augustinus, etc. *Cancel query.*

Lambeth Palace,   13.   *Add* [*Cf. cat.* 272e].

21.   *Add* [*Leche,* 31].

+   29.   *m*Cassiodorus. s.xiii. [*Cf. cat.* 60].[3]

55.   *Read* fos. i, ii, 1–156, 162.

56.   *Read sm*Gregorius. *Cancel query..*

---

[1] B.L. Arundel 36, Cotton Vesp. B.xi, fos. 84–125, 125* and Royal 13 A.xxi, fos. 151–92 formed one volume: see A. G. Watson, *The Manuscripts of Henry Savile of Banke* (1969), pp. 74–7.

[2] Footnote 5, p. 108 of 1964 edn. applies also to this MS.

[3] For Lambeth Palace, 29 and other entries marked with the siglum *m*, see N. R. Ker, in E. G. W. Bill, *A Catalogue of Manuscripts in Lambeth Palace Library, MSS. 1222–1860* (Oxford, 1972), p. 11, footnote 1.

London (*contd*)

+   Lambeth Palace,   61, fos. 1–117. *m*A. Nequam. s.xii/xiii. [*Cat.* 55].

           71. *Read* fos. i, 1–118.

+   77. *m*Ezechiel et Daniel glo. s.xiii in. [*Cf. cat.* 14].

           80. *For* 246 *read* 244, also in 1964 edn., p. 108, footnote 5, p. 109, footnote 7 and p. 111, footnote 6.

           81. *Read m*Job et Daniel glo.

           85. *Read m*Libri regum glo.

+   102. *m*Lucas et Johannes glo. s.xii/xiii. [*Cf. cat.* 19].

+   110. *m*Exodus glo. s.xii ex [*Cf. cat.* 26, 27].

+   114. *m*Judicum-Judith glo. s.xii. [*Cat.* 20].[1]

         119. *Read m*J. Lanthoniensis. The binding leaves, two leaves of a commentary on St Matthew, in Latin and Irish, s.x, are kept separately as MS. 1229, nos. 7, 8.

+   134, fos. 97–245. *m*Jeremias, etc. glo. s.xii. [*Cat.* 21].[2]

+   137. Bartholomaeus Anglicus. s.xiv. [*Leche*, 41].

         138. *Read* fos. i, ii, 1–44, also in 1964 edn., p. 108, footnote 5, p. 109, footnote 7, and p. 111, footnote 6.

         145. *Read* fos. i, ii, 1–137.

         148. *Read es*Beda. The *ex libris* is on a binding leaf now kept separately as MS. 1229, no. 10.

+   153, fos. 1–6. Praef. in Bibliam. s.xii.[1]
+   153, fos. 7–88. *m*Isaias glo. s.xii.[2]

         161. *Read m*Bernardus.

+   164. *m*Epp. Pauli glo. s.xii. [*Cf. cat.* 155, 156].

+   200, fos. 168–75. 'Sermo de latrone crucifixo', etc. s.xii.[2]

+   200, fos. 176–217. Sermones. s.xii.[3] ?

         218. *Read* 1–89, also in 1964 edn., p. 108, footnote 5, p. 109, footnote 7, and p. 111, footnote 6.

         335. *Read* fos. 1–228. *m*Cantica, etc. glo.

         343. *Read m*Deut. et Josue glo.

         345. *Read* fos. 97–227.

---

[1] Lambeth Palace 114 and 153, fos. 1–6, formed one volume.
[2] Lambeth Palace 134, fos. 97–245, 153, fos. 7–88, and 200, fos. 168–75, formed one volume.
[3] Lambeth Palace 200, fos. 176–217 (and perhaps further) probably formed one volume.

London (*contd*)

    Lambeth Palace, 365. *Read* fos. i, ii, 1–119.

                  378. *Read* fos. i, ii, 1–56, 125–65, also in 1964 edn., p. 108, footnote 5, p. 109, footnote 7, and p. 111, footnote 6.

\+   379, fos. 1–68. Galfredus Monemutensis. s.xii/xiii.[1]

                  395. *Read* fos. i, ii, 1–52, 141–72.

\+   425, fos. i, 1–21. Cicero. s.xii/xiii.[2]

\+   431, fos. i, 1–7, 16–88. Misc. theol. s.xii.[2]

                  431. *For* fos. 146–60 *read* 145–60.

                  437. *For* 72 *read* 73.

                  449. [*Cf. cat.* 266].

                  475. *Read* fos. 111–79.

\+   1229, nos.14, 15. De ritibus ecclesiae in Cena domini, etc. s.xii.[3]

\+ Oxford, Bodleian, Auct. D.2.1. *m*'Liber psalmorum secundum glosulam Clementis Lantoniensis ecclesie prioris'. s.xii. [*Cat.* 49].

\+   Rawl. C.163. P. Lombardus. s.xiii. [*Cf. cat.* 249, 272].

\+   C.331. *c*Registrum brevium, etc. s.xiii ex.

    Corpus Christi Coll., 139. *Read ms*Cassiodorus, etc. s.xii. [*Cf. cat.* 211].

    Queen's Coll., 309. *Add* [*Cat.* 168].

    Trinity Coll., 33. *Add* [*Cat.* 117].

                  39. *Read m*Gregorius.

\+   40. *m*Gregorius. s.xii med.

                  51. *Add* [*Cf. cat.* 158].

                  69. *Read cm*Jeronimus.

P. 112 of 1964 edn. paragraph beginning 'M. R. James suggests', *cancel* (Lambeth Palace), 29, 61, 77, 102, 110, 114, 164, 335, 425 *and* (Trinity Coll.) 40, *all now in the addenda above. Add* fos. i, ii, 1–222 *after* Lambeth Palace 18; *add* (fos. 1–100) *after* 139; *read* 142 (fos. 1–123); *read* 176 (fos. ii, 1–120); *read* 217 (fos. i, 1–85 and 127–268); *read* 378 (fos. 57–124); *read* 395 (fos. 53–138); *in line 10 read* like 9 of the Corpus Christi MSS. listed above (not 154) belonged.

LAUNCESTON, Cornwall. *Aug. priory of St Stephen.*

Little Malvern, Mr W. Berington. Now Mr T. M. Berington, deposited in Birmingham U.L.

LEICESTER. *Collegiate church of B.V.M.*

\+ Leicester, Wyggeston Hospital, 10D34/13. *e*J. Felton, Sermones. s.xv med. ?

---

[1] Lambeth Palace 379, fos. 1–68, and Lambeth Palace 357 almost certainly formed one volume.

[2] Lambeth Palace 425, fos. i, 1–21, and 431, fos. i, 1–7, 16–88, formed one volume, earlier at **LLANTHONY**, q.v.: footnote 5 on p. 108 of 1964 edn. applies to it. Footnote 6 on p. 111 also applies to both MSS.

[3] Probably once at the end of Lambeth Palace 372.

LEIGHS, LITTLE, Essex. *Aug. priory.*

+ *Untraced:* Sotheby sale, 21 June 1965, lot 103 (pr. bk). Augustinus, Opuscula. Venice, A.D. 1491.[1]

LEOMINSTER, Herefordshire. *Ben. priory of St Peter.*

+ Gloucester, Cathedral, 1. *c*Vitae sanctorum. s.xiii in[2].
+ Lincoln, Cathedral, 149.[2] s.xii$\frac{3}{4}$.
+   150.[2] s.xii med.

LESMAHAGOW, Lanarkshire. *Ben. priory of St Machutus.*

+ Edinburgh, N.L., Acc. 2710. *l*Missale. s.xiii.

LESSNESS, Kent. *Aug. abbey of St Thomas the Martyr.*

Cambridge, Trinity Coll., 1236. *Cancel entry and transfer to* **STAFFORD**.

LETHERINGHAM (Crew), Suffolk. *Aug. priory of B.V.M., cell of St Peter's Ipswich.*

Alter the entry to Rejected: Cambridge (U.S.A.), Harvard Law School, 25.

LICHFIELD, Staffordshire. *Cathedral church of B.V.M. and St Chad.*

Heading: *after c.* 1622 *add* Lichfield Cathedral, MS. 39 *and that* Shrewsbury Public Libr., MS. 2, a transcript made in 1789 of a Lichfield Chapter Act Book of *c.* 1430–51, contains on fos. 95^v–6 an inventory of the Sacristy 1450–1 which lists 112 service and 10 other books.

Lichfield, Cathedral, Evangelia.   Now MS. 1.
                   Decretales.   Now MS. 31.
                   Chronica, etc.   Now MS. 28.

LICHFIELD. *Cathedral chantries.*

Read New York, Mrs Phyllis Gordan.

LICHFIELD. *Franciscan convent.*

+ Tokyo, Prof. T. Takamiya, 15. *e*Mirror of Life, etc. (in English). s.xv[1]. ?

LINCOLN. *Cathedral church of B.V.M.*

Lincoln, Cathedral,   9.   *For* s.xii *read* s.xii in.
                 13.   *For* s.xi *read* s.xi ex.
                 15.   *Read* [*Cat.* 86; *old cat.* 73; Leland].
                 29.   *Read* 29, fos. 201–20.[3]
                 42.   *For* s.xiv *read* s.xiii in.
                 43.   *For* s.xiv *read* s.xii ex.

---

[1] Bears signature of Richard Vowel, prior, 1510–14.
[2] A three-volume set: see *MMBL* ii, 934–9, on the Gloucester volume. Confirmation from Dr R. M. Thomson.
[3] MS. 29, fos. 201–20, and MS 136 formed one volume, which can be added to list of Salysbury MSS. in footnote 9, p. 116, of 1964 edn.

Lincoln, Cathedral (*contd*)

	67.	*For* s.xi/xii *read* s.xii ex.
+	71.	Decretales abbreviatae. s.xiv. [*Cat.* 49].
	77.	*Add date* s.xii.
	86.	*Add* [*Cat.* 5].
	96.	*For* s.xii *read* s.xii med.
	116.	*For* s.xiii *read* s.xiii in.
	134.	*For* s.xii *read* s.xii in; *and for* [*old cat.* 4] *read* [*old cat.* 14].
	135.	*For* s.xiv *read* s.xiii in.
+	136.	Decretales Gregorii IX. s.xiii.[1]
	137.	*For* [*Cat.* 137] *read* [*Cat.* 41].
	139.	*For* s.xiii *read* s.xiii in.
+	142.	Omelie. s.xii med. [*old cat.* 20 or 39].[2]
	146.	*For* s.xii *read* s.xii ex; *add* [?*old cat.* 83].
	147.	*For* s.xii *read* s.xii ex.
	153.	*For* s.xiii *read* s.xii ex.
	154.	*For* s.xv *read* s.xiv.
+	158.	Omelie. s.xi ex. [*old cat.* 20 or 39].[2]
	160.	*For* s.xiii *read* s.xii ex.
	163.	*Read* [Leland].
	164.	*For* s.xiv *read* s.xv.
	171.	*For* s.xii *read* s.xii med; [add *old cat.* 77].
	174.	*For* s.xii ex *read* s.xii med. [*Cat.* 97; *old cat.* 80; Leland].
+	178.	Exodus glo. s.xii.[3]
	182.	*Add footnote 4* MS. 184, fo. 1 was formerly part of MS. 182.
+	184, fo. 1.	See MS. 182 above.
	201.	*Read* cSermones lxv. s.xii med. [cat. 85; old. cat. 62].

+ Dean & Chapter Muniments. Di/20/2/B1, fos. 22–5. Officium Johannis de Dalderby. s.xiv[1].

+ Rome, Vatican, Ottob. lat. 308. cProcessionale sarisburiense. s.xiv ex. ?

LINCOLN. *Franciscan convent.*

Heading: add that the pressmark is illustrated in A. C. de la Mare, *Catalogue of the Collection of Medieval Manuscripts Bequeathed to the Bodleian Library Oxford by James P. R. Lyell* (Oxford, 1971), pl. 36a.

London, B.L., Add. 54231: formerly London, Dr E. G. Millar.

LINCOLN. *Convent of Austin friars.*

+ Rome, Vatican, Vat. lat. 4954. eAugustinus. s.xii.

---

[1] MS. 29, fos. 201–20, and MS 136 formed one volume, which can be added to list of Salysbury MSS. in footnote 9, p. 116, of 1964 edn.

[2] MS. 158 is the exemplar of MS. 142.

[3] MSS. 172, 178 and 187 are annotated in the same hand, probably that of Petrus de Melida.

LINDISFARNE (Holy Island), Northumberland. *Ben. priory of St Peter.*

+London, B.L., Cotton Tib. C.ii. *i*Beda, Hist. ecclesiastica. s.viii ex.[1] ?

LINGFIELD, Surrey. Collegiate church of St Peter.

Heading: *after* printed *add* from a manuscript in the Loseley collection.

LITTLE LEIGHS see **LEIGHS, LITTLE.**

LLANBADARN FAWR, Dyfed. *'Celtic' monastery, later Ben. priory, cell of Gloucester.*

+Cambridge, Corpus Christi Coll., 199. Augustinus. s.xi.[2]

+Dublin, Trinity Coll., 50. Psalterium. s.xi.[2]

+London, B.L., Cotton Faustina C.i, fos. 66–93. Macrobius. s.xii.[3]

LLANDAFF, Dyfed. *Cathedral church of St Peter and St Teilo.*

Lichfield, Cathedral: *cancel entry.*[4]

LLANDEILO-FAWR, Dyfed. *'Celtic' monastery.*

+Lichfield, Cathedral, 1. *c*Evangelia ('Codex S. Ceadde'). s.viii in.

LLANFAES, Gwynedd. *Franciscan convent.*

London, B.L., Add. 54232: formerly London, Dr E. G. Millar.

LLANTARNAM, Gwent. *Cist. abbey.*

Transfer to here entry under **CAERLEON.**

LLANTHONY (prima), Gwent. *Aug. priory of St John the Baptist; cell of Lanthony (secunda) from* A.D. 1481.

London, Lambeth Palace, 96. *For 243 read 244.*[5]

+   145, fos. 257–64. Homiliae. s.xii.

                      356 and 1964 edn., p. 120, footnote 6: *for* 75–125 *read* 125–75.

                      431 and 1964 edn., p. 120, footnote 7: *for* fos. 1–7, 16–88 *read* fos. i, 1–7, 16–88.

LLANVAES, Gwynedd: *see* **LLANFAES.**

---

[1] In Bede's preliminary letter an almost contemporary hand wrote *nostro* between *patre* and *et antistite cudberchti* on fo. 4.

[2] See M. Lapidge, *Studia Celtica*, viii/ix (1973–74), 70–6.

[3] See A. Peden, *Cambridge Medieval Celtic Studies*, ii (1981), 21–45.

[4] This manuscript is now Lichfield, Cathedral, 1. For provenance, Llandeilo-Fawr until s.x[1] and then Lichfield, see *Jnl. Nat. Libr. of Wales*, xviii (1973), 135–46. An entry made in Old English at Lichfield in s.xi[1] is on p. 4: see Ker, *Cat. Anglo-Saxon MSS.*, no. 123.

[5] Lambeth Palace, 96, fos. 113–243, and Lambeth Palace, 145, fos. 257–64, formed one volume.

LONDON. *Cathedral church of St Paul.*

N. R. Ker, 'Books at St Paul's Cathedral before 1313', *Studies in London History presented to P. E. Jones*, ed. A. E. J. Hollaender and W. Kellaway (1969), pp. 41–72; reprinted in Ker, *Books, Collectors and Libraries*, pp. 209–42.

Heading line 3: *for* Booklists *read* Lists of books, mainly service. Line 7: *after* but *add* a version of it made in 1255. Line 8: *for* fos. 131–34. Another text A.D. 1295 *read* fos. 112–15 printed by Ker, pp. 49–60 (pp. 215–30 in reprint). The latter list exists also in MS. W.D.3, fos.3ᵛ, 12–13ᵛ and. Line 9: *after* 181–84 *add* whence it is ptd. by Ker, pp. 60–66 (pp. 230–36 in reprint).

London, St Paul's Cath., 1.   *Read* [cf. *inv. 1295* (4a); *cat.* 1486 (23)].

          2.   *Read* [*Inv. 1295* (4); *cat.* 1486 (33)].

+   4, fos. iv, v.   'Liber sermonum diversorum. Liber dispensationum' (flyleaves only). [*cat.*0.(8)].

     Lambeth Palace,   8.   *Read* [*Inv. 1295* (117); cat.F.(1)].

          1106.   *For* i *read* fos. 1–110.

+   Society of Antiquaries, 136C, fos. 1–36.   *e*Liber niger scaccarii, etc. s.xiv med–xiv ex.

LONDON. *Charterhouse of the Salutation of the B.V.M.*

Blackburn. *For* Public Libr. *read* Art Gallery and Museum.

+Coleraine, Univ. of Ulster Libr., 1R4 (pr. bk).   *e*R. de S. Victore, etc. Basel, A.D. 1494.

Downside Abbey, 48253 (Clifton 12) (formerly Partridge Green).   *e*Preces, etc. s.xv.

Edinburgh, N.L., 9999: formerly London, Charterhouse, s.n.

Partridge Green, St Hugh's Charterhouse.   *Cancel entry and substitute amended entry under Downside Abbey above.*

Yale U.L.   *Read* New Haven, Yale U.L., Beinecke 286.

LONDON. *Abbey of B.V.M. and St Francis, without Aldgate, of Franciscan nuns.*

For Wellington (N.Z.), Bible House *read* Wellington (N.Z.), Turnbull Libr.[1]

LONDON. *Aug. priory of Holy Trinity, Aldgate.*

Cambridge, Emmanuel Coll., 252.   *For* s.xii ex *read* s.xiii in.

+ London, B.L., Add. 10052.   Speculum spiritualium, etc. s.xv med.[2]

+ San Marino, Huntington Libr., HM 112.   *i*W. Hilton (in English). s.xv med.[2]

LONDON. *Aug. priory of St Bartholomew, Smithfield.*

+ London, B.L., Add. 10392.   *s*Misc. theologica. A.D. 1432.   ?

London, St Bartholomew's Hosp.   Pressmark is now Misc. 10.

+ Wolfenbüttel, Herzog August Bibl., Extravagantes 25.1.   *e*Biblia. s.xiv.

LONDON. *Franciscan convent.*

List of 2 books, s.xvi[1], in Rome, Vatican, Reg. lat. 2099, fo. 305.

---

[1] On permanent loan from Bible Society of New Zealand.
[2] B.L., Add. 10052, 10053 and Huntington Libr., HM112 formed one volume.

LONDON. *Carmelite convent.*

Glasgow, U.L., BD.19.h.9 (now Euing 26) and London, B.L., Add. 29704, 29705, 44892: another volume of cuttings has been found in London, Private Collection 2.

+ Oxford, Magdalen Coll., lat. 43. Directorium ad passagium in terram faciendum, etc. s.xv in. [M.32ᵐ]. ?

LONDON. *Convent of Austin friars.*

San Francisco, John Howell. Now London, Dr B. Lawn, 22.

LONDON. *Priory of Knights Hospitallers of St John of Jerusalem, Clerkenwell.*

+ Dublin, Trinity Coll., 500. *c*Brut Chronicle (in French). s.xiv. ?

LONDON. *Guildhall.*

London, Guildhall Libr., 244. Footnote 8: *for* belonged to the library *read* belonged to the Corporation of London.

LOUTH PARK, Lincolnshire. *Cist. abbey of B.V.M.*

Flackwell Heath, Mr R. Allison. Now *Untraced.*

LYNN, KING'S, Norfolk. *Hospital of St Mary Magdalen.*

Ripon, Mr H. L. Bradfer-Lawrence. Now Norwich, Norfolk and Norwich Record Office, B-L ixb.

MALLING, Kent. *Abbey of B.V.M. and St Andrew, of Ben. nuns.*

Blackburn. *For* Public Libr. *read* Art Gallery and Museum.

MALMESBURY, Wiltshire. *Ben. abbey of B.V.M. and St Aldhelm.*

On William of Malmesbury's handwriting see now also R. M. Thomson, *William of Malmesbury* (Woodbridge, 1987), pp. 76–98. Pls. 3–5 illustrate Malmesbury pressmarks.

+ Cambridge, U.L., Ii.3.20. *s*W. Malmesburiensis. s.xii in.[1] ?
      Corpus Christi Coll., 330. *Delete* fos. 1–87. *For* s.xii in *read* ss.xii ex, ix in.

+ London, B.L., Cotton Tib. A.xv, fos. 175–80. *cs*Junilius. s.viii in. ?
+   Vit.D.xvii, fos. 1–3. Vitae sanctorum. s.xi ex.[2] ?
+   Harley 3140. *i*Medica quaedam. s.xiii.
+   Royal Appx. 85, fos. 25–6, J. Scotus, was part of Cambridge, Trinity Coll., 1301.

Oxford, Bodleian, Bodl. 852. *For* s.xi *read* s.xi–xii in.
+   Rawl. G. 139. *sm*Cicero, etc. s.xii in.[1]
      Merton Coll., 181. *Read* *eb*Beda, etc.

+ Sankt Gallen, Stiftsbibl., 26. *l*Psalterium, etc. s.xiv.
+ Urbana, Univ. of Illinois Libr., 128 (2 fos.). *cm*Sylloge inscriptionum. s.x.

---

[1] Perhaps written at Malmesbury for another house. 1964 edn., p. 128, footnote 9 applies to this MS.
[2] Cotton Vit.D.xvii, fos. 1–27, fos. 1–3 before the fire of 1731, is part of Oxford, Bodleian, Bodl. 852.

MALVERN, GREAT, Worcestershire. *Ben. priory of B.V.M. and St Michael.*

Helmingham Hall, 49. Now Prof. T. Takamiya, Tokyo, 14.
+ Oxford, Bodleian, Bodl. 619. *i*G. Chaucer, On the astrolabe. s.xv.

MARGAM, West Glamorgan. *Cist. abbey.*
+ Dublin, Trinity Coll., 507. Annales de Margam. s.xiii. ?

MARKYATE, Hertfordshire. *Hermitage, later priory of Ben. nuns.*

Sürth bei Köln, Dr J. Lückger. Now Cologne, Schnütgen Museum, M694.

MARLBOROUGH, Wiltshire. *Mayor and Corporation.*
+ Trowbridge, Wiltshire Record Office, W.R.O. 12.30. *e*Statuta Angliae; Registrum brevium. *c.* A.D. 1316.

MEAUX, Yorkshire. *Cist. abbey of B.V.M.*

Chicago, Univ. of Chicago Libr., 654. *For* [Y.xviiii] *read* [I.xviiii].

MEREVALE, Warwickshire. *Cist. abbey of B.V.M.*
+ *Untraced:* J. S. Hawkins sale, Fletcher's, 8 May 1843, no. 2640. *i*Vitae sanctorum. s.xiv.

MISSENDEN, Buckinghamshire. *Aug. (Arrouaisian) abbey of B.V.M.*

Chicago, Art Institute, 23.420. *Read c*Speculum humanae salvationis, etc. s.xiv ex.
+ Lincoln, Cathedral, 196. *e*Speculum Gregorii. s.xii.

MONKLAND, Herefordshire. *Ben. alien priory (cell of Conches).*
+ Cambridge, Trinity Hall, 4. *i*Flavius Josephus, Antiquitates Judaicae. s.xii med. ?

MONTACUTE, Somerset. *Cluniac priory of St Peter and St Paul.*
+ London, B.L. Cotton Tib. A.x, fos. 145–76, 179–88. *c*Annales. s.xiv in.

MOTTENDEN, Kent. *Trinitarian convent.*

Oxford, Hertford Coll., Mr C. A. J. Armstrong. Now Oxford, Somerville Coll., Dr A. E. Armstrong.

MOUNT GRACE, Yorkshire. *Charterhouse of the Assumption of the B.V.M.*
+ Cambridge, Ridley Hall, R.H.L. E.2 (pr. bk). *e*Opera beati Anselmi. Strasbourg, after A.D. 1496(?).
Mayfield, Capt. M. Butler-Bowdon. Now London, B.L. Add. 61823.
Ripon, Cathedral. *Read* 6. *e*Bonaventura. A.D. 1400.
            Mr H. L. Bradfer-Lawrence. Now London, B.L., Add. 62450.
+ *Rejected: add* Aberystwyth, N.L., Porkington 19.[1]

---

[1] Porkington 19 has the same inscription as the rejected Cambridge MS. ('Scriptus finaliter in M . . .').

MUCH WENLOCK, Shropshire: *see* **WENLOCK, MUCH.**

MUCHELNEY, Somerset. *Ben. abbey of St Peter and St Paul.*
+ London, B.L., Add. 21927. *l*Psalterium. s.xii.

NEATH, West Glamorgan. *Savigniac and (1147) Cist. abbey of B.V.M.*
+ London, P.R.O., E.164/1. *c*Annales, etc. s.xiii/xiv.

NEWBATTLE, Midlothian. *Cist. abbey of B.V.M.*
+ *Untraced:* now Glasgow, Mitchell Libr., 308876.

NEWCASTLE-UPON-TYNE. *Dominican convent.*
read Ripon, Cathedral, 2. *e*Anselmus, etc. s.xiii.

NEWENHAM, Devon. *Cist. abbey of B.V.M.*
Heading: *read* List of 12 books . . . 53ᵛ; also in the cartulary, Oxford, Bodleian, Top. Devon. d.5, fo. 6ᵛ.

NEWSTEAD, *Nottinghamshire. Aug. priory of B.V.M.*
+ Oxford, Bodleian, Laud. Misc. 285. *s*Bernardus. s.xii/xiii.[1] ?
Newbury, Prof. H. A. Ormerod. Prof. Ormerod is deceased. The MS. has been transferred from Nottingham Public Libr. to the Castle Museum, Nottingham.

NOCTON PARK, Lincolnshire. *Aug. priory of St Mary Magdalen.*
Insch, Mr C. A. Gordon. Now Cambridge, Trinity Coll., B.11.33.

NORTHAMPTON. *Cluniac priory of St Andrew.*
+ Cambridge, U.L., Add. 3060. *cl*Manuale. s.xiv/xv.

NORTHAMPTON. *Dominican convent.*
London, Sion College. Now Oxford, Bodleian, Lat. class. d.39.

NORWICH. *Ben. cathedral priory of Holy Trinity.*
Heading: Ker, 'Medieval manuscripts from Norwich Cathedral Priory', reprinted in Ker, *Books, Collectors and Libraries*, pp. 243–72. The Norwich MS. now Cambridge, U.L., Ii.1.18, fo. 3, has a list of 26 titles, service books and others, of s.xvi in. 'In alt'' or 'alter'' has been added to most entries.

+ Aberystwyth, N.L., 21878E. *e*Biblia. s.xii. (Previously *Untraced*).
Brussels, Bibl. Royale, IV.328: formerly London, Messrs Maggs.
Cambridge, U.L., Ii.2.23. Footnote 1: *for* some other Norwich MSS. *read* CUL, Ii.1.27 and Norwich, Cathedral, 2.
              Ii.3.32. *For* [X.ccxxvii] *read* [X.ccxxviii].
+   Trinity Coll., 884. *c*Dares Phrygius, etc. s.xii–xv.[2]

---

[1] Footnote 7 on p. 134 of 1964 edn. applies to this MS.
[2] The older part of Trinity Coll. 884, fos. 1–10, 82–8, was apparently at **HORSHAM ST FAITH** in s.xii (cf. annals of 1134 and 1147) before moving to Norwich (cf. annals of 1172 and 1175).

London, B.L., Add. 15759. *Alter footnote 4 to read* Lambeth Palace 188, fos. 175–9, and 192, fo. 44 (flyleaf) have been detached apparently from B.L., Add. 15759.

+   Harley 957. *i*Alcuinus, etc. s.xii–xiv.

        Lambeth Palace, 188. For alteration to footnote 4 see B.L., Add. 15759 above.

+   192, fo. 44. A leaf detached from B.L., Add. 15759, *q.v.* above.

        Messrs. Maggs: now Brussels, Bibl. Royale, IV.328.

New York, Columbia U.L. *For* Plimpton 269 *read* Plimpton 308. *Cancel query.*

Norwich, Cathedral. *Entries should read:*
        Norwich Cath., 1. *gc*Barth Cotton. s.xiii ex. [C.xi, C.xix].[1]
        Norwich Cath., 2. *e*Joh. Boccatius, etc. s.xv. [F.lxxv].[1]

+   Norfolk and Norwich Record Office, binding leaves in Norfolk Archdeaconry Wills Register 16 (Beales), 1556–8. *l*Consuetudinarium (frag., 4 fos.). s.xii/xiii.

Oxford, Wadham Coll., s.n. *Read* A.5.28.

Untraced: now Aberystwyth, N.L., 21878E.

NORWICH. *Dominican convent.*

London, Middle Temple, s.n. *Read* 54.7.

+ Wantage, Oxon., Lord Astor. *e*Psalterium, etc. s.xiv.

+ *Untraced:* J. and J. Leighton, cat., April 1916, item 785 (pr. bk). *i*J. Canonicus. Venice, A.D. 1516.[2] P. M. Barnard, cat. 64 (1912), no. 98 (pr. bk). *i*Aegidius Aurifaber. Deventer, A.D. 1481.[3]

NORWICH. *Hospital of St Giles.*

+ London, B.L., Add. 57534. *e*Processionale. s.xiv ex. ?
        Harley 1688. Psalterium. s.xv.[4]

NOSTELL, Yorkshire. *Aug. priory of St Oswald.*

+ Lampeter, St David's University Coll., 47F (pr. bk). *e*Erasmus, De ratione studii ac legendi. Strasbourg, A.D. 1524.

+ Toronto, U.L., RB 9689 (pr. bk). *e*Biblia, I, cum comment. N. de Lyra. Nuremberg, A.D. 1487.

---

[1] On deposit in the Norfolk and Norwich Record Office, DCL1, 2.

[2] The Leighton item was in the Sherbrooke sale at Sotheby's, 27 June 1912, lot 458, when it was bound after *Recollecte Gaietani super octo libros Physicorum*, Venice, A.D. 1500: the latter was detached and appeared in a Sotheby sale, 14 Nov. 1918, lot 751, to Ellis.

[3] For the inscription 'conventus Norwici' cf. Middle Temple 54.7.

[4] Calendar contains 'dedicatio ecclesie Norwicensis', obits of Norfolk families and 'obitus hugonis prior hospicii', i.e. Hugh Acton, Master, 1437–64 (*VCH Norfolk*, ii, 446).

NOTLEY, Buckinghamshire. *Aug. abbey of B.V.M. and St John the Baptist.*

+ *Untraced:* Sotheby and Wilkinson sale of Bodleian Libr. duplicates, 21 May 1862, lot 915 (pr. bk). *i*D. Mancinus (in Latin and English). (London, A.D. 1518?)

NUNEATON, Warwickshire. *Priory of B.V.M. of nuns of Fontevrault.*

Douai, Bibl. Mun., 887. *Cancel query.*

OSNEY, Oxfordshire. *Aug. abbey of B.V.M.*

Cambridge, Gonville and Caius Coll., 297, 481. *Read* Hugo de S. Caro.

+ Oxford, New Coll., 22. *e*Isaias et Jeremias glo. s.xii/xiii. [P].

+ *Untraced:* Oxford, Bodleian, Twyne XXI, p. 264, contains notes made by Brian Twyne 'Ex manuscripto episcopi Oxon [John Bridges, bp. 1604–18] apud Staunton Harcot: in folio. . . .' It contained Speculum theologie Johannis Methensis and two chronicles, the second of which continued to Henry VI.

OXFORD. *Aug. priory of St Frideswide.*

+ Coulsdon, Surrey, Mr D. L. Cumming (pr. bk). *e*Joh. Balbus, Catholicon. Venice, A.D. 1497/98.[1] ?

+ London, B.L., Arundel 157. *l*Psalterium. s.xiii in. ?

+ *Reject:* Baltimore, Johns Hopkins U.L., W.15.

OXFORD. *Franciscan convent.*

London, Mr E. M. Dring. Now Oxford, Bodleian, Lat. misc. b.18.
+   Royal College of Physicians (pr. bk). *i*Opera agricolationum. Reggio, A.D. 1496.

+ Manchester, John Rylands U.L., Box of fragments, no. 9. *e*Interpretationes nominum hebraicorum (2 fos.). s.xiii ex.

+ Oxford, Bodleian, Auct. 4.Q.4.9 (pr. bk). *i*Duns Scotus, Aurea quarti sententiarum. Paris, A.D. 1497.
             Lat. misc. b.18: formerly London, Mr E. M. Dring.

OXFORD. *Dominican convent.*

Heading: *for* Oriel Coll., MS. 30 fo. 111 *read* Oriel Coll., MS 30, fo. iii. List of 4 books, s.xvi[1], in Rome, Vatican, Reg. lat. 2099, fo. 307[v].

Oxford, Mr N. R. Ker. Now Oxford, Bodleian, Lat. bib. d.9.

OXFORD. *Carmelite convent.*

+ Stockholm, Kungl. Bibliotek, A.140. Irenaeus. s.xiv ex. [Leland].[1] ?

---

[1] *Ex dono* inscription of Wm. Wyssheter is followed by later note in another hand that he had sold it to Wm. Moll for 2*s*. 6*d*.: whether it ever reached St Frideswide's is therefore uncertain.

[2] Copied 'iussu Burelli Oxonii' from the MS. now Leyden, Voss. lat. F.33, which was brought 'ex anglia' by Lawrence Burrell, provincial of Narbonne, and given by him to the Carmelites of Paris in 1494. The Stockholm MS. may be the copy which Leland saw in Oxford (*Collectanea*, iv (1774), 59).

OXFORD. *University.*

The lists of Duke Humphrey's gifts in 1439, 1441 and 1444 printed by A. Sammut, *Unfredo duca di Gloucester e gli umanisti italiani* (Medioevo e umanesimo xli, 1980), pp. 60–84. The 1444 gift is of 135 volumes, not 134: Anstey omitted no. 29.

London, B.L., Cotton Nero E.v. *For 47 read 48.*
Oxford, Bodleian, Duke Humphrey d.1. *For 74 read 75.*
    Hatton 36. *For 93 read 94.*
  Magdalen Coll., lat. 37. *For 107 read 108.*
Paris, B.N., lat. 7805. *For 73 read 74.*
+ Rome, Vatican, Vat. lat., 10669. Plato (in Latin). s.xv. [*cf. Dk. H. 1444, 133*]. ?

OXFORD. *All Souls College.*

The catalogues in Archives Misc. 209, the P.R.O. list, and the catalogues and lists in the 'Vellum Inventory' printed by N. R. Ker, *Records of All Souls College Library* (Oxford Bibliographical Society, Oxford, 1971).

Antwerp, Plantin-Moretus, 12. *Add* [*Cat. 209, 434*].
     26. *For* [*Cat.*, p. 478, line 13] *read* [*Cat. 209, 96*].[1]
     30. *For* [*Cat.*, p. 480, line 22] *read* [*Cat. 209, 430*].
     144. *Add* [*Andrew* 25].
+   341, fos. 15–22. Augustinus. s.xii.[1]
Exeter, Cathedral, 3506. *Read* [*Cat. 209, 134; inv. fo. 25*].
London, The Robinson Trust. Now Oxford, Bodleian, Lat. misc. c.75.
Oxford, Pembroke Coll., 2. Given in 1551, therefore omit.

OXFORD. *Balliol College.*

List of 16 books, s.xvi[1], in Rome, Vatican, Reg. lat. 2099, fos. 306[v]–7.

+ Antwerp, Plantin-Moretus, 109+343, fos. 1–3 (flyleaves). *d*J. Felton, etc. s.xv.
Oxford, Bodleian, Digby 29. *Add that* Balliol Coll., 219, fo. 105, is part of this MS.

OXFORD. *Brasenose College.*

St Albans School. Now London, Mr J. P. Getty.

OXFORD. *Canterbury College; cell of Christ Church, Canterbury.*

Heading line 4: *after* 1510 *add* 1521. List of 3 books, s.xvi[1], in Rome, Vatican, Reg. lat. 2099, fo. 306[v].

+ Durham, U.L., Bamburgh Sel. 40. II Esdras, Esther, Tobit glo. (2 frags.). s.xii ex [*cf. list 1501*, 110].[2]
+ Oxford, Bodleian, Lat. misc. b.19, B.47–9. Job glo. (frag.). s.xii ex. [*cf. list 1501*, 111; etc.].[2]
+ Windsor, St George's Chapel, 5. *e*Gregorius. s.xii. [*List 1501*, 26 etc.].

---

[1] Plantin-Moretus 341, fos. 15–22, is a detached quire of Plantin-Moretus 26.
[2] See also above under **CANTERBURY**. Assigned to Canterbury College on the basis of being binding fragments from books bound in Oxford, s.xvi in: see de Hamel, *Glossed Books*, p. 42.

OXFORD. *Corpus Christi College.*

+London, B.L. 1073.1.4 (pr. bk). *e*H. Barbarus, Orationes. Paris, A.D. 1509.[1] ?

OXFORD. *Durham College; cell of Durham Cathedral priory.*

On use of ¶ in this section see heading to **DURHAM**. Lists of books sent there from Durham in 1315, *c.* 1400, and in 1409, printed from rolls in the Durham Cathedral Muniments by H. E. D. Blakiston, *Oxf. Hist. Soc. Collectanea*, iii (1896), 36–41; second folios given in the second and third lists, which are printed also in *Cat. Vet. Eccles. Dunelm.*, pp. 39–41. Another list, *c.* 1390–1400, is printed by W. A. Pantin in H. E. Salter, *Oxford Formularies* (Oxford Hist. Soc. N.S., iv, 1942), 241–44, from Durham, Dean and Chapter Muniments, 2.6.Ebor.5. 1 book listed, s.xvi[1], in Rome, Vatican, Reg. lat. 2099, fo. 307.

¶ Cambridge, King's Coll., 22. H. de S. Victore. s.xii.[2] [C *over erased* F; *cat. 1409*, F].

+Durham, Cathedral, A.I.12. H. de S. Caro, s.xiii. [H,1ª.2ⁱ.B; *cat. 1409*, H].

¶ London, B.L., Harley 1924. *c*Beda. s.xii [D; ?*cat. 1315*, 22].[3] ?

¶ Oxford, Bodleian, Digby 41, fos. 91, 91*, 92, 101. *c*Reliquie Dunelm., etc. s.xii.[3] ?

Laud Lat. 12. *e*Biblia. s.xiii.[2] [B *corr. from* C].

+Ushaw Coll., XVIII.A.4.1 (pr. bk). *e*J. Nyder, Preceptorium. Paris, A.D. 1478.

Rejected: Oxford, Bodleian, Aubrey 31.

OXFORD. *Exeter College.*

List of 25 books given by William Rede, bishop of Chichester, 22 Oct. 1374, among muniments of Exeter College, E.v.2/1: second folios given. List of 45 books given by William Rede for the use of his kinsmen which appear to have come to Exeter College in 1400 after the death of Richard Pestour, among muniments of Exeter College, E.v.2/2: second folios given.

Douai, Bibl. Mun., 860. *Add* [*List 1374*].

+Oxford, Merton Coll., 224. Avicenna. s.xiv. [*List 1374*]. ?

+ 257. 'Proverbia Senece', etc., s.xiii. [*List 1400*, 41].

OXFORD. *Gloucester College; cell of Gloucester.*

+Oxford, New Coll., 49. *bs*Petrus Johannes Olivi. s.xv.[4]

---

[1] Title-page bears *ex libris* in italic hand of s.xvi[1] but whether it was at the College before 1540 is uncertain. See T. A. Birrell, *The Library of John Morris* (1976), p. xviii, pl. v and no. 107. 14 other short tracts of about the same date, bound with this item until s.xix, are probably covered by the *ex libris*. See Birrell, nos. 157–68, 919, 1113 for present pressmarks.

[2] King's Coll. 22 and Laud lat. 12 were earlier at **DURHAM**, *q.v.*

[3] Bodleian, Digby 41, fos. 91, 91*, 92, 101, was part of BL, Harley 1924. The manuscript was used by T. Gascoigne, perhaps at Oxford.

[4] New Coll., 49 is evidently a present from John Whethamstede, abbot of St Albans, like London, Bodleian and Worcester Coll. manuscripts: like them it is identifiable in Whethamstede's booklist in London, B.L., Arundel 34 (see under **ST ALBANS**): see D. R. Howlett and R. W. Hunt, *BLR*, x (1982), 225–8.

OXFORD. *Lincoln College.*

List of 9 books, s.xvi¹, in Rome, Vatican, Reg. lat. 2099, fo. 307ᵛ.

+ Cambridge, St John's Coll., 54.   *s*Virgilius. s.xv. [*Cat.* 73].
+ Edinburgh, N.L., Adv. 33.3.1.   Scala mundi, etc. s.xv. [*Cat.* 106].
+   U.L., 200.   Pseudo-Acron in Horatium. s.xv. [*Cat.* 76].
+ London, B.L., Burney 138.   *s*Cicero. s.xv. [*Cat.* 66].
+   Royal 15 C.xv.   Caesar. s.xv. [*Cat.* 72].
+ Oxford, Bodleian, Auct. F.2.25.   Curtius Rufus. s.xv. [*Cat.* 71].
+   Queen's Coll., 202.   *s*Horatius. s.xii. [*Cat.* 85].

OXFORD. *Magdalen College.*

List of 16 books, s.xvi¹, in Rome, Vatican, Reg. lat. 2099, fo. 306ᵛ.

+ Oxford, Bodleian, Bodl. 455.   *b*Augustinus, etc. s.xii.   ?

OXFORD. *Merton College.*

The election lists of 1372 and 1375 also printed by N. R. Ker, 'The books of philosophy distributed at Merton College in 1372 and 1375', *Medieval Studies for J. A. W. Bennett*, ed. P. L. Heyworth (Oxford, 1981), pp. 347–94, reprinted in Ker, *Books, Collectors and Libraries*, pp. 331–78. Heading line 6: *for* †1385 *read* †22 Oct. 1374 *and add after* 1941 and is printed by J. R. L. Highfield in *BLR*, x (1982), 14–19, from the papers of H. W. Garrod.

+ London, B.L., Cotton Tib. B.ix, fos. 1–4, 225–35.   R. Bacon, etc. s.xiv.¹   ?
+   Harley 625.   *s*Geber, etc. s.xiv.¹
   Oxford, Bodleian, Bodl. 365.   *Read* [*Cat. T.* 184; cf. *electio* 1519, Norice 20].
                  Digby   10.   *For* 10 *read* 19.
                        176.   *Add* [*Reg. Coll.*, *sub anno* 1483, 37].
+   178, fos. 1–4, 88–115.   *s*Euclides, etc. s.xiv.¹
+   179.   *s*Ptolomaeus, etc. s.xiv.
                        216.   *Add* [*Reg. Coll.*, *sub anno* 1483, 37].
                  Savile 19.   *Read* [*Cat. D.*22; *electio* 1519, Barlow 11].
   1964 edn., p. 147, footnote 7: the four leaves at Merton are in the binding of Seneca, Paris, 1587, 23.dd.11.
+ *Reject*: Oxford, Trinity Coll. 47.²

OXFORD. *New College.*

List of 18 books, s.xvi¹ in Rome, Vatican, Reg. lat. 2099, fo. 307. List of 13 books, A.D. 1489, in Oxford, Bodleian, MS Digby 31 ('. . . hec infra in studiis scolarium Wintonie Oxon' reperta sunt'), printed in *Catalogus codicum MSS Bibl. Bodl.*, ix (1883), col. 29.

+ Cambridge (U.S.A.), Harvard Coll., Houghton Libr. (pr. bk).   *e*Politianus. Venice, A.D. 1498.
+ London, B.L., Cotton Calig. A.xvi.   C. Salutati. s.xv. [Leland].   ?
+   Mr N. J. Barker.   *e*Jeronimus, Epistolae. s.xv.
   Oxford, Bodleian, Bodl. 809.   *For* P. Blesensis *read* P. de Waltham.
                  Digby 31.   *Read* Cessolis and transfer to **WIN-CHESTER,** *Ben. cathedral priory.*
+ *Rejected:* Oxford, All Souls Coll., SR 81.a.15 (pr. bk).

¹ Harley 625, Digby 178, fos. 1–14, 88–115, and probably Cotton Tib. B.ix, fos. 1–4, 225–35, formed one volume given to Merton College by Simon Bredon (Powicke, no. 385): see A. G. Watson, *BLR*, ix (1976), 207–17.
² See Ker, 'The books of philosophy distributed at Merton College'.

OXFORD. *Oriel College.*

London, Sion College. Now Oxford, Bodleian, Lat. class. d. 39.

OXFORD. *The Queen's College.*
An indenture in the College archives lists 10 books and an astronomical instrument, apparently the 'electio' of Mag. Henry Scayf in 1445.[1]

London, The Robinson Trust. Now Oxford, Bodleian, Lat. misc. c.75. 1964 edn., p. 149, footnote 6: for Ker's note on the MS. see now also Ker, *Books, Collectors and Libraries*, pp. 411, 436.

OXFORD. *University College.*
List of 21 books, s.xvi[1], in Rome, Vatican, Reg. lat. 2099, fos. 307[v]–8.

PERTH. *Charterhouse of Vallis Virtutis.*
+Edinburgh, N.L., Adv. 35.6.7. *e*J. Fordun, Scotochronicon (abridged). s.xv ex. [0(?) ix].

PERTH. *Franciscan convent.*
Wolfenbüttel. *For* Ducal Libr. *read* Herzog August Bibl. *and add* [F.21].

PETERBOROUGH, Northamptonshire. *Ben. abbey of St Peter and St Paul and St Andrew.*

Helmingham Hall, 6. Now Liverpool, Public Libr., f091 RAB.
+London, Dulwich College, A.3.f.3 (pr. bk). *i*Biblia cum glo. N. de Lyra, III. Nuremberg, A.D. 1497.
London, Lambeth Palace, 335 and footnote 3. *For* 76 *read* 77.
+Norwich, St Peter Mancroft Church. *e*Epp. Pauli glo. s.xii/xiii.
+Oxford, Bodleian, Rawl. C.677. *g*Logica. s.xv. ?
Peterborough, Cathedral. The manuscripts are now on permanent loan in Cambridge, U.L.

PIPEWELL, Northamptonshire. *Cist. abbey of B.V.M.*

Deene Park. Now Oxford, Bodleian, Lat. th. d.35.
Dublin, Chester Beatty Libr. Now Düsseldorf, private collection.
Peterborough, Cathedral. Now deposited in Cambridge, U.L.

POLSLOE, Devon. *Convent of Ben. nuns.*
+Oxford, Bodleian, BB 200 (pr. bk). *i*Breviarium Sarisburiense. Paris, A.D. 1519.[2]

QUEENBOROUGH, Kent. *Mayor and Corporation.*
+Queenborough, Corporation. *e*Statuta Angliae; Registrum brevium. s.xiv in.[3]

---

[1] *Sic* Ker's notes. I have been unable to identify the document. (A.G.W.)
[1] On endleaf is 'Polslow' with list of Polslow nuns, emended in late 1530s, after death of Margaret Trow (after 16 Oct. 1535) and before surrender, 19 Feb. 1538: cf. list in G. Oliver, *Monasticon Exon* (Exeter, 1846), p. 168.
[2] Deposited in Kent Archives Office, Maidstone, Qb/AZ 1.

RAMSEY, Huntingdonshire. *Ben. abbey of B.V.M. and St Benedict.*

Deene Park. Now London, B.L., Add. 54184.

London, B.L., Cotton Vit. A.vii. *Cancel the entry and list as Rejected: see now under* **EXETER.**

+   Vesp. A.xviii, fos. 87–149 (and 150–67?). *c*De abbatia de Ramesia. s.xiii.

The Robinson Trust. Now Oxford, Bodleian, Lat. misc. c. 75.

Rejected: Mount Stuart, Marquess of Bute, now London, B.L., Add. 62777. *Add* London, B.L., Cotton Vit. A.vii.

READING, Berkshire. *Ben. abbey of B.V.M.*

Belvoir, Duke of Rutland. Now London, B.L., Add. 62925.

Cambridge, Gonv. and Caius Coll., 177. *Cancel the entry and substitute e*Vita Caroli Magni, etc. s.xii ex. [*Cat.* p. 120].[1]

Cambridge (U.S.A.), Harvard Law School, 64. *Cancel the entry and list as Rejected.*

Glasgow, U.L. *For* BE.7.e.24 *read* Gen.335.

+ Leyden, U.L., Bibl. Publ.Gr.16J. *e*Josephus. s.xi[2]. ?

+ London, B.L., Add. 30898: formerly *Untraced,* Puttick and Simpson. *Add date* s.xii ex.

                         54230: formerly London, Dr E. G. Millar.

                         62925: formerly Belvoir, Duke of Rutland.

+   Cotton Vit A.viii, fos. 5–100. Gesta Normannorum Ducum. s.xii ix. [*Cat.* p. 120].[1]

Dr E. G. Millar: now London, B.L., Add. 54230.

Morcombelake, Mr J. S. Cox: now St Peter Port, Guernsey, Mr J. S. Cox.

Oxford, Bodleian, Bodl. 713. *Add query.*

+   Laud Misc. 578. Bachiarius, etc. s.xii ex. [*Cat.* p. 121].

                  Worcester Coll. *For* 213 *read* 213+213*.[2]

Portsmouth, Roman Catholic Bishopric. Now Reading Museum and Art Gallery, 40.74.

St Peter Port, Guernsey, Mr J. S. Cox: formerly Morcombelake, Mr J. S. Cox.

+ Woolhampton, Douai Abbey. *s*lVersarius (frag.). s.xii in. ?

1964 edn., p. 156, footnote 3: *for* xvi(?) *read* s.xvi, post-Dissolution(?).

Untraced: +Sotheby sale, 7 Dec. 1964, lot 149 (property of R. J. R. Arundell, Wardour Castle), to H. M. Fletcher for a client. *l*Preces privatae. s.xv.; Puttick and Simpson 5 July 1877, now London, B.L., Add. 30898.

Rejected: Portsmouth, Roman Catholic Bishopric, Virtue and Cahill 8451, now Durham (U.S.A.), Univ. of North Carolina Libr., 103; *add* Cambridge (U.S.A.), Harvard Law School, 64.

---

[1] Cotton Vit. A.viii, fos. 5–100, formed one volume with Cambridge, Gonv. and Caius Coll., 177: see E. M. C. van Houts, *Gesta Normannorum Ducum* (Groningen, 1982), pp. 239–41.

[2] Two binding leaves of polyphonic music, s.xiii[2], are now kept separately as MS. 213*.

READING, Berkshire. *Franciscan convent.*
List of 35 books, s.xvi[1], in Rome, Vatican, Reg. lat. 2099, fo. 305[r-v].

RIEVAULX, Yorkshire. *Cist. abbey of B.V.M.*
+London, B.L., Add. 63077. *e*Genesis glo. s.xii ex.
Cotton Vit. D.v. and 1964 edn., p. 159, footnote 9: *read*
Cotton Vit. D.v fos. 1–16.
+ Vesp. D.xiii, fos. 181–201. Abbey of Holy Ghost
(in English), etc. s.xv.[1]

ROBERTSBRIDGE, Sussex. *Cist. abbey of B.V.M.*
+Aberystwyth, N.L., 13210D. *e*G. Monemutensis, etc. s.xiii in.[2]
+London, Private Collection 1. *s*W. Malmesburiensis. s.xiii in.[2]
+Oxford, Bodleian, Laud Misc. 109. *s*Bernardus, Opera. s.xii.
+*Untraced:* Sotheby sale, 25 Nov. 1969, lot 455, to Dawson. *s*Giraldus
Cambrensis. s.xiii in.[2]

ROCHE, Yorkshire. *Cist. abbey of B.V.M.*
Manchester. *Cancel* Rylands, lat. 186 *and list as Rejected.*
Yale U.L., Prof. N. H. Penrose. Now New Haven, Yale U.L.,
Beinecke 590.
Rejected: Manchester, John Rylands U.L., lat. 186.

ROCHESTER, Kent. *Ben. cathedral priory of St Andrew.*
Heading: line 3, *for* 120 ff *read* 122ff. *Add that* 13 books lent by the prior and
convent, 1 June 1390, are listed in a model form of indenture 'de libris liberandis de
libraria' in London, B.L., Cotton Faustina C.v, fo.50: third, fourth, fifth, sixth or
seventh folios are given, and the names of donors. A new edition of all the
catalogues and lists by A. G. Watson is in preparation for the British Academy's
Corpus of British Medieval Library Catalogues.

Cambridge, St John's Coll., 70. *Add* [Faustina List 10].
Eton College. *Read* (*e*)*s*Jeronimus. s.xii.
London, B.L., Royal 4 A.xii. *Add* [*Cat.II.* 129].
4 E.v. *Add* [Faustina list 2].
5. B.xiii. *Read* [*Cat.I*, p. 123; *II*.19; Faustina
list 12].
10 C.xii. *Add* [Faustina list 6].
Lambeth Palace, 76. *Read* fos. i, 1–147. *Add* [*Cat.I*, p. 123].
Messrs Maggs (pr. bk). Now sold and untraced.
+Maidstone, Kent Archives Office, U1121/M2. *s*Boethius (2 fos.). s.xii in.
+Oxford, Bodleian, Laud Misc. 624. *e*W. de Pagula. s.xiv.
Rochester, Cathedral. Augustinus, s.n. *Read* A.3.16.
'Textus Roffensis'. Deposited in Maidstone,
Kent Archives Office, DRc/R1.

---

[1] Cotton Vesp. D.xiii, fos. 181–201, Cotton Vit. D.v and Corpus Christi Coll.
Oxford, 155 formed one volume.
[2] Three parts of one volume, Phillipps 26233 (Aberystwyth), 26641 (London,
formerly Bristol Baptist College), 26642 (*Untraced*), sold respectively at Sotheby's
30 Nov. 1971, lot 499; 21 Nov. 1972, lot 539; 25 Nov. 1969, lot 455. The London
section (Phillipps 26641) is now deposited in Edinburgh, N.L., Acc. 9193/13.

+ Rome, Vatican, Reg. lat. 458, fos.1–36. *s*Osbernus, Vita S. Elphegi; etc. s.xii in.[1] [*Cat.I.*77].

+   598, fo. 8. Missa de S. Elphego. s.xii in.[1] [*Cat.I.*77].

+   646, fos. 1–49. Osbernus, Vita S. Dunstani; etc. s.xii in.[1] [*Cat.I.*77].

+ Salisbury, Cathedral, Y.2.16 (pr. bk). *e*Seneca, Lucubrationes omnes. Basel, A.D. 1515.

Untraced: London, Messrs Maggs (pr. bk), above. London, J. & J. Leighton, *Cat. of Early Printed Books*, pt. xiii (before 1908), no. 7251 (pr. bk). *e*P. Comestor, Scolastica historia. Paris, A.D. 1518.

ROTHERHAM, Yorkshire. *Jesus College.*

+ Cambridge, Trinity Coll., 1270. R. Grosseteste, Dicta. s.xv ex. [*cf. Cat.,* p. 6].

+ York, Minster, XVI.A.6. *c*R. Grosseteste. s.xv ex. [*Cat.* p.6, (6)].

ST ALBANS, Hertfordshire. *Ben. abbey of St Alban.*

    The burnt fragments of book lists of abbot Whethamstede in London, B.L., Cotton Otho B.iv are partly printed by T. Tanner, *Bibliotheca Britannico-Hibernica* (1748), pp. 441–2. R. W. Hunt, 'The library of the Abbey of St Albans', *Ker Essays*, pp. 151–77, lists Bale's excerpts from the 'indiculus' of Walter the Chanter, s.xii ex (pp. 269–71) and an imperfect borrowers' list of c. 1430 which formed part of the pad of a book belonging to Gonville and Caius College, Cambridge (pp. 273–6). R. M. Thomson, *Manuscripts from St Albans Abbey 1066–1235* (Woodbridge, 1982), ii, pls. 174, 240, illustrate St Albans titles and pressmarks, pls. 12, 13, 15, 48, 172, 173, 175, 258 illustrate St Albans *ex libris.*

+ Cambridge, U.L., Ee.4.20. *c*Formularium. s.xiv–xv.[2]

+   Emmanuel Coll., 244. *s*Palladius, De agricultura. s.xii med. ?

           Fitzwilliam Mus. *Cancel the entry and add to Rejected.*

+   Trinity Coll., 62. *s*Epp. Pauli glo. s.xii med. ?

+   147. *sc*Biblia. s.xii med. ?

     Eton Coll., 103. *For* N. de Gorran *read* P. de Tarentasia.

+ Hertford, County Record Office, Gorhambury XD4/B, C. Lectionarium (frag., 4 fos.). s.xi ex.[3] ?

     London, B.L., Add. 26764. *m*J. Whethamstede, etc. s.xv in.

                  62777. Formerly Mount Stuart, Marquess of Bute.

+   Arundel 11, fos. 1–182. *cs*J. Whethamstede, etc. s.xv in.

+   201, fos. 44–97. *c*Verses (in Latin). s.xiii in.

+   Cotton Jul. D.iii, fos.125–96. *c*Verses (in Latin), s.xiii in. ?

+   Tib. D.v, part 1. *s*J. Whethamstede. s.xv in.

+   Nero C.vi. *s*J. Whethamstede. s.xv in.

+   Dr C. F. R. de Hamel. *b*Biblia (1 fo.). s.xiv[1].[4]

---

[1] Three parts of one manuscript.

[2] Bears signature of Robert Blakeney, last prior of Tynemouth, cell of St Albans.

[3] See Thomson, i, 77.

[4] For other leaves see *Fine Books and Book Collecting: Books and Manuscripts acquired from Alan G. Thomas*, ed. C. de Hamel and R. A. Linenthal (Leamington Spa, 1981), pp. 10–12. Another leaf, now also in private hands, is Quaritch cat. 1036 (1984), no. 76. Dr de Hamel has a record of many others.

Mount Stuart, Marquess of Bute. Now London, B.L., Add. 62777, above.

+New York, Pierpont Morgan Libr., 926. /Vita Johannis Elemosinarii, etc. s.xi ex–xi/xii.

+Oxford, Bodleian, Bodl. 331. gOdo Morimundensis super iv libros Moysi. s.xiii in. ?

+   585, fos. 1–47. Excerpta historica. s.xv.[1]

              752. 1964 edn., p. 165, footnote 3 also applies to this MS.

+   Douce 299. Historia Alexandri magni. s.xv.[2]

              Rawl. C.562.⎫

+   C.568.⎬ cJoh. Beleth, etc. s.xiii in.[3] ?

+   C.569.⎭

Stonyhurst Coll. 10. *For* 10 *read* 7 (10).

Sürth bei Köln, Dr J. Lückger. Now Cologne, Schnütgen Museum.

+Urbana, University of Illinois Libr., 74. /Breviarium. s.xiv.

+*Rejected:* Cambridge, Fitzwilliam Museum, 274; London, Lambeth Palace, 102; Oxford, Magdalen Coll., Lat. 53, pp. 145–68; Verdun, Bibl. Mun., 70.

ST ANDREWS, Fife.   *Aug. cathedral priory of St Andrew.*

Wolfenbüttel. *For* Ducal Libr. *read* Herzog August Bibl.

              Helmst. 538. *For* s.xiv *read* s.xv.

              628. *For* s.xiv *read* s.xiii.

ST DAVID'S, Dyfed.   *Cathedral church of St David.*

Cambridge, Corpus Christi Coll., 199.   *Cancel entry and add to Rejected.*

ST OSYTH (Chich.), Essex.   *Aug. abbey of St Peter, St Paul and St Osyth.*

Helmingham Hall, 2.   *Cancel entry. See now* **STOKE-BY-CLARE.**

London, B.L., Add. 56252: formerly Helmingham Hall, 3.

New York, Pierpont Morgan Libr., G.65: formerly New York, Mr W. S. Glazier.

SALISBURY, Wiltshire.   *Cathedral church of B.V.M.*

    N. R. Ker, 'The beginnings of Salisbury Cathedral Library', *Medieval Learning and Literature: Essays Presented to Richard William Hunt*, ed. J. J. G. Alexander and M. T. Gibson (Oxford, 1976), pp. 23–49, reprinted in Ker, *Books, Collectors and Libraries*, pp. 143–72. Ker, 'Salisbury Cathedral MSS and Patrick Young's Catalogue', repr. ibid., pp. 175–208.

Cambridge, Trinity Coll., 717, fos. 44–71.   Cancel the entry and add to *Rejected.*

+London, B.L., Cotton Vit. A.xii, fos. 4–78. sRabanus Maurus, etc. s.xi ex. [Leland].

+   Harley 3237. eJeronimus. s.xv ex.[4]

---

[1] Cambridge, U.L., Dd.6.7 and Bodleian, Bodl.585, fos. 1–47, formed one volume.

[2] Bodleian, Douce 299 and Rawl. D.358 formed one volume.

[3] Bodleian, Rawl. C.562, C.568 and C.569 formed one volume.

[4] B.L., Harley 3237 and Salisbury Cath. 143 are companion volumes.

London (*contd*)

+ B.L., Royal 5 F.xiii. *s*Ambrosius, Epistolae. s.xi ex.
+ 5 F.xviii. *s*Tertullianus, Apologeticus, etc. s.xi/xii.
+ 6 B.xv. *s*Cyprianus. s.xi/xii. [*Young* 155?].
+ 8 B.xiv, fos. 154–6ᵛ. *s*In cantica canticorum (frag.). s.xi ex.
  15 B.xix. *Cancel query.*
+ 15 C.xi, fos. 1–58, 113–94. *s*Cicero, Plautus. ss.xii in, xi ex.

Oxford, Bodleian. Fell 1, 3, 4, e Mus. 2. These MSS. were permanently restored to Salisbury Cathedral Libr. in 1985, with numbers 222, 223, 221 and 224 respectively.

+ Keble Coll., 22. *s*Epp. Pauli glo. s.xi ex. [*Young* 135?].

Salisbury, Cathedral, 65 and 138, and footnote 3, p. 173 of 1964 edn. *Footnote should read* Salisbury Cath. 138 appears to be the exemplar of 65.

109. In 1964 edn., p. 174, footnote 1, and p. 174, footnote 5, add this MS. to MSS. 114 and 128. All three are from the same MS. of Augustine on Genesis, s.xi ex.

117. In 1964 edn., p. 175, footnote 3, note that the Bodmer leaves are now owned by Prof. T. Takamiya, Tokyo (MS. 21).

132. *Cancel query.*

138 and 1964 edn., p. 175, footnote 6. *Footnote should read* Salisbury Cath. 138 appears to be the exemplar of 65.

+ 198. *es*Augustinus. s.xi/xii. [*Young* 131].[1]

Rejected: add Cambridge, Trinity Coll., 717, fos. 44–71.

SALISBURY, Wiltshire. *Franciscan convent.*

+ Oxford, Bodleian, Digby 68. *e*Tabulae astronomicae, etc. s.xiv. [R. II].

SALISBURY, Wiltshire. *Dominican convent.*

+ London, Dr C. F. R. de Hamel (pr. bk). *e*Sermones Meffreth (2 vols.). Basel, before 11 July 1486.

+ **SCARBOROUGH**, Yorkshire. *Dominican convent.*

Cambridge, U.L., Rel.d.51.15 (pr. bk). *i*Epistolae Pauli (etc.). recognitae per Erasmum Roterodanum. Louvain, A.D. 1519.

SCARBOROUGH, Yorkshire. *Grange or 'domus' dependent on the abbey of Cîteaux.*

Prof. Ormerod is deceased and the MS. cannot now be traced.

SELBY, Yorkshire. *Ben. abbey of B.V.M. and St German.*

+ London, B.L., Add. 36652C. *c*Tabula paschalis. s.xii/xiii.

---

[1] Footnote 1 on p. 171 and footnote 5 on p. 173 of 1964 edn. apply to this MS.

SEMPRINGHAM, Lincolnshire. *Gilb. priory of B.V.M.*

+ Rome, Vatican, Barberini 2689. *c*English chronicle (in French). s.xiv.

SHAFTESBURY, Dorset. *Abbey of B.V.M. and St Edward of Ben. nuns.*

+ Cambridge, U.L., Ii.6.40. *i*Fervor amoris, etc. (in English). s.xv.
+ Salisbury, Cathedral, 150. *l*Psalterium. s.x ex. ?

Steyning, Sir Arthur Howard ⎰ These entries in the 1964 edn. refer to
Wellington, J. Hasson ⎱ one MS., now London, Lambeth Palace, 3285.

SHEEN, Surrey. *Charterhouse of Jesus of Bethlehem.*

Chandlers Cross, Mr W. L. Wood. Sold (Traylen, *Cat. 81* (1970?), no. 11) and now untraced.
+ Claremont (U.S.A., Cal.), Claremont Colleges, Honnold Libr., Crispin 5. *c*Psalterium. s.xiv ex.

Dublin, Trinity Coll., 281. ⎰ The Vesp. leaves are a detached
London, B.L., Cotton Vesp. D.ix, ⎱ fragment of the Dublin volume.
fos. 44–9, 167, 168.

Footnote 6, p. 178 of 1964 edn. On Grenehalgh and for a list of all MSS. known to have passed through his hands see M. G. Sargent, *James Grenehalgh as Textual Critic* (Analecta Cartusiana lxxxv, 1984).

SHERBORNE, Dorset. *Ben. abbey of B.V.M.*

Alnwick, Duke of Northumberland. Deposited in London, B.L., Loan 82.

London, B.L., Cotton Faustina A.ii. *Read* Faustina A.ii, fos. 2–98. Loan 82. Formerly Alnwick, Duke of Northumberland.

SHOULDHAM, Norfolk. *Gilbertine priory of Holy Cross and B.V.M.*

+ York, Minster Libr., XVI.N.3. Pierre de Packham, Lumiere as lais; etc. s.xiii ex.[1] ?

SHREWSBURY, Shropshire. *Ben. abbey of St Peter and St Paul.*

London, Prof. F. Wormald. Now Cambridge, Fitzwilliam Museum, 88-1972 (218).

SHREWSBURY, Shropshire. *Franciscan convent.*

Leicester, Bernard Halliday. Now Kyoto (Japan), U.L., 039.7-Isi (183787).

SNAPE, Suffolk. *Ben. priory of B.V.M.*

Cancel title and entry. See now under **COLCHESTER.**

SOUTHAMPTON, Hampshire. *Aug. priory.*

London, B.L., Royal 5 E.vii. *Read* 5 E.vii, fos. 102–45.

[1] See *Manuscripts of Fourteenth Century English Polyphony*, ed. F. Harrison and R. Wibberley (1981), p. xiv.

SOUTHAMPTON, Hampshire.   Franciscan convent.

List of 12 books, s.xvi [1], in Rome, Vatican, Reg. lat. 2099, fos. 305ᵛ–6.

SOUTHAMPTON.   *Hospital of God's House (Domus Dei).*

13 books listed in inventory of 1362 and 10 books 'ordinati pro studio prioris sociorum collegie ac capellanorum commorantium in hospitali domus dei Suth'', listed in inventories of 1414–15 among muniments of The Queen's College, Oxford, R.230, R.457, printed in Southampton Record Society xix (1976), pp. xci–ii. Second fos. and values given in 1362 list and most second fos. in 1414–15 list. Mun. R.458 of 1416–17 adds a bible and R.462 of 1418–19 adds two more, with donors' names (op. cit., p. xvii, note 1).

+**SOUTH MALLING,** Sussex.   *College of St Michael.*

Norway, Mr M. Schøyen.   *i*Biblia. s.xiii med.

SOUTHWARK, Surrey.   *Aug. priory of St Mary Overy.*

Canterbury, Cathedral, 101.   *For* 101 *read* Lit.E.10 (101).

Guildford, Mrs F. E. O'Donnell.   Now London, B.L., Add. 63592.

+London, B.L., Add. 59855. Missale. *c.* 1410–20.[1]   ?

+   62105. *c*Horae. s.xv.

          63592. Formerly Guildford, Mrs F. E. O'Donnell.   ?

Royal 7 A.xix.   *Read* 7 A.xix, fos. 1–65.

+   Jesuit House, 1508 I (pr. bk). *e*Jeronimus, Epistolae.   Lyon, A.D. 1508.

Oxford, Bodleian, C.1.5.Linc.   *For* De vita et moribus sacerdotum *read* J. Clichtoveus.

+Ushaw College, Lisbon Collection (pr. bk). *e*J. Faber Stapulensis. Basel, A.D. 1523.

Yale U.L.   *Read* New Haven, Yale U.L., Beinecke Marston 243.

SPINNEY (Wicken), Cambridgeshire.   *Aug. priory of B.V.M. and the Holy Cross.*

+*Untraced:* Dawson cat. 200 (1969), no. 2. *e*Cassiodorus, In cantica canticorum. s.xiii.

STAFFORD.   *Aug. priory of St Thomas the Martyr.*

+Cambridge, Trinity Coll., 1236. *e*Gregorius. s.xiii ex.[2]   ?

---

[1] Probably the 'large new missal' bequeathed by John Gower to the altar of the chapel of St John Baptist in St Mary Overy, where Gower was buried. On fo. 9ᵛ is a kneeling man with a coat of arms as on Gower's tomb in the church and as in the MS. of his Latin poems, Glasgow U.L., Hunterian MS. T.2.17 (59). For translation of will see G. C. Macaulay, *The Complete Works of John Gower*, iv (Oxford, 1902), pp. xvii–xviii.

[2] Listed under Lessness in 1964 edn. on basis of *ex dono* inscription to house of St Thomas the Martyr, but Stafford is perhaps more likely: see N. R. Ker, 'The English manuscripts of the Moralia of Gregory the Great', *Kunsthistorische Forschungen Otto Pächt zu seinem 70. Geburtstag*, ed. A. Rosenauer and G. Weber (Salzburg, 1972), pp. 77–89.

STAMFORD, Lincolnshire. *Ben. priory of St Leonard; cell of Durham.*
Deene Park. Now Durham Cathedral C.III.22.

STAMFORD. *Carm. convent.*
Yale U.L. *Read* New Haven, Yale U.L., Beinecke Marston 118.

STOKE-BY-CLARE, Suffolk. *College of St John the Baptist.*
+Private collector, c/o Quaritch, London. *l*Ambrosius, Exameron etc.
  s.xii (listed in 1964 edn. under **ST OSYTH**, Helmingham Hall, 2).

STONELEIGH, Warwickshire. *Cist. abbey of B.V.M.*
  A list of service books of 9 Richard II (1385–86) is in P.R.O., E.154/1/41 ('in
  libraria abbatis nichil').

SUDBURY, Suffolk. *Collegiate church of St Gregory.*
  List of goods in 1391, including 35 service books, in Elveden Hall, Iveagh
  Collection, 373/1 (Phillipps 24002), now in the Suffolk Record Office, Bury St
  Edmunds.

SYON, Middlesex. *Bridgettine abbey of St Saviour, B.V.M. and St*
  Bridget.
  Heading: *add at the end* See the reduced facsimile in Sotheby cat., 12 July 1971,
  opposite the description of lot 36.
+Ampleforth Abbey, C.V.130 (pr. bk). *i*The tree & 12 fruits of the
  Holy Ghost. London, A.D. 1535.
Bury St Edmunds. Now San Marino, below.
+Brussels, Bibl. Royale, IV.481 (previously *Untraced*, London, Maggs,
  1935). *l*Psalterium, etc. s.xv ex.
+Cambridge, U.L. Add. 7634. *l*Breviarium (frag.). s.xv.
+   Ff.6.18   *l*Officia. s.xvi in.   ?
+   Ff.6.33   *c*The boke of the 12 patriarkys, etc. s.xv
                      med.
+   Emmanuel Coll., 32.6.49 (pr. bk). *b*Henricus VIII adversus
                      Lutherum, etc. London, A.D. 1523, etc.
+Durham, U.L., Cosin V.v.12. *i*Sawter of mercy (in English). s.xv/xvi.
+   Dr A. I. Doyle (pr. bk). *i*B. Senensis, Sermones. Basel, s.a.
+   (pr. bk). *i*T. à Kempis. Paris, A.D. 1523.
+Firle Park, Sussex, Lord Gage. *l*Psalterium, etc. s.xv med.
Göttingen, U.L. *Add pressmark* 4° Theol. Mor. 138/53.
+Karlsruhe, Badische Landesbibl., Skt Georgen in Villingen 12.
  Sanctilogium salvatoris. s.xv in. [*Cat.* M.2.].
  Lincoln, Cathedral, 60. *For e*W. de Alvernia. s.xv *read e*W. Peraldus,
  A.D. 1453.
+London, B.L., Harley 1298. R. Grosseteste, etc. s.xv in. [*Cat.* E.67].
+   Dr C. F. R. de Hamel. *l*Preces, etc. s.xv.
+   *l*Horae, etc. s.xv ex.

Morcombelake, Mr J. S. Cox. Now St Peter Port, Guernsey, Mr J. S. Cox.

+ Oxford, Bodleian, Bodl. 62. *l*Horae. s.xiv^2.

+ 346. *c*Revelationes S. Brigittae. s.xv^1.

+ Brasenose Coll., 16. *l*Psalterium. s.xv.

+ St John's Coll., 187. *l*Officia. s.xv. ?

St Peter Port, Guernsey, Mr J. S. Cox: formerly Morcombelake, Mr J. S. Cox.

+ San Marino, Huntington Libr., HM35300: formerly Bury St Edmunds, Cathedral, 1.

Syon Abbey, 3. *Cancel the entry and footnote 7: list as Rejected.*

Xanten, Stiftsbibl. *For pressmark read* 3970B [Inc.] 241.

+ *Untraced:* Sotheby sale (Ashburnham Appx.), 1 May 1899, lot 17, to Ellis. *l*Officia, s.xv (107 fos.); Sotheby sale 12–14 Dec. 1932 (J. M. Falkner sale), lot 413, to Marks & Co. *l*Psalterium et cantica, s.xv (120 fos.); Sotheby sale, 11 July 1966 (Mowbray sale), lot 223, Dawson, cats. 200 (1969), no. 15, and 218 (1971), no. 11. *l*Psalterium, s.xv ex (205 fos.).

+ *Rejected:* Syon Abbey, 3.

TARRANT KEYNSTON, Dorset. *Abbey of B.V.M. of Cist. nuns.*

Redlynch, Major J. R. Abbey. Now Stockholm, National Mus., NMB 2010. *i*Psalterium. s.xiii.

Stonyhurst College, 12. *For* 12 *read* 9, fos. 1–3, *and for e*Psalterium. s.xv *read e*Kalendarium. s.xiii ex.

TAVISTOCK, Devon. *Ben. abbey of B.V.M. and St Rumonus.*

Colchester Museum. Now London, B.L., Add. 62122. Cancel 1964 edn., p. 188, footnote 2.

TEWKESBURY, Gloucestershire. *Ben. abbey of B.V.M.*

Gloucester, Cathedral (pr. bk). The inscription is on a binding leaf now kept separately as MS 36/4.

THETFORD, Norfolk. *Dominican convent.*

+ Chapel Hill, Univ. of N. Carolina Libr., 522. *c*W. Reede, etc. s.xiii–xv.

THREMHALL, Essex. *Aug. priory of St James.*

Gloucester, Cathedral. *For* D.3.18 *read* D.3.16.

THURGARTON, Nottinghamshire. *Aug. priory of St Peter.*

+ Washington, D.C., Library of Congress, Incun. X.5.7 (Rosenwald Collection) (pr. bk). *i*John Wotton, Speculum Christiani. London, A.D. 1486? ?

TONBRIDGE, Kent. *Aug. priory of St Mary Magdalen.*

+ Stockholm, Kungl. Bibliotek, A.182. *l*Psalterium, etc. s.xv. ?

TYNEMOUTH, Northumberland. *Ben. priory of B.V.M. and St Oswin.*

+ Cambridge, U.L., Ee.4.20. Formularium. s.xiv–xv.[1]   ?
+   Kk.6.45. Diurnale. s.xv in.[2]   ?
+ Cambridge, Fitzwilliam Mus., 274. *l*Psalmi, etc. s.xiv ex.[3]
+   1-1973. *l*Breviarium. s.xiv ex.[3]
        Pembroke Coll., 82. The binding leaves are kept separately as MS. 313/82.
+ Oxford, Bodleian, Digby 20, fos. 62–168. *c*Misc. theologica. s.xiii.
             Gough liturg. 18. *For* Processionale *read* Psalterium.
+   Magdalen Coll., lat.171. *e*Galfredus Monemutensis. s.xii.

TYWARDREATH, Cornwall. *Ben. alien priory of St Andrew.*

St Austell, Mr P. S. Rashleigh. Now Par, Mr P. S. Rashleigh. The Cornwall County Record Office call no. is DD.R(S)60.
+ *Rejected:* London, B.L., Add. 44949.

VALLE CRUCIS, Clwyd. *Cist. abbey of B.V.M.*

+ Aberystwyth, N.L., Peniarth 20. *c*Chronicle (in Welsh), etc. s.xv.

WALSINGHAM, Norfolk. *Franciscan convent.*

+ London, B.L., Harley 2818. *e*Biblia. s.xiii.
Oxford, Keble Coll. *After* Keble Coll. *add* 32.
+ *Untraced:* Sotheby sale, 21 June 1965, lot 585 (pr. bk). R. Zamorensis. Speculum vitae humanae. Paris. A.D. 1510.[4]

WALTHAM, Essex. *Aug. abbey of Holy Cross.*

Heading, para. 2 line 1: *for* Mr H. C. Drayton's MS. *read* the Passmore Edwards Museum MS.

London, Dr E. G. Millar. Now London, B.L., Add. 57532.
Whepstead, Mr H. C. Drayton. Now London, Passmore Edwards Museum, LD PEM AD/AY 0001.

WARDEN, Bedfordshire. *Cist. abbey of B.V.M.*

+ *Rejected:* Oxford, University Coll., 4.

WARWICK. *Dominican convent.*

+ Cambridge, Fitzwilliam Museum, 3-1967 (205). *i*Collectarium. A.D. 1523.

WARWICK. *Collegiate church of B.V.M.*

Heading: *for* Exch. K.R. Misc. bks. 22 *read* E.164/22 fos. 201ᵛ, 203ᵛ, 204, *and add that* the original of the 1464 list is P.R.O., E.154/1/46.

+ Oxford, Bodleian, Eng. misc. c.291, fo. 1. *e*Statuta Anglie.[5]

---

[1] A St Albans Abbey formulary, but bearing the signature of Robert Blakeney, last prior of Tynemouth, cell of St Albans.
[2] The proper of Saints includes St Oswin.
[3] Fitzwilliam Mus. 274 and 1-1973 formed one volume.
[4] Bears signature of Richard Vowel, prior 1514–38.
[5] One bifolium previously used as a wrapper, with 'Colleg de Warr'' on front and 'Liber de nouis et veteris statutis' on back, both s.xv.

WELBECK, Nottinghamshire.   *Prem. abbey of St James.*

Manchester, John Rylands U.L., Lat. 179.   Now Eng. 109.
+ Norwich, Cathedral, 5 (8 fos.).   Sermones. A.D. 1432.[1]

WELLS, Somerset.   *Cathedral church of St Andrew.*

+ Cambridge, Sidney Sussex Coll., 75.   Miscellanea. s.xiii in. [Leland].
+ Oxford, Bodleian, Add. A.44.   Poemata, satira, etc. s.xiii in. [Leland].
+ Paris, B.N., lat. 3381.   R. Dymock, W. Woodford. s.xv in. [Leland].

WENLOCK, MUCH, Shropshire.   *Cluniac priory of St Werburga.*

+ Cambridge, St Catharine's Coll., Inc.38 (pr. bk).   *i*N. Panormitanus.
    Basel, A.D. 1477.
+ Oxford, Bodleian, Bodl. 921.   *e*Northern verse psalter. s.xiv.[2]
Rejected: Holkham Hall, 39.   Now London, B.L., Add. 49363.

WESTMINSTER, Middlesex.   *Ben. abbey of St Peter.*

Heading: *after* 111 *add* fos. 9, 11ᵛ, 24ᵛ–25, 49ʳᵛ. At end add Service books in list
of Lady Chapel goods, A.D. 1304, printed from WAM 23180 by H. F. Westlake,
Westminster Abbey (1923), pp. 502–3; list of books in Lady Chapel, 1485, WAM
23258; list of service books at St Edward's shrine, 1467 and 1479, WAM 9477, 9478.

Cambridge, Corpus Christi Coll., 139, and 1964 edn., p. 196, footnote
    7: *add* and may not have been at Westminster before 1541.
London, B.L., Egerton 3775: formerly London, Dr E. G. Millar.
            Royal   2 A.xii.   *Read* 2 A.xxii.
+   10 A.xvii.   *i*Petrus Lombardus. s.xiii med.
+   K.8.k.8 (paper leaf).[3]
+   Jesuit House, 1507 I (pr. bk).   *i*L. de Saxonia. Lyon, A.D. 1507.
+   Society of Antiquaries, 136C, fos. 39–42.   *e*On the order of
                        knighthood, etc. (in French). s.xiv/xv.
+   Westminster Abbey, 34/2.   *b*De scismate. s.xiv/xv. [cf. Leland].
+   33327, fos. 1–2 (frag.).   *l*Liturgical poly-
                            phony. s.xiv.[4]   ?
        Dr E. G. Millar.   Now London, B.L., Egerton 3775, above.
+ *Rejected:* Sotheby sale, 27 Feb. 1951, lot 183 (pr. bk).   *i*Missale romanum.
    Paris, 1506;[5] Colchester, Harsnett Libr., K.d.2 (pr. bk).

---

[1] Norwich Cath., 5, is part of Rylands, Eng. 109.
[2] Bears an erased *ex libris* with a monastic anathema. Over '< > de <Wen?>lok'
is written 'hugoni de Wolast<on?>'. There are three places called Wollaston not
far from Wenlock of which that near Shrewsbury is closest and perhaps the one
mentioned here.
[3] Inscription on the leaf refers to a now missing volume in the binding of which
this leaf of *STC* 20700.3 was used: see *The Library*, 5th series xxvi (1971), 209 and
pl. II.
[4] See *Manuscripts of Fourteenth Century English Polyphony*, ed. F. Harrison and
R. Wibberley (1981), p. xii.
[5] Said in sale cat. to bear signature of John Whyttingham, abbot of Westminster.
No abbot or monk of that name is recorded by E. H. Pearce, *The Monks of
Westminster* (Cambridge, 1916).

WETHERALL, Cumberland. *Priory of Holy Trinity, B.V.M. and St Constantine; cell of St Mary's, York.*

Bridgnorth. Now deposited in Shrewsbury, Shropshire Libraries, Local Studies Dept.

New York. Pierpont Morgan: *add after Morgan* 30780.

WHALLEY, Lancashire. *Cist. abbey of B.V.M.*

Canterbury, Cathedral, 73. *For* 73 *read* Lit. B.1 (73).

WHITBY, Yorkshire. *Ben. abbey of St Peter and St Hilda.*

+Paris, B.N., lat. 7410. *e*Canones in tabulas Alphonsi regis. s.xv.

Untraced: Lt.-Col. Moss's psalter has been split up. One bifolium is owned by Prof. T. Takamiya, Tokyo, and four leaves by Mr S. J. Keynes, London.

WHITLAND, Dyfed. *Cist. abbey of B.V.M.*

+Exeter, Cathedral, 3514. *c*Historica. s.xiii ex. ?

WILTON, Wiltshire. *Abbey of B.V.M. and St Edith, of Ben. nuns.*

London, B.L., Cotton Faustina B.iii. *For* 194 *read* 199.

WINCHCOMBE, Gloucestershire. *Ben. abbey of St Kenelm.*

Sudeley Castle, Mrs Dent-Brocklehurst. Now Oxford, below.

+London, Dr C. F. R. de Hamel. *b*Origen in Numeros. s.xii ex.

Oxford, Bodleian, Lat. th. d. 46: formerly Sudeley Castle.

WINCHESTER, Hampshire. *Ben. cathedral priory of St Peter, St Paul and St Swithun.*

List of 12 books, s.xvi[1], in Rome, Vatican, Reg. lat. 2099, fo. 306.

Le Havre 330. Cancel the entry and add to *Rejected. See now* **HYDE.**

+London, B.L., Add. 60577. *i*Miscellanea (English and Latin). s.xv ex–xvi med.

+Oxford, Bodleian, Digby 31. Jacobus de Cessolis. s.xv.[1]

+   112. *c*Vitae sanctorum; Liber proverbiorum Galfridi prioris Winton. s.xii in. ?

Rejected: Le Havre, Bibl. Mun., 330.

WINCHESTER. *New Minster:* see **HYDE.**

WINCHESTER. *Franciscan convent.*

List of 2 books, s.xvi[1], in Rome, Vatican, Reg. lat. 2099, fo. 306.

WINCHESTER. *Dominican convent.*

List of 2 books, s.xvi[1], in Rome, Vatican, Reg. lat. 2099, fo. 305.

---

[1] In 1964 edn. listed under Oxford, New Coll. On fo. 188 is a list of books at New College in 1489 (for which see above, **OXFORD,** *New College*), which is as likely to have been written in Winchester as in Oxford. The book belonged to Wm. Manwode, presumably the deacon of that name ord. Winchester 1484 (see *Hampshire Record Society* vii (1892), 478, and was certainly at St Swithun's in the 1530s, when it was owned by Thomas Dackombe, monk and later minor canon.

WINCHESTER. *Hospital of Holy Cross.*

London, B.L., Add 39976, fos. 83–4, is a transcript by J. F. Baigent of a list in a lost cartulary of books 'in antiqua libraria' and additions in the time of John de Campeden, warden (†1410), all but three of them service books; second folios given. Book list, *c.* 1400, second folios given, in Hospital's *Liber secundus*, fos. 81ᵛ–3, in Hampshire Record Office.

WINCHESTER. *Hospital of St Mary Magdalene.*

Inventory, *c.* 1400, in London, B.L. Harley 328, fos. 26–8, including 15 service books and a Legenda sanctorum, ptd. *Vetusta Monumenta* iii (1796), 11: see also summary in *VCH Hants.* ii, 198–9.

WINDSOR, Berkshire. *Royal collegiate chapel of St George.*

Heading: *for para 2 substitute* Inventories of about 60 service books 'in choro', a dozen books 'diuersarum scientiarum' chained 'in ecclesia', no doubt a reference collection, and about 20 law books, a Bible and a biblical concordance, 'in armario'; printed from Bodleian, Ashmole Rolls 47 (1384–5) and 36 (1409–10) by M. F. Bond, *The Inventories of St George's Chapel Windsor Castle 1384–1667* (Windsor, 1947), pp. 32–8, 102–8; second or third folios given of the books 'in armario'. List of 11 service books, lately Lord Scrope's, given by Henry V, on dorse of Precentor's compotus 1415–16 (Windsor, Dean and Chapter Muniments, Erary xv.56.22), printed *loc. cit.*, pp. 122–4; third folios given. Books noted by J. Bale, *Index* (p. 579).

Langley Marish, Parish Church. *Add* [*Inv. 1384–5*, 21(?); *Inv. 1409–10*, 64].

London, Mr A. Ehrman. Now Oxford, Bodleian, Broxb. 34.5.

Princeton. *For 89 read* Princeton 89.

WORCESTER. *Ben. cathedral priory of B.V.M.*

Heading: line 13, *after* List of *add* about 100; line 16, *for* 54 *read* 34.

+ Birmingham, U.L., 11/v/10. *i*Medica. s.xiv¹.
+ Cambridge, St John's Coll., 42. Homiliae. s.xii in.
+ Edinburgh, N.L., Adv. 18.5.3. *e*Anticlaudianus. s.xii. ?
  Gloucester, Cathedral, 25. *Read* †Gloucester, Cathedral, 25.
+ London, B.L., Cotton Nero C.iii, fos. 241–6. *s*Augustinus. s.xii in. ?
+   Harley 3066. *i*Augustinus, etc. s.xii in.
         Royal 5 E.xiii. *Read* [R.cxcii *(altered to* R.xxvii); *Young* 333].
      Lambeth Palace, 238. *Read* Senatus, etc. s.xiii in.¹
      Mr A. Ehrman. Now Oxford, Dr D. M. Rogers. *Cancel* [*Young* 37 *or* 38].
+ Oxford, Merton Coll., 32. *m*Augustinus. s.xii med.
+ Rome, Vatican, Reg. lat. 1351. *c*Baldricus Dolensis. s.xii in.
  Worcester, Cathedral, F.68. *Read e*Aristoteles, etc.
+   F.140, part of a leaf found in. *e*.²

---

¹ In the contents-list the Worcester author Senatus Bravonius is described as 'Senatus prior', whereas in the text he is called 'Senatus monachus Wigornensis ecclesie'. The Worcester Cath. MS. of the *Anticlaudianus* of Alanus de Insulis, F.147, is a direct copy of the text in this MS.
² The flyleaf of a now missing copy of the Ethics and Politics of Aristotle in the translation of Leonardo Bruni.

WORCESTER. *Dominican convent.*

Helmingham Hall, 49. Now Prof. T. Takamiya, Tokyo, 14.

YORK. *Cathedral church of St Peter.*

Heading, line 5: *for* books bequeathed *read* about 76 books bequeathed absolutely or (39–76) conditionally.

+ Ampleforth Abbey, C.V.65 (pr. bk). *e*Antoninus, Secunda pars summae. Venice, A.D. 1480.

+   C.V.66 (pr. bk). *e*Antoninus, Quarta pars summae. Venice, A.D. 1480.

Cambridge, Trinity Coll., 728, flyleaf 4. *Read* [*Newton*, 21].

Lincoln, Cathedral, 101.   ⎱ *Cancel query* and in 1964 edn., p. 216, foot-
                    102. ⎰ note 1, *for* a similar note in MS. 101 *read*
                           similar notes in MSS. 101 and York Minster, XVI.A.8.[1]

Oxford, Bodleian, Rawl. B.199. *Read* [*Newton*, 30].

                       B.200. *Read* [*Newton*, 30].

                       C.162. *Read* [*Newton*, 30].

+ York Minster, XVI.A.8. *s*Boethius, De trinitate, etc. s.xii.

+   XVI.P.5–7. Bartholomaeus de Saxoferrato, A.D. 1401. [*cf. Newton* 72, 73, 38].

+   XVI.P.8. Cino da Pistoia. s.xiv [*cf. Newton* 37].

            XVI.Q.13. *Read* XVI.Q.15.

YORK. *Ben. abbey of B.V.M.*

Heading, line 4: *after* 1*a–c add* and from Bodleian, Lyell 17, by A.C. de la Mare, *Catalogue of the Collection of Medieval Manuscripts bequeathed to the Bodleian Library Oxford by James P. R. Lyell* (Oxford, 1971), pl.35e.

Bridgnorth. Now deposited in Shrewsbury, Shropshire Libraries, Local Studies Dept.

Deventer, Mr J. P. L. van der Lande. Now Urbana, Univ. of Illinois Libr., below.

+ Edinburgh, N.L., H.24.f.10 (pr. bk). *i*Rupertus abbas. Nuremberg, A.D. 1525.

Leeds, U.L., Brotherton Collection, 29: formerly Ripon, Mr H. L. Bradfer-Lawrence.

+ Lincoln, Cathedral, 228. *e*Pseudo-Bonaventura. s.xv.

+ London, B.L., Cotton Ch. xiv.4. Genealogia regum. s.xiii/xiv.[2]

+ Oxford, Bodleian, Rawl.C.553. *l*Horae. s.xv.[3]

Ripon, Mr H. L. Bradfer-Lawrence. Now Leeds, U.L., above.

+ Rome, Vatican, Ottob. lat. 177. *e*P. Lombardus. s.xii/xiii. [In G. *altered to* D(?) 25].

Urbana, Univ. of Illinois Libr., q.251 Sp.31.1481: formerly Deventer, Mr J. P. L. van der Lande.

YORK. *Franciscan convent.*

London, Mr Raymond Russell. Now in another private collection.

---

[1] The front flyleaves of MS. 102, at least in s.xvii, were the present frag. 3 in Lincoln Cath. 298, a bifolium from a noted Antiphoner, s.xi in.

[2] Cotton Ch. xiv.4 and Bodley Rolls 3 formed one volume.

[3] See *Trans. Cumberland and Westmorland Arch. Soc.*, lxxx (1980), 33, n. 15.

YORK. *Convent of Austin friars.*

A new edition of the catalogues and lists by K. W. Humphreys is in preparation for the British Academy's Corpus of British Medieval Library Catalogues.

Liverpool, Merseyside County Museums, 12036. cEugippius, etc. s.xiii/xiv. [T; *Cat.* 84].

+London, B.L., Cotton Vesp. B.xix, fos. 83–163. cHildebertus, Opuscula, etc. ss.xii ex–xiii. [*Cat.* 104].

Untraced: briefly seen in New York in 1980 but now again untraced.

APPENDIX

Books formerly owned by parish churches and chapels

+ **BEDWYN, GREAT,** Wiltshire. Cambridge, U.L. Add. 8333. *e*Graduale. s.xiii[1].
+ **BERWICK-ON-TWEED,** Northumberland. Chapel of St George (?). Ampleforth Abbey, C.V.221 (pr. bk). *ce*Missale Sarisb. Paris, A.D. 1514.
 BRECON, Powys. *Cancel entry,* which relates to **BRECON,** Ben. priory.
+ **CAMBRIDGE,** Great St Mary's. Several inventories of church goods, including service books, printed from Cambridge, Corpus Christi Coll., 204, in Cambridge Antiquarian Society Octavo Publications x (1869).
+ **CANTERBURY,** Kent. St Andrew's. 50 books (second folios given) listed under A.D. 1485 in churchwardens' accounts printed by C. Cotton, *Archaeologia Cantiana,* xxxii (1917), 181–246.
+ **COTTENHAM,** Yorkshire. Ripon, Dean and Chapter Archives 432. *c*Kalendarium Ebor. (frag.). *c.* 1400.
+ **DESFORD,** Leicestershire. Southwark, Roman Catholic Metropolitan See, 1. Breviarium. s.xv in.[1]
+ **ESH,** Co. Durham. Parish chapel. Ushaw Coll., 5. *e*Missale. s.xv$^{\frac{3}{4}}$.
 FARNWORTH, Lancashire. Now Manchester, John Rylands U.L., Christie 3.f.19.
+ **FORNCETT,** Norfolk. *Untraced:* Thomas Martin sale (Booth and Bury, Norwich, 5 June 1773, lot 4463), 'de virtutibus et de vitiis.'
+ **HADDENHAM,** Cambridgeshire. Oxford, New Coll., 98. *c*W. de Monte, etc. s.xiii.[2]
+ **HALSALL,** Lancashire. Boston (U.S.A.), Public Libr. (pr. bk). *e*Missale Sarisb. Rouen, A.D. 1509.
+ **HAMBLETON,** Leicestershire ('Hameldon'). Manchester, John Rylands U.L., Lat. 119. Missale. s.xv in.[1]
 HAREWOOD, Yorkshire. Now York, Minster Libr., Add. 70.
+ **HEADCORN,** Kent. Chantry attached to Lady Chapel. Oxford, Bodleian, Bodl. 110. *e*Misc. theol. s.xv.
+ **HONITON,** Devon. Aberystwyth, N.L., Peniarth 162(i). *e*P. Quivil, etc. s.xv.
+ **HORNINGSEY,** Cambridgeshire. List of 18 service books, s.xiv, in W. E. Clay, *A History of the Parish of Horningsey* (Cambridge Antiquarian Society Octavo Publications, ix, 1865), 35.

---

[1] Calendar contains the dedication of the church.
[2] See Dorothy Owen in *Reading Medieval Studies* xi (1985), 121–31.

+**IKEN,** Suffolk. *l*Psalterium. *c.* A.D. 1300. Now split up. It appeared intact in a Sotheby sale, 10 Dec. 1969, lot 36, and in Traylen's cat. 77 (1972), no. 77, but one leaf appeared in Quaritch cat. 1036 (1984), no. 16, and is now in private hands.

+**LANCHESTER,** co. Durham. Ampleforth Abbey, C.V.144 (pr. bk). *c*Portiforium (pars aestivalis), s.l., s.a.

+**LANTEGLOS,** Cornwall. Aberystwyth, N.L., 22253A. Breviarium, s.xv[2].[1]

+**LLANBADARN-FAWR,** Dyfed. Aberystwyth, N.L., b.31P(5F) (pr. bk). Missale Sarisb. Paris, A.D. 1531.[1]

+**LONDON,** St Christopher-le-Stocks. Inventory of the late 1480s in London, Guildhall Libr., MS. 4424, fo. 29, printed in *Archaeologia,* xlv (1880), 118. Second folios given.

+**LONDON,** St James Garlickhithe. Inventory of 1449 is Westminster Abbey, Muniment 6644.

+**LONDON,** St Margaret New Fish St. Inventory of 1472 in London, Guildhall Libr., MS. 1174, fos. 8–14, part illustrated in C. Words-worth and H. Littlehales, *The Old Service Books of the English Church* (1904), pl. II.

+**LONDON,** St Martin le Grand. List, largely of service books *tempore* Henry VIII, in Westminster Abbey, Muniment 9487.

LONDON, St Peter Cornhill. The London, Guildhall Libr., pressmark is 4158[A].

+**LONDON,** St Peter Westcheap. Inventory of 1431 with later additions in London, Guildhall Libr., MS. 645/1, fo. 173.

+**LONDON,** St Sepulchre, Holborn. London, B.L., Harley 2942. *ce*Pro-cessionale Sarisb. s.xv in.

+**LYDD,** Kent. Munich, Staatsbibl., Clm. 705. Missale. A.D. 1384.[1]

+**MERE,** Wiltshire. Inventory of church goods, A.D. 1405, including 11 books other than service books, in Reg. Chandler et Sydenham (Trowbridge, Wiltshire County Record Office, D5/1), fos. 65[v], 66, printed *Wiltshire Record Society,* xxxix (1984), nos. 119, 121.[2]

+**MORLEY,** Derbyshire. Canterbury, Cathedral, Plumptre Deposit. Missale. s.xiv/xv.[1]

NORTON, Suffolk. Cambridge, U.L., Ee.5.13: the footnote reference number on p. 222 of 1964 edn. should be 7. The Downing Coll. fragment has been reunited to Cambridge, U.L., Ee.5.13.

ORPINGTON, Kent. Now Syracuse (U.S.A.), U.L., Uncat. 1.

+**PIRTON,** Worcestershire. London, B.L., Harley Charter 83.A.37. *i*Missale (1 fo.). s.xiii in.

+**SALISBURY,** Wiltshire, St Edmund's. Inventory of 1472 (including 52 books, mostly service books) printed by H. J. F. Swayne, *Church-wardens' Accounts of S. Edmund and S. Thomas, Sarum 1443–1702* (Salisbury, 1896), p. 2.

SALTFLEETBY, Lincolnshire. *Read* **SALTFLEETBY,** All Saints.

---

[1] Calendar contains the dedication of the church.
[2] See also ibid., nos. 116–28, 130–88 (fos. 65–84[v]) for inventories made at the same visitation of 1405 for 67 named churches and 2 unidentified churches. All mention service books but no other books.

+ **SANDWICH,** Kent, St Mary's. Inventory of 1473 printed in W. Boys, *Collections for an History of Sandwich* (Canterbury, 1792), pp. 376–7.

+ **SEAVINGTON ST MICHAEL,** Somerset. Liverpool Cathedral, Radcliffe Libr., 27. Psalterium, etc. s.xiii/xiv.[1]

  SHEPTON BEAUCHAMP, Somerset. *Read* Liverpool Cathedral, Radcliffe Libr., 29.[2]

  SHERE, Surrey. Acquired, split up and sold by Duschnes, New York.

+ **SPRINGFIELD,** Essex. Cambridge, U.L., Add. 2602. Antiphonale. s.xiii.[3] ?

+ **TAWSTOCK,** Devon. London, U.L., 906. Horae. s.xv.[4]

+ **THAME,** Oxfordshire. Inventory of 1447 in Oxford, Bodleian, DD Par. Thame c.5, fo. 28.

  WEALD, SOUTH, Essex. Now owned by Mr H. C. Pratt, London.

+ **WISBECH,** Suffolk. Wisbech, Museum, 1. *c*Statuta synodalia diocesis Eliensis; etc. s.xiv[1].[5]

  WINGFIELD, SOUTH, Derbyshire. *For* Capetown, U.L., 1 *read* Cape Town, South African Libr., 1.

  WOLLATON, Nottinghamshire. Now on permanent deposit in Nottingham U.L.

+ **WOODRISING,** Norfolk. *Untraced:* Graduale, s.xv med, belonging to Rev. H. G. Morse (cf. W. H. Frere, *Graduale Sarisburiense* (1894), p. lxiii). ?

  WORCESTER, St Helen. On p. 223 of 1964 edn. add footnote reference number 3. *Delete query.*

  WRITTLE, Essex. *Read* Liverpool Cathedral, Radcliffe Libr., 51.[2]

  YORK, All Saints, Pavement. +London, B.L., Harley 2369. Computistica, s.xv.[4] York Minster, xvi.G.5: *read* XVI.K.6.

---

[1] Deposited in Liverpool U.L. Contains obits of Stone family of Seavington.
[2] Deposited in Liverpool U.L.
[3] Found in wall of Springfield church in 1867: see W. H. Frere, *Antiphonale Sarisburiense*, Introduction pt. 2 (1925), p. 78.
[4] Calendar contains the dedication of the church.
[5] See Dorothy Owen in *Reading Medieval Studies* xi (1985), 121–31.

Donors, Scribes and Other Persons concerned before 1540 with the Books recorded on pages 1–71

For the principles of arrangement see 1964 edition, pp. 225–6, from which the following list departs in only two respects. First, the use of roman and italic type to distinguish words derived from inscriptions in the books (roman) and information added from other sources (italic) has been abandoned: roman is used throughout, with quotation marks to indicate that the words are derived from the book. Second, an attempt has been made to provide some kind of date or identification for people mentioned (including many unidentified in the 1964 edition) and to indicate the source.

Much of the information about sources is derived from a draft typescript found among Neil Ker's papers, apparently made for him in the early or mid 1970s by someone who has not been identified. Judging from Ker's own typescript he had intended to make only limited use of this and not to include the references to sources but it has seemed worth while to use it more fully. All references in it to printed sources have been checked but it has not been possible to check folio references in unpublished bishops' registers. For some people only a selection of dates and sources is given. Thus, when the dates of a man's ordination as acolyte and/or subdeacon and/or deacon and/or priest are known, only the highest of these is mentioned, and when the same fact is recorded in several sources (some perhaps interdependent) only one source is mentioned, e.g. Chambers or *VCH* or *LP* or *DK Rep. 8*. To save space the titles of books are given in abbreviated form involving a reference to E. L. C. Mullins, *Texts and Calendars: an Analytical Guide to Serial Publications* and *Texts and Calendars II: an Analytical Guide to Serial Publications 1957–1982* published in 1958 and 1983 as nos. 7 and 12 respectively in the Royal Historical Society's Guides and Handbooks series. Thus *TC* 14.44 and *TCS* 54.41 indicate volumes 44 and 41 in the series of publications numbered 14 and 54 in *Texts and Calendars* and its supplement respectively. The volumes cited in this way are listed above, pp. xvi–xviii. For the location of original episcopal registers cited see David M. Smith, *Guide to Bishops' Registers of England and Wales* (Royal Historical Society, Guides and Handbooks no. 11, 1981).

A warning is necessary about the exclusion of names from this list and from the list in the 1964 edition. Neither list includes all the names, even all the medieval names, found in the books, even when ownership is clearly implied: they include only such names as are relevant to the book's acquisition by the institution under which it is listed. A better title for the lists might in fact be 'Persons associable with the acquisition of a particular institution's books'.

As in the 1964 edition, * before a name indicates that it is to be found in Emden's *Biographical Register of the University of Oxford* (*BRUO*) and ** indicates that it is to be found in his *Biographical Register of the University* *of Cambridge (BRUC).* *** is new in this Supplement and indicates Emden's *A Biographical Register of the University of Oxford A.D. 1501 to 1540* (Oxford, 1974). + before a name indicates that the name appears for the first time in this Supplement: the absence of a + indicates that the entry contains an addendum or corrigendum to the 1964 list.

ABERDEEN, *King's College*
+ Braidfut, R.:
    Edinburgh, N.L., Adv. 18.3.10 (signs as scribe of fos. 1–99).

ABINGDON
***Buckland, Willelmus:
    + Charlecote (inscription as in (a) in Pembr. Coll. 4.18.8).
***Crystalle, John:
    + Shrewsbury School F.vi.5 (name).
***Rowland, Thomas:
    + Shrewsbury School F.vi.5 ('T. Rolhand est possessor').

ANGLESEY
Bromptoun, Willelmus de, 'rector de Bircham' (Bircham Magna, Norfolk; adm. 1322. vac. 1364 (?): Blomefield, x, 294).

ASHRIDGE
Hyle, Thomas: lic. to hold benefice, etc. 1540 (Chambers, p. 204).
+ ***Waterhouse, Thomas, 'Rector A.' 1529–39:
    London, Dulwich Coll., A.3.f.13 (g).

AXHOLME
Chamberlayne, dom. Jo.: monk at surrender, 1538 (*DK Rep. 8*).
    One of same name at Hinton, at surrender, 1539 (ibid.).

BABWELL
Fakynham: *read* *Fakynham . . . magister . . . *and transfer to* **LYNN**, Franciscan convent.
Hepworth, fr. Nicholaus de:
    + New Haven, Yale U.L., Beinecke Mellon 37 ('ex dono——').
Medilton: transfer to **LYNN**, Franciscan convent.

BARDNEY
Fuldon, Rogerius de: *for c.* 1285–76 *read c.* 1255–76 (*Fasti I*, iii, 26, 70).

BARKING
+ Fabyan, Martha: nun at surrender, 1539 (*LP*, xv, p. 547):
    London, Lambeth Palace, 1495.4 ('Thys bouke belongyth to——').

BARLINGS
Edenham, dom. Galfridus de, 'canonicus Lincoln', 1333–49 (*Fasti II*, i, 50, 106, 107).

BASINGWERK
+ Pennant, Thomas, abbot 1481–1522 (*Bull. of the Board of Celtic Studies*, xxiv (1971), 216):
    Aberystwyth, N.L., Peniarth 356 (name as scribe).

BATH
Saltford, Fr. Willelmus: ord. d. 1421 (*TC* 61.49, p. 127), sacrist 1447, 1449 (*TC* 61.50, pp. 434, 435); or Salford, Fr. Willelmus: precentor 1524, 1525 (*TC* 61.55, pp, 32, 81).

BATTLE
Nuton, dom. Johannes, 'abbas B.' 1463–90, prior of St Nicholas, Exeter (cell of Battle), adm. 1459 (B.L., MS. Harley 3586, fo. 13).

BEAUVALE
*Ruwe: *for* Trinity Coll. *read* Trinity Hall.

BEDFORD, *Franciscan convent*
Grene, fr. Johannes:
  + London, Mr N. Barker ('Liber—Emptus Oxon'); + Cambridge, Emmanuel Coll., MSS. 4.1.14 ('liber——Emptus ex elemosinis amicorum suorum Anno 1489').

BELVOIR
Belvero: adm. prior 1333 (*VCH Lincs.*, ii, 125, 127).

BILSINGTON
Johannes, dom., 'vicarius de Newecherche: perhaps J. Whetyng, V. of N., 1403 (*Archaeologia Cantiana*, xiii (1880), 464–5).

BODMIN, *Franciscan convent*
Pole, fr. Ricardus, O.F.M.: recorded 1390 (Reg. Brantyngham, Exeter, ii, fo. 608).
Werdour, fr. Galfredus (Geoff. de Werthor, Warthorr): ord. pr. 1312 (Reg. Stapledon (Exeter) fo. 487).

BORDESLEY
Northewode, Johannes: ord. acol. 1389 (*TCS* 69.50, p. 204).

BOURNE
+ Orrm, O.S.A.:
  Oxford, Bodleian, Junius 1 (*composed and probably wrote*).

BOXLEY
Gotfridus, Johannes: 1538 (Chambers, p. 123).
Heriettsham, dom. Johannes: *ord. subd. 1345* (*TC* 14.49, p. 1111); *read* *Renham nuper rectoris de Holyngbourne (†*by Nov. 1376*).

BRECON, *Dominican convent*
+ Paynot, Dom. Thomas, 'de Brechonia':
  Oxford, Bodleian, Laud Misc. 667 (constat).
Texerii, fr. Bartholomaeus, O.P.: Master-General, O.P., 1426–47 *C. Pap. L.*, vii, 514–15.

BRIDGWATER, *Franciscan convent*
Blo[. . .]worth: *read* **Blo[ckes]worth, fr. Walterus de (46th lector, Cambridge, *c*. 1324).

BRISTOL, *St Mark*
Colman, Johannes: *read* ***Colman. Master at surrender, 1539 (*LP*, xiv (ii), p. 241).

BROMFIELD
Sebrok: *read* ***Sebrok.

BRUISYARD, *Franciscan nunnery*
Bakon: in Campsey Priory, 1514 (*TC* 32.43, p. 134).

BUCKFAST
Dove: ord. subd. 1409 (*Reg. Stafford*, ed. F. C. Hingeston-Randolph (1886), p. 95).

BUILDWAS
Gnowsal: occurs as abbot 1428–43 (*VCH Salop*, ii,59).

BURTON-UPON-TRENT
+ *Bate, Walterus, mag. by 1445:
  Oxford, Lincoln Coll., lat. 113 ('deliberatus——per instanciam Ric'
  [. . .] eiusdem monasterii nono die Octobris mcccc quadrin[. . .]').
Edys: *read* ***Edys.
Elkyn: sacrist 1518, 1521 (*TCS* 62.78, pp. 26, 68), 3rd prior and sacrist
  (ibid. p. 146).

BURY ST EDMUNDS
(T) indicates that the source is R. M. Thomson, 'Obedientiaries of St Edmund's Abbey', *Proc. Suffolk Inst. of Arch. and History*, xxxv pt. 2 (1982), 91–103, who records the offices held.

Baldewinus: prior by 1114 (T). *For* feri *read* fieri.
Barwe: occurs 1403/4, 1407 and later (T).
Bryngkeley: *read* **Bryngkeley.
+ Colcestr', fr. Willelmus de (s.xiii/xiv):
  Oxford, Bodleian, Lat. hist. d. 4 ('de empcione').
Cranewys: occurs 1402, 1426, 1434, after 1441 (T).
Curteys: occurs 1417, prior 1426, abbot 1429 (T).
+ Dellyng, Robertus (s.xv):
  London, B.L., Harley 5442 ('quod——' in hand of text).
Denham: occurs 1312 (T).
Dersham: occurs 1498, before 1503, after Oct. 1504 (T).
Feningham: occurs 1521–24 (T).
Gosford: occurs 1381, prior 1382, 1405 (T).
Halliwell: *read* *Halliwell, fr. J., monachus B. (scholar, Gloucester Coll., 1354).
Hemlington: occurs 1325, prior 1328 (T).
Hesset: *read* ***Hesset, Thomas, 'monachus B.' at surrender, 1538 (*LP*, xv, p. 546).
Ikelyngham: occurs before 1390, prior 1406 and after 1425 (T).
Kyrkestede: occurs as prior 1362/3; out of office by 1374/5 (T):
  + London, B.L., Harley 4025 ('de empcione').
Langham: occurs 1358–61 (T). *For* Dublin, Chester Beatty W.26 *read*
  San Marino, Huntington Libr., HM31151.
Mildenall, dom. Willelmus: *see* Ryngsted.
+ Myldenhale, dom. Robertus, (2) prior (1504) (T):
  London, B.L., Harley 5388 (name), (2) Harley 5442 (liber).
Rokeswell: ord. pr. 1356 (Reg. de Lisle, Ely, fos. 101, 101ᵛ).
Ryngsted: occurs as prior etc. 1517–22, 1533–35 (T):
  + London, B.L., Harley 1206 ('d. Willelmus Mildenall dedit——').
Swaffham: occurs before March 1472 till after Feb. 1489 (T).
Wesingham: occurs 1435 (London, B.L., Add. 14848 fo. 131). *After*
  procurauit *add* suis sumptibus et expensis.
Wickham, Johannes: ord. pr. 1454 (Reg. Gray (Ely) fo. 201).
Wirlingworthe: occurs *c.* 1362–3 (T).
W[. . .]spet: perhaps John Wolspeth *al.* Buknam, monk at surrender, 1539 (*LP*, xiv (ii), p. 168).

BUTLEY

Thetford, John: canon of B., B.Cn.L. (*TC* 32.43, pp. 131,133) presumably same as John Thetford, prior of Thetford, 1520, 1526, 1532 (*TC* 32.43, pp. 155, 242, 303). He was a benefactor to Botley (*VCH Suffolk*, ii, 98).

Wodebrigge: subprior 1514, still in 1532 (*TC* 32.43, pp. 54, 131, 178, 217, 285).

CAMBRIDGE, *Franciscan convent*

+ **Hindringham, fr. T. de (Cambridge conv., 41st lector, *c.* 1321):
London, B.L., Add. 9831 (name in genitive).

+ **Kemp, fr. Roger (Cambridge conv. 1485–9):
Rome, Vatican, Ottob. lat. 1276 ('emptus per me——a Willelmo Godyrson Stacioner' and '——est possessor huius libri').

+ **Walsham, fr. Johannes (Cambridge conv., 73rd lector. *c.* 1353); *see* Wychingham.

+ Wychingham, fr. Rogerus de:
London, B.L., Add. 9831 (*a* 'emit——de elemosinis amicorum suorum prec' 1 marc''); *b* 'emit fr. Johannes Walsham magister de——pro 1 marca et tantum dedit pro illo Oxon' ex parte predicti fr. Rogeri').

CAMBRIDGE, *Dominican convent*

+ **Crafford (John C., Cambridge conv. in 1411 and 1412):
Rome, Vatican, Vat. lat. 7095+Ottob lat. 187 (marginalia signed by). Ottob lat. 208 (marginalia signed by).

+ Horsythe, fr. Johannes (g):
Rome, Vat. lat. 3056.

Picwurth: Ottob. lat. 758: *read* ('liber——de perquisito').

+ **Rywel, fr. Thomas (g) (Cambridge conv. in 1412):
Rome, Vatican, Vat. lat. 3056.

**Yx[. . . .]: *cancel* **.

CAMBRIDGE, *Convent of Austin friars*

+ *Bury, fr. Johannes:
Rome, Vatican, Ottob. lat. 468 (liber).

+ **Clara, fr. Johannes de (Cambridge conv. in 1304; prior provincial 1307 and 1328):
Rome, Vatican, Ottob. lat. 200, 202, 211, 229, 342, 427 (all 'liber').

+ **Crome, mag. Walterus (fellow of Gonville Hall, 1420–27): *see* Stokton.

+ Denton, fr. Adam *fl. c.* 1388: F. Roth, *The English Austin Friars 1249–1538* (Cassiciacum vi, New York, 1966), p. 532.
Rome, Vatican, Ottob. lat. 116.

+ Ludham, mag. Johannes:
Rome, Vatican, Ottob. lat. 468 ('Caucio——exposita cist' s. trinitatis' 22 March 1400 and supplement, 1401).

+ **Massingham, Benedictus de, 'vicarius de Luton' (1366): *see* Tuylett.

**Mendham:
Rome, Vatican, Ottob. lat. 186 (name and 'conventus C.').

+ **Nekton, mag. Johannes (fellow of Corpus Christi Coll., 1376; master, 1389–98):
Rome, Vatican, Ottob. lat. 326 (name, as donor?).

+ + **Pakenham, mag. Radulphus de, D.Th. by *c.* 1350:
  Rome, Vatican, Ottob. lat. 214 ('ex dono————').
+ **Stokton, mag. Henricus, O.E.S.A. (Cambridge conv. in 1417):
  Rome, Ottob. lat. 73 ('Istum librum accepit mag. Walterus Crome
  a——in festo sancti Martini A.D. 1425 et dedit sibi in pignus librum
  suum proprium de mineralibus Alberti').
Swyllyngton: D.Th. inc. 1518–19, prior in 1520; bp. of Philadelphia 1532:
  †1546 (Roth, 'Sources', pp. 416*, 426*, 436*, 441*).
+ **Tuylett[1] (fr. John. prior C. in 1350):
  Rome, Vatican, Ottob. lat. 182 ('Iste liber est – quousque vic' de
  Luton Magister Benedictus [. . .]').
[. . .], Johannes de, fr., O.E.S.A.:
  Rome, Vatican, Ottob. lat. 196 ('Caucio————exposita ciste de
  Neel . . .', 23 March 1346).

CAMBRIDGE, *University*
+ **Holler, Willelmus, mag. by 1420:
  Cambridge, Gonville and Caius Coll., 364 (619) (recorded as his gift in
  cat.).
+ **Butler, fr. Nicholas
  Cambridge, Gonville and Caius Coll., 414 (631) ('————emit, 1406').

CAMBRIDGE, *King's College*
Hartwell: *for* super *read* nuper.
+ *Humphrey, duke of Gloucester, †1447:
  London, B.L., Harley 1705 ('Cest liure est A moy————du don P.
  Candidus secretaire du duc de Milan').
Langport: *read* **Langport, Johannes, S.T.P. (fellow 1446, † in or after
  1494).

CAMBRIDGE, *King's Hall*
+ **Bothe, Robert, dean of York, †1488:
  Chicago, Newberry Libr., 33.1.

CAMBRIDGE, *Michaelhouse*
Filey, W.: †1549 (*AC*):
  + Cambridge, Trin. Coll., D.8.122, VI.15.35.
Hunkes, mag. Johannes (s.xvi in):
  London, Dulwich Coll., A.3.f.12 ('Iste liber pertinet ad collegium diui
  Michaelis ex dono——').

CAMPSEY
Babyngton: still subprioress 1532 (*TC* 32.43).

CANTERBURY
For the monks see W. G. Searle, *Christ Church, Canterbury* (Cambridge
Antiquarian Society Octavo Publs., xxxiv, 1902).

Beket: monk in 1511 (*EHR*, vi (1891), 20) and at surrender, 1540 (*LP*,
  xv, p. 186).
Bereham: *read* *Bereham.
Bockyng, dom. Edwardus: *read* ***Bockyng, dom. Edwardus.

---

[1] *BRUC* wrongly gives the name as Julyet.

+ Bockyng, Johannes de: ord. pr. 1480 (*TCS* 14.55, p. 450).
 Cambridge (USA), Harvard Univ., Houghton Libr., Typ.3 (g).
Bockyng, Thomas de: monk in 1349 (Canterbury Cath. Reg. G, fo. 36ᵛ).
Bonington: † by 1488 (Canterbury Cath. Reg. N, fo. 255).
Boolde: ord. pr. 1449 (Reg. Stafford (Canterbury), i, fo. 203ᵛ).
Broke: ord. pr. 1464 (*TCS* 14.55, p. 388).
Cawston: ord. pr. 1456 (*TCS* 14.55, p. 366).
Chelmington: *read* Chelmynton *and for* (name, and date 1461 *read* (name, and dates 1452 and 1461).
+ *Copton, Richardus, doctor (monk 1520 or 1521) *see* Coptun, Jasper.
+ ***Coptun, Jasper (monk, professed 1506):
 Oxford, New Coll., .13.2 ('attinens ad——ex dono doctoris Coptons').
Covintre: ord. d. 1465 (*TCS* 14.55, p. 390), chancellor 1486, 1493 (Canterbury Cath. Reg. S, fos. 362ᵛ, 383ᵛ).
Dover: pr. 1455 (*TCS* 14.55, p. 362).
+ *Dryffeld, mag. Thomas: *see* Estry.
+ *Estry, dom. Robertus, monachus C. (professed 1473):
 Canterbury, Cath., Lit. B.1(73) (name in memorandum; perhaps acquired by, from mag. Thomas Dryffeld in payment of debt).
Fro: *for* perquisicione *read* perquisito.
Goleston (Goldston): *read* *Goleston.
Gyllingham: *read* ***Gyllingham.
Hadley: *read* ***Hadley.
Hartey: *read* ***Hartey.
Holyngbourne, Robertus: ord. pr. 1496 (Reg. Morton (Canterbury), ii, fo. 144).
Humphrey: *read* *Humphrey.
Ingram, William: ord. d. 1485 (*TCS* 14.55, p. 452).
Ivyngho: pitancer 1314 (Canterbury Cath. S.V. Reg. Q, fo. 92ᵛ).
London, dom. W.: ord. d. 1391 (Reg. Courtenay (Canterbury), fo. 312).
+ Lyghfyld, dom. Willelmus, 'monachus C.' (at surrender, 1540: *LP*, xv, p. 186).
 Untraced (g).
Northwico: subprior 1306, cellarer 1314 (Canterbury Cath. S.V. Reg. Q, fos. 43, 92ᵛ).
+ *Permisted, Arnaldus, 'monk C.', †1464:
 Cambridge (USA), Harvard Univ., Houghton Libr., Typ.3 ('si hic perdatur——restituatur').
Stone, Johannes: † by 1488 (Canterbury Cath. Reg. N, fo. 254ᵛ).
Stureya, Thomas de, subprior 1270:
 + Lincoln Cath. 139 (name).
Sudbury: ord. d. 1491 (Reg. Morton (Canterbury), ii, fo. 140ᵛ).
+ Trussell, mag. Thomas (s.xiv: perhaps the rector of Lamport, North-ants., 1332 and 1334, appointed to a canonry of London (*C. Pap. L.*, ii, 359, 399) and the borrower of a book recorded in the Christ Church register printed by James, *Anc. Libs.*, p. 149, 'defectus librorum in manibus secularium').
+ *Wodnysbergh, Johannes, 'subprior C.', †1457:
 Manchester, John Rylands U.L., Lat. 474 (name).
Wynchelse:
 + Cambridge, Trinity Coll., 382–5 (recorded as his gift in cat.).

CANTERBURY, *St Augustine*

For further details and sources for all names below *except Oftwelle*, and for other names in 1964 edn., pp. 243–6, see A.B. Emden, *Donors of Books to S. Augustine's Abbey Canterbury* (Oxford Bibliographical Society, Occasional Publication no. 4, 1969).

Adam, subprior: sacrist *c*. 1215.
Alulphus: perhaps Alulphus de Bocton
Arnold: ord. acol. 1368.
    + Oxford, Bodleian, Fr.e.32 ('liber fr.——').
Bertelot: ord. subd. 1356.
Bracher: at surrender, 1538.
Byholt:
    + Aberystwyth, N.L., Peniarth 28 (name).
Cantuaria: treasurer 1334.
Clara:
    + Oxford, Bodleian, Ashmole 341 fos. 1–144 (wrote).
Cokerynge: treasurer 1287.
Dittone: ord. d. 1332.
Elham: ord. d. 1355 (Reg. Sheppey (Rochester), fo. 264).
Godcheap: monk by 1302.
Godmersham: ord. pr. 1484; dispensation to hold benefice 1535 (Chambers, p. 11).
Hakynton: subprior 1332.
Hileghe: *fl*. 1287.
Lenham: ord. pr. 1464.
Leybourn: †1367.
London, Johannes de (*fl*. 1310):
    + Cambridge, Trinity Coll. 903 + London, B.L., Egerton 823 and 840A (recorded as his gift in cat.).
Lovente: ord. d. 1299.
Mankael: †1334.
Maydeston: ord. pr. 1447.
Northgate: *after* hand *add* A.D. 1340.
Oftwelle, T.:
    Cologny-Genève, Bodmer II (recorded as his gift in cat.).
Radulphus: *fl*. s.xii ex.
Retlyng: ord. d. 1299.
Ridderne: *read* Riddenne; ord. pr. 1295.
Robertus, abbas: i.e. Robertus de Bello.
Rogerius, abbas: elected 1176.
Sancto Georgio: ord. acol. 1286.
Taneto, R. de: ord. pr. 1320.
Thomas, abbas:
    + London, B.L., Cotton Cleop. A.v (recorded as his gift in cat.).
Thomas, prior: *fl*. 1297(?).
Tylmanstone: subprior 1375.
Wilmintone: prior 1272.
Wyvelsburgh: *fl*. 1320.

CANTERBURY, *Dom. conv.*

+ Valoynes, fr. Anselmus de, *fl*. 1349? (see p. 13, n. 3 above):
    Oxford, Bodleian, Digby 203 ('Concessus———ad terminum vite').

CARLISLE, *Dominican convent*
Kyrby: possibly fr. Ricardus de Kirkeby, ord. subd. in St Nicholas, Newcastle-on-Tyne, 1370 (Emden, *Dominicans*, p. 222).

CHERTSEY
Ocham: abbot's attorney and steward *c.* 1279–1305 (*TC* 63.12, p.lxv).

CHESTER
Clarke: *read* ***Clarke.
Ricardus, abbas C.: Ricardus de Seynesbury, abbot before 1350, resigned 1362 (*VCH Cheshire*, iii,145).
+ Thomas, abbas:
  London, B.L., Sloane 285 (g).

CHESTER, *Benedictine nunnery*
Byrkenhed: nun 1521, 1524 (*TCS* 62.78, pp. 52, 129).

CHESTER, *Franciscan convent*
Wyche: in 1404 (Reg. Burghill (Coventry and Lichfield), fo. 152ᵛ).

CHICHESTER
+ **Crucher, mag. Johannes, 'decanus', †1453:
  Oxford, Univ. Coll., 148 ('de novo ligatus per').

CHICKSANDS
Gowshille: probably same as Simon, prior 1316 (*VCH Beds.*, i, 313).

COLCHESTER, *Augustinian priory*
Depyng, dom. Johannes (de Ping): prior, transferred to St Osyth *c.* 1434 (*C.Pap. L.*, viii, 253).

COLCHESTER, *Franciscan convent*
Baldwyn: vicar of Ardleigh, Colchester, 1506–22 (R. Newcourt, *Repertorium ecclesiasticum parochiale Londinense* ii (1710), 12.
+ Francis, Dom. John (monk C):
  Untraced (Kraus): (name).

COVENTRY
Crosseley: prior 1412 (*C. Pap. L.*, vi, 382).
+ ***Knyghton, fr. Thomas (monk of C., B.Cn.L. 1523) 'scolaris reverendissimi. . .pastoris eccl. cath. B.M. Coventrie studendi gracia opibus sacris literis exhibitus'):
  Oxford, Bodleian, 4°V.16(2) (name).
Luffe: subprior in 1414 (*C. Pap. L.*, vi, 353).

COVENTRY, *Franciscan convent*
Duffild: *read* ***Duffild.

COVENTRY, *Carmelite convent*
Kenton: *read* **Kenton.

CROWLAND
Bardenay: at surrender 1539 (Chambers, p. 208).
London: *cancel query*. At surrender 1539 (Chambers, p. 208).
Slefurth: at surrender 1539 (*LP*, xiv (ii), p. 230).

CROXDEN
Chalner: *read* ***Chalner, St Bernard's Coll., 1529.

DALE
North: D.Cn.L., inc. Cambridge, 1525 (Cambridge University Grace Book B.ii p. 281).

DARLEY
Grovis (Greves, etc.), Thomas, *al.* Rag: occurs 1514, 1521, abbot 1524
and at surrender 1538 (*TCS* 62.78, pp. 23, 64, 151–3).

DARTFORD
+ Cressener, Elizabeth, prioress 1487 until death in 1536 (*LP*, xi,
pp. 533–4).[1]
Oxford, Bodleian, Bodl. 255, fos. 1–44 (arms).
Wyntyr, soror Emma:
+ Oxford, Bodleian, Rawl, G.59 (name).

DENNY
Throgkmorten: at surrender 1539 (*LP*, xiv (ii), p. 159).

DEREHAM, WEST
+ Capgrave, John, O.E.S.A.:
San Marino, Huntington Libr., HM55 (composed and wrote: P. J.
Lucas, *TCBS*, v (1972), 3ff).
+ Lawmlay, John:
Dublin, Trinity Coll., 223 ('——[1 word] in thys hows off Westderan').
+ Wygenhale, John, *als.* Saresson, abbot 1429–55 (*VCH Norfolk*, ii, 418):
San Marino, Huntington Libr., HM55 (received presentation of):
P. J. Lucas, *TCBS*, v (1972), 3ff).
+ Martyn, *als.* Wysbech, John, 'abbot D.' (occurs 1488, successor elected
1511: *VCH Norfolk*, ii, 418):
untraced, Rosenthal (name).

DORE
+ Cluberuus (Thomas Cleobury, abbot D. 1516–*c.*1523) (*TC* 14.27,
pp. 231–2, *TC* 14.28, p. 139):
London, B.L., Harley 218 ('constat – iam dudum Dorensi A. 1526').
+ Hartylbury, dan John, monk D. (ord. pr. 1511) (*TC* 14.27, p. 256):
London, B.L., Harley 218 (name).
+ Redborn, Johannes, abbas D. 1529 and at surrender, 1536 (*TC* 14.28,
p. 208; *LP*, xiii (i), p. 476).
London, Westminster Abbey, F.4.21 ('Liber——, emptus in cimiterio
Sancti Pauli London' A.D. 1535').

DOVER
Whytefelds: ord. pr. 1368 (*TC* 14.53, p. 392).

DUNFERMLINE
+ Spendluffe, J. (monk D. 1492):
Oxford, Bodleian, Fairfax 8 (name).

DURHAM
The dates given below for monks of Durham are derived from various sources;
those that begin '*c.*' refer to the period from a monk's profession as deduced from
his position in the *Liber Vitae* and other lists, until his death, while those that
begin '*fl.*' refer to his first and last occurrence in the records.

---

[1] To be distinguished from one of the same name, nun at surrender, 1539 (*LP*,
xiv (i), p. 251), who became prioress of the convent in exile (*VCH, Kent*, ii,
188–9).

+ Abyndun, Stephanus de:
  Cambridge, Jesus Coll. 29 ('liber constat (*expunct*: Petro)——': scribe's colophon, s. xiv).
Adington (Edigton), mag. Robertus de (s.xii ex.):
  Durham, Cath., A.III.2, 5, 16 (also 'liber mag. Roberti de dunelmo'), 17, 19, 24; A.IV.4 (all 'de' or 'ex dono'). York, Minster, XVI.Q.5 (presumed gift of).
+ Admudeston, Willelmus:
  Durham, Cath., C.I.5 (name, s. xiv or xv; *cf.* Clowttesham).
+ Alwerton, fr. Rogerus de (monk of D., *c.* 1342–80/1):
  Durham, Cath., B.IV.26 ('ex procuracione', cf. Wessyngton).
*Appylby, fr. Willelmus de (monk of D., *c.* 1373–1409):
  Durham, Cath., B.III.31, C.IV.20B (both 'ex procuracione——assignatus communi armariolo'). Cf. B.III.14 ('Appleby'): Oxford, Bodleian, Laud Misc. 392 ('Appelby').
+ Arderne, Symonis de. *See* Haylesburi.
Aristotil, mag. Gilbertus (rector of Branxton (Northumb.) before 1253):
  Durham, Cath., A.II.22 ('de dono').
+ Ascleby, Johannes. *See* Lumly.
+ ate Wynne, Symon. *See* Wynterbourne.
Athelstan (king of England, †940):
  Cambridge, Corpus Christi Coll., 183 (presumed gift of). London, B.L., Cotton Otho B.ix ('ic—cyning selle þas boc into sancto Cudberhte').
*Aukland, Johannes, 'prior' (of D., 1484–94):
  The inscription in Cambridge, Jesus Coll., 45, 54 (also 'ex dono'); Sid. Sussex Coll., 56 (cf. Bell, Ricardus); Durham, Cath., B.I.7 (also liber, *see* Elwick), B.I.28, 32 (cf. Est[.]by); B.III.18 (cf. Bell, Ricardus), B.III.26 (cf. Bell, Ricardus); B.IV.30 (cf. Ebchester, Willelmus); C.III.18; C.IV.22 (cf. Shyrborn); Inc. 4a, 13a–b (cf. Law), Inc. 14c (? also '*ex dono*'), 22, 35, 62; London, B.L., Cotton Titus A.xviii + Vesp.B.x, fos. 1–23 + Frags. xxix; Oxford, Bodleian, Laud Misc. 368 (cf. Bell, Ricardus): York, Minster, XVI.D.9 is 'Assignatur novo almariolo in claustro per'; also cf. Cambridge, Jesus Coll., 13 (strip cut out); Durham, Cath., B.II.36 (prior's name erased). London, B.L., Cotton Titus D.xix ('liber dom Thome la[.]son monachi ex dono'). York, Minster, XIX.C.5 ('assignatur registro ecclesie. . .ex donacione'). *See also* Bell, Ricardus.
+ Bake, Robertus. *See* Haylesburi.
Bamburgh, dom. Robertus de (? monk of D. *c.* 1305–53/4):
  Durham, Cath., C.III.10 ('liber Sancti Cuthberti de dunolm' accomodatus R. Harpyn' per').
+ *Banastre, fr. Johannes, S.T.P.:
  Durham, Cath., B.IV.3 ('Tradatur . . . dom. Willelmo [. . .] Thesaurio Calesii ex parte', cf. Doncastre).
Barneby, dom. Reginaldus de (monk of Durham. *c.* 1265–1313/4):
  London, Dulwich Coll., 23 ('datus Comuni Armariolo per').
+ Barwe, Petrus. *See* Wynterbourne.
+ Baseford *or* Daseford, fr. Robertus de, O.P.:
  Durham, Cath., A.IV.23 (g.).
+ *Baylle[y], dan Roberte (monk of D. *c.* 1478–1500/1):
  Durham, Cath., Inc. 61 ('To——' on back cover).

+ *Baynbrygg, [. . .] (? James. fellow of Univ. Coll.). *See* Hertilpoll.
+ *Bel, Elyas:
 Oxford, Brasen. Coll., 4 (caucio, 1482, cf. Roxborth).
*Bell, Ricardus, (1, 3, 5) 'prior' (of D. 1464–79: † 1496):
 (1) Cambridge, Sid. Sussex Coll., 56 ('liber dom. Willelmi Law monachi
 D. ex dono'; cf. Seton, Aukland). Durham, Cath., B.III.18 ('Emanuel
 maria Ric bell' in E of 'Explicit'); B.III.26 ('liber sancti Cuthberti
 et——', cf. Aukland); (3) B.IV.41 ('liber dom. Ricardi Byllyngham
 ex dono, 1466', cf. Dalton, Willelmus; Elwick; Masham); B.IV.42
 ('liber beati Cuthberti et——et ipse contulit . . . mag. Roberto
 Ebchestr'). (5) Nottingham, U.L. ('liber Johannis Aukland monachi
 Dunelm' ex dono', cf. Launcell). Oxford, Bodleian, Laud Misc. 368
 ('liber sancti Cuthberti et——', cf. Emylton, Aukland). *See also*
 Seton.
***Bell, dom. Rogerus, monachus D. (*c.* 1515–39; canon, as Roger
 Watson, 1541–61):
 Untraced Bible (liber: cf. Cornforth).
***Bennett, mag. Willelmus. S.T.P. (incepted 1535), 'prior de Finchal'
 (monk of D., *c.* 1518–39; canon of D. 1541–79). *See* Wylom.
+ Bentlay:
 Durham, Cath., C.IV.21, fos. 251ᵛ–276 (wrote).
+ Berton, Ricardus de. *See* Haylesburi.
*Beverlaco, (1–4) fr., (5–7 mag. Johannes de, (1) 'monachus D'. (*fl.*
 c. 1320–49):
 Durham, Cath., (1) B.II.12 ('ex procuracione'); C.I.20 (Caucio,
 'communitati fratrum minorum oxon' pro exposicione abbatis Ioachim
 super apocalipsim' s.xiv in., 1315, 1318, (5) 1319, 1320, (7) 1322; cf.
 Beverlaco, Rob.; Quitbi).
+ Beverlaco, Robertus de:
 Durham, Cath., C.I.20 (caucio, 1313, cf. Beverlaco, Joh.). *See also*
 Haylesburi.
Blaklaw, dom. Robertus, S.T.B., 'sub-prior D.':
 Durham, Cath,. A.I.3 ('scripte per manum Willelmi de Stiphol ex
 precepto——', A.D. 1386).
***Blunte, fr. Christopherus, S.T.B., 'quondam terrarius D.' († in office
 1534):
 Cambridge, U.L., Rel.b.51.3 ('liber dompni Johannis Blyth ex dono',
 cf. Marley, Stephanus).
Blyth, dom. Johannes (monk of D. *c.* 1531–39). *See* Blunte; and cf.
 Marley, Stephanus.
*[Boldon], fr. Uthredus [de], 'monachus D.' (1341–97):
 Cambridge, Pembr. Coll., 241 ('ex procuracione'). Durham, Cath.,
 C.IV.17 ('ex procuracione', cf. Wynterton). London, B.L., Burney
 310 (*a* 'ex procuracione'; *b* 'scriptus per manum Guillermi dicti du
 Stiphel de Britania pro——A.D. 1381 in Fincal'. cf. Hemmyngburgh).
+ Bolton, Hugo. *See* Lumly.
Bolton, dom. Johannes de (monk of D., '1353'–1407/8):
 Oxford, Univ. Coll., 86 (liber).
+ Boston.
 Oxford, Magd. Coll., lat. 162 (constat, s.xv, cf. Cokken).
+ [B]othal, fr. Rogerus de (? O.F.M. *fl.* 1312). *See* Novo Castro.
+ Boyle, Robertus. *See* Haylesburi.

Brakenbyri, Robertus (1–5, 8) de (monk of D., *c.* 1342–91):
  (1) Durham, Cath., B.I.9 ('liber', cf. Elwyk), (2) B.IV.15 ('liber'), (3) C.I.19, fos. 128–233 (g.), (4) C.II.3 ('liber'), (5) C.IV.12 (liber). (6) London, B.L., Harley 491 ('liber'). Oxford, Bodleian, Laud Misc. 603 ('liber'), (8) 641 ('liber——pro tempore vite sue'). *See also* Lumlei.
Brantyngham, dom. Willelmus (monk of D., *c.* 1521–39). *See* Wyllye.
+ Brisconet*tes*, Willelmus. *See* Wynterbourne.
*Burnby, mag. Johannes, 'prior' (D. 1456–64):
  London, Lambeth Pal., 483 ('usus conceditur dom. Roberto Ebchester per').
*Byllyngham, dom. Ricardus (monk of D., *fl.* 1445–72):
  Durham, Cath., A.IV.8, fos. 79–138 (*a* 'liber'; *b* 'liber dom. J[. .] Manby ex dono [. . .]yllyngham'; fos. 1–52, *see* Warner); B.I.7 ('liber dom. Willelmi Elwyk ex dono——in recompensione certe summe pecunie mutuate'). *See also* Bell, Ricardus; Seton.
+ Byrtley, dom. Johannes (? monk of D., *fl.* 1423–50):
  London, B.L., Add. 24059 (name in red).
+ Cadebur, Johannes. *See* Wynterbourne.
*Cale, T. (monk of D., *fl.* 1441–78):
  London, B.L., Harley 4688 (name). *See also* Ebchester, Willelmus.
+ *Caly, dom. Ricardus monachus (D. *fl.* 1485–1526):
  London, Law Soc. 107.d ('emptus sumptibus assignatis——', the name erased, with 'Wi*llelm*o Wylom' in its place).
*Castell, dom. Thomas, (1, 8) 'monachus D.' (two contemporary namesakes *c.* 1473–1519 and *fl.* 1495–1511), (1, 2, 3, 6) 'quondam custos collegii Dunelm' [Oxon.]' (both monks held this office, the senior on his election as prior, the junior when he last occurs), (4) prior (D. 1494–1519):
  (1) Cambridge, U.L., Inc. 1049 (*a* 'liber, precium iii s' iiii d''; *b* 'pertinet'), (2) Rel. *c.* 50.8 ('liber'; *cf.* Wylom). (3) Durham, Cath., Inc. 48 ('pertinet'); (4) U.L., Cosin V.ii.5 ('liber dom. Thome Lawson ex dono'). (5) Oxford, Bodleian, Tanner 4 (name, in g. or dative); (6) St John's Coll., P.4.46 ('pertinet'). Ushaw Coll., XVII.F.4.12 (g., '5 Marcii 1511', cf. Wyllye). (8) York, Minster, X.A.7 ('liber').
Castro *Bernardi*, fr. Johannes de, 'monachus D.' (*i: fl.* 1298–1311: *ii: c.* 1351–81):
  Durham, Cath., C.III.16 ('ex procuracione', cf. Luceby). Oxford, Bodleian, Rawl. C.4 ('ex procuracione', ? *ii*, ? wrote).
Castro, dom. Thomas de (? monk of D. *c.* 1269–1313/14):
  Durham, Cath., B.I.1.('Sentencie date Communi Armariolo').
*Cawthorn, dom. Willelmus (*fl.* 1478–1520):
  Durham, Cath., Inc. 1f ('liber', *cf.* Manbe, Werdall).
+ Charleton, Rogerus de. *See* Haylesburi.
+ Chilton, Michael de (monk of D.). *See* Elwyk.
*Chirden, mag. Alanus de, 'S.T.P. quondam vicarii de alverton' (adm. 1323, vac. by 1332):
  Durham, Cath., A.I.11 ('ex colacione').
+ Cliff, mag. A. de:
  Durham, Cath., A.III.30 (g., s.xiii: cf. Lund).

+ Clowttesham, Robertus:
Durham, Cath., C.I.5 (caucio, 'et Roberti Redeness, 1383'; cf. Admudeston).

Clyffe, dom. T. (monk of D., *fl.* 1495–1513). *See* Cornforth.

*Cokken, dom. Willelmus, 'monachus D.' (*fl.* 1444–60):
Oxford, Magd. Coll., 162 (wrote, cf. Boston).

+ Colby, Johannes. *See* Luceby.

+ Colwitho, Johannes de:
Durham, Cath., B.I.27 (name, s.xiv).

+ Constabill, Robertus (monk of D. *c.* 1362–79/80):
Durham, Cath., C.IV.26 ('constat').

+ Corbrige, dom. Hugo de:
Durham, Cath., C.I.12 ('dom.——, Willelmus Herike, Thomas de M[. . .]', s.xiii/xiv, cf. Insula).

Cornforth, dom. Georgius (monk of D., '1463'–1507):
Untraced Bible ('liber dom. T. Clyffe ex dono'; cf. Bell, Rogerus).

Crosby, dom. Ricardus, 'monachus D.' (*fl.* 1517–39). *See* Whytehed.

Cuthbert, Willelmus (monk of D., namesakes: *c.* 1437–74 and *fl.* '1460'–96). *See* Dalton, Willelmus.

+ Dale, dom. Thomas:
Durham, Cath., A.I.6 (name in ablative, s.xv in., cf. Langley; Ebchester, Willelmus).

Dalton, dom. Henricus (monk of D.):
Cambridge, Trin. Coll., 1227 ('in insula sacra ex dono——prioris eiusdem A.D. 1513'; cf. Ebchester, Willelmus).

*Dalton, dom. Willelmus, 'monachus D.' (*fl.* 1420–61):
Durham, Cath., B.IV.41, fos. 33–7, 115–17 (wrote, cf. Bell, Ricardus); B.IV.42 ('liber'). Untraced Cassiodorus ('liber Willelmi Cuthbert ex dono'). *See also* Hoveden.

+ Danby, J:
London, Coll. of Arms, Arundel 25 (name, ? s.xv).

+ Daseford. *See* Baseford.

+ *Dilyngton, mag. Thomas (*c.* 1300):
Durham, Cath., B.I.26 ('liber').

+ Ditensale, mag. Johannes de:
Durham, Cath., C.IV.20A ('Explicit . . . a——A.D. 1283').

*Doncastre, mag. Willelmus, 'decanus de Aukelande' (1435–9):
Durham, Cath., B.IV.3 ('ex dono', cf. Banastre), C.I.2 (ex dono, cf. Lyndewode), C.III.12 ('ex dono', s.xviii inscription).

*Dune, dom. Thomas, 'monachus D.' (*fl.* 1489–96). *See* Manbe.

Dunelm', Petrus de, 'monachus D.' (*fl.* 1351–68):
Durham, Cath., B.IV.34 ('liber').

+ Dunelmo (*als.* ? Adington, *q.v.*), mag. Robertus de:
Durham, Cath., A.III.16 ('liber').

+ Dunelm', Robertus de (monk of D., *fl. c.* 1287–1324):
Oxford, Bodleian, Lat. misc.b.13 fo. 51 (caucio, 'et Roberti [. . .]', s.xiv in.).

Dunelmo, mag. Willelmus de († 1249):
Durham, Cath., A.II.7 (ex dono).

+ Durward [John], monk of D., *fl.* 1411–61):
London, B.L., Add. 24059 (name).

*Ebchester, (2) mag. R. (incepted 1470/1), dom. Robertus, (1) 'monachus
D.' (c. 1455–84, prior 1479–84):
(1) London, B.L., Arundel 332 ('liber', cf. Hertylpull). (2) Oxford,
Brasen. Coll., 4 ('redemit', cf. Stroder, Manbe). See also Bell,
Ricardus; Burnby; Ebchester, Willelmus; Figy.
*Ebchester, mag. (by 1426), (3a) dom., Willelmus, (3a) 'monachus D.'
(c. 1403–62/3), (1, 7) 'quondam', (9) 'nuper', 'prior' (1446–56):
(1) Cambridge, Trin. Coll., 1227 ('liber dom. W. Elwyk ex dono').
Durham, Cath., A.I.6 ('ex procuracione'. cf. Dale, Langley);
A.III.27 (2a 'liber——ex empcione iiii marc', cf. Sixt[. .]; b 'assignatur
librarie monachorum D. per'); B.III.12 ('assignatur . . .', as A.III.27);
B.III.19 ('assignatur . . .', as A.III.27, cf. Lethum); B.IV.29 ('assignatur . . . , as A.III.27'); (7) B.IV.30 ('usus conceditur dom. Roberto
Ebchester per'; cf. Aukland); C.III.11 ('assignatur . . .', as A.III.27;
cf. Westmerland). (9) London, B.L., Harley 3049 ('fecit fieri et
assignavit librarie A.D. 1458'); Harley 5234 ('liber dom. Thome Caly
ex dono', cf. Mody).
*Elwick, dom. Willelmus, 'monachus D.' (c. 1440–1499/1500), (3) 'sub-
prior' (1483–7):
Durham, Cath., B.I.7 ('liber dom. Johannis Aukland ex dono', cf.
Byllyngham); B.I.18 ('liber dom. Roberti Wardell ex dono'); (3)
B.IV.41 ('liber dom. Johannis Manbe Monachi D. ex dono', cf.
Bell, Ricardus). See also Ebchester, Willelmus.
+ *Elwyk, (1) dom., (2, 3) mag., Gilbertus de, (3) 'monachus D.':
Durham, Cath., B.I.9 (caucio, (1) 'et Michaelis de Chilton, 1310'; (2)
'1320'; cf. Brakenbyri). (3) Oxford, Bodleian, Lat. misc.b.13 fo. 51
(caucio, 1312).
*Emylton, (1, 2, 7) Robertus, (junior, monk of D., fl. 1423–48):
Cambridge, (1) Fitzwilliam Mus., McClean 169 (wrote); (2) Jesus
Coll., 70 (wrote); Sid. Sussex Coll., 32 (name). Durham, Cath.,
A.III.29 (name); C.IV.23, fos. 129–40ᵛ (wrote). Oxford, Bodleian,
Laud Misc. 368 (name, cf. Bell, Ricardus). (7) York, Minster,
XVI.I.1 (wrote, cf. Wardell).
Est[.]by, Johannes, 'vicarius de Bannebury':
Durham, Cath., B.I.32 ('fecit fieri A.D. 1448'; cf. Aukland).
+ Eyrsden, dom. Johannes (monk of D., c. 1507–39: minor canon until
1548):
London, B.L., Harley 4843 ('liber', cf. Tode, Hacfurth).
*Farn, mag. Thomas, 'vicarius ecclesie sancti Oswaldi Dunelm.' († by
1519):
Durham, Cath., Inc. 32–34, 43, 47a, 53. York, Minster, XIV.B.22. All
'ex dono', and, except 47a, A.Ch. 1519.
Figy, dom. W(illiam, monk of D., c. 1432–85/6):
Edinburgh, N.L., Adv.18.6.11 ('liber sancti Cuthberti dunelm c[ui]us
usus conceditur dom. Roberto Ebchester per').
*Fishborne (5) Junior ?, (2a, 3) Johannes de, 'monachus D.' (senior
c. 1394–1434, junior fl. 1402–11/12):
Durham, Cath., B.IV.36 (name); (2) B.IV.45 (a 'liber'; b wrote
fos. 85–101); (3) C.I.11 ('liber'); C.I.13 (name); (5) C.III.8 (name);
C.IV.23, fos. 57–126 (wrote). London, Lambeth Pal., 12 ('quod', cf.
Pooll).
Fossor, dom. J., 'prior D.' (1341–74). See Hextildesham.

Gisburne, [. . .] Willelmus de, 'quondam electus [1321] in priorem', (monk of D. *c.* 1281–1337/8):
Durham, Cath., C.IV.24 ('donatus communi armariolo per').

+ Gloucestr', Ricardus de. *See* Wynterbourne.

*Graystanes, fr., (2*d*, 9*b*) mag., Robertus de, (8) 'subprior' (occurs 1333), (monk of D. *c.* 1304–33/4):
Durham, Cath., A.I.2, (2) B.I.10 (caucio, 1306, 1323, †1325), B.II.19 (cf. Lund), 20, 28, C.I.18; U.L., Cosin V.i.8. (all 'ex procuracione'). (8) Nottingham, U.L. (name, cf. Launcell). (9) Oxford, Bodleian, Lat. misc.b.13 fo. 51. (caucio, 1324, *b* 1325).

+ Graystanys, Thomas de (monk of D.):
Durham, Cath., B.I.10 (caucio, 'et Roberti de hexildisham, 1317').

+ *Gregfort, mag. W[illelmus], of Univ. Coll., 1453/4 (†1487/8):
Oxford, Brasen. Coll., 4 (renewed caution, cf. Roxborth).

+ Gretham, T:
Durham, Cath., C.II.7 (name. £4, s.xiv).

Gretham, W. de:
Durham, Cath., C.III.2 ('ex dono', s.xiii ex.).

+ *Gylyott, mag. [Willelmus], fellow of Univ. Coll., 1478/9 (†1489):
Oxford, Brasen. Coll., 4 (renewed caution, cf. Roxborth).

Hacfurth, dom. Willelmus, (2) 'monachus D.' (*c.* 1516–39, minor canon 1541–59):
London, B.L., Harley 4843 ('sir Willm Hacfurth', cf. Eyrsden). (2) York, Minster, XII.J.22 ('liber').

Halidene (Halidon), fr. Robertus de, 'monachus D.' (*c.* 1330–49):
Durham, Cath., C.I.14 ('ex procuracione'), C.II.10 ('liber').

+ Hallughton, Johannes de (monk of D., *c.* 1347–84/5):
Cambridge, Jesus Coll., 41 ('Orate pro anima——').

Hamsterly, Johannes, 'monachus D.' (two: *c.* 1476–1501, and *c.* 1510–39). *See* Warner.

+ *Hamsterly, Willelmus. *See* Lumly.

Harpyn, R[icardus], monk of D., *fl.* 1340–3:
Durham, Cath., C.I.16 ('assignatus——per priorem D.', cf. Hemmyngburgh). *See also* Bamburgh.

+ Harwe, Johannes, 'advocatus':
Oxford, Brasen. Coll., 4 ('liber Sancti Cuthberti de D. comodatus ——', cf. Rowlande, Roxborthe).

+ Hawkwell, dom W[illiam] (monk of D., *fl.* 1486–1522):
Ushaw Coll., XVII.F.4.12 ('liber dom. Stephani Marly ex dono', cf. Wyllye).

+ H[a]w[t]wys[e]ll, . . . Willelmus de, 'monachus D.':
Durham, Cath., C.III.9 (caucio, 'M. Nicholai de Luceby et——', 1339; 'M. N[. . .] et——, 1341'; cf. Lund).

+ Haylesburi, mag. Johannes de:
Durham, Cath., C.I.1 (caucio, with Symonis de Arderne, mag. Ricardi Reygne[. .], fr. Willelmi de Wynterbourne, Walteri de Kelmeston, Stephani Herebert, Roberti Bake, Rogeri de Charleton, Johannis de Wygornia, Roberti Boyle, Galfridi de Mersten, Ricardi de Berton, Roberti de Beuerlaco, Hugonis de Preston, Mauricii de Lews et Walteri dela mor', 1324; cf. Loughtburgh, Wynterbourne).

+ *He*m*lyngtun, mag. Johannes de (fellow of Merton). *See* Mala[. . .].

Hemmyngburgh, dom. Johannes de, 'quondam prior D.' (1391–1416):
  Durham, Cath. B.II.23, 27; B.III.4, fos. 1–162; C.I.16 (cf. Harpyn): (each 'assignatus communi armariolo', or 'com. alm. claustri, per'). London, B.L., Burney 310 (damaged inscription as Durham Cath., B.II.23; cf. Boldon).
+ Hepden, mag. Thomas. *See* Westmerland.
Herbertus, mag., 'medicus':
  Cambridge, Jesus Coll., 44 ('ex dono', s.xii/xiii. cf. cat., p. 8/1–6). Edinburgh, N.L., Adv.18.6.11 (cat., p. 7).
+ Herebert, Stephanus. *See* Haylesburi.
+ Herike, Willelmus. *See* Corbrige.
+ *He*rtilpoll, mag. Robertus (fellow of Univ. Coll.):
  Oxford, Brasen. Coll., 4 (caucio, with 'mag. Henrici [. . .] Baynbrygg Christofori Stakhus', 1455 'luat he*r*tilpoll'', cf. Stroder).
Hertylpull, dom. Willelmus, 'monachus D.' (*fl.* 1501–36):
  London, B.L., Arundel 332 ('liber', cf. Ebchester, Robertus).
+ Hesylden, Thomas (? monk of D., *fl.* '1466'–94/5):
  Durham, Cath., B.II.26 (name).
Hextildesham, fr. Robertus de, (3) 'hostillarius D.' (1344–48; monk *fl.* 1337–57/8):
  Dublin, Trin. Coll., 349 ('usus conceditur'). Durham, Cath., A.II.18 ('usus conceditur'); (3) B.III.7 ('communi armaliolo assignatus per dom. J. Fossor priorem D. per procuracionem——'). *See also* Graystanys, Thomas de.
Hilton, dom. Robertus de:
  Durham, Cath., A.II.12 ('liberetur').
+ Holm, Alexander de:
  Durham, Cath., C.I.19, fos. 64–127 ('Iste liber est mag. `Johannis´ de [. . .] en holderness filii adopptiui salamonis quondam idem quod——', cf. Ward).
+ Horneclif, T de:
  Durham, Cath., B.IV.8 ('karissimis amicis suis francis et anglis——', s.xii).
Hoton, Johannes, 'monachus' (*of D., fl. 1428–70*). *See* Wessyngton.
+ Houlla, fr. Rolandus de, 'carmelita':
  Durham, Cath., C.IV.22, fos. 41–138 ('scriptus in conventu Stanfordie A.D. 1449', cf. Shyrborn).
*Hoveden, (2) S, Stephanus, 'subprior D.' (1420–40; monk c. 1389–1444/5):
  Durham, Cath., A.IV.5 ('liber dom. Willelmi Dalton ex dono'). (2) London, Lambeth Pal., 23 ('ex dono').
*Howlande, *recte* Rowlande.
Hugo, episcopus. *See* le Puiset.
+ *Hull, mag. Johannes (fellow of Univ. Coll.). *See* Stroder.
+ Hylton, mag. *See* Toppyng.
+ Hynton, T.:
  Ushaw Coll., XVIII.A.3.5 (name deleted, cf. Wyllye).
Insula, dom. Johannes de, (1) 'miles':
  Durham, (1) Cath. A.II.9 ('ex dono', s.xiii/xiv); U.L., Cosin V.ii.5 (name). Cf. Durham, Cath. C.I.4 (cf. Lumly), 6, 9, uniform vols. (the first and third inscribed as the property 'trium puerorum de

Insula scilicet Henrici, Ricardi ac Johannis fratrum', likewise C.I.12, cf. Corbrige).

+ Jarwe, Johannes de:
Durham, Cath., A.IV.14 ('ex dono', s.xii/xiii).

Kaugi, Adam de:
Durham, Cath., C.I.7 ('ex dono', s.xiii in.).

Kedwely, Willelmus de:
Durham, Cath., B.IV.36, fos. 149–195 ('scriptum a').

+ Kellau, Robertus de (monk of D., *fl.* 1334–62):
Durham, Cath., C.IV.1 ('liber').

+ Kelmeston, Walterus de. *See* Haylesburi.

+ *[Kempe], dom. Johannes, 'cardinalis [1439], Ebor' archiepiscopus' (trans. Canterbury 1452):
Durham, Cath., B.III.20 ('liber', cf. Pykerynge).

+ Kirkby, Willelmus, 'monachus D.' (*c.* 1426–39/40):
London, B.L., Harley 4688 (name).

+ Kornsow, Adam de:
Oxford, Bodleian, Laud Misc. 277 (name, s. xiv).

+ Kybbyll, Willelmus:
Durham, Cath., B.III.22 (g., s.xiii/xiv, cf. Rome).

Kyllerby, fr. Willelmus de, (monk of D., *fl.* 1368–92/3):
Cambridge, U.L., Mm.3.14 (ex procuracione; he kneels before St Cuthbert in an initial inscribed 'confessor vere Kyllerby gaudia quere').

Kyppier, fr. Godefridus de:
Durham, Cath., A.III.28 ('ex dono', s.xiii in.).

+ la mor', Walterus de. *See* Haylesburi.

+ Lamsley, Alexander de, 'monachus D.':
Oxford, Bodleian, Lat. misc.b.13, fo. 51 (caucio, 1313).

*Langchester, Robertus de, 'cancellarius et postea feretrarius D.' (*c.* 1356–1406/7: chancellor, 1391; librarian, 1381–92; feretrar 1392–7):
Durham, Cath., C.IV.25 ('quondam g.').

Langley, dom. Thomas, episcopus D. (1406–37):
Durham, Cath., A.I.5 ('ex dono', cf. Wykingeston); A.I.6 (arms include his).

*Lasynby, Willelmus, 'monachus D.' (*fl.* 1412–20):
Durham, Cath., B.IV.42 ('tradatur'; cf. Bell; Dalton, Willelmus).

+ Launcell, dom. Th. (monk of D., *c.* 1355–1408/9):
Nottingham, U.L. (Biblia, cf. Graystanes; Bell, Ricardus).

*Law, (2–4) mag. (incepted 1477–80), Willelmus, 'monachus D.' (*fl.* 1460–81):
Durham, Cath., C.IV.23, fos. 57–128 ('liber'); (2) Inc. 1a–d ('liber'); (3) Inc. 13 a, b ('liber——et a dicto sancto Cuthberto nunquam alienandus', cf. Aukland); (4) Inc. 20b ('liber'). *See also* Bell, Ricardus.

Lawson, dom. Thomas, 'monachus D.' (*c.* 1478–1513/14):
Durham, U.L., GSAD A92K ('liber'). *See also* Aukland, Castell.

Le Berwby (Borwby):
Durham, Cath., A.I.4, fos. 90ᵛ–228 (name: wrote cf. Stiphol).

***Lee, (6) mag. (incepted 1522), dom. Petrus, 'monachus D.' (*fl.* 1510–27):

Dublin, Trin. Coll. 440 ('constat'). Durham, Cath., P.V.16–17 (17: 'liber——precium istius cum altra parte x s"). Oxford, Oriel Coll., C.e.20 ('liber——precium huius vii s"). Ushaw Coll., XVII.E.4.6–10 (annotated by); XVII.E.5.9. ('liber———precium III s' viii d''); (6) XVII.F.4.5 ('liber——precium iii s''; cf. Marley, Stephanus); XVIII.B.4.24 (annotated by, *also* Swalwell; XVIII.B.5.2 (annotated by); XVIII.B.5.15 ('liber——precium vi s''; cf. Marley, Stephanus); XVIII.B.7.6 ('liber——precium cum aliis duabus partibus vj s''; cf. Marley, Stephanus); XVIII.G.3.10–11 ('liber——precium istius cum aliis duabus partibus xi s'' on both; cf. Wylom).

[le Puiset], Hugo of, 'episcopus' (1, 2) 'D.' (1153–95).
  Durham, Cath., (1) A.II.1, (2) 19, A.III.7, A.IV.1, 10 (all 'liber'); B.III.13 (recorded as his gift in cat.); C.IV.5 ('liber'); U.L., Cosin V.ii.1 (presumed gift of). Cambridge, Trin. Coll., 1194 (g). London, B.L., Add. 16616 ('lib*er*').

+ Lethum, Johannes (? monk of D., *fl.* 1394–1431):
  Durham, Cath., B.III.19 ('Nomen scriptoris Johannes plenus Amoris Muhtel').

+ Lews, Mauricius de. *See* Haylesburi.

+ *Lougthburgh, mag. T.:
  Durham, Cath., C.I.1 (caucio, 1426, cf. Haylesburi, Maynsforth).

+ *Luceby, (1) dom., mag. Nicholaus de (master of Balliol 1328), (2c) 'monachus' (D., *fl.* 1331–49), (1) 'prior domus sancti Leonardi iuxta Stamford' (cell of D., 1338–46):
  Durham, Cath., (1) B.IV.43, fos. 2–16ᵛ ('Explicit tabula quam composuit'); (2) C.III.9 (caucio, 'et Johannis de Colby, 1325'; 1328; c 'et domini Willelmi [de Hau]tw[i]s[e]ll 1339)'; C.III.16 ('Caucio Johannis de Colby[?], 1327', 'tradatur mag. Nic[. .] de L?[. . .]').

Lu*m*lei, Emericus de (monk of D., *fl.* 1306–44):
  Durham, Cath., A.III.7 ('liber Roberti de Brakenbiri ex dono'; cf. le Puiset).

+ Lumly, Willelmus:
  Durham, Cath., C.I.4 (caucio, with Johannis Ascleby, Hugonis Bolton, 1[.]76; with Willelmi Ha*m*st*er*ly et Thome Spens, 1378; cf. Insula).

*Lund, fr. Thomas de (monk of D., *c.* 1309–49/50):
  Durham, Cath., B.I.2, B.II.25 (cf. Sutton), B.III.27 (all 'ex procuracione'); C.III.9 (caucio, 1330, cf. Hawtwysell). *Annotated:* Durham, Cath., A.III.30 (cf. Cliff); B.I.23, 29; B.II.15, 19 (cf. Graystanes, Robertus), 26, 32 (cf. under **COLDINGHAM**); B.IV.16; C.II.13; C.III.2. Oxford, Bodleian, Laud Misc. 546.

+ Lyndewode, Willelmus:
  Durham, Cath., C.I.2 ('constat', s.xv in. ?; cf. Doncastre).

+ Mainesford (Rogerus de, monk of D., *c.* 1369–1409/10). *See* Quitbi.

+ Mala[. . .], Robertus [et] Walterus frater eius:
  Durham, Cath., B.I.5 (caucio, 1317 'et tradatur Magistro Johanni de He*m*lyngtun').

*Manbe, dom. Johannes (monk of D., '1463'–94/5):
  Durham, Cath., B.III.20 ('Manby', cf. Pykerynge); B.IV.40 (*a* 'liber ——emptus de dom. Roberto Sotheron'; *b* 'ex dono——assignatus communi armariolo D.'): Inc. 1f ('liber'; cf. Cawthorn); Inc. 11a ('liber'; cf. Werdall); Inc. 12 (*annotated by*; cf. Werdall). Lincoln, Cath., 240 (*annotated by*). Liverpool, County Mus., 12036 (*a*

annotated by; *b* caucio, 1475). Oxford, Bodleian, Douce 129 ('liber dom. Thome Dune monachi D. ex dono'); Lyell 16 ('liber'); Brasen. Coll., 4 ('liber [. . .] Manby [. . .]', cf. Ebchester, Robertus; Rowlande). Ushaw Coll., XVIII.B.1.2 (*annotated by*; cf. Swalwell). *See also* Byllyngham, Elwick.

***Marley, (1) dom., (9) dom. (*erased*) Nicholaus, (2) S.T.P. (monk of D., 1529–39, canon 1541–60. Some books listed here may have come into his hands after the Dissolution: cf. R. de Sancto Victore, Paris, 1510 (Oxford, Bodleian, Broxb.29.13 (R.1327)) inscribed 'liber dompni Nicholai Marley ex dono Thome Tempest anno 1560', and two printed books, a Driedo of 1543 and a Cyril of 1546. (Ushaw Coll., XVII.F.4.8 and F.4.9–10) 'liber Nicholai Marley'):

(1) Durham, Cath., Inc. 25 ('liber——ex dono nullius sed care emptus 1536'); (2) Inc. 45 ('liber'; cf. Swalwell, Whytehed). Ushaw Coll., XVII.E.4.1 ('to dean——yn Duram abbay delyver thes'); XVII.E.5.6 ('to dean——'); XVIII.A.3.12 ('liber'; cf. Whelden); XVIII.B.3.6 (name, cf. Swalwell); XVIII.B.3.8 (g., cf. Swalwell); XVIII.B.3.10–11 (name); (9) XVIII.B.6.7 ('liber——precium iiii s''). *See also* Marley, Stephanus; Wylom.

***Marley, (1, 7) S, (1) 'sacerdos', (3, 4, 6, 8) dom. (3–6, 8, 9) Stephanus, (2, 3, 9) 'monachus D.'' (*c*. 1515–39, canon 1541–72. Some books listed here may have come into his hands after the Dissolution):

(1) Cambridge, U.L., Rel. b.51.3 (name on lost fly-leaf; cf. Blunte). (2) Durham, Cath., P.x.40 ('liber——1530 prec' iii s' iiii d''). Ushaw Coll., (3) XVII.E.4.10 (name, 1526); (4) XVII.E.5.4 ('liber'; cf. Swalwell); (5) XVII.F.4.5 ('liber dom Nycholai Marley ex dono'; cf. Lee); (6) XVIII.B.5.15 ('liber'; cf. Lee); (7) XVIII.B.7.6 ('liber'; cf. Lee); (8) XVIII.C.5.11 ('liber'; cf. Swalwell); (9) XVIII.C.5.15 (name; cf. Swalwell). *See also* Hawkwell, Swalwell.

*Masham, (1, 2) Robertus (monk of D., *fl.* 1391–1418):
Durham, Cath., (1) B.IV.41, fos. 41–50 ('collegit et fecit scribi' *sic*, but s. xii/xiii, and cf. Wyuistou; *cf*. Bell, Ricardus); (2) B.IV.43, fos. 24ᵛ, 88ᵛ–90ᵛ, 123–42, 160–67ᵛ and 172ᵛ–86ᵛ (wrote). London, B.L., Harley 3858 (wrote; cf. Wessyngton).

+ *Maynsforth, mag. Johannes (fellow of Merton):
Durham, Cath., C.I.1 (caucio, 1438, 1439, cf. Loughtburgh).

*Melsaneby, mag. Alanus de (s.xiii in.):
Durham, Cath., B.I.33 ('ex dono').

Melsaneby, mag. Henricus de (s.xiii):
Durham, Cath., A.II.15, A.III.15, A.III.22 (all 'ex dono').

+ Melton, Ricardus (? monk of D., *fl*.1343–5):
Aberdeen, Forbes of Boyndlie ('scripsit', according to note added s.xiv).

Merley (?), fr. Johannes de (monk of D., *c*. 1410–22):
Durham, Cath., B.I.11 ('liber——et reddatur sibi').

+ Mersten, Galfridus de. *See* Haylesburi.

Middleton, Bertramus de, 'prior D.' (1244–58):
Cambridge, Trin. Coll., 8 ('ex dono' but with use for life reserved to his chaplain Roger; cf. Wessyngton). Durham, Cath., A.I.12, 16; A.III.12, 21, fos. 1–90; B.IV.23. *All* 'ex dono'. Durham, Cath., A.I.15 ('ex procuracione' *cat., p. 44*).

+ Milthorpp, Johannes. *See* Whorton.

+ *Mody, mag. Johannes, 'subprior' (D., 1443/4–46):
London, B.L., Harley 5234 ('liber', cf. Wlveston; Ebchester, Willelmus).
+ *Morby, R[obertus], monk of D., *fl.* 1410–47:
Durham, Cath., B.IV.42, fos. 1–104ᵛ (wrote).
+ Muhtel. *See* Lethum.
Nigellus, dom., (*b*) 'quondam vicarius de Stichil' (s.xiii ex.):
Durham, Cath., B.III.17 (*a* 'liber', *b* 'ex dono').
Norham, Radulfus de:
Durham, Cath., A.IV.12 ('liber iste inscribitur——' in hand *of s.*xviii).
+ Novo Castro, fr. Hugo de:
Durham, Cath., B.I.13 ('liber [. . .]orum fratris——et assignatur per
cap' fr. Rogero de [.? B]othal, s.xiv in.).
+ Pikering, Robertus de:
Durham, Cath., C.IV.17 ('suplementum caucionis', s.xiv in., cf.
Wynterton).
*Poklyngton, dom. Willelmus, 'monachus D.', B.Th. (by 1406; †1442/3):
Durham, Cath., B.II.29 (assignatur communi librarie per'). Oxford,
Bodleian, Wood empt. 24 ('Poklyngton', cf. Strygete). *See also*
'Poklyngton' added against entries in 1416 Spendement catalogue.
+ Pooll, dom. Ricardus, (2) 'monachus D.' (*fl.* 1495–1522):
London, Lambeth Pal., 11 ('Poole'), (2) 12 (name, cf. Fishborne,
Wrake). Ushaw Coll., XVIII.B.4.4. ('liber', cf. Swan).
+ Preston, Hugo de. *See* Haylesburi.
Puiset. *See* le Puiset.
+ *Pykerynge, dom. Thomas (monk of D., *c.* 1458–86/7):
Durham, Cath., B.III.20 ('liber dom. iohannis [. . .] monachi D.
emptus de', cf. Kempe, Manbe).
+ Quitbi [Willelmus], ('monk of D.', *c.* 1381–1411/12):
Durham, Cath., C.I.20 ('Memento finis et esto amabilis deo et hominibus
quod Quitbi': 'Fac hoc et vivos ineternum quod Mainesford', cf.
Beverlaco, Joh.; Wessyngton).
Qwelden. *See* Whelden.
R., 'prior de Finchale':
Durham, Cath., A.I.7 ('ex dono', s.xiii).
*Radlee, Petrus (*fl.* 1410). *See* Wessyngton.
Rana, mag. Johannes de (s.xii ex.):
Durham, Cath., A.III.3, fos. 63–173; A.III.23 (both 'liber').
+ Redeness, Robertus. *See* Clowttesham.
Reginald of Durham:
Durham, Cath., Hunter 101 (? author's autograph, s.xii).
+ Rey(g)nbyr, mag. Ricardus. *See* Haylesburi, Wynterbourne.
Riddell, dom. Ricardus (monk of D., *fl.* 1487–1504). *See* Rok.
**Ridley, Robertus († *c.* 1536):
Durham, Cath., B.V.58 ('dono datus A.D. 1533'); D.VII.23–4 ('ex
dono A.D. 1534'). Hereford, Cath., A.ix.2–3 (gave in 1532). Lin-
coln, Cath., F.1.14 ('ex dono A.D. 1532/3'). His name is written in
Durham, Cath., D.VII.1 (first vol. of a set of Jerome), D.VII.6–11
(Augustine), P.V.2 (Nausea, Homeliae), P.V.5–8 (Dionysius Car-
thusianus), P.V.31 (N. Gorran, Super epistolas Pauli); Ushaw Coll.,
XVIII.B.6.10 cf. Swalwell; and York, Minster, VIII.F.7 cf. Tutyng.
+ Riple, Salamon de:
Durham, Cath., C.I.1 (caucio, s.xiv in; cf. Wynterbourne.

Robertus, dom., 'prior' (R. de Walworth, prior of D. 1374–91):
Durham, Cath., C.I.19, fos. 234–97 ('A.D. 1388 assignatus . . . communi armariolo D. per—ut nulli extra claustrum accomodetur').
Rogerus capellanus. *See* Middleton.
Rok, dom. Robertus (monk of D., *c.* 1487–1512/13):
Durham, Cath., A.IV.29 (name). Winchester, Cath., 10 ('liber dom. Ricardi [Rid]dell de empcione a').
*Rome, fr. T., S.T.P. (incepted 1412/13; monk of D., 1383–1425):
Durham, Cath., B.III.6, 22 (cf. Kybbyll). Oxford, Bodleian, Laud Misc. 389. All 'ex procuracione'.
+ *Rowlande, Thomas, 'monachus D.' ('1466'–87):
Oxford, Brasen. Coll. 4 ('liber'; cf. Manby, Harwe).
+ *Roxborth, mag. Johannes (fellow of Univ. Coll.):
Oxford, Brasen. Coll., 4 (caucio, 1481, cf. Bel, Gregfort, Gylyott, Harwe).
*Rypon, (1, 2) dom. Johannes de, (1, 2) 'monachus D.' (1371–1413/14), (2) 'medicus':
Durham, Cath., (1) B.IV.32, fos. 1–49, + B.IV.39B, fos. 1–3 ('ex procuracione'); (2) B.IV.32, fos. 50–145 ('constat——ex propturacione propria'); C.IV.4 ('constat'). Oxford, Bodleian, Laud Misc. 392 (name).
St Calais, William of, bishop of D. († 1096):
Identifiable with his gifts recorded in cat., pp. 117–18:
Cambridge, Peterhouse, 74. Durham, Cath., A.II.4, A.III.29, B.II.2, 6, 9–11, 13, 14, 16, 17, 21, 22, 35, B.III.1, 9–11, 16, B.IV.13, 24. Oxford, Bodleian, Laud Misc. 546. ? Shrewsbury, Shrewsbury Sch., XXI.
Segbrok, Richard de (monk of D., '1353'–96/7):
London, B.L., Arundel 507 (presumed owner).
*Seton, (3, 4) dom., (2) mag., Willelmus, 'monachus D.' (1428–65):
Cambridge, Sid. Sussex Coll., 56, pp. 145–382 (wrote; cf. Bell, Ricardus). (2) Durham Cath., B.II.5 ('liber quondam——assignatus communi librar' D. per Ricardum Bell priorem A.D. 1465'); (3) B.III.29 ('fecit fieri, complete factus A.D. 1438'; *b* (fos. 70–82) 'quod'). (4) Oxford, Bodleian, Tanner 4 ('liber constat dom. Ricardo byllynham ex dono').
*Shyrborn, Ricardus, monachus D. (*fl.* 1441–72):
Durham, Cath., C.IV.22, fos. 141–215ᵛ (wrote, cf. Aukland, Houlla).
Shyrburn, fr. Gilbertus de (? monk of D., *fl. c.* 1255–1300):
Durham, Cath., C.II.2 ('ex dono').
+ Sixt[. .], mag. T:
Durham, Cath., A.III.27 (caucio, 1412, cf. Ebchester, Willelmus).
Sotheron, dom. Robertus. *See* Manbe.
+ Spens, Thomas. *See* Lumly.
+ *Stakhus, Christoforus. *See* Hertilpoll, Stroder.
Stanlawe, dom. Robertus de (? monk of D., *fl.* 1283–1317):
Durham, Cath., C.III.5 ('liber', cf. Wyuistou).
+ *Staplay (? Thomas, monk of D., *c.* 1380–1420/1):
Durham, Cath., A.III.29 (name).
Stiphol (Stiphel), Willelmus de (4, 'Guillermus dictus du—de Britania'):
Durham, Cath., A.I.3 (wrote in 1386; *see* Blaklaw); A.I.4, fos. 1–76ᵛ (name: wrote; cf. Le Berwby). Cambridge, Trin. Coll., 365, fos. 7–37ᵛ

(name: wrote). (4) London, B.L., Burney 310 (wrote in 1381; *see* Boldon).

+ *Stroder, mag. (3) H, (1, 2) Henricus (fellow of Univ. Coll.):
Oxford, Brasen. Coll., 4 (caucio, (1) *with* M Johannis Hull, Christofori Stakhus, 1460; et Hull, (2) 1463, (3) 1[4]64 'luat M H*er*tylpoll', 1468; 1471; 1472. Cf. Hertilpoll; Ebchester, Robertus).

*Strother, dom. Robertus, 'monachus D.' (*fl.* 1490–1521):
York, Minster, VII.G.4 ('liber'). Cf. Downside Abbey, 960 ('Strother' on tail). *See also* Whytehed.

+ Strygete, dom. Willelmus de, 'capellanus':
Oxford, Bodleian, Wood empt. 24 ('liber dom. Johannis de [. . .] ex collacione'. s.xiv/xv; cf. Poklyngton).

+ Sutton, mag. Thomas de:
Durham, Cath., B.II.25 (g.,'pro postil' super lucam', s.xiv).

*Swalwell, dom., (2, 9, 13*b*, 19, 22–4, 27, 31–2) mag. (incepted 1503), Thomas, (1, 3, 10–12, 14, 17, 21, 25, 35, 40) 'monachus D.' (entered *c.* 1483, † *1539*):
(1) Aberystwyth, N.L., bo5 P3 (5F) ('liber——1519 prec' 8 s''). Cambridge, (2) U.L., Kk.5.10 ('assignatur almariolo noviciorum per'); (3) Corpus Christi Coll., EP.S.3 ('liber emptus 1537/8. cf. Wylom). Downside Abbey, 970 (name, price and date 1510), 18274 ('liber——emptus die 11 Januarii 1512'). Durham, Cath., A.II.9 (name); A.IV.8, fos. 79–138 ('per——registro seu usui cancellarii limitatus'); C.I.4 (name); (9) Inc. 3 ('liber dom. Stephani Marley ex dono—A.D. 1537'); (10) Inc. 21b (name); (11) Inc. 45 ('liber——5 s''; cf. Marley, Nicholaus; Whytehed); (12) Inc. 47b ('liber——prec' 6 s' 8d''). (13) Gredington (*a* 'liber', *b* 'liber dom. Stephani Marley ex dono mag. Swalwell A.D. 1526'). London, B.L., (14) Add. 28805 ('liber'); Harley 4725 ('liber emptus per——12 die Junii 1513'); Lincoln's Inn, Hale 114 ('liber'). (17) Los Angeles ('liber'). Toronto (name). Ushaw Coll., (19) XVII.E.4.2 ('liber'); XVII.E.5.4 ('liber ——emptus die 10 Junii 1524 20 d''; cf. Marley, Stephanus); (21) XVII.F.4.1 ('liber'); (22) XVII.G.4.3 ('liber dom. Stephani Marley ex dono—1 die Januarii A.D. 1526'); (23) XVII.G.4.5 ('liber dom. Stephani Marley ex dono—A.D. 1536'); (24) XVIII.A.3.15 ('liber dom. Stephani Marley monachi ex dono—A.D. 1534'); (25) XVIII.B.1.2 ('liber', cf. Manbe); XVIII.B.3.5 (*annotated by*); (27–32) XVIII.B.3.6–11 (6, 10–11: 'liber', 7–9: *annotated by*; cf. Marley, Nicholaus); XVIII.B.4.24 (*annotated by, also* Lee); XVIII.B.6.10 (*annotated by*, cf. Ridley); (35) XVIII.C.2.9 ('liber——et jam datus est dom. Stephano Marley 1534'); XVIII.C.4.11 (*annotated by*); XVIII.C.5.2 ('liber——emptus 1517 prec' iiii s' iiii d''); XVIII.C.5.10 (*annotated by;* cf. Toppyng); XVIII.C.5.15 (*annotated by;* cf. Marley, Stephanus). York, Minster, (40) XI.G.4 ('liber——prec' v s' 4 d' 1510'); XV.A.12 ('liber'). *See also* Byllyngham. Many other books from the monastic collections contain annotations in Swalwell's distinctive hand.

Swan, dom. Willelmus, 'monachus D.' (*fl.* 1512–18):
Ushaw Coll., XVIII.B.4.4 ('liber', cf. Pooll).

*Thew, dom. Henricus, 'monachus D.' (*fl.* 1486–1526):
Durham, U.L., Mickleton & Spearman, 89 ('liber sancti Cuthberti et——').

+ Tode, John (? monk of D., *fl.* 1519–21):
  Oxford, Bodleian, Laud Misc. 277 (named in note, fo. 165).
Tode, dom. Willelmus, 'monachus D.' (? senior, *fl.* 1522–38):
  London, B.L., Harley 4843 (wrote, 1528; cf. Eyrsden).
+ ***Toppyng, mag. Ottwelus:
  Ushaw Coll., XVIII.C.5.10 ('possessor est——teste mag. Hylton precium iiii s''; cf. Swalwell).
***Tutyng, Johannes, 'monachus D.' (1529–39; canon 1541–60. London, Soc. of Antiquaries, MS. 7 and Ushaw Coll., XVII.E.4.3–5, a three-vol. copy of Bersuire's Dictionarium (Nuremberg, 1499), are inscribed 'liber Johannis Tutyng 1541'; his name is on Ushaw Coll., XVII.F.4.7, the first volume of T. Walden's Doctrinale fide (Paris, 1532), and Durham, U.L., S.R.8 A.30, while York, Minster, VIII.F.7 is inscribed 'a prebendario Tuting emit Adamus Halliday', cf. Ridley; X.G.13 'Johannes tutyng 1553', cf. Wylom, and XIII.K.3 'Johannes tutyng 1557'):
  Bristol, Central Public Libr., EPB 353 ('liber precium xiii s'').
Uthred. *See* Boldon.
[*]Wakerfeud, mag. Alanus de (rector of Branxton (Northumb.) 1235):
  Durham, Cath., A.III.14 ('ex dono').
Walworth, Robertus de. *See* Robertus.
+ Wanetinge, fr. Thomas de. *See* Wynterbourne.
+ Ward, mag. [. . .]:
  Durham, C.I.19, fos. 64–127 (caucio, [. . .], s.xiv/xv, cf. Holm).
*Wardell, dom. Robertus, 'monachus D.' (? senior, *fl.* 1456–91; junior, *see* Werdall):
  York, Minster, XVI.I.1 ('liber'; cf. Emylton). *See also* Elwick.
+ Warner, dom. Johannes, (1) 'monachus D.' (1423–78/9):
  (1) Cambridge, Jesus Coll., 61 ('liber——', the second name erased, with 'Hamsterly' in its place; cf. Whytehed). Durham, Cath., A.IV.8, fos. 1–52 ('liber constat dompno Ricardo byllyngham ex dono').
Watson, *see* Wylom.
Werdall (Weyrdal), dom. Robertus, (2, 3) junior (cf. Wardell) 'confrater D.', (1) 'monachus' (*fl.* 1489–1522):
  (1) Cambridge, U.L., Inc. 264+778 ('liber'). (2) Durham, Cath., Inc. 1f, ('assignatus novo armariolo in claustro D. per——A.D. 1513'; cf. Cawthorn, Manbe), (3) 11a ('assignatus . . .', *as* Inc. 1f; cf. Manbe); Inc. 12 ('Wardell', cf. Manbe). Hilversum, Messrs C. de Boer ('liber'). *See also* Cambridge, Jesus Coll., 15 ('Datus novo armarialum in claustro per benivolum confratrem ac commonachum D Ro W').
+ Werkwrth, R. de:
  Plymouth, City Mus., C1/S37/11 (wrote).
+ Wermouthe, dom. Adam de (? subsequently monk of D., *fl. c.* 1325–54):
  Durham, Cath., B.I.5 (Caucio, 1323, 'tradatur alicui monacho dulnemie'). Oxford, Bodleian, Lat. misc.b.13, fo. 51 (caucio, 1323). *See also* Wermouthe, Johannes de.
+ Wermouthe, Johannes de:
  Oxford, Bodleian, Lat. misc.b.13, fo. 51 (caucio, 'et Ade de Eadem, tradatur alicui monacho D.', 1320, 1321, 1322).

*Wessyngton (Wesyngton), dom. Johannes (3) de, (1, 2*a*, 4, 5, 7–10, 13–15) 'prior' (D. 1416–46; professed 1390, †1451):
    (1) Cambridge, U.L., Ff.4.41 ('liber Johannis Hoton monachi ex dono'); (2) Trin. Coll., 8 (*a* 'De communi libraria per', *b* 'liber—— accomodatus Petro Radlee'; cf. Middleton). (3) Durham, Cath., A.III.35 ('assignatus communi armariolo per fr.——'); (4) B.I.14 ('per'); (5) B.I.30 ('assignatus 'communi librarie' per'); B.III.30 ('per——pro parte laborata'); (7) B.IV.26 ('assignatur librarie infra capellam prioris per', cf. Alwerton); (8) B.IV.39 A + B ('assignatur claustro per'); (9) B.IV.43 ('assignatus communi librarie per J W Priorem'); (10) C.I.20 ('ex procuracione', cf. Quitbi); C.III.17 ('liber'). London, B.L., Cotton Claud. D.iv (arms); (13) Harley 3858 ('assignatum communi librarie per'); (14) Lansdowne 397 ('liber'). (15) Oxford, Bodleian, Laud Misc. 262 ('per'); Laud Misc. 748 (autograph ?).

*Westmerland, Robertus, 'monachus D.' (*fl.* 1423–48):
    Durham, Cath., C.III.9 ('liber', cf. Hawtwysell); (2) C.III.11 ('liber— ——quem emit de executoribus mag. Thome Hepden'; cf. Ebchester, Willelmus).

Whelden (Qwelden), dom. Ricardus, 'monachus' (D., d. 1539):
    Ampleforth Abbey, C.V.72 ('liber——emptus A.D. 1513 precium iiii s' 4 d"). Ushaw Coll., XVIII.A.3.12 ('liber——emptus A.Ch. 15[.]3'; cf. Marley, Nicholaus). *See also* Whytehed.

Whitby. *See* Quitbi.

Whorton, Johannes, de Kirkebythore:
    London, B.L., Cotton Titus A.xviii ('liber——ex legacione Johannis Milthorpp auditoris in testimonio suo etc. post obitum ejusdem—— liberetur priori et conventui abbathie D. precepto suo speciali', s. xv).

***Whytehed (except 1), mag. (incepted 1513) Hugo (monk of D., *c.* 1497–1539), (1, 5) 'prior D.' (1519–39; dean, †1551):
    Cambridge, (1) Jesus Coll., 61 ('assignatur almariolo noviciorum per', cf. Warner). Durham, Cath., Inc. 2 ('liber dom. Roberti Strother ex dono'); Inc. 45 ('liber dom. Ricardi Whelden ex dono'; cf. Marley, Nicholaus; Swalwell). Hawkesyard Priory ('liber dom. Christofori Wyllye monachi ex dono——A.D. 1521'). (5) London, B.L., Harley 4664 ('liber dom. Ricardi Crosby monachi ex dono——A.D. 1521'). Oxford, Bodleian, Laud Misc. 359 (name). Ushaw Coll., XVII.G.4. 1–2 ('emptus sumptibus——anno salutis 1513').

Wlton (? Wolviston), fr. Ricardus de (? monk of D., *fl.* 1331–49):
    Durham, Cath., B.III.8 ('ex procuracione').

Wlveston, fr. T. de (monk of D., *fl.* 1274–1300):
    London, B.L., Harley 5234 ('ex dono et labore', *c.* 1284, cf. Mody).

+ Wrake, dom. Johannes (monk of D., *c.* 1495–1515):
    London, Lambeth Pal., 12 (name, cf. Pooll).

+ Wygornia, Johannes de. *See* Haylesburi.

+ Wykingeston, Jon:
    Durham, Cath., A.I.5 (scribe, s. xiv ex.; cf. Langley).

***Wyllye, dom. Christoferus, 'monachus D.' (*c.* 1502–30), (2, 5) S.T.B. (2) 'quondam camerarius' (left office 1524/5):
    Dublin, Trin. Coll., Ff.dd.4,5 ('liber'). (2) Oxford, Bodleian, Auct. 1.Q.5.1 (*a* 'liber'; *b* 'liber dom. Willelmi Brantyngham monachi ex

dono'). Ushaw Coll., XVII.F.4.4 ('liber——emptus anno 1519 precium v s''); XVII.F.4.12 ('liber', cf. Castell, Hawkwell); (5) XVIII.A.3.4–5 (*a* 'liber', *b* 'ex dono——'; cf. Hynton); XVIII.C.3.13(ii) ('liber'). *See also* Whytehed.

***Wylom (Whylom), dom. Willelmus, (2–4, 6, 9) 'monachus D.' (*c.* 1513–39; *as* Watson, canon 1541–56, *see* Cambridge, Corpus Christi Coll., EP.S.3 'liber——quondam monachi D.'):

Cambridge, U.L., Inc. 4163 (*annotated*); (2) Rel. c.50.8 ('liber', cf. Castell; 'Sum nicholai Marley 1560'). Durham, Cath., (3) Inc. 15a ('codex——A.Ch.1536'), (4) 44 ('liber——1534'); D.VI.37 ('liber d.——ex dono mag. Wyllelmi Bennett S.T.P. doctoris et de Fynkhall' Prioris 1536. `nunc autem dom. Nicholai Marley ex dono ejusdem ——qui obiit A.D. 1556 et 18° Septembris''). Ushaw Coll., (6) XVII.F.4.3 ('codex——1515 cuius precium iii s' viij d''); XVIII.B.4.3 (*annotated both items*); XVIII.G.3.10, 11 ('liber'; cf. Lee). (9) York, Minster, X.G.13 ('liber——precium xii d''; cf. Tutyng). *See also* Caly, Ricardus.

+ Wynterbourne, fr. Willelmus de:
Durham, Cath., C.I.1 (caucio, 'et Ricardi Reynbyr, fr. [. . .], Petri Barwe, Willelmi brisconett*es*, Ricardi de Gloucestr', fr. [. . .]ande, fr. Thome de Wanetinge, [. . .] de W[. . .]synton, Petri de W[. .], Willelmi [. .]ammel, Johannis Cadebur, Symonis ate Wynne, Willelmi de [. .]selingham, 1323'; cf. Riple). *See also* Haylesburi.

+ Wynt*er*ton, mag. Robertus de:
Durham, Cath., C.IV.17 (Caucio, 1308; [. . .], '1309 et tradatur——', cf. Pikering, Boldon).

Wyuistou (Wivestou), Thomas de (monk of D., *fl.* 1283–1321):
Durham, Cath., C.III.14 (g., 'MCClxx[. . .]'). See prefatory note to Durham section, 1964 edn., pp. 60–1, sub Thomas de Wyniston, for his purchase of some 25 books listed in Cambridge, Jesus Coll., 57; *also* M. R. Foster, 'Durham Cathedral Priory 1229–1333'. (Cambridge Ph.D. thesis, 1979), pp. 395–402, identifying in the list Durham, Cath., A.III.13, 31; B.I.6, 17, 21 (all annotated by him). *Also annotated:* Durham, Cath., B.IV.41, fos. 41ᵛ–50 (cf. Masham); C.III.5 (cf. Stanlawe); C.III.13, fos. 2–110.

ELY

Norwico: ord. pr. 1341 (Reg. Montacute (Ely) fo. 107ᵛ).
Stewarde: elected prior 1522, still at surrender 1539 (*VCH Cambs.*, ii, 210).

ETON

Borowe: *read* *Bonour, †1467
Elys: *read* *Elyot. Viceprovost, †1499.

EVESHAM

Alcetur: ord. pr. 1513 (*TC* 14.27, p. 263):
+ Aberystwyth, N.L., Peniarth 339 ('constat'). *For* London, Mr Philip Robinson ('constat') *read* Evesham, Almonry Museum ('constat').
Joseph: *read* ***Joseph.

EXETER

Bobych: literate, with a notarial certificate, 1444 (*TCS* 14.62, p. 346).

Brounst: *delete* 1417. *Add* Vicar Choral 1441 (*TCS* 14.63, p. 36), still in 1452 (*TCS* 14.60, p. 125), rector of a moiety in Ermington, 1432 (*TCS* 14.66, p. 29).

+ London, B.L., Harley 1003 ('librarie vicariorum . . . dedit et assignauit volens insuper quod non extra hostium librarie mutuatur nec infra se ipsos cameratim occupetur sed si quis studere voluerit in eodem ibidem sedeat et permaneat donec intencionem ad voluntatem perfecerit').

EYE

Stowe: *delete* monk, fl. 1525. *Add* Monk 1514, sacrist 1526 (*TC* 32.43, pp. 141, 184, 222).

FERRIBY, NORTH

+ **Anlaby, Thomas (donor in 1454):

London, B.L., Cotton Faustina A.ii, fos. 99–175 ('Et pro me – dignare preces fundere. . .': cf. *BRUC*, p. 13).

FOUNTAINS

Cotone: presumably Mag. R. de Cortuna, said to have been archdeacon of Durham, †1255 (*Fasti I*, ii, 39).

+ Hayton, fr. Willelmus:

Untraced (name: Hayton 'of Fountains Abbey' according to sale catalogue).

Kydde: prior at surrender, 1539 (*LP*, xiv (ii), p. 209).

Smythe: *read* *Smythe. Admitted rector of Wath, 1488.

Thyrske: *read* ***Thyrske.

Young: *delete* s.xvi in. At surrender, 1539 (*LP* xiv (ii), p. 209).

GLASTONBURY

Langley: ord. pr. 1461 (*TC* 61.50, pp. 532).

Selwode: abbot 1456–92 (*VCH Somerset*, ii, 99).

Taunton: occurs 1466 (*C. Pap. L.*, xii, 818).

Wylton: occurs 1500 (*TC* 61.54, p. 48).

GLOUCESTER

*Arndell: at Oxford 1498, Gloucester 1510, 1514.

Boure: ord. d. 1375 (*TC* 69.8, p. 342), occurs 1394 (*C. Pap. L.*, iv, 497).

Hortone: cf. Thomas H., occurs 1350 (*C. Pap. L.*, iii, 403).

Malvern: *read* ***Malvern; *for* Hunt *read* Hunter.

Nuton: *read* *Nuton: abbot 1510–14.

Temese: ord. d. 1350 (*TC* 14.8, p. 511).

GUISBOROUGH

Hemmyngburth: occurs 1302, 1308/9 (*TC* 41.138, p. 134, *TC* 41.153, p. 238).

HAILES

Acton: *read* ***Acton *and for* D.D. *read* B.Th.

Bristow, Johannes: occurs 1468 (*C. Pap. L.*, xii, 632).

Coscom: *read* ***Coscom.

Huddleston: cancel the entry.

Urswyck: *read* Wells, Cath., Psalter and Chrysostom (written at expense of and given to Hailes by, A.D. 1516–17 and A.D. 1517–18 in memory of Sir John Huddleston (1512) and his wife Joan).

HARROLD
+ Simon, a priest ('obitus——qui fecit librum').

HATFIELD PEVEREL
Bebseth: prior 1401 (*VCH Essex*, ii, 107).

HAUGHMOND
Corvesar: abbot at surrender, 1539 (*DK Rep. 8*).

HEREFORD
Castyll: occurs 1414–30 (see *BRUO*, p. 368, foot of col. 2).

HEREFORD, *Diocesan Registry*
Bothe: *read* **Bothe.

HEREFORD, *Franciscan convent*
Chalbenor (Chabbenore):
   + London, B.L., Harley 3901 ('dedit fr. W. de la Mare de licencia
     Ministri fr. R. de Denemede ita quod post decessum dicti fr. W. de
     la Mar redeat ad communitatem fratrum H.').

HERTFORD
Nigellus: prior *c*. 1200 (*VCH Herts.*, iv, 421).

HINTON
Fletcher: at surrender, 1539 (*DK Rep. 8*); *for* † at Sheen, 1559 *read*
   apparently † at Sheen before Nov. 1558 (M. E. Thompson, *The
   Carthusian Order in England* (1930), p. 508).

HOLME ST BENETS
Skothole: prior 1532 (Scottowe) (*TC* 32.43, p. 279).

HUNTINGDON
Laurentius: archdeacon 1181 and 1198 (*Fasti I*, iii, 42).

HYDE + ***Bowre, 'baccularius, prior' (Walter B., prior, 1536):
   Chichester, Cath.; Naworth; Oxford, Brasenose Coll., Oriel Coll.;
   York, Minster.

ILCHESTER
Yvelcestria: priest 1322 (Emden, *Dominicans*, p. 492).

KEYNSHAM
Arnolld: occurs 1530 (Chambers, p. 175)

KING'S LANGLEY
Mylys: *read* ***Mylys. . . (prior K. 1522, and of Warwick, Doms., 1519),
   and for Oxford, Blackfriars *read* Cambridge, Fitzwilliam Mus.,
   3–1967.

KIRBY BELLARS
Brokesby: *For* 1427 *read* 1437.
+ Womyndham: in 1534 (*DK Rep. 8*):
   London, Lincoln's Inn, Hale 68 (composed and probably wrote part:
     'finis descripcionis——non ut videt set sicut audivit').

KYME
Streyl: in 1525 (Steille) (*TC* 52.35, p. 177).

LANCASTER, *Dominican convent*
*Urswyck, Christopher:
   + Oxford, Bodleian, Vet. F1.c.90 ('ex dono——quondam Helemo-
     synarii H. 7').

LANGLEY, *Premonstratensian abbey*
+ Dechingham, John, canonicus regularis de Claxton:
Cambridge, Mrs A. Pedley (name). *See also* Rockelande.
+ Rockelande, Sr. Elizbeate de:
Cambridge, Mrs A. Pedley ('Johannes Dechingham de Claxton dedit
. . . Suster————.' *See also* Dechingham.

LANTHONY
+ Jeram, Humfridus, 'canonicus et cellarius' at suppression, 1539 (*LP*,
xiv (i), p. 596):
Durham, Cath., Inc. 58 (name).
Leche
+ London, Lambeth Palace, 137 (recorded as his gift in cat.).
Morganus
+ Cambridge, Corpus Christi Coll., 390 (name).

LEEDS
Eggerton: in 1509 and 1511 (*EHR*, vi (1891), 31; *TC* 59.74, p. 130).

LEICESTER
Charyte: canon s.xv ex, compiler of the library catalogue and registers.

LEICESTER, *Collegiate church*
Becansaw: *read* ***Becansaw.

LEIGHS, LITTLE
+ *Vowell, dom. Ricardus (prior 1510–14: *VCH Essex*, ii, 156).
Untraced (owned).

LEISTON
Galfridus: archdeacon of Norwich 1200, bp. of Ely 1225–8 (*Fasti I*, ii,
p. 64).

LESSNESS
Colman: abbot in 1472 (*VCH Kent*, ii, 167).
Mere: *read* dom. Eudo de M. Perhaps the book was a gift to Stafford,
not Lessness: for the MS see now **STAFFORD**, Aug. convent.
Sandwyco: ord. pr. 1332 (*TC* 14.49, p. 1160).

LEWES
Burghersch: occurs 1403 (*C. Pap. L.*, v, 564).
OK': prior 1397–1409 (*VCH Sussex*, ii, 70).

LICHFIELD, *Franciscan convent*
Bottisham: *read* **Bottisham.

LINCOLN
+ Foxton, John de. (*c.* 1240):
Lincoln Cath., 28, 42, 116, 139 (all in the list of his books in MS 139,
fo. 2ᵛ, printed by R. M. Woolley, *Cat. of the MSS of Lincoln
Cathedral* (Oxford, 1927), p. 98, under name of 'John de Sexton).
+ Hamo: can. and chanc., *c.* 1148–1182: (*Fasti I*, iii, 16):
Lincoln, Cath., 174 (in cat. as his gift).
+ Hugh of Avalon: bp. 1180–1200: (*Fasti I*, iii, 3):
Lincoln, Cath., 107, 147 (both in cat. as his gift).
+ Jordanus: treasurer. *c.* 1147–56 (*Fasti I*, iii, 18–19):
Lincoln, Cath., 171 (in cat. as his gift).

+ Melida, Petrus: can. *c.* 1163–1180 (*Fasti I*, iii, 133–4):
   Lincoln, Cath., 79, 172, 187 (all in cat. as his gift).
+ Radulfus medicus: 1150s–1170 (*Fasti I*, iii, 135–6):
   Lincoln, Cath., 146, 176 (both in cat. as his gift).   ?
Salysbury: *for* 29 *read* 29, fos. 201–22 + MS 136.
+ Samson of Newark: can. *c.* 1132–1189 (*Fasti I*, iii, 144):
   Lincoln, Cath., 80 (in cat. as his gift).
Warsop:
   + Lincoln, Cath., 77 (g).

LINCOLN, *Franciscan convent*
Tatewic: occurs 1300 (Reg. Dalderby (Lincoln), iii, fo. 19ᵛ).

LONDON, *Cathedral church of St Paul*
Cornhell: dean 1234–54 (*Fasti I*, i, 7).

LONDON, *St Mary of Graces*
Langton: still in 1511 (*VCH London*, i, 464).
Wroksam: *read* *Wroksam (Wrixham), †1505.

LONDON, *Charterhouse*
+ Brigarn, Johannes, 'monachus et sacerdos L.':
   Coleraine, Univ. of Ulster Libr.: ('Orate pro anima——per quem hic
   liber adquiritur').
Burgoyn: in 1538 (Chambers, p. 161).
Chawncy: *read* ***Chawncy. *After* exarauit *insert* sanctus.
Rowst: *read* Bakster. *For* Partridge Green, St Hugh's Charterhouse *read*
   Downside Abbey, 48253 (Clifton 12).

LONDON, *Holy Trinity Aldgate*
Pery:
   + San Marino, Huntington Libr., HM112 ('quod——': partly wrote).

LONDON, *St Bartholomew*
Cok, fr. Johannes:
   + London, B.L., Add. 10392 (name; 'scripto a——A.D. 1432'; 'quod
   ——qui scripsit'); Wolfenbüttel, Herzog August Bibl. (He added
   summaries in 1463–4 when aged 68 and 69).
Colyer: occurs 1424 (*Cal. Pap. L.*, vii, 375.
Gray: *read* ***Gray.
+ Wakeryng, mag. Johannes (magister hospitalis): *see* Whyt.
+ Whyt, fr. Johannes, 'quondam magister hospitalis, †15 Jan. 1423':
   Wolfenbüttel, Herzog August Bibl. ('——dedit hanc bibliam mediante
   magistro Johanne Wakeryng successorum suum ad opus ipsius hos-
   pitalis ibidem in perpetuum permansuram').

LONDON, *Franciscan convent*
Kelle: *read* ***Kelle
Man: *read* ***Man.

LONDON, *Dominican convent*
Beauchamp: ord. pr. 1334, D.Th. (Emden, *Dominicans*, p. 275).
Rokesle: ord. d. 1304, occurs 1335 (Emden, *Dominicans*, p. 437).

LONDON, *Augustinian convent*
Andrew: in 1509 (Roth, 'Sources', ii, 395*).
Frere: in 1509 (Roth, 'Sources', ii, 414*).
Tame: ord. d. 1369 (Roth,'Sources' ii, 231*).

LONDON, *St Thomas of Acon*
Jacobus, comes Ormundiae: *for* 1539–46 *read* † 1461.

LYNN, *Franciscan convent*
+ *Fakynham, fr. Nicholas, mag, † 1407:
London, B.L., Add. 47214 ('quaternus fr. Johannis de Medilton de dono——').
+ Medilton, fr. Johannes: see Fakynham.

MALMESBURY
+ Gryfod(?), Johannes, 'monachus M.':
London, B.L., Harley 3140 ('Hunc librum emit frater——pro xiiis iiijd A.D. 1371').

MALVERN, GREAT
+ More,—, 'monachus M.':
Oxford, Bodleian, Bodl. 619 ('Constat More de Mychelmalvarn monoch'').

MARLBOROUGH
Bastabyll: will proved 1502 (P.C.C. 16 Blamyr).

MEAUX
Dapton: *read* Barton *and for* Lowdip de Daynton *read* Lowdir de Baynton.

MEREVALE
Brantyngthorp: ord. subd. 1349 (*TCS* 69.47, p. 341).

MERTON
Ramsey: *read* ***Ramsey.

MONKLAND
+ Monkland, fr. Willelmus de:
Cambridge, Trinity Hall, 4 ('liber———').

MOTTENDEN
Lansyng: ord. pr. 1456 (*TCS* 14.54, p. 364).

MOTTISFONT
Vitriaco: *for* s.xiii *read* fl.1250 (*C. Pap. R.*, i, 261).

NEWARK
Rosse: 1539 (Chambers, p. 170).
Thecher: 1539 (ibid).

NEWCASTLE, *Reclusory*
Lacy: ord. subd. 1397 (Reg. Scrope (Coventry and Lichfield) fo. 157).

NEWNHAM
Henricus, dom., prior: in 1493 (*VCH Beds.*, i, 381).
Renhall: prior 1477 and 1490 (ibid.).

NORWICH
Attleborough: warden of Hoxne, 1492 (Reg. Goldwell (Norwich), fo. 195ᵛ).
Causton: 1285, 1294 (Saunders, p. 193).
Chaumpneys: occurs 1458–63 (Saunders, p. 199).
Donewico: dates from Saunders, pp. 194–5.
Elingham, Johannes: occurs also 1418–22, 1425–27 (Saunders, pp. 197–8).
Elingham, Radulfus de: still cellarer 1285 (Saunders, p. 193).

Elsyngge: also 1379 (Saunders, pp. 196–7).

Fretenham: also until 1280 (Saunders, p. 193).

Hyndringham: also 1413, 1418, 1422 (Saunders, pp. 197–8)

Jernemuth: occurs 1353 (*C. Pap. L.*, iii, 506).

Lakenham: also 1282–3 (*TCS* 54.41, p. 7), prior 1289–1309 (Norwich Cath. Priory Reg. iv, fo. 132).

Morton: 1520, 1532 (*TC* 32.43, pp. 193, 264, 266, 269).

Plumpstede: occurs 1299–1309 (Saunders, p. 194).

Steward: adm. Rector 1471 (Blomefield, iv, p. 51).

Stratton: occurs 1288–1322 (Saunders, pp. 193–4).

Walsham: occurs 1431–7, 1441–52 (Saunders, pp. 198–9).

Wroxham: occurs 1303 (Saunders, p. 194).

NORWICH, *Dominican convent*

+ Bryggs, fr. Thomas, 'conventus N.' (prior N. 1534: Blomefield, ii, p. 725:
   Untraced (i) ('pertinet ad——').

+ Clyffton, domina Johanna de, † 15 Nov. A.D. 1540:
   Wantage, Lord Astor ('———per procuracionem fr. J. Gillyngham contulit').

Doggett: *read* ('possessor teste Manu propria precium iiˢ 1530').
   Occurs 1538 (Emden, *Dominicans*, p. 326).

NOTLEY

Brehyll: in 1487 (*TC* 32.43, p. 255).

+ Hyll, dom. Johannes, 'prior N.':
   Untraced ('emit A.D. 1518').

NOTTINGHAM, *Franciscan convent*

Ryppon: occurs 1539 (Ripton) (Chambers, p. 182).

OSNEY

Abbendune: inscription, now lost, in Magd. Coll., 123, is recorded in W. D. Macray, *A Register of . . . St Mary Magdalen College, Oxford* (1897), ii, 213.

Bloore: at surrender, 1539 (*DK Rep. 8*).

Holbeche: in 1445 (*TC* 32.43, p. 263).

Wrthe: in 1236 (*TC* 59.89, p.x).

OXFORD, *Franciscan convent*

Bryngkeley: *read* **Bryngkeley.

+ **Collys, fr. Edmundus (O. convent in 1525):
   London, Royal Coll. of Physicians ('liber——A.D. 1525').

+ *Kyngton, Dr John, †1536:
   Oxford, Bodleian, Auct. 4.Q.4.9 ('Liber——').

OXFORD, *Convent of Austin friars*

Soppethe: *read* ***Soppethe.

OXFORD, *Balliol College*

+ *Wyrthyngton, Mag. T., vicarius de Schyrburne, †1476:
   Antwerp, Plantin-Moretus Museum, 109 + 343, fos. 1–3 ('legauit ad usum sociorum').

OXFORD, *Canterbury College*

Bockyng: *read* ***Bockyng.

OXFORD, *Exeter College*
*Rede:
+ Oxford, Merton Coll., 224 (recorded as his gift in 1372).

OXFORD, *Lincoln College*
+ *Flemmyng, Robert, dean of Lincoln, †1483:
    Cambridge, St John's Coll., 54; Edinburgh, U.L., 200; London, B.L.,
    Burney 138; Royal 15 C.xv; Oxford, Bodleian, Auct. F.2.25, Queen's
    Coll., 202 (all recorded as his gifts in catalogue).
+ Mabulthorpe, mag. Johannes, † in or after 1471:
    Edinburgh, N.L., Adv. 33.3.1 (wrote and signed with his initials:
    recorded as his gift in catalogue).

OXFORD, *Magdalen College*
Stanbrig: *read* ***Stanbrig.

OXFORD, *Merton College*
+ *Bredon, Simon de, fellow, †1372:
    London, B.L., Harley 625, etc. (wrote part of; bequeathed). Oxford,
    Bodleian, Digby 178 (wrote part of; probably bequeathed).
Giddyng: *read* *Geddyng *and for* 489 *read* 490, no. 15.

OXFORD, *New College*
+ *Holes, mag. Andreas, socius 1414–20, †1470:
    London, Mr N. Barker ('Hic liber collegii [. . . .] magistri——socii').
+ Longolius, Christophorus, †1522:
    Cambridge (U.S.A.), Harvard Coll., Houghton Libr. (signature in).

OXFORD, *Oriel College*
Tumensis: *read* *Cornysh, Thomas, Tinensis (fellow, bp. of Tine 1485,
    †1513).

PETERBOROUGH
Bird: ord. d. 1520 (Reg. Atwater (Lincoln), fo. 132):
    + London, Dulwich Coll., *see* Kirkton; Norwich, St Peter Mancroft
    Church ('liber fr.——monachi').
Clyffe: ord. pr. 1518 (Reg. Atwater (Lincoln), fo. 124ᵛ).
Exton, W., "prior" (?*W.E., prior 1447):
    Oxford, Bodleian, Rawl. C.677 (g).
Gloucester: subd. 1529 (Reg. Longland (Lincoln), i, fo.23ᵛ).
Kirkton: ord. pr. 1473 (Reg. Rotherham (Lincoln), fo. 142):
    + London, Dulwich Coll., A.3.f.3 ('liber fr. Rogeri Byrd ex dono——
    A.D. 1526').
Lecester: ord. pr. 1515 (Reg. Atwater (Lincoln), fo. 116ᵛ).
Natures: ord. d. 1529 (Reg. Longland (Lincoln), i, fo. 23ᵛ).
+ Nouelle, Robertus de (s.xii/xiii):
    Norwich, St Peter Mancroft Church (g). *See also* Bird.
Wodeforde, dom. Willelmus de: abbot 1295 (*TC* 52.43, pp. 131–2).
Wytelese: occurs 1349 (*C. Pap. L.*, iii, 330).

RAMSEY
Keturing: ord. subd. 1343 (Reg. Montacute (Ely), fo. 109ᵛ).
Lyncoln: ord. 1504 (Reg. Smith (Lincoln), ii, fo. 47).
Sentyves: ord. pr. 1504 (Reg. Smith (Lincoln), ii, fo. 44).
Wellis: ord. pr. 1365 (*TC* 14.38, p. 35).
Weston: ord. d. 1504 (Reg. Smith (Lincoln), ii, fo. 43ᵛ).

READING
Chilmark: ord. d.1398 (Reg. Mitford (Sarum), fo. 156^v).
Hendele: in 1403 (Henle) (*C. Pap. L.*, v, 550).
Staunton: in 1415 (*C. Pap. L.*, vi, 357).
Wokyngham: ord. subd. 1398 (Reg. Mitford (Sarum), fo. 156).

RIEVAULX
+ Gyllyng, Richardus, 'mon. R.': (in 1538: Chambers, p. 156):
  London, B.L., Add.63077 (name).

ROBERTSBRIDGE
Wodecherche:
  + Aberystwyth, N.L., 13210D ('scripsit').

ROCHESTER
A., 'prior': possibly Alex. de Glanville, 1242–52 (Fielding, p. 410).
A., 'vicarius de Stoke': possibly Adam de Sevenoke, 1349, vac. 1367
  (Fielding, p. 264).
Bambrogh: *read* **Bambrogh, 'Vicarius de Malling' (1517–24).
  + *Untraced* (Leighton).
Bradewell: rector of Shoreham, Kent, 1355 till death, 1383 (Fielding,
  pp. 255, 341).
Bruyn: possibly Thos. Brown, subprior 1400, vac. 1412 (London, B.L.,
  Cotton Faustina C.v, fos. 103^v, 123^v).
Cranebroke: in *c.* 1391 (ibid. fos. 50, 50^v).
Gelham: occurs 1323, 1329, 1339 (*TC* 14.49, pp. 122, 241, 510, 533).
Horstede: in *c.* 1391 (London, B.L., Cotton Faustina C.v, fos. 50, 50^v).
Mallinges: in 1384 (ibid., fo. 21).
Sotton: occurs 1409, 1412 (ibid., fos. 121^v, 129).

ST ALBANS
+ Blakeney, Robert: prior of Tynemouth at surrender, 1538 (Chambers,
  p. 122):
  Cambridge, U.L., Ee.4.20 (name).
Chenley: *read* Shenley.
Huswyff: *read* *Huswyff.
Kyrkeby: precentor in 1492 (*TC* 33.45, p. 233).
La Mare: in 1349–96 (*VCH Herts.*, iv, 415).
Ware: ord. acol. 1394 (Reg. Fordham (Ely), fo. 233).
Whethamstede, John:
  + London, B.L., Add.26764; Cotton Nero C.vi; Cotton Tib. D.v, pt.1
    (all contain marginalia in hand of; also Cotton Claud D.i).
Wylum: ord. pr. 1376 (Reg. Arundel (Ely), fo. 118^v).

ST OSYTH
Busshe: at surrender, 1539 (*DK Rep. 8*).
Joly: at surrender, 1539 (*DK Rep. 8*).

SALISBURY
Fadir: rector of St. Sampson, Cricklade, Wilts, adm. 1430 (T. Phillipps,
  Institutiones clericorum in comitatu Wiltoniae (Middle Hill, 1825),
  p. 120); vicar of Larkstoke, Wilts., adm. 1433, vac. 1435 (ibid.,
  pp. 124, 126).

Fydyon: canon of S. and preb. of Lyme and Halstock, 1456, etc., †1474
(*Fasti II*, iii, 65, 45):
+ London, B.L., Harley 3237 ('ex dono magistri——canonici ecclesie
cath. Sarum').
+ *Hegham, Radulphus de, 'cancellarius S.' (*c.* 1241–*c.* 1271):
See **SALISBURY**, *Franciscan convent*, Wudeston.
La Wyle: *cancel* Oxford. . .(legauit). (La Wyle's 'legauit' is on a flyleaf of
Oxford, Bodleian, Bodl. 516, but that leaf did not originally belong to
the MS.)

SALISBURY, *Franciscan convent*
*Wudeston: transfer to here the entry under **SALISBURY**, *Dominican
convent*.

SALISBURY, *Dominican convent*
+ *Dogood, mag. Johannes, †1501:
London, Dr C. F. R. de Hamel ('ex dono——').
Heskynus: in 1538 (Chambers, p. 167).
*Wudeston: transfer the entry to **SALISBURY**, Franciscan convent.

+ SCARBOROUGH, *Dominican convent*
Hardyng, fr. Roland, 'prior S.' (occurs Stamford, 1511, Newcastle 1539
(Emden, *Dominicans*, p. 356), friar at Scarborough, 1537 (*LP*, xii (i),
p. 464):
Cambridge, U.L., Rel.d.5l.15 (name).

SELBY
Roucliffe: in 1411 or 1426 (*TC* 33.45, p. 228).

SEMPRINGHAM
Cancel all after entry for Glynton in 1964 edn. and transfer to **SHAFTES-
BURY**.

SHAFTESBURY
Insert under this title Awdeley, Champnys and Horder, listed under
SEMPRINGHAM in 1964 edn.
+ Mouresleygh, domina Johanne (nun in 1441 and 1460: J. Hutchins,
History and Antiquities of Dorset, 3rd edn. iii (1868), 30):
Cambridge, U.L., Ii.vi.40 ('constat———').

SHEEN
Bromley: in 1539 (Chambers, p. 195).
Chaffer: in 1539 (Chambers, p. 195).
+ Craneburne, – :
Douai, 396 ('Fratri sacriste venerando traditur liber iste cum gaudio
quod—Anno regni regis Edwardi iiii^{ti} xxj^{o}'). Omitted in error from
this list in 1964 edn., q.v, however, under **SHEEN**, for Douai, 396.
Grenehalgh: *for* Sheen *read* Hull.
Mede: ord. acol. 1417 (*TC* 14.47, p. 322).

SOUTHAMPTON, *Franciscan convent*
Kingestone: in 1318 (*TC* 43.8, p. 85).

SOUTH MALLING
+ Brent, Thomas, 'decani ecclesie. . .' †1515 (*VCH Sussex*, ii, 119):
    Norway, Mr M. Schøyen, ('Liber magistri——decani ecclesie collegialis
    sancti michaelis de suth mallyng Quem contulit eidem thome magister
    Johannes Sterr ultimo die mensis marcii A.D. MCCC lxxxxij'. For
    Sterr cf. *BRUC*.)

SOUTHWARK
+ Gower, John, †1408:
    London, B.L., Add. 59855 (probably bequeathed).
Lecchelade: ord. pr. 1306 (*TC* 14.44, p. 788).
Lichefelde: cf. Richard L., D.Cn. & C.L., †1497 (*BRUO*, pp. 1144–5).

SOUTHWELL
Couton: occurs 1295, 1309, 1314, 1315 (*TC* 41.123, p. 342; *TC* 41.138,
    p. 224; *TC* 41.145, p. 315; *TC* 41.152, p. 379; *TC* 41.153, p. 341).

SOUTHWICK
Kateryngton: ord. pr. 1399 (*TC* 43.11, ii, p. 349).

STAFFORD, *Augustinian convent*
+ Eudo de Mere, dom. (s.xii ex):
    Cambridge, Trinity Coll., 1236 ('fecit scribi et dedit domui beati
    Thome martyris') (under **LESSNESS** in 1964 edn.).

STAMFORD, *Carmelite convent*
Heulla: *read* Houlla.

STRATFORD LANGTHORNE
Huddylstone: in 1538 (*DK Rep. 8*).
Meryot: in 1538 (*DK Rep. 8*).

SUDBURY, *Dominican convent*
Stok': *read* fr. Johannes de, 'rector ecclesiarum de Twyford et Hunede'
    (collated to Twyford 1241: G. Lipscomb, *The History and Antiquities
    of the County of Buckingham* (1847), iii, 133):
    London, Gray's Inn, 20 ('contulerat. . . A.D. 1257', with an anathema
    against alienators 'salvo tamen Johanni de Hundene sacerdoti. . .si
    velit usum dicti libri'. Later at **MELBOURNE**, *Ch*.

SWINE
Wade: in 1483 (*TCS* 14.69, p. 30).

SYON
+ Coderington, Dorothea: in 1539 (*LP*, xiv (ii), p. 206):
    Ampleforth Abbey, C.V.130 (name).
+ **Fewterer, John (at Syon 1513–35, †1536):
    Durham, Dr A. I. Doyle, *Sermones Bernardini* (name *on label and*
    'ad——attinet liber iste').
+ Tressham, Clemence: in 1539 (*LP*, xiv (ii), p. 206):
    Durham, U.L., Cosin V.v.12 (name); Durham, Dr A. I. Doyle, T. à
    Kempis (name and, below, 'yn Syon').
**Westhaw:
    + London, B.L., Harley 1298 (recorded as his gift in cat.).

TARRANT KEYNSTON
Corf: *for* Redlynch, Major J. R. Abbey *read* Stockholm, National
    Museum.

TEWKESBURY
Evesham: ord. d. 1461 (Reg. Carpenter (Worcester), i).

THAME
Forrest: *read* ***Forrest.

THETFORD, *nunnery*
Methwold: occurs 1492, 1514 (*TC* 32.43, p. 91).

THORNHOLM
For Bodl. 565 *read* Bodl. 655.

THORNTON
Forsett: in 1440 (*TC* 52.21, p. 376).

THURGARTON
+ Darby, Henricus, 'canonicus T.':
  Washington, DC (USA), Libr. of Congress, Incun. X.5.7 ('pertinet ad').

TITCHFIELD
Oke: Thomas Coyk is recorded as abbot, without date (s.xiv ex or xv in) in *VCH Hants*, ii, 186.

TYNEMOUTH
Westwyk: ord. d.1370 (Reg. Hatfield (Durham), fo. 109).

WALSINGHAM
*Vowell, dom. Ricardus:
  + *Untraced* (owned).

WALSINGHAM, *Franciscan convent*
Wynbotisham: of Cambridge convent in 1347 (Moorman, p. 224).

WALTHAM
Petrus: archdeacon of London before Dec. 1192 to March 1194 (*Fasti I*, i, 9–10).

WARWICK, *Dominican convent*
Alexander: in 1539 (Chambers, p. 179).
+ ***Mylys, Robert, 'prior W.', in 1519; prior of King's Langley in 1522:
  Cambridge, Fitzwilliam Mus., 3–1967 ('fieri fecit anno Christi 1523).
Norman: in 1538 (Chambers, p. 179).
  + Cambridge, Fitzwilliam Mus., 3–1967 (name).

WENLOCK
Bruge: *read* Brugge:
  + Cambridge, St Catharine's Coll. (name).
+ Wollaston, Hugo de:
  Oxford, Bodleian, Bodl. 921 (name).

WESTMINSTER
For the monks see E. H. Pearce, *The Monks of Westminster* (Cambridge, 1916).
+ ***Cheysman, Robertus, 'monachus W.':
  London, Jesuit House (liber).
+ Emsun, Richardus, 'monachus W.' (*fl.* 1530: Pearce, p. 189):
  London, B.L., K.8.k.8 ('——est custos huius libri').
Felix, John: in 1525/6 (Peatrce, p. 188).

+ Braynt, fr. Johannes: occurs 1373, †1418 (Pearce, p. 114):
  London, Society of Antiquaries, 136C ('ex procuracione').
+ [. . .], dom., 'monachus W.':
  London, B.L., Royal 10 A.xvii ('ex procuracione——A.D. 1477').
+ [. . .], Johannes, 'monachus W.':
  London, B.L., K.8.k.8 ('——est custos huius libri').

WESTMINSTER, *Collegiate church of St Stephen*
+ Morland, William, canon of St S. 1470–76, etc., †1492 (*Fasti II*, iii, 31, *II*, v, 34):
  London, B.L., Add. 63787.

WETHERALL
Hartley: in 1538 (Chambers, p. 157).

WHALLEY
Lindelay: occurs 1354 (*C. Pap. L.*, iii, 534).

WHITBY
+ Colson(?), dom. Willelmus, 'monachus W.':
  Paris, B.N., lat. 7410 ('per manus——').

WINCHCOMBE
Augustinus: ord. pr. 1512 (Reg. Gigli (Worcester), fo. 161).
Benedictus: ord. d. 1514 (ibid., fo. 167^v).
Benet: ord. d. 1503 (ibid., fo. 209^v).

WINCHESTER
Avyngton: *read* ***Avyngton. Subprior 1528–39.
Basynge: *read* ***Basynge.
+ Brynstane: John B. (sacrist W., ord. d. 1520): *see* Buryton.
+ Buryton, Johannes, 'monacus W.' (sacrist W., 1536–7: *TC* 43.7, pp. 106, 201).
  London, B.L., Add. 60577 (name *and* 'y bowthe hym of brynstane cost me 3^s 4^d').
Cramborne: in 1392 (*TC* 43.7, p. 165).
+ Manwode, William: ord. subd. 1484 (*TC* 43.7, p. 478):
  Oxford, Bodleian, Digby 31 (name).
Morton: ord.d. 1499 (*TC* 43.7, p. 479).
Sylksted: occurs 1471–2, 1524 (*TC* 43.7, p. 105; *VCH Hants.*, ii, 115).
Tarente: in 1308 (*TC* 43.7, p. 98).

WOBURN
Hobs: in 1529 (*VCH Beds.*, i, 370).

WORCESTER
Clemens: *read* Clement *de Hertford*, 'quondam rector ecclesie de Chaddesleye' [Corbett] (in 1303); †by Feb. 1306 (*TC* 69.22, pp. 76, 147).
Cliva: occurs 1411 (*C. Pap. L.* vi, 275), 1428 (ibid., viii, 54), 1340 (ibid. viii, 185).
Dikklesdon: in 1308 (Ducleston) (*TC* 69.39, p. 2).
Fouke: in 1339 (*TC* 69.8, p. 269).
Gloucester: in 1373 (ibid., p. 290).
Hambory: in 1374 and 1401 (ibid., pp. 304, 372).
Hatfield: in 1373, 1395, 1401, 1407, 1419 (ibid., *passim*):
  + Birmingham, U.L., 11/v/10 ('Iste liber est——').
Kelminton: *read* *Kelminton.

Meldenham: ord. d. 1481 (*TC* 14.26, p. 163).
Mor': occurs 1373, 1374, 1401 (*TC* 69.8, pp. 290, 322, 373).
More: *read* *More.
Seggesberwe: †1401 (ibid., p. 42).
Temedelyn (Temedebur, Teimebur, Teinedebiry): in 1364, 1350 (ibid., pp. 220–1: *C. Pap. L.*, iii, 380).
Webley, dom. Humfridus: *read* ***Webley.
Webley, Johannes: ord. subd. 1490 (Reg. Morton (Worcester)).
Westbury: in 1339 (*TC* 69.8, pp. 259, 466).
Wyke: in 1305 (*TC* 69.39, pp. 2, 58, 92), 'ultimus prior' in 1317 (*TC* 69.40, p. 2).

WORCESTER, *Franciscan convent*
Joseph: *read* ***Joseph, Johannes, O.F.M., W. (Warden 1533).

WORCESTER, *Dominican convent*
Prechett: *read* ***Prechett, fr. Thomas, O.P., W. (Oxford convent in 1508 and 1509).
Toroldus: in 1528 (C. F. R. Palmer, *The Reliquary*, xx (1879–80), 28.

WORKSOP
Philippus: cf. Philip, canon of Lincoln 1178/80, † soon after 1186 (*Fasti I*, iii, 134).

YORK
**Neuton:
  + York, Minster, XVI.P.5–XVI.P.8 (all recorded as of his bequest).
+ **Scheffeld (Cheffeld), Mag. William:
    Ampleforth Coll., C.V.65–66 ('. . .fuit——olim ecclesie Cathedralis Sancti Petri Ebor decani et ex dono magistri Roberti appilgarth dudum executoris dicti magistri ex procuracione istorum fratrum scilicet ricardi gosberkirk, Iohannis robynson AD M° quincentessimo tercio [66: Cheffeld, gosberkirke]').

YORK, *Ben. abbey of St Mary*
Arrows: ord. subd. 1509 (Reg. Bainbridge (York), fos. 104ᵛ, 106).
+ Braystanes, fr. Christophorus, 'commonachus' (cf. **BEAUVALE**, 1964 edn.).
    Lincoln, Cath., 228 ('Liber monasterii [. . . .] Claustr[. .] eiusdem ordinis [. . .] ex dono fratris——commonachi . . . eiusdem').
Brudford: *read* *Brudford (*BRUO*, p. 264, Bridford).
Staveley:
  + Edinburgh, N.L., H.24.f.10 ('acquisitus per dom.——baccalarium monasterii E.'; Deventer: now Urbana, Illinois (*and for* owned *read* acquisitus per).
Wellys: *read* *Wellys.

113

APPENDIX

Donors and other persons concerned with books formerly owned by parish churches and chapels

+ **BERWICK-ON-TWEED**
[. . .], Robert, of the Citie of London:
  Ampleforth Abbey, C.V.221 (gave in 1526 or 1527).

CRICH
Bankes: *read* ***Bankes.

+ **HALSALL,** Lancashire
Askew, Thomas, priest:
  Boston (U.S.A.), Public Libr. ('William Welding borowed this boke of Sir——prest to be delyvered agayne. . .to halsall chirch').
Halsall, Sir Henry:
  Boston (U.S.A.), Public Libr. ('———Knight dyd geve. . .to halsall chirch').

HEADCORN
+ Camyl, Willelmus (first chaplain of chantry at St Mary's altar founded by *Robert and *Thomas Kent, instituted 1467: *TC* 14.54, p. 288). *See* Cleve.
+ *Cleve, Willelmus, nuper rector de Clive (Cliffe-at-Hoo, Kent, † by Dec. 1470):
  Oxford, Bodleian, Bodl. 110 ('contulit——dom. Willelmo Camyl huius cantarie capellano et successoribus suis perpetuis').

LONDON, St Sepulchre, Holborn
Lorde, mag. Johannes, 'Curie Cantuarie procurator generalis et Ursula uxor ejus.'
  London, B.L., Harley 2942 ('Orate pro animabus——et—, Simonis Briggeman, Marione uxoris ejus et omnium benefactorum eorundem cum quorum bonis iste liber conparatus fuit et datus huic ecclesie per media Willelmi Taylard').

PENWORTHAM
For Bournemouth, A. G. Thomas *read* London, B.L., Add. 52359.

Glossary of Words Used in References to Books and Ownership recorded on pp. 76–114 above, and in Addenda and Corrigenda to 1964 edition, pp. 326–31. Entries marked § refer to entries on pp. 76–114 above, the others to 1964 edition.

accipere. *Add* §**CAMBRIDGE**, *Aug. friars*, Stokton.

accomodare. *Cancel* **SALISBURY**, Wudeston. *For* **SALISBURY**, *Dom. conv., Coppere read* **SALISBURY**, *Dom. conv.*, Wudeston.

acquirere. E.g. §**LONDON**, *Charterhouse*, Brigarn; §**YORK**, *St Mary*, Staveley.

armariolum. *Add* §**DURHAM**, Appylby.

afferre. *For* **LONDON**, *Charterhouse*, Rowst *read* **LONDON**, *Charterhouse*, Bakster.

assignare. *Before* Snetesham *add* Brounst.

attinere. *Before* Sellyng *add* Coptun. *Add* §**SYON**, Fewterer.

cameratim. *Add* §**EXETER**, *Vicars Choral*, Brounst.

cautio. *For* implegiare *read* impignorare. *Add* §**CAMBRIDGE**, *Aug. friars*, Johannes de [. . .], Ludham; §**DURHAM**, Clowtessham, R. de Dunelm, Graystanes, R. de and T. de, Gregfort, Gyllyott and many others.

confirmare. *Add* **CANTERBURY**, *Fran. conv.*, Hertepol.

custos. *Add* §**WESTMINSTER**. Johannes [. . .], Emsun.

deliberare. *Add* **EXETER**, Gybbys; §**BURTON-UPON-TRENT**, Bate.

emere. (4) *Add* at London, see §**DORE**, Redborn.

expensum. *Add* §**BURY**, Wesingham.

exponere. *Add* §**DURHAM**, Beverlaco.

gaudium. *Add to last sentence* Cambridge, St John's Coll., 147; B.L., Roy. 12 B.iii (fo. 166^v), Manchester, Rylands Eng. 85; Oxford, Magd. Coll., lat. 162.

instancia. *Add* §**BURTON-UPON-TRENT**, Bate.

licentia. *For* **LONDON**, *Charterhouse*, Rowst *read* **LONDON**, *Charterhouse*, Bakster. *Add* §**HEREFORD**, *Fran. conv.*, Chabbenore.

ligare, colligare. *Add* §**CHICHESTER**; §**DURHAM**, Masham.

manus. *Add* (7) *accomodatus per manus* §**WHITBY**, Colson.

memoriale. Other examples of 'memoriale. . .pro' are Oxford, Bodleian, Bodl.156, Laud Misc. 209, Balliol Coll., 317, Merton Coll., 55.

mutuare. *Add* §**EXETER**, *Vicars Choral*, Brounst.

occupare. *Add* §**EXETER**, *Vicars Choral*, Brounst.

opus. *Add* §**LONDON**, *St Bartholomew*, Whyt.

pertinere. *Add* §**NORWICH**, *Dom. conv.*, Bryggs.

pignus. *Add* §**CAMBRIDGE**, *Aug. friars*, Stokton.

procurare. *Add* §**DURHAM**, Alwerton, Appylby, Beverlaco, Graystanes, R.; §**NORWICH**, *Dom.conv.*, Clyffton; §**WESTMINSTER**, Braynt; §**YORK**, Scheffeld.

quaternus. *read* §**LYNN**, Fakynham; *in quaterno* **ST ALBANS**, Ware.

recompensatio (recompensio). *Add* §**DURHAM**, Byllingham.

redimere. *Add* **BURY**, Swaffham.

redire. *Add* §**HEREFORD**, *Fran. conv.*, Chabbenore.

restituere. *Add* §**CANTERBURY**, Permisted.

studere. *Add* §**EXETER**, *Vicars Choral*, Brounst.

sumptus. *Add* §**BURY**, Wesingham; §**DURHAM**, Caly.

supplementum. An additional pledge: §**CAMBRIDGE**, *Aug. friars*, Ludham.

tradere. *Add* §**DURHAM**, Banastre: §**SHEEN**, Craneburne.

INDEX OF MANUSCRIPTS

Manuscripts listed in the 1964 edition which are the subject of corrections in this Supplement are not usually indexed, being already traceable in the 1964 index. Changes in the location and/or ownership of a manuscript recorded on pp. 1–74 above are, however, indexed, as are reattributions from one medieval owner to another (e.g. B.L., MS. Harley 603), and renumberings of manuscripts within the same repository (e.g. Manchester, John Rylands University Libr., MS Lat. 179 changed to Eng. 109). All 'rejected' manuscripts listed for the first time are indexed, as are all manuscripts listed in the 1964 edition which are now listed as 'rejected' for the first time. Since the Durham section on pp. 16–34 above has been completely revised all Durham manuscripts have been indexed, either individually or, as under Durham and Ushaw, as the total number of Durham manuscripts in the collection recorded on pp. 18–28.

As in the 1964 edition, in index references to the main list a place-name without further specification refers to the first entry under each place-name in the list: thus *London* stands for St Paul's, London, *Colchester* for St John's, Colchester. A † indicates a 'rejected' ascription. References to the Appendix of books from parish churches, etc. are indicated by *Ch.* following the place-name.

ABBEY   *cancel*

ABERDEEN
Univ. Libr.
  7   *read* †London
  11   *read* †London
  Forbes of Boyndlie   Durham

ABERFORD   *cancel*

ABERYSTWYTH, *Dyfed*
Nat. Libr. of Wales
  +735C   Ely (see above,
                 p. 35 n.1)
  +9852C   Beverley
  +13210D   Robertsbridge
  17520   *for* Caernarvon, *Ch.*
        read Llanbeblig, *Ch.*
  +21878E   Norwich (formerly
                untraced)
  +22253A   Lanteglos, *Ch.*
  +Llanstephan 176   Hyde
  +Peniarth 20   Valle Crucis
  +   28   Canterbury,
                St Aug.
  +   162(i) Honiton, *Ch.*
  +   339   Evesham
  +   356   Basingwerk
  + Porkington 19
             †Mount Grace

ALLISON   *cancel*

ALNWICK CASTLE, *Northumb.*
Duke of Northumberland
  The Sherborne MS. is now
    London, B.L., Loan 82.

ANTWERP, *Belgium*
Museum Plantin-Moretus
  +M.55 (341) Oxford, All Souls
  +M.183 (109) Oxford, Balliol
  +   (343) Oxford, Balliol

ASTOR, Lord *see* **WANTAGE**

BALTIMORE, *U.S.A., Maryland*
Johns Hopkins Univ. Libr.
  +W.15 †Oxford, St Frideswide

BARKER, Mr N. J. *see*
  LONDON

BATH, Marquess of *see*
  LONGLEAT

BEAUMONT COLLEGE, *Berks.*
               cancel

BELCHAMP HALL, *Essex*
               cancel

BELVOIR CASTLE, *Leics.*
Duke of Rutland
  The Reading MS. is now Lon-
    don, B.L., Add. 62925

BERINGTON, Mr T. M. *see*
  MALVERN, LITTLE

BERLIN (WEST), *Germany*
STAATSBIBL.: *now* Staatsbibliothek
der Stiftung Preussischer Kulturbesitz. *Cancel footnotes, 1964*
edn., p. 333.

BIRDSALL HOUSE, *Yorks.*
LORD MIDDLETON
The Durham MS. is now de-
posited in Nottingham Univ.
Libr., Middleton MS. L.M.5

BIRMINGHAM
UNIV. LIBR.
+11/v/10   Worcester
                Launceston
(deposited by Mr T. M.
Berington, Little Malvern)

BLACKBURN *read* Art Gallery
and Museum

BODMER, Dr M. *see*
COLOGNY-GENÈVE

BRADFER-LAWRENCE *cancel*

BRINKLEY   *cancel*

BRISTOL
BAPTIST COLL.
Z.c.23   *cancel*
Z.d.5   *cancel*
Z.e.38   *cancel*
BRISTOL RECORD OFFICE
—   Bristol Corporation
CENTRAL PUBLIC LIBR. (omitted
              from 1964 index)
2   Bristol
3   Bristol, Fran.
5   Glastonbury
6   Bristol, Hosp. of St Mark
12   Kingswood

BRUDENELL   *cancel*

BRUSSELS, *Belgium*
BIBL. ROYALE
+1103 (444–52)
        Canterbury, St Aug.
IV.328   Norwich (formerly
           London, Maggs)
+IV.481   Syon (formerly
          untraced: London,
           Maggs, 1935)
IV.1008   †Bury (formerly
         Bury St Edmunds,
              Cath., 3)

BURNETT-BROWN, Mr A. S.
  see **LACOCK ABBEY**

BURY ST EDMUNDS
GRAMMAR SCHOOL
now   deposited   Bury   St
Edmunds, West Suffolk Record
                    Office
ST JAMES'S CATH.
1, 3, 4   *cancel*
WEST SUFFOLK RECORD OFFICE
E 5/9/408.7   Bury (formerly
          Bury St Edmunds,
            Grammar Sch.)
+A 8/1   Bury

BUTE, MARQUESS OF *cancel*
BUTLER-BOWDON, Capt. M.
  see **MAYFIELD**

CAMBRIDGE
UNIV. LIBR.
+Add. 2602   Springfield, *Ch.*
+   3060   Northampton,
                St Andrew
     3303   Durham
+   4406 pt. 1   Bury
+   7634   Syon
+   8333 Bedwyn, Gt., *Ch.*
+   8335   Denny
+Dd.1.17   Glastonbury
+Dd.9.5   †Kirkham
+Ee.4.20   St Albans,
               Tynemouth
+Ff.3.10   Canterbury
Ff.4.41   Durham
+Ff.6.18   Syon
+Ff.6.33   Syon
Gg.3.28   Durham
Gg.4.33   Durham
+Hh.1.10   Exeter
+Ii.3.20   Malmesbury
+Ii.6.40   Shaftesbury
Kk.1.24   *read* †Ely
Kk.5.10   Durham
+Kk.5.34   Hyde
             Glastonbury
+Kk.6.45   Tynemouth
+Mm.2.8   Belvoir
+Mm.2.9   Barnwell
Mm.3.14   Durham
+Mm.6.17   Evesham
EDC 1   Ely (deposited
   by Dean & Chapter of Ely

TRINITY COLL. (*contd*)
 1227 (0.3.55) Durham
 +1270 (0.3.40) Rotherham
 1369 (0.7.41)   *read*
   Colchester, †Snape
TRINITY HALL
 +4   Monkland
DR S. KEYNES, TRINITY COLL.
 — Glastonbury (formerly
  Brinkley, Sir G. Keynes)

CAMBRIDGE, *U.S.A., Mass.*
HARVARD LAW SCH.
 25 *read* †Letheringham
 64   *read* †Reading

CANTERBURY
CATH. LIBR.
 +Lit. B.1 (73) Canterbury
 +Plumptre Deposit Morley,
  Ch. (deposited by
  Mr J. H. Plumptre,
  Nonington)
 s.n. (Epp. Pauli glo.)
  Canterbury, St Aug.
  (formerly Redlynch,
  Major J. R. Abbey)
 Box ABC *read* Add. 128
 Box CCC, no. 19a *read*
   Add. 20, no. 19a
 Box CCC, no. 23 *read*
   Add. 127/15
 p. 346 cols. 1, 2
  before A, B, C, D, E
   add Lit.

CAPE TOWN, *South Africa*
for UNIV. LIBR. *read*
  SOUTH AFRICAN LIBR.

CASHEL, *Republic of Ireland*
DIOCESAN LIBR.
 +2   Darley
CHANDLERS CROSS *cancel*

CHAPEL HILL, *U.S.A.,*
 N. Carolina
UNIV. OF NORTH CAROLINA LIBR.
 +522   Thetford

CHICAGO, *U.S.A., Illinois*
NEWBERRY LIBR.
 +33.1 Cambridge, King's Hall

CLAREMONT, *U.S.A.,*
 California

CLAREMONT COLLEGES
 +Honnold Libr., Crispin 5
     Sheen
COLCHESTER *cancel*
COLOGNE, *Germany*
SCHNÜTGEN MUSEUM
 M694 Markyate, St Albans
  (formerly Sürth bei Köln,
   Dr J. Lückger)
COLOGNY-GENÈVE,
 Switzerland
FONDATION MARTIN BODMER
 +Bibl. Bodmeriana 11
   Canterbury, St Aug.
 Cancel reference to Salisbury
 MS., now in Tokyo (see above,
      p. 61)

COLUMBIA, *U.S.A., Missouri*
UNIV. OF MISSOURI LIBR.
 +Rare-L/PA/3381.A1/F7, no.14
      Bury

COX, Mr J. S. *see* **ST PETER'S
 PORT**

DAVIS   *cancel*
DEENE PARK   *cancel*
DENT-BROCKLEHURST
      cancel

DOUAI, *France*
BIBL. MUN.
 +171 (14)   †Bury
DOWNSIDE ABBEY, *Stratton-
 on-the-Fosse, Som.*
 48253 (Clifton 12) London,
  Carth. (formerly
  Partridge Green)

DRAYTON   *cancel*
DUBLIN, *Republic of Ireland*
CHESTER BEATTY LIBR.
 W.26, W.27, W.34, W.45
      cancel
TRINITY COLL.
 +A.4.20 (50) Llanbadarn-Fawr
 +B.10.12(223) Dereham, West
 C.5.15 (349) Durham
 D.4.26 (440) Durham
 +E.2.33 (500) London,
   St John of Jerusalem
 +E.4.23 (507) Margam
 +E.5.10 (516) Jervaulx

GENEVA see
COLOGNY-GENÈVE

GLASGOW
Mitchell Libr.
+308876 Newbattle (formerly
untraced, Sir J. Home-
Purves-Hume-Campbell,
in 1913)
Univ. Libr.
BD.19.h.9   *read* Euing 26
BE.7.b.8   *read* Gen. 333
BE.7.e.24   *read* Gen. 335
BE.8.y.7   *read* Gen. 1126
p. 350 col. 2   *for* Hunterian
                   read Hunterian
                   Museum Libr.
(kept in the Univ. Libr.)
+Hunterian S.1.7 (7)   †Bury
T.4.2 (85) Durham

GLOUCESTER
Cath. Libr.
+ 1   Leominster
+36/4   Tewkesbury

GORDAN now **NEW YORK**,
Mrs P. G. Gordan

GORDON now Miss J. Gordon:
see **EDINBURGH**

GORHAMBURY
Earl of Verulam
+—   St Albans (deposited in
Hertford, Herts.
Record Office)

GUILDFORD
Mrs F. E. O'Donnell
—   Southwark (omitted from
1964 index: now London,
B.L., Add. 63592)

HARLECH, Lord see
TALSARNAU

HARVARD UNIVERSITY see
CAMBRIDGE, *U.S.A., Mass.*

HASSON   *cancel*

HAVRE (LE), *France, Seine-Mer*
Bibl. Municipale
330   *read* Hyde; †Winchester

HELMINGHAM HALL, *Suff.*
Lord Tollemache
2, 3, 6, 49, 72   *cancel*

HEREFORD
Cath. Libr.
+O.vi.8   †Bury

HERTFORD
Herts. Record Office
Gorhambury XD4/B,C
St Albans (deposited by
Earl of Verulam)

HOLKHAM HALL, *Norf.*
Earl of Leicester
39   *cancel*

HOWARD   *cancel*

INSCH   *cancel*

KARLSRUHE, *Germany*
Badische Landesbibl.
+345   Coupar Angus
+Skt Georgen in Villingen 12
Syon

KEYNES, Sir G.   *cancel*
—, Dr S.   see **CAMBRIDGE**,
Dr S. Keynes
—, Mr S. J.   see **LONDON**,
Mr S. J. Keynes

KINGSTON LACEY,
The National Trust
+—   Jarrow (deposited in
London, B.L.)

KÖLN see **COLOGNE**

KYOTO, *Japan*
Univ. Libr.
309.7-Isi (183787) Shrewsbury,
Fran. (formerly Leicester,
Bernard Halliday)

LACOCK ABBEY: now Mr A. S.
Burnett-Brown

LAWN, DR B. see **LONDON**

LEEDS
Public Libr.   *cancel*
Univ. Libr.
+Brotherton Coll. 16 Beverley
29   York,
St Mary (formerly
Ripon, Mr H. L.
Bradfer-Lawrence)

BRITISH LIBR. (*contd*)

	48984	*read* Llantarnam
	49363	†Wenlock
		(formerly Hoikham
		Hall, 39)
+	53710	Canterbury,
		St Aug.
	54184	Ramsey
		(formerly Deene Park,
		Mr G. Brudenell)
	54229	Canterbury,
		St Aug.
		(formerly London,
		Dr E. G. Millar)
	54230	Reading
		(formerly London,
		Dr E. G. Millar)
	54231	Lincoln, Fran.
		(formerly London,
		Dr E. G. Millar)
	54232	Llanfaes
		(formerly London,
		Dr E. G. Millar)
	56252	St Osyth
		(previously Helming-
		ham Hall, 3)
	57337	Canterbury
	57337	Canterbury
	57532	Waltham
		(formerly London,
		Dr E. G. Millar)
	57533	†Burton-upon-
		Trent
		(formerly London,
		Prof. F. Wormald)
+	57534	Norwich,
		St Giles
+	59616	Canterbury
	59839	†Glastonbury
+	59855	Southwark
+	60577	Winchester
	61823	Mount Grace
		(formerly Mayfield,
		Capt. M.
		Butler-Bowdon)
	61901	Beverley
		(formerly Ripon,
		Mr H. L.
		Bradfer-Lawrence)
+	62104	Exeter
+	62105	Southwark

BRITISH LIBR. (*contd*)

	62122	Tavistock
		(formerly London, Prof.
		L. S. Penrose, on loan
		to Colchester Museum)
	62129–62132B	
		Fountains (formerly
		Studley Royal,
		Mr H. Vyner)
	62450	Mount Grace
		(formerly Ripon,
		Mr H. L.
		Bradfer-Lawrence)
	62452	Byland
		(formerly Ripon,
		Mr H. L.
		Bradfer-Lawrence)
	62777	†St Albans
		(formerly Mount Stuart,
		Marquess of Bute)
	62925	Reading
		(formerly Belvoir,
		Duke of Rutland)
+	63077	Rievaulx
	63592	Southwark
		(formerly Guildford,
		Mrs F. E. O'Donnell)
+	63787	Westminster,
		St Stephen
+Arundel	11	St Albans
+	157	Oxford,
		St Frideswide
+	201	St Albans
	332	Durham
	507	Durham
+Burney	138	Oxford,
		Lincoln Coll.
	310	Durham
+Cotton Julius	A.i	Bury
	A.vi	Durham
+	D.iii	St Albans
	D.iv	Durham
	D.vi	Durham
+	Tib. A.x	Montacute
+	A.xv	
		Malmesbury
	B.v	*read* †Ely
+	B.ix	Oxford,
		Merton Coll.
+	C.ii	Lindisfarne
+	D.v	St Albans
+	D.vi	Byland

BRITISH LIBR. (*contd*)

	4843	Durham
+	4887	Eynsham
	4894	Durham
	5234	Durham
	5289	Durham
+	5388	Bury
+	5442	Bury
+	5977	Exeter (above,

p. 36, footnote 1)

+Charter 83.A.37 Pirton, *Ch.*
+Roll Y.6 Crowland
Henry Davis Gift M.49

Fountains
(formerly London,
Mr H. Davis)

Lansdowne 397 Durham
+ 431 Chichester

Barnwell
+Loans 29/333 Guisborough
(deposited by Duke of
Portland, Welbeck)
74 Durham (deposited
by The Trustees for Roman
Catholic Purposes Registered)
81 Jarrow (deposited
by The National Trust)
82 Sherborne
(deposited by Duke of
Northumberland, Alnwick)

+Royal	5 F.xiii	Salisbury
+	5 F.xviii	Salisbury
	6 A.v	Durham
+	6 B.xv	Salisbury
	7 A.vi	Durham
+	7 B.xiv	Arundel
+	8 B.xiv	Salisbury
+	10 A.xvii	Westminster
+	12 C.xxiii	Glastonbury
+	13 A.xxi	Kirkham
+	15 C.xi	Salisbury
+	15 C.xv	Oxford,

Lincoln Coll.
+Appx. 85 Malmesbury
+Sloane 285 Chester
1044 *read* †Ely
Stowe 930 Durham
Yates Thompson 26 Durham
BRITISH RECORDS ASSN. *cancel*
COLLEGE OF ARMS
Arundel 25 Durham

DULWICH COLL.
23 Durham
GUILDHALL LIBR.
4158A London, St Peter's
Cornhill, *Ch.*
LAMBETH PALACE

	10	Durham
	11	Durham
	12	Durham
	23	Durham
+	29	Lanthony
+	61	Lanthony
+	77	Lanthony
	102	*read* Lanthony

†St Albans

+	110	Lanthony
+	114	Lanthony
+	134	Lanthony
+	137	Lanthony
+	145	Llanthony (prima)
+	153	Lanthony
+	164	Lanthony
+	192	Norwich
+	200	Lanthony
	325	Durham
+	379	Lanthony
+	425	Lanthony
+	431	Lanthony
	483	Durham

+1229, nos. 14, 15 Lanthony
+1510, nos. 20, 21 Byland
3285 Shaftesbury (formerly
Steyning, Sir A. Howard
and Wellington, Mr J.
Hasson, the same volume)
LINCOLN'S INN
Hale 114 Durham
PASSMORE EDWARDS MUS.
LD PEM AD/AY 0001
Waltham (formerly Whep-
stead, Mr H. C. Drayton)
PUBLIC RECORD OFFICE
+E.164/1 Neath
ST BARTHOLOMEW'S HOSP.
Misc. 10 London,
St Bartholomew's
ST PAUL'S CATH.
+4 London
+8 Droitwich
SION COLL.
L.9 (i.e. Arc. L.40.2/L.9)
cancel

SION COLL. (*contd*)
L.21 (i.e. Arc. L.40/2.L.21)
     cancel
SOCIETY OF ANTIQUARIES
7   Durham
136C   London
SOUTHWARK, ROMAN CATHOLIC
    METROPOLITAN SEE
+1   Desford, *Ch.*
UNIVERSITY OF LONDON LIBR.
+906   Tawstock, *Ch.*
VICTORIA AND ALBERT MUS.
661   *after* Canterbury
    add (see p. 33,
     footnote 6)
WELLCOME HISTORICAL MEDICAL
       LIBR.
801ᴬ   Bury (previously
    Bury St Edmunds
     Cathedral, 4)
WESTMINSTER ABBEY
+34/2   Westminster
+36/17–19 Exeter
    (above, p. 36,
     footnote 1)
+33327   Westminster
+F.4.21   Dore
MR N. J. BARKER,
  22 CLARENDON ROAD, W.11
+ —   Carlisle
+ — Oxford, New Coll.
MR H. DAVIS   *cancel*
DR C. F. R. DE HAMEL.
    c/o Sotheby & Co.
+ —   Amesbury
+ —   Canterbury
+ —   Croxden
+ —   St Albans
+ —   Syon
+ —   Syon
+ —   Winchcombe
MR E. M. DRING *cancel*
MR S. J. KEYNES Whitby
DR B. LAWN, OLD ESSEX HOUSE,
    BARNES, S.W.13
22 London, Aug. friars
   (formerly San Francisco,
    John Howell)
MAGGS BROS. LTD. *cancel*
DR E. G. MILLAR *cancel*
PROF. L. S. PENROSE *cancel*

MR H. C. PRATT,
399–401 HIGH ST, STRATFORD
     E15 4RF
+ — Bury (formerly untraced,
    Maggs Bros., 1949)
— Weald, South, *Ch.*
  (formerly Belchamp Hall,
    Mrs Raymond)
MR P. L. ROBINSON
—   Bury (formerly
   The Robinson Trust,
    Helmingham 58)
— Cambridge, Clare Coll.
  (formerly The Robinson Trust,
    Helmingham 15)
PRIVATE COLLECTION 1
 — Harrold (formerly Bristol,
    Baptist Coll.)
+ —   Robertsbridge
 (deposited in Edinburgh, N.L.).
PRIVATE COLLECTION 2
+ —   London, Carm.
PRIVATE COLLECTOR,
    c/o Quaritch
—   Stoke-by-Clare
THE ROBINSON TRUST *cancel*
MR RAYMOND RUSSELL *cancel*
PROF. F. WORMALD *cancel*

LONGLEAT, *Wilts.*
MARQUESS OF BATH
13   Durham
+55   Bath Corporation

LOS ANGELES, *U.S.A.,*
California
DR P. F. SLAWSON, UNIV. OF
  CALIFORNIA, LOS ANGELES
+ — Kirkham (formerly
   untraced, Davis and
    Orioli, 1921)

LOUGHLINSTONE, *Republic of*
Ireland
SIR J. GALVIN Kirkstead
   (formerly Beaumont
    Coll., VI)

LÜCKGERS, DR J. *cancel*

MADRID, *Spain*
BIBLIOTECA NACIONAL
 V.3.28 *read* Vitr. 23–8
PALACIO NACIONAL
+II.2097   Dunfermline

MAIDSTONE
KENT ARCHIVES OFFICE
DRc/R1   Rochester
    (deposited by Dean and
    Chapter of Rochester;
    formerly Rochester
    Cath. Libr.)
+Qb/AZ 1   Queenborough
    Corporation (deposited
    by Mayor and Corporation
    of Queenborough)
+S/Rm.Fae.2   Canterbury
+U 1121/M2   Rochester
MUSEUM
1   *read* All Saints P.5
2   *read* All Saints A.13

MALVERN, LITTLE
MR W. BERINGTON: now MR
T. M. BERINGTON and deposited
in Birmingham Univ. Libr., *q.v.*

MANCHESTER
JOHN RYLANDS LIBR.: now JOHN
      RYLANDS UNIV. LIBR.
Christie 3.f.19   Farnworth,
    Ch. (formerly
    Manchester Univ. Libr.)
Eng.109   Welbeck (formerly
    Lat. 179)
Lat. 22   *read* †Beverley
    23   *read* †Roche
+   119   Hambleton, *Ch.*
   179   *read* Eng. 109
   186   *read* †Beverley
          †Roche
   474   Canterbury
    (formerly Manchester,
    Northern Congregational
    Coll., 1)
+Box of Fragments, no. 9
    Oxford, Fran.
Northern Congregational Coll.
    cancel
Univ. Libr.   *cancel*

MAYFIELD, *Suss.* Capt. M.
Butler-Bowdon
Cancel the second item (Mount
Grace)

MORCOMBELAKE, *Dorset: read*
ST PETER PORT, *Guernsey*

MOSTYN HALL   *cancel*

MOUNT STUART   *cancel*

MUNICH, *Germany*
STAATSBIBL.
+Clm. 705   Lydd, *Ch.*
lat. 835   *read* Clm.835
         †Gloucester

NATIONAL TRUST, THE *see*
KINGSTON LACEY

NEW HAVEN, *U.S.A., Conn.*
YALE UNIV. LIBR.
  Read Beinecke 286
      London, Carth.
+   426
      Bermondsey
    590   Roche
  (formerly New Haven,
    Prof. N. H. Pearson)
Marston 118
      Stamford, Carm.
Marston 243   Southwark
+Mellon 37   Babwell
Prof. N. H. Pearson   *cancel*

NEW YORK, *U.S.A., New York*
ACADEMY OF MEDICINE
+ —   Canterbury, St Aug.
COLUMBIA UNIV. LIBR.
Plimpton 269 *read* Plimpton 308
PIERPONT MORGAN LIBR.
  521   *After* Canterbury *add*
  724   (see p. 33, footnote 6)
+926   St Albans
+G.43   Ely
p. 373 col. 1 *cancel the words*
William S. Glazier's collection *and*
the footnote, and add G. *before*
    18, 19, 39, 53, 65
PHILIP C. DUSCHNES   *cancel*
EXECUTORS OF THE LATE MR
WILLIAM S. GLAZIER   *cancel*

NEWBURY   *cancel*

NIJMEGEN, *Holland*
UNIV. LIBR.
+194   Barking

NONINGTON, *Kent*
MR J. H. PLUMPTRE, LITTLE
      FREDVILLE
+ —   Morley, *Ch.* (deposited
    in Canterbury Cath. Libr.)

BODLEIAN LIBR. (*contd*)

4	now Salisbury, Cath.	
	Libr., 221	
+Fr.e.32	Canterbury, St Aug.	
+Junius 1	Bourne	
Lat. bib. d. 9	Oxford, Dom.	
	(formerly Oxford,	
	Mr N. R. Ker)	
+	d. 10	Exeter
Lat. class. d. 39		
	Northampton, Dom.;	
	Oxford, Oriel Coll.	
	(formerly London,	
	Syon Coll.)	
+Lat. hist. d. 4	Bury	
+Lat. liturg. d.42	Chertsey	
+	e.38	Exeter
	(p. 36, footnote 1)	
+	e.39	Chertsey
	(formerly untraced,	
London, Francis Edwards)		
	f.5	Durham
Lat. misc. b. 13	Durham	
	(formerly London,	
British Records Assn.)		
+	b. 18	Oxford,
	Fran. (formerly	
London, Mr E. M. Dring)		
+	b. 19, B.47–9	
	Canterbury;	
Oxford, Canterbury Coll.		
	c. 75	Oxford,
All Souls Coll.; Oxford,		
Queen's Coll.; Ramsey		
(formerly London, The		
Robinson Trust)		
+	e.118	Hyde
Lat. th. d.35	Pipewell	
(formerly Deene Park,		
Mr G. Brudenell)		
+	d.40	Haughmond
	d.46	Winchcombe
(formerly Sudeley Castle,		
Mrs Dent-Brocklehurst)		
Laud Lat. 12	Durham;	
	Oxford,	
	Durham Coll.	
36	Durham	
Laud Misc. 52	Durham	
+	85	Bury
+	109	
	Robertsbridge	

BODLEIAN LIBR. (*contd*)

	262	Durham
	277	Durham
	285	Newstead
	344	Durham
	345	Durham
	348	*cancel*
	359	Durham
	368	Durham
	389	Durham
	392	Durham
	402	Durham
	413	Durham
	489	Durham
	491	Durham
	546	Durham
+	578	Reading
	603	Durham
+	624	Rochester
	641	Durham
	667 *read* Brecon,	
	Ben. priory	
	†Brecon, *Ch*.	
	700	Durham
	720	†Durham
	748	Durham
	758	Bury
Lyell 16	Durham	
e Mus. 2	now Salisbury,	
	Cath. Libr., 224	
+Rawlinson A.371		
		Bermondsey
+	B.150	Battle
	C.4	Durham
+	C.163	Lanthony
+	C.331	Lanthony
+	C.553	York,
		St Mary
+	C.562	St Albans
+	C.568	St Albans
+	C.569	St Albans
+	C.677	
		Peterborough
	D.338	Durham
+	G.59	Dartford
+	G.139	
		Malmesbury
+Tanner 4	Durham	
Wood empt. 24	Durham	
BRASENOSE COLL.		
4	Durham	
+16	Syon	

READING, *Berks.*
MUSEUM AND ART GALLERY
40.74   Reading
(formerly Portsmouth,
Roman Catholic Bishopric,
Virtue and Cahill 8473)

REDLYNCH   *cancel*

REYKJAVIK, *Iceland*
NAT. LIBR.
+IB 363 8ᵛᵒ   Carrow
+Lbs. frag. 51   Carrow
NAT. MUSEUM
+4678   Carrow

RIPON
CATHEDRAL LIBR.
read 6   Frieston
        Mount Grace
read 3–4   Bridlington
read 2   Newcastle, Dom.
DEAN AND CHAPTER ARCHIVES
+432   Cottenham, *Ch.*
MR H. L. BRADFER-LAWRENCE
        cancel

ROCHESTER, *Kent*
CATH. LIBR.
A.3.16   Rochester
Textus Roffensis   Rochester
(deposited in Maidstone,
Kent Archives Office)

ROME, *Italy*
BIBLIOTECA ANGELICA
+1084 Cambridge, Aug. friars
BIBLIOTECA APOSTOLICA VATICANA
+Barberini 2689 Sempringham
+Ottoboni lat. 73 Cambridge,
        Aug. friars
+   85 Cambridge,
        Dom.
+   104 Cambridge,
        Dom.
+   116 Cambridge,
        Aug. friars
+   177   York,
        St Mary
+   181–2   Cam-
        bridge,
        Aug. friars
+   186 Cambridge,
        Aug. friars

BIBLIOTECA APOSTOLICA (*contd*)
+   187   Cambridge,
        Dom.
+   188   Cambridge,
        Aug. friars
+   193–4   Cambridge,
        Aug. friars
+   196   Cambridge,
        Aug. friars
+   200   Cambridge,
        Aug. friars
+   202   Cambridge,
        Aug. friars
+   208   Cambridge,
        Dom.
+   211   Cambridge,
        Aug. friars
+   214   Cambridge,
        Aug. friars
+   229   Cambridge,
        Aug. friars
+   235   Cambridge,
        Aug. friars
+   271   Cambridge,
        Dom.
+   308   Lincoln
+   323   Cambridge,
        Aug. friars
+   326   Cambridge,
        Aug. friars
+   331   Cambridge,
        Aug. friars
+   342   Cambridge,
        Aug. friars
+   357   Cambridge,
        Aug. friars
+   426   Cambridge,
        Aug. friars
+   427   Cambridge,
        Aug. friars
+   468   Cambridge,
        Aug. friars
+   612   Cambridge,
        Aug. friars
+   630   Cambridge,
        Aug. friars
+   1276   Cambridge,
        Fran.
+   1407   Cambridge,
        Aug. friars
+   1603   Cambridge,
        Aug. friars

BIBLIOTECA APOSTOLICA (*contd*)

+	1757	Cambridge, Aug. friars
+	1764	Cambridge, Aug. friars
+	2071	Cambridge, Aug. friars
+Reg. lat.	458	Rochester
+	598	Rochester
+	646	Rochester
+	1351	Worcester
+Vat. lat.	3056	Cambridge, Dom.
+	4954[1]	Lincoln, Aug. friars
+	7095	Cambridge, Dom.
+	10669	Oxford Univ.

ROUEN, *France*
BIBL. MUNICIPALE
+231 (A.44)   Canterbury, St Aug.

RUTLAND, DUKE OF *see*
BELVOIR CASTLE

ST AUSTELL   *cancel*

ST PETER PORT, *Guernsey*
MR J. STEVENS COX (formerly
MORCOMBELAKE)
—   Reading
—   Syon

SALISBURY, *Wilts.*
CATH. LIBR.
+150   Shaftesbury
+198   Salisbury
221–4   Salisbury (formerly Oxford, Bodleian, Fell 4, 1, 3, e Mus. 2)

SAN FRANCISCO, *U.S.A.,*
California
JOHN HOWELL   *cancel*

SAN MARINO, *U.S.A.,*
California
HENRY E. HUNTINGTON LIBR.
+HM 55   Dereham, West
+HM 112   London, Holy Trinity
+HM 27187[2]   King's Langley

HUNTINGTON LIBR. (*contd*)
HM 30319   Battle (formerly London, The Robinson Trust)
HM 31151   Bury (previously Dublin, Chester Beatty Libr.)
HM 35300   Syon (formerly Bury St Edmunds, Cath.)
HM 45717   Bury (previously London, Sion Coll.)

SANKT GALLEN, *Switzerland*
STIFTSBIBL.
+26   Malmesbury

SCHØYEN, Mr M. (Norway)
South Malling

SHEFFIELD, *Yorks.*
CENTRAL LIBR.
+MD3500   Beauchief

SHERBROOKE: *read* Mrs R.,
Sherbrooke, Oxton Lodge, Newark, Notts.

SHREWSBURY, *Shrops.*
SHREWSBURY SCHOOL
+XXI   Durham
+XXX   Haughmond

SLAWSON, Dr P. F. *see* **LOS ANGELES**

STEYNING   *cancel*
STOCKHOLM, *Sweden*
KUNGL. BIBL.
—   *read* A.135
+A.140   Oxford, Carm.
A.182   Tonbridge
NAT. MUSEUM
NMB 2010   Tarrant Keynston (formerly Redlynch, Major J. R. Abbey)

STONYHURST COLLEGE,
Lancs.
for s.n., 6, 9, 10, 11, 12
read 55, 3, 6, 7, 8, 9
respectively
55   Durham (deposited in London, B.L.)

STUDLEY ROYAL   *cancel*
SUDELEY CASTLE   *cancel*

---

[1] Also (correctly) entered under **CAMBRIDGE**, Aug. friars in 1964 edn.
[2] Also (correctly) entered under **KING'S LANGLEY** in 1964 edn.

SÜRTH *cancel*

SUTHERLAND, DUKE OF,
see **DUNROBIN**

SYON ABBEY, *Devon*
read 1, 2, 4, 6   Syon
read 3   †Syon

SYRACUSE, *U.S.A.,* *New York*
UNIV. LIBR.
Uncat. 1   Orpington, *Ch.*
(formerly Portsmouth,
Roman Catholic Bishopric,
Virtue and Cahill 8433)

TALSARNAU, *Gwynedd*
LORD HARLECH   Bury (formerly
    OSWESTRY, Lord Harlech)

TOKYO, *Japan*
PROF. T. TAKAMIYA, DEPT. OF
ENGLISH, KEIO UNIV., MITA,
    MINATOKU, TOKYO 108
14   Great Malvern
     Worcester, Dom.
     (formerly Helmingham
     Hall)
+15   Lichfield Fran.
21   Salisbury (formerly
     Coligny-Genève,
     Mr M. Bodmer)
+55   Canterbury
—   Whitby

TOLLEMACHE, LORD, *see*
HELMINGHAM HALL

TROWBRIDGE, *Wilts.*
WILTS. RECORD OFFICE
+W.R.O. 12.30   Marlborough,
     Corporation

TRURO, *Corn.*
CORN. RECORD OFFICE
DD.R(S) 60   Tywardreath
     (deposited by
     Mr P. S. Rashleigh, Par)

URBANA, *U.S.A.,* *Illinois*
UNIV. OF ILLINOIS LIBR.
—   *read* 139
+ 74   St Albans
+128   Malmesbury
+132   Furness
139   Flaunden, *Ch.*

USHAW, *Co. Durham*
+5   Esh, parish chapel

VATICAN *see* **ROME, VATICAN**

VERDUN, *France, Meuse*
BIBL. MUNICIPALE
+70   †St Albans

VERULAM, EARL OF, *see*
GORHAMBURY

VIENNA, *Austria*
NATIONALBIBL.
1274 (Theol. 351)   †Durham

VYNER *cancel*

WANTAGE, *Oxon.*
LORD ASTOR, GINGE MANOR
—   Norwich, Dom.

WELBECK ABBEY, *Notts.*
DUKE OF PORTLAND
—   Guisborough
     (deposited in London,
     B.L., Loan 29/333)

WELLINGTON, *Som.*   *cancel*

WELLINGTON, *New Zealand*
ALEXANDER TURNBULL LIBR.
+MS Papers 2 (P. Watts Rule)
     Canterbury
—   Holme Cultram (formerly
     untraced, Yarmouth, Isle of
     Wight, Mr F. Rowley, 1941), on
     permanent loan from Bible
     Society of New Zealand
—   London, Fran. (on
     permanent loan from Bible
     Society of New Zealand)

WELLS, *Som.*
CATH. LIBR.
read 3   †Exeter
4   †Hailes
5   Hailes
6   Hailes
VC/II   Garendon
s.n.   Glastonbury
s.n.   Wells
VICARS CHORAL HALL   *cancel*

WENTWORTH WOODHOUSE
The Barlings MS. is deposited in
     Magdalene Coll., Cambridge

WHEPSTEAD *cancel*

WINCHESTER, *Hants.*
CATH. LIBR.
10   Durham

WINDSOR, *Berks.*
CASTLE
— *read* Jackson Collection, 3
ST GEORGE'S CHAPEL
+5   Oxford, Canterbury Coll.

WISBECH, *Suffolk*
MUSEUM
1   Wisbech, *Ch.*

WOLFENBÜTTEL, *Germany*
HERZOG AUGUST BIBL.
+Extravagantes 25.1
        London, St Bartholomew

WOLLATON, *Notts.*
MS. now on deposit in
        Nottingham Univ. Libr.

WOOLHAMPTON, *Berks.*
DOUAI ABBEY
+—   Reading

WORCESTER
CATH. LIBR.
+F.140   Worcester

YORK
MINSTER LIBR.
xvi *should read* XVI *throughout*
                        entry
+XVI.A.6   Rotherham
+XVI.A.8   York
XVI.D.9   Durham
XVI.G.5   *read* XVI.K.6
XVI.I.1   Durham
XVI.I.12   Durham
XVI.K.4   Durham
+XVI.N.3   Shouldham
XVI.N.8   Durham
+XVI.P.5–8   York
XVI.Q.5   Durham
XVI.Q.13   *read* XVI.Q.15
s.n. covers three items, Add. 1
(Evangelia), Tabula 1 (Historia
eccles. Ebor.) and Tabula 2 (De
        aetatibus mundi, etc.).
—   *read* Add. 70 (deposited
        by Sir A. D. F. Gascoigne,
                        Aberford)

135

INDEX OF PRINTED BOOKS

This has been compiled on the same principles as the Index of Manuscripts on pp. 117–35, above.

136

HAWKESYARD PRIORY,
Rugeley, Staffs.
—   Durham

HEREFORD
Cath. Libr.
A.ix.2.3   Durham

HEYTHROP COLLEGE address
now 11–13 Cavendish
Square, London W1

HILVERSUM, *Holland*
Messrs C. de Boer
—   Durham (formerly
Gouda, Messrs Koch
and Knuttel)

INSCH   *cancel*

KENYON, Lord, *see*
GREDINGTON

LAMPETER, *Dyfed*
St David's Univ. Coll.
+47F   Nostell

LINCOLN
Cath. Libr.
F.1.14   Durham
V.5.11 (MS. Flyleaves)
Exeter (above,
p. 36, footnote 1)

LONDON
British Museum *read* British
Library
British Libr.
+1073.1.4   Oxford,
Corpus Christi Coll.
+C.77.d.17   Burton-upon-
Trent
+K.8.k.8   Westminster
Dulwich Coll.
+A.3.f.3   Peterborough
+A.3.f.12   Cambridge,
Michaelhouse
+A.3.f.13   Ashridge
Jesuit House, Farm St.
+1507 I   Westminster
+1508 I   Southwark
Lambeth Palace
— (Syon)   *read* **H890.G8
+1495.4   Barking
Law Soc.
107.d   Durham

MIDDLE TEMPLE
— (Norwich)   *read* 54.7
Royal Coll. of Physicians
+ —   Oxford, Fran.
Westminster Abbey
+F.4.21   Dore
Mr N. J. Barker, 22 Clarendon
Road, W.11
+ —   Bedford, Fran.
Dr C. F. R. de Hamel, c/o
Sotheby & Co.
+ —   Salisbury, Dom.
Mr A. Ehrman   *cancel*
Mr J. P. Getty   Oxford,
Brasenose Coll. (formerly
St Albans Sch.)
Messrs Maggs   *cancel*
Mr P. Robinson   *cancel*

LOS ANGELES, *U.S.A.,*
California
Univ. of California
Biomedical Libr.
+ —   Durham

MANCHESTER
John Rylands Libr. now John
Rylands Univ. Libr.

NAWORTH CASTLE, *Cumb.*
Earl of Carlisle
+ —   Hyde

NEW YORK, *U.S.A., New York*
Pierpont Morgan Libr.
— (Wetherall) *read* PML 30780

NOTTINGHAM
Univ. Libr.
—   Kingston-upon-Hull
(formerly Oakham Ch.;
deposited by churchwardens)

OAKHAM, *Rutl.*
Parish Ch.
—   now deposited in
Nottingham Univ. Libr.

OXFORD
Bodleian Libr.
Auct. I.Q.5.1   Durham
+Auct. 4.Q.4.9 Oxford, Fran.
+BB 200   Polsloe
Broxb. 34.5   Windsor
(formerly London,
Mr A. Ehrman)
+4° V.16(2) Th.   Coventry

BODLEIAN LIBR. (*contd*)
+Vet. Fl.c.90 Lancaster, Dom.
University Coll. d.6
Leominster (entry misplaced
in 1964 edn.)

ALL SOULS COLL.
+SR 81.a.15   †Oxford,
                     New Coll.

BRASENOSE COLL.
+Latham B.4.6   Hyde

NEW COLL.
+Ω.13.2   Canterbury

ORIEL COLL.
C.e.20   Durham
+2F.f.14   Hyde

ST JOHN'S COLL.
P.4.46   Durham

UNIVERSITY COLL.   *cancel*

DR A. E. ARMSTRONG,
         SOMERVILLE COLL.
Mottenden (formerly Oxford,
Mr C. A. J. Armstrong)

DR D. M. ROGERS, c/o BODLEIAN
         LIBR.
Worcester (formerly London,
Mr A. Ehrman)

PEDLEY, Mrs A., *see*
CAMBRIDGE

PETERBOROUGH, *Northants.*
CATH. LIBR.
D.8.17   now deposited in
         Cambridge, U.L.
M.6.6   missing since 1902

ROGERS, Dr D. M., *see*
OXFORD

ST ALBANS   *cancel*

ST ANDREWS, *Fife*
UNIV. LIBR.
Forbes d.34 Hailes (formerly
Edinburgh Theological Coll.;
deposited by Coll.)

SALISBURY, *Wilts.*
CATH. LIBR.
+Y.2.16   Rochester

SHREWSBURY, *Shrops.*
SHREWSBURY SCH.
+F.vi.5   Abingdon
SHROPS. LIBRARIES, LOCAL
        STUDIES DEPT.
—   Wetheral; York, St Mary

SHROPS. LIBRARIES (*contd*)
(formerly Bridgnorth,
St Leonard's Ch.;
deposited by churchwardens)

STONOR PARK, *Oxon.*
HON. S. STONOR *read* LORD
                CAMOYS

TOKYO, *Japan*
PROF. T. TAKAMIYA, DEPT. OF
ENGLISH, KEIO UNIV., MITA,
      MINATOKU, TOKYO 108
      Fountains (formerly
    Cambridge, Union Soc.)

TOLLERTON   *cancel*

TORONTO, *Canada*
PONTIFICAL INST.
+A.1.10   Durham
UNIV. LIBR.
+RB 9689   Nostell

URBANA, *U.S.A., Illinois*
UNIV. OF ILLINOIS LIBR.
q.251 Sp.31.1481   York,
                St Mary
(formerly Deventer,
Mr J. P. van der Lande)

USHAW COLLEGE,
Co. Durham
53 books   Durham
+ — (Lisbon
Collection)   Southwark
+XVIII.A.4.1   Oxford,
          Durham Coll.

VAN DER LANDE   *cancel*

WASHINGTON, *U.S.A., District
of Columbia*
LIBR. OF CONGRESS
+Incun. X.5.7   Thurgarton

WINCHESTER, *Hants*
PRESBYTERY   *cancel*

XANTEN, *Germany*
STIFTSBIBL.
3070B   *read* 2970B [Inc.]241

YORK
MINSTER LIBR.
vii, x etc. *should read* VII, X
     etc. *throughout entry*
8 books   Durham
+II.N.1   Hyde
XIV.K.3   †Durham

INDEX OF UNTRACED
MANUSCRIPTS AND PRINTED BOOKS

This index is a conflation of the list on pp. 403–4 of the 1964 edition and of new entries marked (+). The arrangement is alphabetical by the name of the last known owner or, failing that, of the last known place where the book was recorded.

+ ABINGDON
—— in 1665   Kirby Bellars
+ ALLISON, R. W.
—— in 1964   Louth Park
BABRA, S. (bs., Barcelona)
—— in 1923 Cambridge, Fran.
BAILLARDEAU, LEWIS
—— in 1726   Crowland
BARKER, –
—— in 1734   Mount Grace
+ BARNARD, P. M. (bs., Manchester)
—— in 1912   Norwich, Dom.
+ BEIJERS, J. L. (bs., Utrecht)
—— in 1959   Hounslow,
                    Trinitarians
BOLLANDISTS, SOCIETY OF
—— in s.xvii   St Albans
+ BRIDGE, JOHN, bp. of Oxford
—— in s.xvii in   Osney
+ BRISTOL, BAPTIST COLLEGE
—— in 1964   Crowland
BUDDICOM, –
—— in 1913   Winchcombe
+ CHRISTIE'S (auctioneer, London)
—— in 1981   Canterbury
CLARENDON, HENRY, EARL OF
—— in 1697   London, Carth.
COCHRAN, JOHN (bs., London)
—— in 1837   Darley
COLERAINE, LORD
—— in 1734   London,
                    Aug. friars
+ COLOGNE(?)
—— in 1718   Kingston-
          upon-Hull, Carth.

COOLIDGE, T. J.
—— in 1911   Byland
DAVIS AND ORIOLI (bs., London)
                    cancel
+ DAWSON, WM., AND SONS
                    (bs., London)
—— in 1969   Spinney
—— in 1969   Robertsbridge
—— in 1971   Syon
DULAU AND CO (bs., London)
                    cancel
+ DUSCHNES, P. B. (bs., New York)
—— in 1964   Shere, Ch.[1]
EDWARDS, FRANCIS (bs., London)
—— in 1946   cancel
+   —— in 1970   Fountains
+ ELLIS
—— in 1899   Syon
+ ELMSTONE RECTORY, KENT
—— in 1964   Canterbury,
                    St Aug.
+ FLETCHER, H. M. (bs., London)
—— in 1843   Merevale
—— in 1964   Reading
GAEBELEIN, REV. A. C. (U.S.A.)
—— in 1937   Reading
GÖRLITZ, OBERLAUSITZISCHE
GESELLSCHAFT DER
     WISSENSCHAFTEN (D.D.R.)
—— missing since 1943
                    Waltham
GOUGH, RICHARD
—— in s.xix in   Doncaster,
                    Fran.

[1] Dismembered: some fragments traced.

140

INDEX OF PERSONAL NAMES

All the names occur in the lists on pp. 76–114. The names of scribes are in italics. Spellings of well-known names have been modernized and standardized in a common form, e.g. Middleton. Spellings of little-known names have been altered to coincide with a modern name only if the change does not interfere or hardly interferes with the alphabetical sequence, e.g. Alcester for Alcetur, but Quitbi, not Whitby, or if the form of the name can be readily modernized, e.g. Embleton for Emylton. The letter *i* has been generalized for *y* if a consonant follows in the same syllable, e.g. Winterbourne, unless the spelling with *y* is the generally recognized spelling (Blyth); also *ck* for *k*. Names preceded by + are additions to the 1964 list; other entries refer to additional information or corrections.

Abingdon, R. de	Osney
+ Abingdon, S. de	Durham
Acton	Hailes
Adam	Canterbury, St Aug.
Adington	Durham
+ Admudeston	Durham
Alcester	Evesham
Alexander, N.	Warwick, Dom.
Alulph	Canterbury, St Aug.
+ Alwerton	Durham
+ Anlaby	Ferriby
Appleby, W. de	Durham
+ Applegarth	York
+ Ardern	Durham
Aristotle	Durham
Arndell	Gloucester
Arnold, J.	Keynsham
Arnold, T.	Canterbury, St Aug.
Arrows	York, St Mary
+ Ascelby	Durham
+ Askew	Halsall, *Ch.*
+ ate Wynne	Durham
Athelstan	Durham
Auckland	Durham
+ Avalon	Lincoln
Avington	Winchester
+ B., W.	Nostell
Babington	Campsey
Bacon	Bruisyard
+ Bailey	Durham
+ Bainbridge	Durham
+ Bake	Durham
Baldwin	Bury
+ Baldwin, J.	Colchester

Bamburgh, J.	Rochester
Bamburgh, R. de	Durham
+ Banastre	Durham
Bankes	Crich, *Ch.*
Bardney	Crowland
Barnby	Durham
+ Barton	Meaux
+ Barwe, P.	Durham
Barwe, W.	Bury
+ Baseford (Daseford?)	Durham
Basing	Winchester
Bastable	Marlborough, Carm.
+ Bate	Burton-upon-Trent
+ Baxter	London, Carth.
Beauchamp, J.	London, Dom.
Bebseth	Hatfield Peverel
Becansaw	Leicester, Coll.
Beccles	Bury
Becket, T., monk	Canterbury
+ Bel, E.	Durham
Bell, Ric.	Durham
Bell, Rog.	Durham
Belvero, W. de	Belvoir
Benet, W.	Durham
+ Bentlay	Durham
Bereham	Canterbury
Bertelot	Canterbury, St Aug.
+ Berton, R. de	Durham
+ Beverley, J. de	Durham
+ Beverley, R. de	Durham
Billingham, R.	Durham
Bird	Peterborough
Birkenhead	Chester, nuns
+ Birtley	Durham

142

+*Cock, J.*	London, St Bartholomew
Cockering	Canterbury, St Aug.
Cokken	Durham
+Colby	Durham
+Colchester	Bury
Colier, R.	London, St Bartholomew
+Collys	Oxford, Fran.
Colman, J.	Bristol, St Mark
Colman, J.	Lessness
+Colson(?)	Whitby
+Colwitho	Durham
+Constable	Durham
+Copton, R.	Canterbury
+Coptun, J.	Canterbury
+Corbridge, H. de	Durham
Corf	Tarrant Keynston
Cornforth	Durham
Cornhill	London, St Paul's
+Cornish	Oxford, Oriel Coll.
Corvesar	Haughmond
Coscomb, Roger	Hailes
Couton	Southwell
Coventry, J.	Canterbury
+Coyk, T.	Titchfield
+Crafford	Cambridge, Dom.
+Craneburn	Sheen
Cranewys	Bury
+Cressener	Dartford
Cristal	Abingdon
Crome, W.	+Cambridge, Aug. friars
Crosby	Durham
Crosseley	Coventry
+Crucher	Chichester
Curteys	Bury
Cuthbert, W.	Durham
+Dale	Durham
Dalton, H. de	Durham
Dalton, W.	Durham
+Danby	Durham
Dapton, *recte* Barton	Meaux
+Darby	Thurgarton
+Daseford, *recte* Baseford(?)	Durham
+Dechingham	Langley
+Delling	Bury
Denham	Bury
+Denton	Cambridge, Aug. friars
Dersham	Bury
Dicklesdon	Worcester
+Dilington	Durham
+Ditensale	Durham
Ditton, T. de	Canterbury, St Aug.
Doggett	Norwich, Dom.
+Dogood	Salisbury, Dom.
Doncaster	Durham
Dove	Buckfast
Dover, W.	Canterbury
+Driffield, T.	Canterbury
Duffield, W.	Coventry, Fran.
Dune	Durham
Dunelm, P. de	Durham
+Dunelm, R. de	Durham
+Dunelmo, R. de (*als.* Adington?)	Durham
Dunelmo, W. de	Durham
+Durward, J.	Durham
Eastry, R.	Canterbury
Ebchester, R.	Durham
Ebchester, W.	Durham
Edenham	Barlings
Eggerton	Leeds
Elham	Canterbury, St Aug.
+Elwick, G.	Durham
Elwick, W.	Durham
+Elyot	Eton
Elys, *recte* Elyot	Eton
Embleton	Durham
+Emson	Westminster
Est[.]by	Durham
Estry	Canterbury
Evesham	Tewkesbury
+Exton	Peterborough
+Eyrsden	Durham
+Fabian, M.	Barking
Fadir	Salisbury
Fakenham	Babwell
Farn	Durham
Feningham	Bury
Fewterer	Syon
Figy	Durham
Filey	Cambridge, Michaelhouse
Fishburn	Durham
Flemming, R.	+Oxford, Lincoln Coll.
Fletcher	Hinton
Forrest	Thame
Forster	Arundel
Fossor	Durham
+Foxton, J. de	Lincoln

Humphrey, duke of Gloucester	+Cambridge, King's Coll.
Humphrey, T.	Canterbury
Hunden	Canterbury, St Aug.
+Hunkes	Cambridge, Michaelhouse
Huswyff	St Albans
Icklingham	Bury
Ilchester (Yvelcestria)	Ilchester
Ingram	Canterbury
Insula, J. de	Durham
+Itringham	Cambridge, Dom.
Ivinghoe	Canterbury
James, earl of Ormonde	London, St Thomas of Acon
+Jarwe	Durham
+Johannes de [.....]	Cambridge, Aug. friars
John, vicar of Newchurch	Bilsington
+Jordanus	Lincoln
Joseph, J.	Worcester, Fran.
Joseph, R.	Evesham
Katerington	Southwick
Kauges	Durham
Kedwely	Durham
+Kellaw	Durham
Kelle	London, Fran.
+Kelmeston	Durham
Kelmington	Worcester
+Kemp, R.	Cambridge, Fran.
+Kempe, J.	Durham
Kenton	Coventry, Carm.
Kettering	Ramsey
+Kibble	Durham
Killerby	Durham
+Kington	Oxford, Fran.
Kirby, R. de	Carlisle, Dom.
+Kirkby, W.	Durham
Kirkstead	Bury
Kirkton	Peterborough
+Knighton	Coventry
Knill	Hereford, Fran.
+Kornsow	Durham
Kydde	Fountains
Kyppier	Durham
La Mare	St Albans
+La Mor', W. de	Durham
La Wyle	Salisbury
+Lamsley	Durham
Langchester	Durham

Langham, S.	Bury
Langley, H.	Glastonbury
Langley, T.	Durham
Langport	Cambridge, King's Coll.
Langton, J.	London, St Mary of Graces
Lasenby, W. de	Durham
+Launcell	Durham
Laurence, archdeacon of Bedford	Huntingdon
Law	Durham
+Lawmlay	Dereham, West
Lawson	Durham
Le Berwby (Borwby)	Durham
Le Puiset, Hugh of	Durham
Leche	Lanthony
Lechlade	Southwark
Lee, P.	Durham
Leicester	Peterborough
Lenham	Canterbury, St Aug.
+Lethum	Durham
+Lews	Durham
Leybourne	Canterbury, St Aug.
+Lighfield	Canterbury
Lincoln, R.	Ramsey
London, J.	Crowland
London, J. de	Canterbury, St Aug.
London, W.	Canterbury
+Longolius	Oxford, New Coll.
+Lorde, J.	London, St Sepulchre, Holborn, Ch.
+Loughborough, T.	Durham
Lovente, R. de	Canterbury, St Aug.
+Luceby	Durham
+Ludham	Cambridge, Aug.
Luffe	Coventry
Lumley, E.	Durham
+Lumley, Wm.	Durham
Lund	Durham
Lupton, R.	Eton
+Lyndewode	Durham
Maidstone, S.	Canterbury, St Aug.
+Mainesford, R. de	Durham
+Mainsforth, J.	Durham
Mala[...], R. and W.	Durham
Malberthorp	Oxford, Lincoln Coll.
Malvern	Gloucester

147

+Robinson	York
Rock	Durham
+Rockland	Langley
Rocksley	London, Dom.
Rogerius	Canterbury, St Aug.
Roger, chaplain	Durham
+Rokeswell	Bury
Rome	Durham
Roucliffe	Selby
Rowland, T.	Abingdon
+Rowland, T.	Durham
Rowst, *recte* Baxter	London, Carth.
+Roxborthe	Durham
Ruwe	Beauvale
+Rywell	Cambridge, Dom.
St Calais (Carilef), W.	Durham
St George	Canterbury, St Aug.
St Ives	Ramsey
+Sainsbury	Chester
+Samson	Lincoln
Scothole	Holme St Benets
Seabrook	Bromfield
Sedgebrook	Durham
Selwood	Glastonbury
Seton	Durham
+Sheffield	York
+Shenley	St Albans
Sherburn, G. de	Durham
Sherburn, R.	Durham
+Shirington	London, St Paul's
+*Simon*	Harrold
+Sixt[..], mag. T.	Durham
Sleaford	Crowland
Smith, R.	Fountains
+Somour	Bridgwater, Fran.
Soppethe	Oxford, Aug.
Sotheron	Durham
+Spendluffe	Dunfermline
+Spens	Durham
Spink	Norwich
+Stakhus	Durham
Stanbridge	Oxford, Magdalen Coll.
+Stanlawe	Durham
+Staplay	Durham
Staunton	Reading
Staveley	York, St Mary
+Sterr	South Malling
Steward, R.	Ely
+Stiphol, W. de	Durham
Stockton	Cambridge, Aug.

Stoke, J. de	Sudbury, Dom.
Stone, J.	Canterbury
Stowe, R.	Eye
Stratton, J. de	Norwich
Streyl	Kyme
+Stroder	Durham
Strother	Durham
+Strygete	Durham
Sturry, T. de	Canterbury
Sudbury	Canterbury
+Sutton, T. de	Durham
Swaffham, J.	Bury
Swalwell	Durham
Swan, W.	Durham
Swillington	Cambridge, Aug.
Tame	London, Aug.
Taneto, R. de	Canterbury, St Aug.
Tarrant	Winchester
Tatewic	Lincoln, Fran.
Taunton	Glastonbury
+Taylard	London, St Sepulchre, Holborn, *Ch.*
Texerius	Brecon
Thetford	Butley
Thew	Durham
Thirsk	Fountains
Thomas, abbot	Canterbury, St Aug.
+Thomas, abbot	Chester
Thomas, prior	Canterbury, St Aug.
Throckmorton	Denny
Tilmanstone	Canterbury, St Aug.
+Tode, J.	Durham
Tode, W.	Durham
Tompson	Warwick, Dom.
+Toppyng	Durham
Toroldus	Worcester, Dom.
+Tresham	Syon
+Trussell	Canterbury
Tuting	Durham
+Tuyllett	Cambridge, Aug. friars
Urswick	+Lancaster, Dom.; Hailes
Uthred	Durham
+Valoynes	Canterbury, Dom.
Vitriaco, A. de	Mottisfont
+Voudon	Welbeck
Vowell	+Leigh; Walsingham
Wackerfield (Wakerfeud)	Durham

AI BOOKS (continued)

Knowledge-Based Programming

Turing Institute Press
Knowledge Engineering
Tutorial Series

Managing Editor   Dr Judith Richards
Academic Editor   Dr Peter Mowforth

The Turing Institute, located in Glasgow, Scotland, was established in 1983 as a not-for-profit company, named in honour of the late Alan M. Turing, the distinguished British mathematician and logician whose work has had a lasting influence on the foundations of modern computing.

The Institute offers integrated research and teaching programmes in advanced intelligent technologies – in particular, logic programming, computer vision, robotics and expert systems. It derives its income from research and training contracts, both governmental and industrial, and by subscription from its Industrial Affiliates. It assists Affiliates with the transfer of technology from research to application, and provides them with training for their technical staff, a wide range of software tools and a comprehensive library and information service.

The Turing Institute is an Academic Associate of the University of Strathclyde, and its research staff work closely with different departments of the University on a variety of research programmes.

Other titles published in association with the Turing Institute Press

Applications of Expert Systems
J. Ross Quinlan (Editor)

Structured Induction in Expert Systems
Alen D. Shapiro

Knowledge-Based Programming

Enn Tyugu

Institute of Cybernetics
Estonian Academy of Sciences
Tallinn, USSR

 TURING INSTITUTE PRESS
in association with

 ADDISON-WESLEY PUBLISHING COMPANY
Wokingham, England · Reading, Massachusetts
Menlo Park, California · New York · Don Mills, Ontario
Amsterdam · Bonn · Sydney · Singapore · Tokyo
Madrid · Bogota · Santiago · San Juan

This book is based on Professor Tyugu's work *Kontseptualnoe programmirovanie*, originally published in the USSR by Nauka in 1984.

This translation © 1988 Addison-Wesley Publishers Limited.
© 1988 Addison-Wesley Publishing Company, Inc.

Cover design by Crayon Design, Henley-on-Thames.
Typeset by Advanced Filmsetters (Glasgow) Limited.
Printed in Great Britain by The Bath Press, Avon.
First printed 1987.

British Library Cataloguing in Publication Data

Tyugu, E.
  Knowledge-based programming. — (Turing
Institute Press Knowledge engineering
tutorial series).
  1. Computer software — Development
  2. Artificial intelligence
  I. Title
  005.1′2   QA76.76.D47

  ISBN 0-201-17815-X

Library of Congress Cataloging in Publication Data

Tyugu, È. Kh. (Ènn Kharal 'dovich), 1935–
  [Kontseptual 'noe programmirovanie. English]
  Knowledge-based programming/E. Tyugu.
    p.   cm. — (Turing Institute Press knowledge engineering
  tutorial series)
  Translation of: Kontseptual 'noe programmirovanie.
  Bibliography: p.
  Includes index.
  ISBN 0-201-17815-X
  1. Artificial intelligence — Data processing.   2. Programming
(Electronic computers)   I. Title.   II. Series.
  Q336.T9813 1988
  006.3—dc19   87-19389
                                                           CIP

Preface

This book is intended for readers who are interested in applying artificial intelligence to programming practice. It shows how a computer can be used even at the problem-specification phase of programming. This approach is called **knowledge-based programming**.

The following features of knowledge-based programming are the most important for us:

- using a knowledge base for accumulating useful concepts;
- programming in terms of a problem domain;
- using the computer in the whole problem-solving process beginning with the description of a problem;
- synthesizing programs automatically.

In order to distinguish our approach to problem solving from the approaches to program development in which knowledge is used for adapting algorithms to particular computers and for selecting data structures suitable for computations, we shall use a more specific term, **conceptual programming**, for our approach, because it extensively uses concepts as pieces of knowledge.

In conceptual programming we define concepts for a computer and then use them to describe the problems which are to be solved on the computer. We also expect the computer to construct automatically the programs for solving problems, using the knowledge we have given to it in the specifications.

It is common knowledge that whereas computer performance has increased about 1000 times, that of programmers has increased only 10 times. This difference in performance cannot be sufficiently improved, either by making software distribution easier, or by increasing the number of people involved in computer programming. There are two quite promising ways of increasing the productivity of programming:

- the development of intelligent software packages;
- the implementation of very high-level languages.

Conceptual programming is a combination of these ways which enables a user to build his own intelligent software capable of understanding the language of the user.

Conceptual programming is a way of using the computer as an intelligent partner for problem solving. It includes:

1.   specifying new concepts to the computer;

2.   representing problems to it in terms of these concepts.

The aim of this book is to introduce conceptual programming to the reader and to teach him how to use the computer as a partner which can understand to a certain degree the problem to be solved. This degree of understanding is determined by two factors:

● the available deductive mechanism;

● the amount of knowledge possessed by the computer.

The user must be aware of the computer's degree of understanding when he specifies problems. This is a difficulty of conceptual programming. Common experience of programming is of no help here. A FORTRAN programmer can be sure that the computer could execute almost any syntactically correct FORTRAN program. In our case the syntactic correctness of a specification of a problem is not sufficient. A problem may be unsolvable because the knowledge included in the specification is incomplete. In this case the specification either of the concepts intended to represent the problem or of the problem itself must be extended. This is a completely new technique of program development, and it is discussed throughout this book and illustrated with a considerable number of examples.

To read this book no deep knowledge of programming or of artificial intelligence is needed. A reader must have a general acquaintance with computers as well as with some programming language. Some knowledge of logic is needed, but only for Section 1.3, in which the logical basis of structural synthesis is explained.

The first chapter contains a discussion of a formal representation of problems, which is followed by a description of automatic program synthesis methods for solving problems. Knowledge representation for program synthesis is considered in the second chapter. A reader not interested in program synthesis can skip the first two chapters, except Section 1.1, where the problems are discussed. However, in this case he must just believe that the problems given as examples in the book can be solved automatically.

The third chapter is a description of a language for conceptual programming, and it must be read thoroughly in order to understand the following chapters, where the conceptual programming technique is presented.

The author is convinced that one can only learn to solve problems by practice in solving them. This book therefore contains a considerable number

of examples from various problem domains and special attention is paid to the specification of useful concepts.

The fourth chapter contains specifications of many concepts from geometry and physics which are taught to children in school. It is hoped that this kind of knowledge will soon be a common part of the knowledge base of every computer. A technique for building large intelligent software systems is presented in the fifth chapter, and in the last chapter this technique is applied to specify concepts in several different domains.

Enn Tyugu
Tallinn, USSR

Contents

Chapter 1

Problems and Programs

Programming can be considered to be the first stage of problem solving, in which a plan of action for solving a problem is developed. Given this view, the process of transcribing a program into a programming language acceptable to a computer is only the last and the simplest task of programming. We may draw an analogy between a programmer and a production engineer who designs a tooling process for a machine part. Both of them must take into account the available facilities and make a reasonable plan to produce a result. The result considered by the production engineer is a machine part, usually specified by a drawing. For a programmer, the result is described by a problem specification. We start this book with a discussion of problems and present a precise definition of computational problems, that is, of those problems the book is intended to deal with.

1.1 Representation of problems

According to the point of view taken in this book, programming starts from a problem and not from an algorithm or a flow chart. Therefore, we must define the notion of problem as precisely as possible. It is a difficult task because the world where the problems arise is extremely diverse, and it may even be impossible to find a universal form applicable to all problems. We shall start with computational problems, and later show that a large number of problems can be represented in a similar way.

1.1.1 COMPUTATIONAL PROBLEMS

Computational problems contain variables and the variables are denoted by identifiers, for instance, AX, $x1$, x, $AREA$. We assume that values of variables are data – in particular, pieces of text and numbers. The values may vary both in form and in meaning, i.e. they may be of various types. A more detailed

discussion of variables, values and data types will be presented in the second chapter. We shall represent a computational problem in the following form:

compute $y1,\ldots,yn$ **from** $x1,\ldots,xm$ **knowing** M.

The identifiers $x1,\ldots,xm$, $y1,\ldots,yn$, M are variables. The words **compute, from** and **knowing** have predefined meanings which must be understood by a problem solver. They show that this is a problem statement and they separate the different kinds of variables from each other:

- input variables: $x1,\ldots,xm$;
- output variables: $y1,\ldots,yn$;
- variable M, the value of which represents the problem conditions.

There are no explicit associations between the problem conditions denoted by M and input and output variables of the problem. Nevertheless, we assume that the problem conditions contain all necessary specifications for the input and output variables. In particular, we assume that problem conditions determine the set of variables from which the input or output variables may be drawn.

The data which constitutes the value of M represents the knowledge needed for solving the problem. Hence, the whole complexity of a problem description is hidden in the value of M. New results in artificial intelligence, especially in knowledge representation, can be used for encoding the knowledge needed for problem solving and this will be discussed in the second chapter.

Let us consider some examples of computational problems.

1.   Compute the area of a triangle from its sides – this problem can be represented using variables S,a,b,c to denote the area and sides of a triangle:

        compute S **from** a,b,c **knowing** *triangle*.

It is important to remember that the concept of a triangle must be specified for the solver before this problem can be solved, and it must contain just the same variables S,a,b,c for the area and sides.

2.   Construct a proof of a formula in a theory: this problem is represented by problem conditions:

        compute *proof* **from** *formula* **knowing** *theory*.

3.   Find the names of all young employees of an institute knowing the staff of the institute and the conditions which determine a young employee. In this case we must take care over the form of output of the problem.

We specify a variable which we shall call

names-of-young-employees.

(This is also an identifier.) This variable will have a set of names of all young employees as the value. Denoting the problem conditions as *staff* we can write the problem as follows:

compute *names-of-young-employees* **knowing** *staff.*

This problem statement does not contain input variables – all the knowledge needed for solving is hidden in problem conditions called *staff.*

Let us introduce a shorter form of a problem representation:

$$(M \vdash x1, \ldots, xm \rightarrow y1, \ldots, yn)$$

where the variables $M, x1, \ldots, xm, y1, \ldots, yn$ have the same meaning as before.
Let us denote the fact that a problem is solvable by writing

solvable $(M \vdash x1, \ldots, xm \rightarrow y1, \ldots, yn)$.

Actually, this is a predicate which has three arguments:

- problem conditions M;
- list of input variables $(x1, \ldots, xm)$;
- list of output variables $(y1, \ldots, yn)$.

It is true if and only if the value of M is such that on its basis a program can be constructed which solves the problem.

Computational problems with identical problem conditions can be compared with each other and some conclusions about their complexity can be drawn. Let $in(P)$ denote a set of input variables and $out(P)$ denote a set of output variables of a computational problem P. We say that a problem $P1$ is less than $P2$ ($P1 < P2$) if and only if $in(P1) = in(P2)$, $out(P1) \subset out(P2)$ and both problems have identical problem conditions. This ordering is reasonable. Indeed, if the problem $P2$ can be solved, then $P1$ can be solved also because, due to $out(P1) \subset out(P2)$, the solution of $P2$ contains the solution of $P1$.

There is also another ordering of problems – $P1 \ll P2$ if and only if $in(P2) \subseteq in(P1)$ and $out(P1) \subseteq out(P2)$, where one of the inclusions is strict and the problems have identical problem conditions. In this case the correspondence between solvability and ordering is not so straightforward. Sometimes a problem with a larger set of input variables may be more difficult to solve due to the redundancy and contradictions of input variables.

1.1.2 OTHER PROBLEMS

Not all computational problems fit directly into the form specified above. For instance, the problem:

compute *everything-that-can-be-computed* **from** $x1, \ldots, xm$ **knowing** M

is different. In order to formalize this problem in our way, we must introduce a new variable – *everything-that-can-be-computed*.

The value of this variable is a set of computable variables with their computed values, i.e. a set of pairs of the form

$\langle$variable name$\rangle = \langle$value$\rangle$.

If we are interested only in a solution of a problem for particular values $v1, \ldots, vm$ of the input variables $x1, \ldots, xm$ and not in a program for computing values of $y1, \ldots, yn$ from any given values of $x1, \ldots, xm$, then we can include the following equations among the problem conditions:

$$x1 = v1,$$
$$\vdots$$
$$xm = vm.$$

Then the problem representation will not contain input variables, being simply

compute $y1, \ldots, yn$ **knowing** M,

or in the abbreviated form:

$(M \vdash y1, \ldots, yn)$.

Introducing new variables can be useful in various cases when something must be computed. One more example of a problem of that kind is

compute *all-that-is-needed* **from** $x1, \ldots, xm$ **knowing** M.

all-that-is-needed must be specified by the value of M. In particular, all changes caused by new values of $x1, \ldots, xm$ may be asked for. (This particular problem is rather difficult to solve.)

There are problems of a quite different nature – the problems in which some real-world activities are needed. For example, to bring a small green box from the leftmost room of a building. Generally speaking, these are not problems for a computer, but a computer can be used to plan the solution of such problems. The plan which is needed can be designated by a variable, and

this will be an output variable of the problem for the computer. However, in this case some difficulties may arise, because the problem conditions may change during the course of action. In other words, the problem conditions are not sufficient to form the whole plan. In this case planning and real-world activities can be performed alternately and repetitively. Planning for a single stage of activities is done with the assumption that the environment does not change, and consequently the problem conditions are fixed for that stage.

In this section we have shown that many essentially different problems can be represented in the form

$$(M \vdash x1, \ldots, xm \rightarrow y1, \ldots, yn).$$

We discussed some modifications of this problem (omitting input variables and asking for all that can be computed) and proposed a method of introducing a new variable to denote the desired result. The main restriction on the use of this problem representation is the requirement that problem conditions must be completely specified before the solution planning begins.

We have barely touched here on the problem conditions M. (We shall also call this problem specification.) The remaining part of this chapter and the second chapter are devoted mainly to the question of how to represent and use knowledge about problems. This subject concerns just the problem conditions M.

1.2 Logical foundations of program synthesis

There are three different approaches to program synthesis:

- **deductive synthesis**, which uses automatic deduction of a proof of solvability of a problem and derives a program from the proof;
- **inductive synthesis**, where a program is built on the basis of examples of input–output pairs or examples of computations;
- **transformational synthesis**, where a program is derived stepwise from a specification by means of transformations.

In this book we shall use deductive synthesis of programs. In this case the way from a problem to a program is as follows:

problem in source form →
problem represented in a formal theory →
proof of solvability of the problem →
program.

The first step – transforming a problem into a language of a formal theory – can be done by means of a translation technique. The most complicated step is the construction of a solvability proof of the problem. In order to discuss

this step we need some knowledge in logic, which will be supplied in the present section.

The last step – derivation of a program from a solvability proof – is a simpler task. A constructive proof of the fact that a solution of a problem exists is itself, in some sense, an algorithm or, at least, it contains the knowledge for finding the desired solution. The trouble is that this algorithm may be extremely inefficient.

If all the three steps of deductive program synthesis are performed automatically (by a correct synthesizer), then a user can be sure that he obtains a correct program for solving the problem which he has specified. But the correctness of the problem specification is up to him, and instead of debugging a program he has to debug the specification. It is easier to do, because it can be done at the conceptual level and a lot of computation-oriented details can be omitted.

1.2.1 FORMAL THEORIES

Here we shall present a brief survey of the concepts of formal logic needed for reading this chapter. Complete definitions can be found in any introduction to logic – for instance, in Lyndon (1966).

Any formal theory has its language of **formulae**. This is a formal language, hence, the formulae can be recognized syntactically.

Besides the formulae, a formal theory has **inference rules** for deriving new formulae from given ones. Let a formula A be derivable from the formulae $A1, \ldots, Ak$ by an inference rule R. We denote this as follows:

$$\frac{A1, \ldots, Ak}{A} (R)$$

and call it a step of derivation where $A1, \ldots, Ak$ are **premises** and A is a **conclusion**.

Any formal theory also has a subset of distinguished formulae called **axioms**. These are formulae which are available *a priori* for deriving new formulae.

A **derivation** of a formula A is a sequence of derivation steps where premises of any derivation step are either axioms or conclusions of preceding steps and the last step has the formula A as a conclusion. A derivation of a formula can also be called a proof of the formula. An example of derivation is shown in Figure 1.1. Only one inference rule is used in this derivation:

$$\frac{F_1, \ldots, F_k, F_1 \& \ldots \& F_k \to F}{F}$$

where $F_1, \ldots, F_k, F$ are formulae.

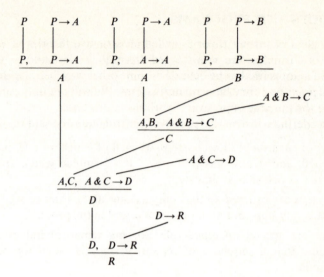

Figure 1.1   An example of derivation.

Now we can explain what we mean by saying that we express a problem in a formal theory. This means that problem conditions are represented as a set of formulae of the theory (we call them **specific axioms**, because they are specific for the problem). One more formula expresses the solvability of the problem; we call it an **existence theorem**, because it states that a solution of the problem exists.

Formulae, axioms and derivations are syntactic concepts which enable us to build a complete syntactic description of a formal theory. But formulae also have a meaning, which is represented by the semantics of a theory. The semantics is given by a mapping which associates a meaning with every formula of the theory. We call this meaning an interpretation of a formula. To represent semantics we need a new collection of objects called interpretations. For example, one such object is 'falsity', denoted by $\perp$. There are many different ways of assigning meanings to formulae even for well-known logical theories – see Mints (1977). We are interested in programs and therefore we are going to use programs as interpretations of formulae.

Note for logicians   Basically, we use the standard interpretation for the intuitionistic system outlined by Kolmogorov (1932) and Heyting (1934), made precise by Kleene (1952) and Gödel (1958) in the form of realizability interpretations, and adapted to the programming context by numerous authors – Manna and Waldinger (1971), Constable (1972), Goto (1978), Martin-Löf (1979), Sato (1979), Nepeivoda (1981).

1.2.2 PROOFS AND PROGRAMS

There is a class of formal theories called **constructive theories** in which the meanings of formulae are constructed from their derivations. Only the meanings of axioms need to be defined in some other way, because the axioms are given *a priori* and they have no derivations. We will use only constructive theories for the purpose of program synthesis in this book.

Considering constructive proofs in general, it can be said that:

1. a proof consists of discrete steps, at each of which an inference rule is applied, and it also has premises – the formulae which are used to prove a conclusion at that step;

2. the steps are ordered so that only axioms and earlier proved facts are used at any step, and no loops are allowed in the proof;

3. there are special inference rules for mathematical induction which assume that a sequence of repetitive steps is taken for deriving a formula;

4. some steps are very complicated in the sense that, proving something at a given step, new subgoals are created and must be proved. A proof of a subgoal is analogous to a proof of a theorem.

In such a proof we can observe a flow of proved facts similar to data flow in a program. These considerations show us the analogy between proofs and programs. A proof may be converted into a program one step at a time and the structure of the program can remain the same as the structure of the proof, because 'the flow of facts' in the proof must satisfy the same requirements as the information flow in the program. The programs derived from proofs are well structured (they do not contain **go to** statements), because the proofs are well structured. Loops may occur in programs if the induction principle is used in a proof.

There are two ways of deriving a program. The first way uses the realizability of formulae of constructive proofs directly. In this case, for every step of the proof, a function $dcl(p,a,c)$ is applied which computes the text of a part of a program from the given inference rule p, the list of premises a and the conclusion c of the step. The complete program is derived from the last step of the proof. If the program is derived in a functional form, it does not contain assignments to variables.

Axiom	Realization
$P \rightarrow A$	$\alpha(t)$
$P \rightarrow B$	$\beta(t)$
$A \& B \rightarrow C$	$\mu(t_1, t_2)$
$A \& C \rightarrow D$	$\delta(t_1, t_2)$
$D \rightarrow R$	$\rho(t)$

Figure 1.2   Realization of formulae.

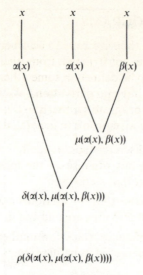

Figure 1.3   The derivation of a functional program.

Let us consider the derivation of a program from the proof shown in Figure 1.1.

A,B,C,D are some meaningful formulae which may even contain the variables x and y. The function *dcl* is defined in Figure 1.2. Figure 1.3 shows the stepwise derivation of a functional program.

The second way of constructing a program is deriving it statement by statement from the proof. In this case special care must be taken with declarations, which must be derived from the variables and constants of the proof. In this case, a derived program will contain assignments (or procedure calls). In Figure 1.4 the statement-by-statement derivation of the example

1. $\dfrac{P, P \rightarrow A}{A}$

2. $\dfrac{P, P \rightarrow B}{B}$

3. $\dfrac{A, B, A \& B \rightarrow C}{C}$

4. $\dfrac{A, C, A \& C \rightarrow D}{D}$

5. $\dfrac{D, D \rightarrow R}{R}$

1. $w_1 := \alpha(x)$

2. $w_2 := \beta(x)$

3. $w_3 := \mu(w_1, w_2)$

4. $w_4 := \delta(w_1, w_3)$

5. $y := \rho(w_4)$

begin real $w_1, w_2, w_3, w_4;$

$w_1 := \alpha(x);$

$w_2 := \beta(x);$

$w_3 := \mu(w_1, w_2);$

$w_4 := \delta(w_1, w_3);$

$y := \rho(w_4);$

end

(a)   (b)   (c)

Figure 1.4   The derivation of a program with assignments.

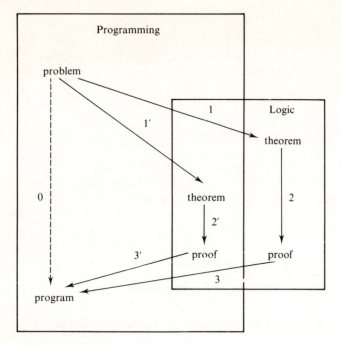

Figure 1.5   The ways from a problem to a program.

program is shown. All declarations are added, and the complete program is formed at the last step.

Here we have considered program synthesis very informally. But it can be described precisely, including a specification of the programming language and its semantics, as well as the description of theories for problem specification and verification of the programs.

Before choosing a suitable class of theories for program synthesis let us consider the general situation in deductive program synthesis as illustrated in Figure 1.5.

This field partly belongs to programming and partly to logic. Programming know-how, accumulated over several decades, considerably shortens the path from problem to program compared with the early days of automatic computing. The first attempts at program synthesis lengthened this distance, because going from problem to an existence theorem means going from programming to logic (1), the process of theorem proving (2) belongs to logic, and the derivation of the program (3) brings one back to programming. The situation can be improved by using special theories for representing knowledge and for proving existence theorems. This enables us to shorten the path from a problem to a program, shifting theorems and proofs from pure logic toward programming in order to simplify the most complicated step – proving the existence theorem (2′). Thereby the

difference between a problem description and an existence theorem may even increase. However, well-developed translation techniques allow us to get existence theorems from problem descriptions quite easily, and thus to take a big step (1′) in the right direction.

1.3 Structural synthesis of programs

The idea of structural synthesis is that a proof of solvability of a problem can be built and that the overall structure of a program can be derived from the proof, knowing very little about the actual properties of the functions used in the program (Tyugu, 1981). We assume that our problem specification contains only information about the applicability of functions for computing values of variables which occur in the problem specification. Some of this information is encoded in implicative formulae of the form

$$A \& \ldots \& B \to C$$

which has a logical meaning '$A, \ldots, B$ implies C' as well as the computational meaning 'C is computable from $A, \ldots, B$'. In the first case $A, \ldots, B, C$ are considered as statements, in the second case as computable objects according to the familiar constructive interpretation of an implication $A \& \ldots \& B \to C$, which is a procedure transforming any realization of $A, \ldots, B$ into some realization of C. Sometimes we shall explicitly indicate this transformation f by writing it under the arrow:

$$A \& \ldots \& B \underset{f}{\to} C \tag{1.1}$$

Such formulae constitute a more restricted language than PROLOG because no free variables are allowed in the statements $A, \ldots, C$. But we also allow nested implications like

$$(A \to B) \& \ldots \& (C \to D) \to (E \to F) \tag{1.2}$$

which add generality to the language. Nested implications allow us to introduce procedures of higher types, since the interpretation of Formula (1.2) is a computation of F from the realizations of $A \to B, \ldots, C \to D$ and of E.

Note for logicians   Formula (1.2) allows us to use objects of all finite types by introducing new propositional variables implicitly through additional transformations and to reduce any propositional formula to a form dealt with by the structural synthesis.

1.3.1 A LANGUAGE FOR REPRESENTING SYNTHESIZED PROGRAMS

Now we are going to describe a language in which programs are automatically constructed. This language, called PL, is not a language for writing programs by hand. It is an internal language of the computer. In this case the convenience of reading and writing programs in it is not as important as the possibility of transforming programs into efficient code. This transformation is trivial, as long as we have only nonrecursive function definitions. The transformation consists of elimination of repetitive computations of identical subexpressions by introducing assignments, and of elimination of computations of unused variables.

PL is a typed functional language. We assume a finite number of primitive types: $\tau, \ldots, \sigma$.

We assume that there exists an infinite number of variables x^σ, y^σ, u^σ, v^σ, $x_1^q \ldots$ for each type σ. Sometimes we omit the type index σ and write $x, y, \ldots$ for variables of primitive types and $\varphi, \psi, \ldots$ for higher types.

We assume the existence of constants of primitive and nonprimitive types: $a, b, f, g, F, G, F_1, \ldots$.

We are defining a functional language. A program in this language is just a term (i.e. an expression).

Terms are built from variables and constants using parentheses and the symbol λ:

1. constants and variables are terms;

2. if t is a term of type $(\sigma_1, \ldots, \sigma_n : \tau)$ and $s_1, \ldots, s_n$ are of types $\sigma_1, \ldots, \sigma_n$, $S = (s_1, \ldots, s_n)$, then $t(S)$ is a term of type τ derived from the value of S by the function which is the value of t;

3. if t is a term of type τ and x is a variable of type σ, then $\lambda x t$ is a term of type $(\sigma : \tau)$; x is a bound variable in this term. In general, t may contain occurrences of x and this is expressed by the notation $t[x]$; $\lambda x t[x]$ is a function yielding $t(a)$ for the given value a of type σ.

Let us use a common meta-notation $t_x[r]$ to express the substitution of r for all occurrences of x in t (with renaming of bound variables to avoid collisions). Then the semantics of λ-terms is given as follows:

$$(\lambda x t)(r) = t_x[r].$$

The constants of PL represent programs which are available to the synthesizer. In this sense the set of constants is potentially infinite. New programs are obtained, and new constants are realized, for instance, when an equation given in a problem specification is translated into the internal language.

At first glance, this programming language prevents a programmer from using the usual constructs of programs (**if–then–else** and **while–do**). In

fact, these constructs can be introduced using constants with a predefined realization (which is not part of PL).

The conditional expression

if p then f else g fi

can be presented by a term

$$\mathbf{C}^{((\mathbf{bool}, \sigma, \sigma): \sigma)} (p^{\mathbf{bool}}, f^{\sigma}, g^{\sigma})$$

where $\mathbf{C}$ is a constant and **bool** is a primitive type. The realization of $\mathbf{C}$ must be supplied by a programmer and must have the properties:

$$t_1 \rightarrow \mathbf{C}(t_1, t_2, t_3) = t_2, \ \neg t_1 \rightarrow \mathbf{C}(t_1, t_2, t_3) = t_3.$$

Recursion can be expressed by means of constants $\mathbf{R}$ of type $(\tau, (nat, \tau : \tau), nat : \tau)$ with a realization given by a programmer and satisfying

$$\mathbf{R}(r,s,\mathbf{0}) = r, \ \mathbf{R}(r,s,\mathbf{next}(u)) = s(u, \mathbf{R}(r,s,u)),$$

where $\mathbf{0}$ is the zero constant, nat is the predefined type for natural numbers and **next** is a constant realized by the successor function.

Let us consider some examples. First of all, an expression can be used as a function specification. If we accept infix notation for functions, then $\lambda x(2 * \sin(x) * \cos(y))$ is a function of x and $\lambda y(2 * \sin * (x) * \cos(y))$ is a function of y. Continuing the example, we can write:

$$\lambda x(2 * \sin(x) * \cos(y))(30°) = \cos(y)$$
$$\lambda y(2 * \sin(x) * \cos(y))(60°) = \sin(x).$$

Our programming language PL, also called **lambda notation**, is convenient for representing functions which have arguments which are also functions.

If we have a program **simps** for integration, we can write **simps**(f,a) instead of $\int_0^a f(x)\,dx$.

But our notation allows us also to show explicitly that the program **simps** has two input parameters: f and a. Then we must write $\lambda f \lambda a \ \mathbf{simps}(f,a)$.

1.3.2A LOGICAL LANGUAGE (LL)

This is an internal language in which theorems are proved. It has only three kinds of formulae:

1. propositional variables: A, B, etc.;

2.   formulae called unconditional computability statements:

$$A_1 \,\&\ldots\&\, A_k \to B \tag{1.3}$$

or in a shorter form: $\underline{A} \to B$;

3.   formulae called conditional computability statements:

$$(\underline{A}^1 \to B^1) \,\&\ldots\&\, (\underline{A}^n \to B^n) \to (\underline{C} \to D)$$

or in a shorter form

$$(\underline{A} \to B) \to (\underline{C} \to D). \tag{1.4}$$

Let us informally explain the meaning of the formulae. A propositional variable is used in one sense only. It corresponds to some variable from the source problem, and it expresses the fact that a value of this variable can be computed.

An unconditional computability statement $A_1 \&\ldots\& A_k \to B$ expresses the computability of (a value of the variable) b corresponding to B from (values) of $a_1, \ldots, a_k$, which correspond to $A_1, \ldots, A_k$.

A conditional computability statement such as

$$(A \to B) \to (C \to D)$$

expresses the computability of d from c depending on the computation of b from a. (As above, the lower-case letters a,b,c,d are the variables corresponding to A,B,C,D.)

Let us encode in our logical language the problem of computing the double integral

$$s = \int_0^a \int_0^b z \, dx \, dy, \qquad z = g(x, y).$$

First of all, propositional variables S,A,B,X,Y,Z and W must be introduced, where W stands for the computability of $w = \int_0^b z \, dx$.

The computability statements are

$$X \,\&\, Y \to Z \qquad \text{(for } z = g(x, y)\text{)},$$

$$(X \to Z) \to (B \to W) \qquad \left(\text{for } w = \int_0^b z \, dx\right),$$

$$(Y \to W) \to (A \to S) \qquad \left(\text{for } s = \int_0^a w \, dy\right).$$

The goal is to prove $A \,\&\, B \to S$.

1.3.3 DERIVATION OF FORMULAE

To complete the description of the class of theories we are dealing with, we define a derivation of a formula and give the inference rules for building the derivations. We use a sequent notation for expressing the derivability of formulae. A sequent $\Gamma \vdash X$, where Γ is a list of formulae and X is a formula, means that the formula X is derivable from the formulae appearing in Γ. The notation Σ, Γ means concatenation of the lists Σ and Γ, with contraction of repetitions of formulae in the resulting list. For any formula X, any list Γ, and any theory considered here, the sequent $\Gamma, X \vdash X$ is an axiom. Traditionally we call it a logical axiom. Beyond this we have axioms in the form of $\vdash X$, where X is a computability statement. These statements are called specific or problem-oriented axioms, because they express specific knowledge about particular problems. Examples are the axioms of double integration:

$$\vdash X \,\&\, Y \to Z; \vdash (X \to Z) \to (B \to W); \vdash (Y \to W) \to (A \to S).$$

The derivation of a formula X is a tree of sequents with the sequent $\vdash X$ in its root. Each sequent in the tree is either an axiom, being a leaf of the tree, or a conclusion of the nodes immediately above it according to one of the following three rules which we call **structural synthesis rules** (SSR):

$$\frac{(\underline{A} \to B) \to (\underline{C} \to V); \Gamma, \underline{A} \vdash B; \Sigma \vdash C}{\Gamma, \Sigma \vdash V} \qquad (\to - -)$$

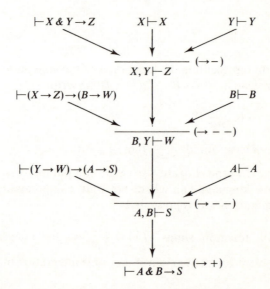

Figure 1.6   Proof of solvability of a double-integration problem.

where $\Gamma, \underline{A} \vdash B$ is a set of sequents for all $\underline{A} \to B$ in $(\underline{A} \to B)$, and $\Sigma \vdash C$ is a set of sequents for all C in $\underline{C}$.

$$\frac{\vdash \underline{A} \to V; \Gamma \vdash \underline{A}}{\Gamma \vdash V} \qquad (\to -)$$

where $\Gamma \vdash \underline{A}$ is a set of sequents for all A in $\underline{A}$,

$$\frac{\Gamma, \underline{A} \vdash B}{\Gamma \vdash \underline{A} \to B} \qquad (\to +)$$

In the rule $(\to - -)$ $\underline{A}$ is a list of propositional variables from $\underline{A}$. That means that B may be computable from fewer variables than is assumed in the conditional computability statement.

In Figure 1.6 the derivation of the goal $A \& B \to S$ is shown, given the double-integration axioms and four logical axioms: $A \vdash A$, $B \vdash B$, $X \vdash X$ and $Y \vdash Y$.

1.3.4 PROGRAM EXTRACTION

Now we extend our logical language (LL) with terms of the programming language which represent programs. Instead of

$$\underline{A} \to B$$

we write

$$\underline{A} \xrightarrow{f} B \qquad (1.5)$$

where f is a term representing the function which computes b from $a_1, \ldots, a_n$. Analogously, instead of $(\underline{A} \to B) \to (\underline{C} \to D)$ we write

$$(\underline{A} \xrightarrow{g} B) \to (\underline{C} \xrightarrow{F(g)} D), \qquad (1.6)$$

where g is a list of terms for all $\underline{A} \xrightarrow{g} B$ in $(\underline{A} \xrightarrow{g} B)$.

Formulae (1.5) and (1.6) are also called computability statements. They constitute a new language LL1, where not only computability but also the means for computations are represented.

Having a function **simps** $(f, v) = \int_0^v f \, du$ for integration, we can express the problem-oriented axioms for double integration in LL1:

$$\vdash X \& Y \xrightarrow{g} Z$$

$$\vdash (X \xrightarrow[\varphi]{} Z) \rightarrow (B \xrightarrow[\text{simps}(\varphi)]{} W)$$

$$\vdash (Y \xrightarrow[\varphi]{} W) \rightarrow (A \xrightarrow[\text{simps}(\varphi)]{} S).$$

The meaning of this notation can be explained as follows. We have already agreed that $A \rightarrow B$ means computability of the proper value of b from a given value of a. Denoting by $\mathbf{A}(x)$ and $\mathbf{B}(y)$ the statements that x is the proper value of a and y is the proper value of b, we can write instead of $A \rightarrow B$ a more detailed formula

$$(\exists x\mathbf{A}(x)) \rightarrow (\exists y\mathbf{B}(y)),$$

or

$$\forall x(\mathbf{A}(x) \rightarrow \exists y\mathbf{B}(y)),$$

which is equivalent.

If we know as well that a term f represents the function which computes b from a, then we can, instead of the last formula, write more precisely

$$\forall x(\mathbf{A}(x) \rightarrow \mathbf{B}(f(x))).$$

This formula is abbreviated to $A \xrightarrow[f]{} B$ in LL1.

Continuing in the same manner, we can introduce the abbreviation

$$(A \xrightarrow[g]{} B) \rightarrow (C \xrightarrow[F(g)]{} D)$$

for the formula

$$\forall g(\forall x\mathbf{A}(x) \rightarrow \mathbf{B}(g(x))) \rightarrow \forall x(\mathbf{C}(x) \rightarrow \mathbf{D}(F(g, x))).$$

A generalization for the formula

$$(\underline{A} \rightarrow B) \rightarrow (\underline{C} \rightarrow D)$$

is obvious.

Due to the one-to-one correspondence between the formulae of LL and LL1, we can immediately conclude that the structural synthesis rules are applicable in LL1 after minor syntactic amendments. These amendments concern the construction of new terms included into derived sequents. The terms appear as follows:

1. Terms in axioms are given. This is obvious for specific axioms and it is true for logical axioms because they have the form $A(t) \vdash A(t)$, where A

is a monadic predicate and t is either a variable or a constant of primitive type.

2.   The application of the rule $(\rightarrow\ -)$ gives a sequent

$$\Gamma \vdash V(f(a_1, a_2, \ldots, a_k))$$

where f is taken from the premise $\underline{A} \xrightarrow{f} V$ and each a_i is taken from $\Gamma_i \vdash A_i(a_i)$.

3.   The application of the rule $(\rightarrow\ -\ -)$ gives a sequent

$$\Gamma, \Sigma \vdash V(F(\lambda \underline{a}^1 b^1, \lambda \underline{a}^2 b^2, \ldots, \lambda \underline{a}^n, b^n)(c_1, \ldots, c_m))$$

where $\underline{a}^i$ are lists of individual variables from $\underline{A}^i(a^i)$, each b^i is taken from $\underline{A}^i \vdash B^i(b^i)$, and each c_i is taken from $\Sigma_i \vdash C_i(c_i)$.

4.   The rule $(\rightarrow\ +)$ yields a sequent

$$\vdash A_k \xrightarrow{\lambda a_1 \ldots \lambda a_k b} b$$

where b comes from $B(b)$ and each a_i comes from $A_i(a_i)$.

Resuming what is said above, we get the inference rules SSR1 for the language LL1:

$$\frac{\vdash (\underline{A} \xrightarrow{g} B) \rightarrow (C \xrightarrow{F(g)} V); \Gamma, \underline{A} \vdash B(b); \Sigma \vdash C(c)}{\Gamma, \Sigma \vdash V(F(\lambda \underline{ab})(\underline{c}))} \qquad (\rightarrow\ -\ -)$$

$$\frac{\vdash \underline{A} \rightarrow B; \Gamma \vdash A(a)}{\Gamma \vdash V(f(\underline{a}))} \qquad (\rightarrow\ -)$$

$$\frac{\underline{A} \vdash B(b)}{\vdash A \xrightarrow{\lambda \underline{ab}} B} \qquad (\rightarrow\ +)$$

We finish the example of double integration by extracting a program from the derivation of $\vdash A \& B \rightarrow S$. We assign terms (free variables x,y,a,b) to the logical axioms: $X(x) \vdash X(x)$, $Y(y) \vdash Y(y)$, $A(a) \vdash A(a)$, $B(b) \vdash B(b)$. The terms of the problem-oriented axioms of this example were constructed at the beginning of this section.

The derivation of $A \& B \rightarrow S$ together with the extraction of a program in LL1 is shown in Figure 1.7.

Let us note that using the constants with a preprogrammed meaning:

recu   for primitive recursion,
min   for unbounded minimization,
0   for the zero function,
next   for the successor function

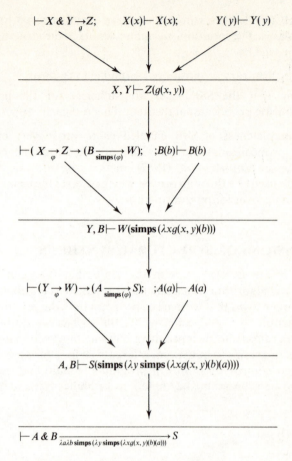

Figure 1.7   The extraction of a double-integration program.

(see Section 1.3.1), we can encode in LL1 any recursive function as soon as we know its partial recursive description, i.e. its representation through primitive recursion and minimization operators. This shows a trivial method for automatic construction of any recursive function from its axiomatic representation in LL1, provided only four operations **recu**, **min**, **0** and **next** are preprogrammed.

1.3.5 COMPLETENESS OF STRUCTURAL SYNTHESIS RULES

One can immediately see that rules ($\rightarrow$ $-$ $-$), ($\rightarrow$ $-$) and ($\rightarrow$ $+$) can be obtained from the familiar natural deduction rules for $\rightarrow$ and & (Gentzen, 1965). So the SSR rules constitute a subsystem of the intuitionistic propositional calculus.

It is surprising that the language LL with quite simple implicative formulae not only allows us to express computability, but is also equivalent to the intuitionistic propositional calculus. Besides that, the formulae of LL are

simple enough to allow an efficient search of proofs needed for automatic program synthesis. The intuitionistic completeness of the structural synthesis rules can be proved by

1.   reducing arbitrary propositional formulae to LL-form;
2.   showing that the SSR rules are sufficient for the proof of any intuitionistic propositional theorem. This is done in Appendix A.

The completeness of SSR enabled us to prove very efficiently all intuitionistic propositional theorems (about 100 formulae) contained in Kleene (1952); see Volozh *et al.* (1982). In this case the existing program synthesizer was used as a theorem prover, which reverses the usual technique of using a theorem prover for program synthesis.

1.3.6 EXTENSIONS OF STRUCTURAL SYNTHESIS

The SSR rules are general rules in the sense that they can be used for synthesizing any algorithm which can be represented as a primitive recursive function. In order to do that we need to program only the primitive recursion operator, function '$+1$' and constant '0'. But in fact we do not intend to synthesize programs from such primitive building blocks, because this would require the set of axioms to be extremely large even for a program of moderate size. The usual control structures of programs (conditional statement and loop) can also be programmed as functions of higher types and used in the axioms

$$(C \xrightarrow[\varphi]{} D) \to (A \xrightarrow[\mathbf{if}(\varphi)]{} B)$$

and

$$(C \xrightarrow[\varphi]{} D \to A \xrightarrow[\mathbf{while}(\varphi)]{} B).$$

In this case, the body of a loop and the statement under the condition are synthesized automatically as realizations of the function φ of the subproblem

$$(C \xrightarrow[\varphi]{} D).$$

There are some simple cases when loops can be synthesized directly from specifications represented in a slightly extended logical language.

Synthesis of loops

Let us introduce sequences of computability statements into the logical language. Let $I, J, \ldots$ be index variables which can have natural numbers as values. We shall extend our language with indexed propositional variables $A[1], B[1], A[2], \ldots, A[I], B[I], A[J], \ldots$ and also $A[I+1], B[I+1], \ldots,$

using only constants, index variables or expressions $I+1, J+1,\dots$ as indices. Let us restrict the usage of indexed propositional variables so that only one index variable can occur in a computability statement. Then, for example,

$$A[I] \rightarrow A[I+1]$$

and

$$A[I] \rightarrow B[I]$$

are formulae of the extended language, but

$$A[I] \rightarrow B[J]$$

is not. We shall assume that any computability statement with indexed variables represents an infinite set of computability statements which are obtained by substituting natural numbers $1, 2,\dots$ instead of the index variable. In particular, the formula

$$A[I] \xrightarrow{f} A[I+1]$$

represents the sequence

$$A[1] \xrightarrow{f} A[2]; A[2] \xrightarrow{f} A[3];\dots$$

It is easy to see that, if the formula

$$A[I] \xrightarrow{f} A[I+1]$$

can be derived by SSR, then so can the formula

$$A[m] \xrightarrow{f^{n-m}} A[n]$$

where m, n are natural numbers, $n > m$, and f^{n-m} means application of f $n-m$ times. This allows us to introduce a new rule applicable to computability statements with indexed propositional variables:

$$\frac{\Gamma \rightarrow B \xrightarrow{f} A[m]; \vdash A[I] \xrightarrow{g} A[I+1]}{\Gamma \vdash B \xrightarrow{f; g^{n-m}} A[n]}$$

where m and n are metasymbols denoting any natural numbers which satisfy the condition $n > m$. Instead of $f; g^{n-m}$ we can also write

$f;$ **for** $i := m$ **step** 1 **until** $n - 1$ **do**
$\langle program\ for\ g \rangle$ **od**.

Restrictions on the indexed variables can be weakened. In particular, we can allow the usage of several indices at any propositional variable, for instance, $A[I, J + 1]$. If, in a computability statement, one and the same index position contains one and the same index variable for all indexed propositional variables, then the inference rule remains applicable for every index position separately. For example, from the following computability statements:

$$B \underset{h}{\rightarrow} A[1, 1]$$

$$A[I, J] \underset{f}{\rightarrow} A[I + 1, J]$$

$$A[n, J] \underset{g}{\rightarrow} A[1, J + 1]$$

where n is a constant, we can derive the program for computing $A[n, m]$

$$\langle program \, for \, h \rangle;$$
$$\textbf{for } J := 1 \textbf{ step } 1 \textbf{ until } m \textbf{ do}$$
$$\textbf{for } I := 1 \textbf{ step } 1 \textbf{ until } n \textbf{ do}$$
$$\langle program \, for \, f \rangle \textbf{ od};$$
$$\langle program \, for \, g \rangle \textbf{ od}.$$

Fixed point of a set of computability statements

One of the principles of the structural synthesis of programs is not to use any other properties of functions except the types of their input and output variables. Strictly following this principle prevents us from solving even some very simple systems of equations, because we cannot check whether the equations are independent or not. For instance, let the equations be

$$y = f(x) \qquad \text{and} \qquad x = g(y).$$

It may happen that the equations uniquely determine the values of x and y, but this depends on properties of the functions f and g. Obviously, these equations give us the computability statements

$$X \underset{f}{\rightarrow} Y \qquad \text{and} \qquad Y \underset{g}{\rightarrow} X,$$

where X, Y are the propositional variables which represent computability of x and y. But these computability statements are not sufficient for building a proof of computability of x and y from the equations. If we have additional knowledge about the functions f and g which allows us to conclude that x and y are computable from the system of equations $y = f(x)$ and $x = g(y)$, then we can add the axioms

$$\underset{G(f, g)}{\longrightarrow} Z; Z \underset{p_1}{\rightarrow} X; Z \underset{p_2}{\rightarrow} Y,$$

where Z represents a new variable $z = (x, y)$, the value of which consists of the values of x and y. A function G of higher order takes functions f and g as arguments and gives out as a result a constant function for the value of z. The functions p_1 and p_2 are projection functions for computing x and y from z.

If we somehow know that a set of equations is solvable for the variables contained in it, then we can use a special inference rule for generating formulae with the function G for the iterative solution of sets of equations. The inference rule is as follows:

$$\frac{\vdash A \xrightarrow{g} B; \qquad \vdash B \xrightarrow{f} A}{\vdash \xrightarrow{G(f,g)} Z},$$

where Z is a new variable which satisfies the axioms $Z \xrightarrow{p_1} A$ and $Z \xrightarrow{p_2} B$.

This is a rule of restricted applicability and it can be applied only if we know that the functions f and g are independent.

1.4 Comments and references

The theoretical possibility of automatic program synthesis follows from the Kleene–Nelson theorem, (Kleene, 1952). Programmers became aware of this from the papers of Constable (1972), Manna and Waldinger (1971) at the beginning of the 1970s. Equivalence of different realizability definitions in logic was demonstrated by Mints (1977). Realizability of intuitionistic formulae in the form of programs was defined by Nepeivoda (1978).

Research in automatic deduction started in the 1960s. One of the first efficient automatic theorem provers was built in Leningrad and was based on Maslov's methods (Maslov, 1964).

Robinson (1965) described the resolution principle, which can be easily used in automatic theorem provers. A good survey of methods based on the resolution principle is presented in Chang and Lee (1973). Practical methods for automatic synthesis of programs appeared at the end of the 1970s. Algorithms for structural synthesis are presented in Tyugu and Harf (1981). A survey of practical methods for program synthesis is contained in Tyugu (1980).

We shall not discuss PROLOG here, although it is undoubtedly the closest language to our own knowledge-based approach. A good book on PROLOG is Bratko (1986). The relation between logic programming and structural synthesis of programs is considered in Tyugu (1986).

Chapter 2
Representation of Knowledge for Problem Solving

We consider programming as an essential part of problem solving, and for problem solving we need knowledge. In the first chapter we described a class of formal theories for knowledge representation. Obviously, formal theories are not suitable for use by humans as knowledge-representation languages. In this chapter we shall discuss other means for representing knowledge about computational problems. We shall start the chapter with a discussion of data types and data specifications in programming languages. There is good reason to think that further development of the means of data specification in programming languages will bring them very close to knowledge-representation languages as developed in the artificial intelligence field.

First of all, let us consider the nature of knowledge. The question may arise, why do we say that knowledge is needed for problem solving – why is it not sufficient to speak about data or information, which are quite well-defined notions? Indeed, knowledge is always encoded in a computer as some kind of data, but we may regard the latter as only a carrier of knowledge, just as some physical media are data carriers. We are unable to define the concept of knowledge precisely. Instead, we can give some examples.

Let us consider a table which represents the budget of the USSR, where all quantities are given in roubles. We may try to make the budget more comprehensible to a Western reader by changing the values from roubles to dollars. Obviously, this is a simple data-processing task which can be performed by means of a very small program. We may also want to translate the names of all items of the budget. Some of them can be translated easily, because a correspondence exists between the budgets of states. Perhaps some programmers would say that this translation is also only a data-processing task. But the translation of some parts of the budget needs deeper analysis, and that, in its turn, needs much knowledge of the Soviet economy. Coming back to converting roubles to dollars we can observe that even here we need some knowledge about foreign currencies, albeit only a very small amount – in fact, only one number is needed.

This example demonstrates that there is no strict difference between data processing and knowledge processing. Besides that, we see that some knowledge can be represented as programs – for example, as a program for changing roubles to dollars.

2.1 Data types

The concept of data type was developed gradually from the concept of primitive types in programming languages. Firstly it described a format (fixed or floating point) of numbers. Very soon, floating-point numbers were called real numbers. Boolean values **true** and **false** appeared which were represented by binary 1 and 0. So the data in the computer acquired additional meaning and also some new properties. Besides the form of physical representation of data, the type began also to denote the functions which could be performed with the data and, some time later, abstract properties of data which could be expressed axiomatically.

When Algol-68 was developed, the importance of precise specification of various new objects became clear. Specifications were needed not only for numbers, strings and arrays, but also for procedures, names and types that were considered as objects as well. Simula-67 was the first language where such objects appeared which were neither data nor procedures, but possessed the properties of both of them. It became more convenient to speak about states of such objects than about their values. For instance, objects like CAR, PROCESS or QUEUE could have states. Later a concept of abstract data type was introduced for representing classes of objects of that kind.

Eventually, a language called UTOPIST made it possible to describe properties of objects in such a way that new functions could be automatically synthesized from a small number of preprogrammed functions. Specifications of objects in the UTOPIST language can be regarded as frames, in the usage of artificial intelligence. In this case a specification of an object in the input language is actually a text in a knowledge-representation language. Internal representation of the specification is a semantic network or a set of axioms of a formal theory.

In the following text we shall follow in more detail the path from primitive and syntactic data types to abstract data types and knowledge-representation languages.

2.1.1 UNINTERPRETED TYPES

Let x be a variable, m_x its domain, i.e. the set of values which it can have. In the simplest case we can say that the type of x is known as soon as we know its domain m_x; we call it the **uninterpreted type**. This definition of a type is sufficient for various purposes in logic. In programming, values of variables are data, and the domain m_x is determined entirely syntactically – by data

formats. For instance, we can distinguish uninterpreted types of binary codes of various lengths, of texts of various lengths and also of binary codes and texts of arbitrary length.

Programming languages usually contain facilities for specifying data formats which can be regarded as means for defining uninterpreted data types. They are used for specifying input and output data.

Uninterpreted types do not partition data into disjoint sets. On the contrary, we can introduce a relation of inclusion of sets which holds between the types t and s if their domains m_t and m_s satisfy the relation $m_t \subset m_s$. For instance, the type 'Algol program' describing all syntactically correct Algol programs is included in the type of all texts. We can see that the uninterpreted type of a value is not determined by the value itself. A value can belong to domains of different types.

One more operation over sets determines a relation between uninterpreted types – the direct product of sets: $m_1 \times m_2 \times \cdots \times m_k$, which is the set of all tuples of k elements where the ith element of a tuple belongs to the set m_i. Let $m_1, \ldots, m_k$ be domains of types $t_1, \ldots, t_k$. We define a new type t with the domain $m_1 \times \cdots \times m_k$ and call it a **structured type** with components $t_1, \ldots, t_k$. We denote it also $t = (t_1, \ldots, t_k)$. Among all uninterpreted types there is one special type which we call **undefined**. This type contains all other uninterpreted types, i.e. any object belongs to the domain of this type.

2.1.2 INTERPRETED TYPES

Now we associate one more set with a variable x – the set q_x of meanings of values of the variable. Let f be a function which enables us to find a meaning of any element of the domain of x. We say that the pair (q_x, f) is an **interpretation** I_x of the variable x. The domain and interpretation of a variable specify the interpreted type of the variable. We can consider primary types of programming languages (**integer, real, bool,** etc.) as **interpreted types**. The meaning of a value of a primary type is not only an abstract object (number, truth, value etc.), but also what can be done with it and what effect this will have. For example, the meaning of the value **true** of the interpreted type **bool** is the following:

1. The operation $\vee$ (disjunction) applied to this value and any other logical value gives the result **true**.

2. If this value appears as the result of the evaluation of expression B in a statement

    while B **do** S **od**;

    then the statement S will be executed and after that the **while** statement will be executed again.

3. The negation operation applied to this value gives the result **false**; etc.

Unfortunately, it is rather difficult to find the precise meanings of objects of real programs even when written in such well-known languages as FORTRAN or Algol.

One of the few languages with well-defined interpreted types is LISP. It has two interpreted types – atoms and expressions. Syntactically, the values of atoms are symbols constructed from characters, and the values of expressions are sequences of atoms with the correct allocation of parentheses. This gives the domains of atoms and expressions. The meaning of a text written in parentheses is determined by the first atom after the first opening parenthesis. This atom must be a name of a function if the text is a program. The name of a function must be known to the system which works with the text. The meaning of an atom is determined by a property list of the atom and also by function specification if the atom is written immediately after the opening parenthesis. This simplicity of types guarantees very good compatibility of data structures in LISP and also good understanding of the meaning of LISP programs.

2.1.3 ABSTRACT DATA TYPES

Very often people informally assign additional meaning to variables of programs, which is not specified by their types. For example, when a queue is used, then the following variables can be specified:

1. l – length of a queue;
2. l_{max} – maximal length of a queue;
3. *elem* – element of a queue;
4. *list*   – list of all elements of a queue.

The question arises whether it is possible to specify precisely the additional meaning of variables which is specific to a particular program. In the case of the queue the variables l and l_{max} can have integer type, but their meaning is obviously different from the meaning of simple integer variables. Attempts to specify meanings of variables of programs more precisely brought programmers to the notion of abstract data types. In this case, type specifications contain in addition knowledge about the properties of objects connected with a particular problem or a class of problems. This knowledge can be represented in the form of axioms. For instance, we can postulate for a queue that $l < l_{max}$. The usual way of representing knowledge about an abstract data type is to specify functions for working with this type. These functions can be specified either axiomatically or by writing programs which are their implementations.

Let us consider a structured type $t = (t_1, t_2, \ldots, t_k)$. We should want to extract an ith component of a structured value. In the case of uninterpreted type we cannot do that immediately. But we can associate a set of functions

with the structured type t:

> *constr*   to construct a structured value from values of components.
>
> $select_i$ $(i = 1, \ldots, k)$ to select a value of the ith component from a structured value.

These functions represent the relation between the whole and its parts, and represent also the meaning of the structured type t.

This is the simplest specification of an abstract data type. In general, a specification of an abstract data type may contain additional functions besides the functions *constr* and $select_i$.

Informally speaking, an **abstract data type** is an interpreted structured type with functions defined for working with components of this type. In order to define an abstract data type we must

1.   give the names and types of its components;

2.   specify functions applicable to the type and to its components.

Besides that, axioms can be specified which determine the properties of objects of that type.

Let us consider once more the type of queue and let us define (informally) *queue* as an abstract data type. Components of the type will be

> *length* : **integer**;
> *maxlength* : **integer**;
> *element* : **undefined**;
> *list* : **undefined**.

We shall define functions, using for that purpose names of preprogrammed procedures:

> *create(maxlength)*   a function for creating a new and empty queue;
>
> *put(element)*   a function for adding a new element to the end of the queue;
>
> *get*   a function for taking the first element from the queue.

All these functions have a side effect – they change the values of the variables *length* and *list*.

Now we can specify some objects of the type *queue* –

> Q : *queue*;
> R : *queue*;

and then do some computations, for example:

> *Q.create*(20);
> *R.create*(100);
> *Q.put*(x);

(Here, for the first time, we use compound names such as $Q . create$, $Q . put$, ...
In general, a compound name $a . b ..... d$ is understood as d **of** ... **of** b **of** a. In
the following text we shall often use compound names for denoting
components of structured objects.)

The representation of functions of an abstract data type by
preprogrammed procedures has one drawback – the meaning of a function is
hidden in a procedure. This is why attempts are being made to specify these
functions axiomatically. For example, for a simpler data type *stack* with
components *list* and *elem* we can easily specify four functions: *create*, *push*, *top*
and *pop*: firstly, representing their types,

$$create: \rightarrow list$$
$$push: list, elem \rightarrow list$$
$$top: list \rightarrow elem$$
$$pop: list \rightarrow list$$

and then specifying properties of the functions completely axiomatically,

$$empty(create),$$
$$top(push(x, e)) = e,$$
$$pop(push(x, e)) = x.$$

Only one predicate, *empty*, has a predefined meaning here which must be
specified elsewhere. (We assume that the meaning of equality is given as a part
of the language of axioms.) Finally we must get realizations of the functions
create, *push*, *pop* and *top* also. We can try to construct them from the
given axiomatic specifications of functions, but it is almost hopeless to do
that automatically for more complicated data types than *stack*. A more
realistic approach is to construct the programs manually, taking into
account systematically the properties of the functions represented by the
axioms.

2.2 Knowledge representation

Here we give only a very brief survey of knowledge representation in natural
language processing. People communicate by means of written or spoken
language, sending each other messages. Using our definitions, we can say that
the uninterpreted type of a message is text. Therefore we start this section
with a discussion of the meaning of texts represented in natural language.
After that we show how meanings of separate messages can be bound
together in a knowledge base. Finally we describe a special kind of frame for
representing computational knowledge. We shall see that frames present

another way for representing properties of objects which we use in programming and, more generally, in computations.

2.2.1 SEMANTIC NETWORKS

Linguists noticed long ago that the structure of a sentence can be represented graphically as a network. The words of the sentence are nodes of the network and arcs bind the words, which are bound by the meaning of the sentence. The type of relation between the words connected by an arc can be denoted on the arc. A network of this kind represents the meaning of a sentence quite accurately, even when the morphological attributes of words are omitted in the network. Let us take as an example the sentence:

'Peter is reading a thick book and laughing loudly.'

The network representing the meaning of this sentence is shown in Figure 2.1, and this is an example of a semantic network. Similar networks can be built for texts containing several sentences. A network can be built not only from these words which are actually in a sentence, but it can also be built using a smaller number of different basic words. In this case some words are represented by several nodes and arcs, i.e. a meaning of a word is represented by a network.

Some knowledge-representation systems exist where the meaning of texts is represented by **semantic networks**. These networks are built from a small number of basic types of nodes (objects) which are connected by means of arcs (relations) of a small number of basic types of relations.

Building a semantic network which represents the meaning of a text can be regarded as a process of understanding the text. Let us consider the

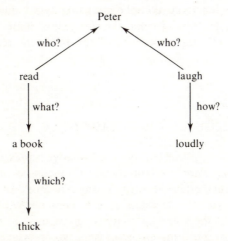

Figure 2.1   The semantic network of a statement.

understanding of a single sentence. This is a complicated process which starts on a formal, syntactical, level with the detection of the morphological attributes of words and the discovery of relations between the words of the sentence. Further on, the processing goes to deeper levels, with semantics involved. Words initially contained in the text are replaced by representations of their meanings in terms of a small number of basic concepts, and relations between the words are expressed explicitly by means of arcs. It is rather difficult to formalize this process. In particular, even text processing on a syntactical level needs some additional semantic information, and several iterations may be needed for extracting a meaning from a text.

Different authors have proposed various kinds of semantic networks, but all these networks are built from objects as nodes connected by means of relations. Objects and arcs can be grouped in several classes. A network represented in Figure 2.2 is taken with modifications from Nariniani (1978) and describes time relations between events. Objects here are time intervals and moments: 3 April, yesterday, today, evening, morning, $time_1, \ldots, time_4$. The objects are connected by inclusion relations (i), time specification relations (t) and succession relations (s). This semantic network represents the time structure of the following text: 'Maximov had a lecture at the university today from 3 p.m. to 4 p.m. In the evening he had a talk with student Voronov about his diploma work. Yesterday morning, before 10 a.m., he edited a report. A week ago, on 3 April, he had a presentation at a conference in Moscow.'

Up to now we have had only binary relations between objects, i.e. the relations which bind exactly two objects. In order to represent relations which bind more than two objects we must introduce nodes into a semantic network also for relations. Any node of a relation is connected by arcs with nodes of objects bound by the relation. Arcs can be marked with names of positions (or roles) which objects have in a relation. The activities of Maximov described in the text above can be represented by a network shown

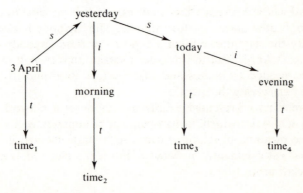

Figure 2.2   A network with binary relations.

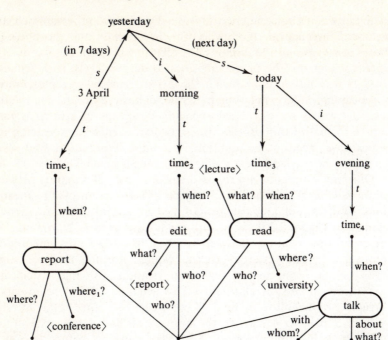

Figure 2.3   The semantic network of a text.

in Figure 2.3. In this network, the relations corresponding to verbs are represented as nodes, but time relations are still represented as arcs.

The advantage of using semantic networks for knowledge representation lies in the fact that semantic networks can be easily used for making inferences. We can build a program which traces associations represented by arcs and answers questions about the meaning of the text represented by a semantic network. For example, using the network in Figure 2.3 we can find out when and where Maximov had lectures, etc. It is possible to get answers to quite complicated questions, for example: 'Did anybody have a lecture in the university the day after editing a report?' or 'Did anybody speak with Voronov after 3 April?' But in this case a substantial amount of additional knowledge is needed to understand the question itself and to construct a procedure for answering the question.

Any relation represented simply as a node of a network may have complicated semantics which, in its turn, can be represented by a semantic network. The meaning of relations can also be implemented in the system which works with semantic networks. For example, the transitivity of succession relation (s),

$$T_1 \underset{s}{\to} T_2 \,\&\, T_2 \underset{s}{\to} T_3 \quad \text{implies} \quad T_1 \underset{s}{\to} T_3,$$

can be known to the system. Also the symmetry of the relation 'talk to' can be known, and, knowing interpretations of these relations, the system can infer that Voronov spoke with Maximov after 3 April.

2.2.2 OPERATIONS WITH SEMANTIC NETWORKS

Any semantic network can be built using only very primitive operations:

- creating an empty network;
- inserting a new object;
- binding some existing objects with a relation.

It is inconvenient to build big semantic networks using only these operations, so we shall describe some more meaningful operations.

Constructing a mapping between elements of networks

Let S_1 and S_2 be semantic networks and X be a set of objects from S_1. The operation we are considering uses some information from the network S_2 and associates with every element of X an object of a network S_2. If S_2 does not contain proper elements for every element of X, then the operation yields no result (is unsuccessful). If the operation is successful, then it builds a mapping

$$w : X \rightarrow Y$$

from a set X of objects from the network S_1 into a set Y of objects from the network S_2.

This operation uses four 'arguments':

- networks S_1 and S_2;
- set of objects X;
- some rules for finding a corresponding object for any element of X.

In practice, we must speak about a set of operations which are determined by the rules for selecting objects of S_2 which correspond to elements of X. If X contains only one element, then we have an operation of pattern matching. In general, the operation of building a mapping is rather complicated – even the pattern matching is a complicated operation.

Union of semantic networks

Let S_1 and S_2 be two semantic networks and

$$w : X \rightarrow Y$$

be a mapping from a set X of objects from the network S_1 into a set Y of objects from the network S_2. The union of the networks S_1 and S_2 in the case

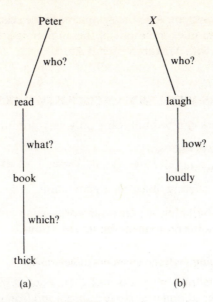

Figure 2.4   Building a semantic network.

of mapping w is a network built as follows:

1.   those objects of S_1 are added to S_2 which do not belong to X;
2.   all those arcs which bind elements of X are added to the new network, but they are added so that instead of $x \in X$ they will bind $w(x) \in Y$.

As an example, we shall consider the last step of building the network shown in Figure 2.1 for the sentence 'Peter is reading a thick book and laughing loudly'. It is built from two separate networks representing the sentences: 'Peter is reading a thick book' and 'X is laughing loudly' where X denotes an unknown person called in natural language 'somebody'. We assume that networks for these sentences are built already: they are shown in Figure 2.4. Now we must understand that X and Peter denote one and the same person. In our terms it means that a mapping w must be built such that $w(X) =$ Peter. Then the resulting network shown in Figure 2.1 can be built as the union of the networks shown in Figure 2.4. In this particular case the mapping $w(X) =$ Peter can be built purely syntactically. But already, in the case of two separate sentences which express exactly the same meaning: 'Peter is reading a thick book. He is laughing loudly', a considerably more complicated analysis of semantics of sentences is needed for understanding that X and Peter are one and the same person.

2.2.3 FRAMES

Semantic networks are a form of representation of the meaning of texts. In some sense, they represent the meaning of a text in a way analogous to the way

floating-point numbers represent the approximate meaning of real numbers. However, we are interested not only in representing the meaning of a text, but also in the representation of knowledge, acquired gradually in the course of interaction with specialists of some problem domain. Obviously, it is not reasonable to look at knowledge in the light of only a single text and store the sum total of knowledge as the meaning of the text.

Marvin Minsky postulated a hypothesis that knowledge can be represented in bundles called frames in intelligent systems (Minsky, 1975). The essence of the **frame** is that it is a module of knowledge about a concept – about a situation, a phenomenon or an object. Frames can be used for representing rather complicated concepts. They can contain various possible actions as well as conditions for applying these actions. Besides that, frames contain **slots** – places to put concrete values or knowledge about other objects which can vary and are related to the concept. The slots are like the formal parameters of macro definition or like the parameters of parameterized data types.

The slots are filled in when a frame is applied to represent a particular situation, object or phenomenon. However, rules for filling slots are much more complicated than rules for binding parameters. Frames can be easily encoded in the form of semantic networks extended with actions and rules for applying these actions, in particular, for handling slots. A slot can be filled by applying sequentially operations with semantic networks described in Section 2.2.2 – constructing a mapping and union of semantic networks.

Semantic networks are not the sole medium for representing frames. As soon as the concept of frame appeared, a question arose: 'Isn't it possible to invent a language in which it would be especially convenient to represent frames?' In other words, 'Wouldn't it be possible to invent a knowledge-representation language?' Indeed, such languages appeared, and references to them are given at the end of this chapter. The UTOPIST language described in the next chapter also belongs to the class of knowledge-representation languages. It is intended for representing a special kind of frames – computational frames containing knowledge about computability.

2.3 Computational models

We have already considered two approaches to knowledge representation. The first is the programmer's approach, which enables us to represent the meaning of concepts only very roughly by means of abstract data types. The goal of the second approach is to represent knowledge explicitly as frames and to encode the frames in the form of semantic networks.

The difference between these two approaches lies in the efficiency of implementation. Abstract data types are developed according to programming traditions and can be implemented efficiently. Semantic networks and frames, on the other hand, were developed by linguists and AI people who were

mainly interested in knowledge-representation principles and not too much in the efficiency of computations.

Now we shall introduce one more form of knowledge representation – computational models. They are intended for representing knowledge about computational problems and must be efficiently applicable for solving these problems. **Computational models** are semantic networks which contain only efficiently implementable relations – the relations which can be used for computations. From another aspect, the computational model is a generalization of the abstract data type which makes it possible to construct functions automatically using structural synthesis of programs.

2.3.1 RELATIONS

In linguistics, a relation is something that binds objects to each other. These relations can have properties which must be somehow known to the system that uses them. We define relations more precisely starting from the common algebraic definition of a relation and adapting it to our purposes. Let $S_1, \ldots, S_k$ be sets. The direct product $S_1 \times \ldots \times S_k$ of the sets is also a set. It consists of all k-tuples $\langle s_1, \ldots, s_k \rangle$ such that $s_1 \in S_1, \ldots, s_k \in S_k$. Any subset of the direct product is a *relation* over $S_1, \ldots, S_k$. It is said that a tuple $\langle l_1, \ldots, l_k \rangle$ satisfies a relation R if and only if $\langle l_1, \ldots, l_k \rangle \in R$.

Most frequently used are relations where $k = 2$. They are called **binary relations**. There are well-known binary relations over numbers, denoted by $=, <, >, \leqslant, \geqslant, \neq$ (equal, less than, greater than, less than or equal, greater than or equal, not equal). It is also well known how to represent relations by means of equations. Let $x_1, \ldots, x_k$ be real variables and f be a function of k real arguments. The equation $f(x_1, \ldots, x_k) = 0$ represents a k-ary relation over the real numbers. It is also said that the equation $f(x_1, \ldots, x_k) = 0$ represents a relation which binds variables $x_1, \ldots, x_k$. We are going to consider just relations between variables.

Let $x_1, \ldots, x_k$ be variables with domains $m_1, \ldots, m_k$ respectively. For any relation $R \subseteq m_1 \times \cdots \times m_k$ over the sets $m_1, \ldots, m_k$ we shall say that it binds the variables $x_1, \ldots, x_k$, and denote it $R(x_1, \ldots, x_k)$ or $R(x)$, where x is a tuple $\langle x_1, \ldots, x_k \rangle$.

For brevity, we shall assume the following:

1. the set of all variables is completely ordered, so that for any pair of variables x_1, x_2 either $x_1 < x_2$ or $x_2 < x_1$. This ordering may be, for instance, the lexicographic ordering of names of variables;

2. any tuple $\langle x_1, \ldots, x_k \rangle$ of variables which we shall use is built in such a way that $x_1 < x_2 < \cdots < x_k$;

3. for any finite set $\{x_1, \ldots, x_m\}$ of variables there exists a variable $x = \langle x_1, \ldots, x_m \rangle$ which is a tuple of these variables;

4. any relation binds variables in the given ordering, so that for $R(x_1, \ldots, x_k)$ always $x_1 < x_2 < \cdots < x_k$. Actually this enables us to write always $R(x)$ instead of $R(x_1, \ldots, x_k)$, where $x = \langle x_1, \ldots, x_k \rangle$.

Given the assumptions made above we can easily extend set-theoretic operations on to the tuples. We shall use the following operations and predicates over tuples of ordered variables:

- union $\cup$
- intersection $\cap$
- difference $\setminus$
- inclusion $\subseteq$
- strong inclusion $\subset$
- inclusion of element $\in$

This enables us to use expressions like $x \subset y, x \cup y, x \setminus y$, where $x = \langle x_1, \ldots, x_k \rangle$, $y = \langle y_1, \ldots, y_m \rangle, x_1 < \cdots < x_k, y_1 < \cdots < y_m$.

Let us consider a relation $R(x)$ which binds variables $x_1, \ldots, x_k$ (here we already implicitly use the fact that $x = \langle x_1, \ldots, x_k \rangle$). Let u, v be tuples of variables and $u \subseteq x, v \subseteq x$. The relation $R(x)$ determines a mapping (generally it is one-to-many mapping):

$$\varphi_{R,u,v} : m_u \rightarrow m_v,$$

that associates with a given value $\mathbf{u}$ of u exactly those values $\mathbf{v}$ of v which satisfy the relation R together with $\mathbf{u}$:

$$\varphi_{R,u,v}(\mathbf{u}) = \{\mathbf{v} \mid \exists \mathbf{e}(\mathbf{e} \in R \,\&\, \mathbf{u} \subseteq \mathbf{e} \,\&\, \mathbf{v} \subseteq \mathbf{e})\}.$$

The set of induced mappings $\varphi_{R,u,v}$ represents potential possibilities of finding values of any variable $v \subset x$ from a given value of any other variable $u \subset x$, i.e. it represents potential computability of variables bound by the relation R.

Actual computation of values according to the mappings $\varphi_{R,u,v}$ is possible only for some simple classes of relations. Restrictions on computations have fundamental reasons as well as practical reasons. For instance, if the relation R is an infinite set then, in general, it cannot be used for computations. But even for finite sets the computations may be practically very time consuming.

On the other hand, a relation itself can be represented by the mappings which it induces. In particular, a relation $R(x)$ can be represented uniquely by any mapping $\varphi_{R,u,v}$, where $u \cup v = x$. Relations can be represented in many different ways – as tables, graphs, equations etc.

As we intend to use relations for computing, we shall represent them by means of the mappings induced by them. But we shall restrict ourselves to mappings which associate at most one value with any value of the argument, i.e. those which are functions. Using the terminology of programmers, we call such mappings operators.

An **operator** is a set of assignments

$$y_i := f_i(x_1, \ldots, x_m), \qquad i = 1, \ldots, n,$$

where $x_1, \ldots, x_m$ are input variables and $y_1, \ldots, y_n$ are output variables of the operator. We denote the sets of input and output variables of an operator φ $in(\varphi)$ and $out(\varphi)$ respectively.

The application of an operator is the execution of all its assignments. We assume that an operator can be applied to any value of its input variables, unless stated otherwise. A set of operators $\varphi_1, \ldots, \varphi_k$ is called unambiguous if no application of any sequence of these operators to any fixed input value gives different values to any variable.

For example, the following two operators (each of which contains only one assignment):

$$x := y + 1$$

and

$$y := x - 1$$

constitute an unambiguous set of operators. But operators

$$x := y + 1$$

and

$$y := x - 2$$

cannot be included in an unambiguous set of operators, because, applying to any value of y firstly the operator $x := y + 1$ and then applying the second operator to the calculated value of x, we obviously obtain for y a value different from the initially given value.

An unambiguous set of operators is called a *partial relation*. The set of variables bound by this relation is the union of input and output sets of variables of its operators.

Obviously, a single operator is unambiguous if $in(\varphi) \cap out(\varphi) = \varnothing$ ($\varnothing$ denotes the empty set) and it can be regarded as a partial relation.

Let us consider a partial relation $R(x)$ represented as a set of operators $\Phi = \{\varphi_1, \ldots, \varphi_k\}$. A variable $u \in x$ bound by the relation R is called

1. an **input variable** if there exists $\varphi' \in \Phi$, where $u \in in(\varphi')$, and there is no φ in Φ with $u \in out(\varphi)$;

2. an **output variable** if there exists $\varphi' \in \Phi$, where $u \in out(\varphi')$, and there is no φ in Φ with $u \in in(\varphi)$;

3.   a **weakly bound variable** if there exist $\varphi' \in \Phi$ and $\varphi'' \in \Phi$, where $u \in in(\varphi')$ and $u \in out(\varphi'')$.

In order to characterize the computational power of a relation, we introduce a numerical characteristic, called the **rank** of the relation. The rank of a partial relation is the minimal number of output variables of an operator of the relation.

Especially useful are partial relations which, for a given rank, contain as many operators as possible with a maximal number of output variables. Every operator of such a relation $R(x)$ has $in(\varphi) \cup out(\varphi) = x$ and $in(\varphi) \cap out(\varphi) = \varnothing$. Obviously, all bound variables of such relations are weakly bound. The number of operators of such a relation is

$$C_r^n = n \cdot (n - 1) \cdot \cdots \cdot (n - r + 1)/1 \cdot 2 \cdot \cdots \cdot r,$$

where r is rank and n is the number of bound variables of the relation. We call these relations **completely symmetric relations**. They are generalizations of systems of equations. In particular, any equation solvable for every variable contained in it is a completely symmetric relation with rank 1.

Generalizations of completely symmetric relations are **symmetric relations**. Every operator of a symmetric relation $R(x)$ has $in(\varphi) \cup out(\varphi) = x$ and number of output variables equal to the rank of the relation. But a symmetric relation may also have input and output variables, i.e. variables which are input (or output) variables for every operator of the relation.

Let k be the number of output variables of a symmetric relation which has rank r. Then output of any operator of the relation has $r - k$ weakly bound variables, and for every $r - k$ bound variables there exists an operator which contains these variables in its output. In the marginal case $k = r$ there are no weakly bound variables and the relation contains only one operator. We see that any relation containing a single operator is a symmetric relation according to our definition.

Let us define another useful class of relations – **structural relations**. Any structural relation has only weakly bound variables, one of which is called a **structured variable**. Let the variables be

$x, x_1, \ldots, x_m$

and let x be the structured variable; then the operators are

$x := (x_1, \ldots, x_m)$

$x_i := select_i(x), \qquad i = 1, 2, \ldots, m,$

where $select_i$ is a selector function which computes the ith component of the argument. (We have met this relation already in Section 2.1.)

2.3.2 SIMPLE COMPUTATIONAL MODELS

Now we are going to investigate semantic networks where objects are variables and relations are partial relations. This special kind of semantic network is suitable for representing knowledge about computability. We call these semantic networks **computational models**. A computational model is a set of variables bound by partial relations. We call a set of partial relations unambiguous if the set of all operators of these relations is unambiguous.

A simple computational model is a set of variables and an unambiguous set of partial relations which bind these variables. Let M be a simple computational model. We denote $var(M)$ its set of variables and $rel(M)$ its set of relations.

We use a graphic notation for computational models as networks. Variables and relations are nodes of a network, and are denoted by dots and circles respectively.

If a variable is bound by a partial relation, then the dot of the variable is connected with the circle of the relation by means of an arc. Connections for all kinds of bound variables (input, output, weakly bound, structured variable) are shown in Figure 2.5(a).

Examples of different kinds of relations are shown in Figure 2.5(b–e): (b) completely symmetric with rank 1; (c) structural; (d) symmetric with rank 2; and (e) containing a single operator.

If we take away a relation containing operators $\varphi_1, \ldots, \varphi_k$ from a computational model and replace it by k different relations, each of which contains one of the operators, then obviously we get a new model with exactly the same computational facilities. This allows us without loss of generality to consider such simple computational models which contain only

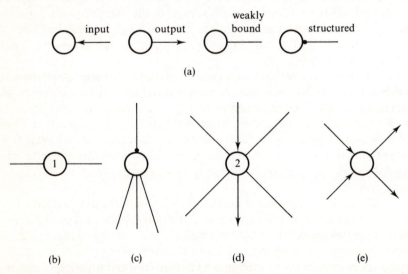

Figure 2.5   Examples of partial relations.

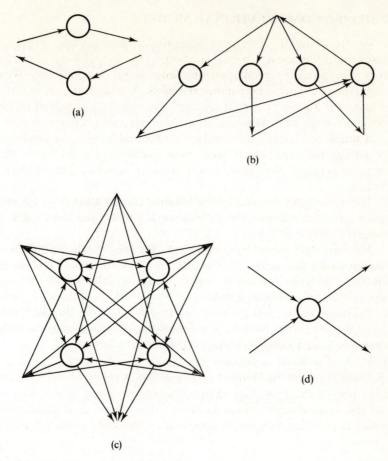

(a)

(b)

(c)

(d)

Figure 2.6   Operator structure of relations.

partial relations in the form of a single operator. We call them **operator models**. But partial relations are practically useful for brevity of representation. Operator models of relations shown in Figure 2.5 are represented in Figure 2.6. We see that even the quite simple symmetric relation shown in Figure 2.5(d) is transformed into a rather intricate network, Figure 2.6(c). Using computational models as semantic networks we try to preserve their expressiveness and, therefore, we use symmetric and structural relations in the models.

What can be represented in the form of computational models? First of all, knowledge about computability in elementary mathematics and physics can be so represented. Let us take the well-known concept of percentage and try to remember what we learned about it at school. By the way, one must agree that it took a lot of time and exercises for the use of percentages in calculations to become automatic. Now we are going to formalize the

following concept of percentage:

> The whole entity is w and constitutes 100%. Part of it, denoted by p, constitutes $c\%$. The rest of the whole is denoted by r and it constitutes, obviously, $(100-c)\%$.

The variables w, p, c, r are bound by the following relations:

1. $w = p + r$
2. $p/w = c/100$
3. $p/r = c/(100 - c)$.

This knowledge can be represented by a computational model shown in Figure 2.7 which contains the variables w, p, c and r and three symmetric relations with ranks equal to 1.

The following example is taken from physics. A body with mass m is moving along a straight line with constant acceleration a in an interval of time from t_1 until t_2. The initial velocity is v_1, the final velocity is v_2, the average velocity is v. The distance between starting point and ending point is Δs, the inertial force is f. The kinetic energy of the body at the beginning of motion is E_1 and at the end is E_2. We denote the velocity gain by Δv and the time between start and finish Δt. So we have 14 variables: $m, a, t_1, t_2, v_1, v_2, v, \Delta s, f, \Delta E, E_1, E_2, \Delta v, \Delta t$.

These variables are bound by 10 equations:

$$f = m * a, \quad \Delta v = a * \Delta t, \quad \Delta s = v * \Delta t, \quad 2 * v = v_1 + v_2$$

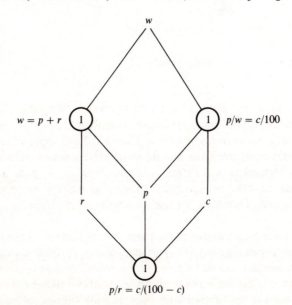

Figure 2.7   A computational model of *percents*.

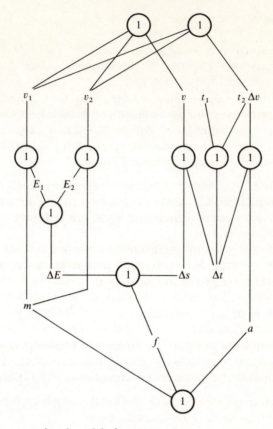

Figure 2.8   A computational model of *motion*.

$$\Delta E = f * \Delta s, \quad \Delta v = v_2 - v_1, \quad \Delta E = E_2 - E_1$$
$$\Delta t = t_2 - t_1, \quad E_1 = m * v_1^2/2, \quad E_2 = m * v_2^2/2.$$

The variables and equations listed above constitute a computational model which contains knowledge about accelerated motion. This model is represented graphically in Figure 2.8.

We recommend the reader to build computational models of some geometric figures. This is a useful exercise. Knowledge about geometric figures can be found in any handbook on elementary geometry.

2.3.3 PROBLEM SOLVING ON COMPUTATIONAL MODELS

Firstly, let us try to solve some problems using the knowledge represented in the computational models which we have already constructed. We denote the computational model of motion with the identifier *motion* and consider the

following problem:

> **compute** v_1, ΔE **from** m, Δt, a, v_2
> **knowing** *motion*.

This problem is represented exactly in the form described in Section 1.1. As the meaning (computational model) of the word *motion* also contains knowledge about the variables v_1, ΔE, m, Δt, a and v_2, the meaning of this problem description must be clear to the reader. But just in case, we shall also give a longer textual representation of the problem:

> a mass m is moving linearly forward during time interval Δt, with a constant acceleration a and it obtains velocity v_2; find the initial velocity v_1 and work ΔE required to accelerate the mass.

Translating a problem specification from one form into another is the duty of linguists and we will not consider it further. Moreover, we shall use an even shorter form of the problem specification:

$$(motion \vdash m, \Delta t, a, v_2 \rightarrow v_1, \Delta E).$$

In trying to solve this problem we must remember that the only means for computation are operators of partial relations of the computational model of *motion*. It is useful to take into consideration the following:

1. Any operator of a simple computational model is applicable as soon as all its input variables have known values.

2. It makes sense to apply an operator only if it computes something new, i.e. some still unknown values of variables.

3. If there are several ways of computing a value of some variable on a simple computational model, then all these ways must give one and the same result; hence it makes no difference which way is chosen.

A simple method exists for solving a problem on a simple computational model and this method can be practically used if the model is small (theoretically, always when the model is finite). We can check the operators of the model one by one and try to find an applicable operator the output of which contains at least one variable with unknown value. Applying this operator we compute some new values, coming closer to the solution of the problem. This process can be repeated iteratively until all results of the problem are computed or after testing all operators it becomes clear that no operator is applicable which computes new values of variables. In the latter case the problem is unsolvable.

Simple computational models have a useful feature – solvability of problems can be checked without actual computations on them, and for any solvable problem a program for solving it can be built before computation.

Indeed, applicability of operators does not depend on values of variables, it depends only on accessibility of the values for the operators.

At any point in the program values of input variables of the program exist (and are accessible) and so do values of output variables of all operators applied before this point was reached.

Using the computational model of motion we can build several different programs for solving our problem. Two of the programs are shown in Figure 2.9.

Simple models cannot contain any information about conditions

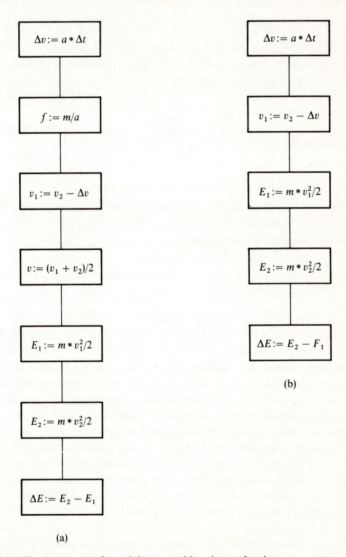

(a)

(b)

Figure 2.9   Two programs for solving a problem in mechanics.

which are dependent on the computed values of variables. Hence the programs built on simple computational models are sequences of operators, without branching and loops. In this case, at any step of the program it is easy to check which variables already have values and which variables are needed for further computations. This allows us to exclude redundant operators (which compute only unnecessary values) from a program. Such operators can appear in a program which is built by the simple method described above.

In order to exclude redundant operators from a program we build two sets of variables for every step of the program: a set w' of variables needed for further computations and a set w of variables with known values. The latter is a union of the set of input variables of the problem and sets of output variables of all operators applied up to this step. The process starts from the end of the program, where the set w' is taken equal to the set of output variables of the problem. Operators are checked one by one. An operator φ is excluded from the program if no output variable of the operator is needed for further computation, i.e. $out(\varphi) \cap w' = \emptyset$.

The set w' is changed only if a current operator φ is not excluded from the program. In this case the new set w' is built as follows:

$$w' := (w' \backslash out(\varphi)) \cup in(\varphi).$$

The program shown in Figure 2.9(b) is obtained from the program in Figure 2.9(a) by means of such a process. The sets of needed variables (from the end of the program to the beginning) are

$$\{v_1, \Delta E\},\ \{v_1, E_1, E_2\},\ \{v_1, v_2, m, E_1\},\ \{v_1, v_2, m\},\ \{v_1, v_2, m\},\ \{v_2, \Delta v, m\},$$
$$\{v_2, \Delta v, m\},\ \{v_2, m, \Delta t, a\}.$$

Let us look at the set of all problems which can be specified on a simple computational model M. We shall denote this set $probl(M)$. On a fixed model a problem is specified by sets of its input and output variables. Let the model M contain n variables. Any subset of $var(M)$ can be taken as a set of input variables of a problem. Thus we have problems with 2^n different inputs. For a fixed input there still exist 2^n different ways for choosing a set of output variables. So we have found the number of problems which can be specified on a simple computational model with n variables: it is 2^{2n}.

On a simple model M with finite sets of variables and operators we can check every problem $(M \vdash u \rightarrow v)$ and find out if the problem is solvable; if it is, then we can also build a program for solving it.

Now we shall investigate how solvability of problems is connected with the ordering which we have already defined as follows:

$$(M \vdash u_1 \rightarrow v_1) \ll (M \vdash u_2 \rightarrow v_2) \qquad \text{iff } u_2 \subseteq u_1 \text{ and } v_1 \subseteq v_2$$

and at least one of these inclusions is strong (see Section 1.1).

From the algorithm for testing the solvability of problems we see immediately that from

$$(M \vdash u' \to v') \ll (M \vdash u \to v) \ \& \ solvable\,(M \vdash u \to v)$$

follows

$$solvable\,(M \vdash u' \to v'),$$

i.e. all problems which are less than a solvable problem are also solvable.

Using the same algorithm, it can be demonstrated that $solvable$ $(M \vdash u \to v_1) \ \& \ solvable\,(M \vdash u \to v_2)$ implies

$$solvable\,(M \vdash u \to v_1 \cup v_2).$$

Note   It may be interesting to notice that the set $probl(M)$ with operations

$$(M \vdash u_1 \to v_1) + (M \vdash u_2 \to v_2) = (M \vdash u_1 \cap u_2 \to v_1 \cup v_2)$$

and

$$(M \vdash u_1 \to v_1) \times (M \vdash u_2 \to v_2) = (M \vdash u_1 \cup u_2 \to v_1 \cap v_2)$$

is a complete lattice with the zero element $(M \vdash var(M) \to \varnothing)$ and unit element $(M \vdash \varnothing \to var(M))$.

Let $sp(M)$ be the set of all solvable problems on a simple computational model M. For any problem $(M \vdash u \to v)$ from $sp(M)$ there exists a program for solving this problem. This program can be considered as a representation of an operator φ with $in(\varphi) = u$ and $out(\varphi) = v$. Let X be an arbitrary set of variables of a simple computational model M. Let us look at the operators which are represented by programs for solvable problems $(M \vdash u \to v)$, where $u \in X$ and $v \in X$. From the definition of a simple computational model it follows that there are no two programs which from the same input compute different output values of variables. Consequently, the set of operators is not contradictory, and it is a partial relation. This partial relation is uniquely determined by the computational model M and the set of variables X. We shall denote this relation $rel(M, X)$.

This result will be useful in the future, because it enables us to encapsulate computational models into the form of partial relations, hiding internal variables and relations of models.

2.3.4 OPERATIONS WITH COMPUTATIONAL MODELS

Computational models can be considered as a special kind of semantic network. Operations defined in Section 2.2.2 are applicable also to computational models. Any computational model can be built from an empty

model, adding variables and relations one by one. The union of models as semantic networks is also a useful operation.

If a problem is specified in a textual form, then a computational model is being built in the same way as any semantic network which represents the meaning of a text. Let us consider the problem with the following text:

> A body with a mass m started moving linearly forward from standstill and the motion continued for time t. For the first $c\%$ of the time the body was influenced by force f_1 and for the remaining time by force f_2. Find the distance s covered by the body.

It is not very easy to understand a text like that. But, as soon as it is understood that there are two linear forward motions with constant acceleration, and the times of the motions are bound by percentages, the task of building the complete model of the problem becomes almost trivial. One must take two copies of the model of motion and one copy of the model of percentages and make a union of them. Using the text of the problem we can build a mapping which binds some variables of the three models. Let us express the mapping in the form of equalities between variables. We must distinguish variables of different copies of models, so we mark them with one prime (′) for the first motion, with two primes (″) for percentage and with three primes (‴) for the second motion. The equalities are:

$$m' = m, \ f' = f_1, \ c'' = c, \ w'' = t, \ m''' = m, \ f''' = f_2, \ v'_2 = v'''_1,$$
$$\Delta t' = p'', \ \Delta t''' = r''.$$

We must take into consideration also two additional relations $v'_1 = 0$ and $s = \Delta s' + \Delta s'''$, which follow from the text.

The union of the models is shown in Figure 2.10. This is the computational model for the whole text of the problem. Let us denote it by M. The problem $(M \vdash m, t, c, f_1, f_2 \rightarrow s)$ is solvable and a program for solving it is

```
v₁' := 0;
c'' := c;
w'' := t;
p'' := (c'' * w'')/100;
f' := f₁;
Δt' := p'';
a' := f''/m'';
Δv' := a' * Δt';
v₂' := v₁' + Δv';
v' := (v₁' + v₂')/2;
Δs' := v' * Δt';
v₁''' := v₂';
```

$$r'' := w'' - p'';$$
$$\Delta t''' := r'';$$
$$f''' := f_2;$$
$$m''' := m;$$
$$a''' := f'''/m''';$$
$$\Delta v''' := a''' * \Delta t''';$$
$$v_2''' := v_1''' + \Delta v''';$$
$$v''' := (v_1''' + v_2''')/2;$$
$$\Delta s''' := v''' * \Delta t''';$$
$$s := \Delta s' + \Delta s'''.$$

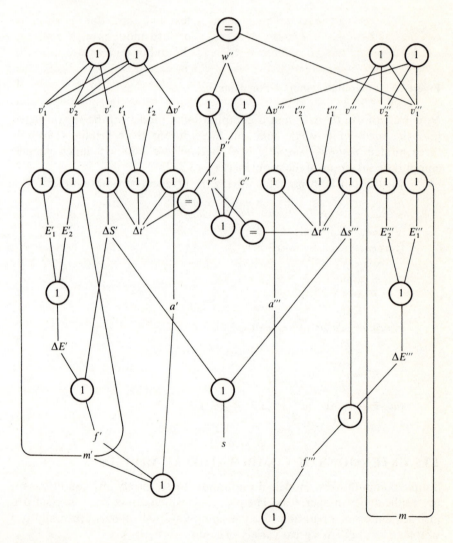

Figure 2.10   A computational model of a compound problem.

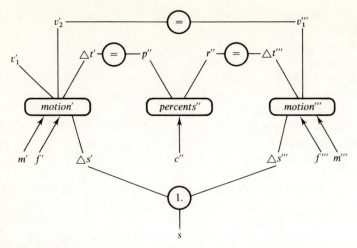

Figure 2.11   A granular computational model.

Now we can use the fact that a computational model can be encapsulated into the form of a single relation. Substituting three relations for our three models *motion'*, *percents''* and *motion'''* we obtain a much simpler computational model of the problem (Figure 2.11).

In addition, a program for solving the problem becomes simpler:

$$w'' := \Delta t;$$
$$c'' := c;$$
$$(percents'' \vdash c'', w'' \rightarrow r'', p'');$$
$$\quad \Delta t' := p'';$$
$$\quad m' := m;$$
$$\quad f' := f_1;$$
$$\quad v_1' := 0;$$
$$(motion' \vdash \Delta t', m', f', v_1' \rightarrow v_2', \Delta s');$$
$$\quad m''' := m;$$
$$\quad f''' := f_2;$$
$$\quad v_1''' := v_2';$$
$$\quad \Delta t''' := r'';$$
$$(motion''' \vdash \Delta t''', m''', f''', v_1''' \rightarrow \Delta s''');$$
$$\quad s := \Delta s' + \Delta s'''.$$

2.3.5 EXTENSIONS OF COMPUTATIONAL MODELS

Simple computational models do not allow us to specify any conditions on the applicability of operators. The programs which can be built on them are just sequences of operators. Simple computational models are really too simple to be useful in a great variety of cases.

Regarding computational models as semantic networks, we can extend

them by introducing new types of nodes and arcs. Let us do it in the following way. In addition to variables and relations we introduce new kinds of nodes – control nodes (or controls) which are connected to those relations whose applicability they influence. A control node can also be connected to a variable, and this means that the control depends on the value of the variable. In general, a control restricts the applicability of relations, and this restriction is determined by the type of the control. We shall always show the type of a control node. If a relation is not connected to any control node, then we shall use it in the same way as in a simple computational model.

The first control which we shall use is concatenation of relations. It binds two relations, and shows that one of the relations must be applied immediately after the other has been applied. (To apply a relation means to apply one of its operators.) Figure 2.12(a) shows concatenation of the relations r and q, where q must be applied always after r. The second relation bound by a concatenation is an operator which simply assigns the values of some temporarily used variables $x'_1, \ldots, x'_k$ to the variables $x_1, \ldots, x_k$, bound by the first relation. We shall denote a pair of such concatenated relations briefly as shown in Figure 2.12(b). The variables $x_1, \ldots, x_k$ are called in this case strongly bound variables. A useful example of a relation (operator) with strongly bound variables is obtained as the concatenation of operators

$$i' := i + 1;$$
$$i := i';$$

Its graphical representation is really simple, as we see in Figure 2.12(c). The following type of control, called *cond*, is designed for representing logical conditions on applicability of operators. It has one bound variable of boolean type, a control variable, and it is connected also with one relation (Figure 2.13(a)). This control means that the relation is applicable if its input

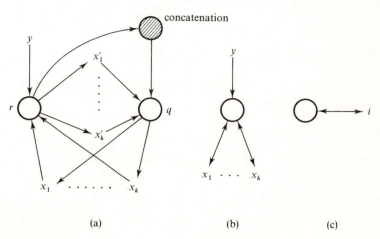

| (a) | (b) | (c) |

Figure 2.12 Control types.

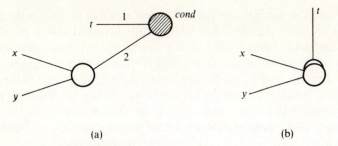

(a)   (b)

Figure 2.13   A conditional relation.

variables have values and the value of the control variable is **true**. For this control we also use a simpler graphical representation where the control variable is directly bound with the relation (Figure 2.13(b)). In this case we assume that the control variable is a bound variable of the relation.

It is interesting to notice that extending computational models with the control of *cond* type we obtain computational models which are expressive enough to represent any algorithm which has the form of an interpreted program schema.

A pair of relations, one of which has a single output variable which is a control variable for the other relation (Figure 2.14) represents a production as used in knowledge bases. In particular, this allows us to use computational models with control variables for representing knowledge in various expert systems.

One more type of control is *sub*, which binds a relation R of computational model M with a relation from $rel(M)$. The latter is specified implicitly by its input and output variables and is called a *subproblem* of the relation R. Let us look at an example where a computational model must represent the following relation:

$$z = \int_0^x y \, du.$$

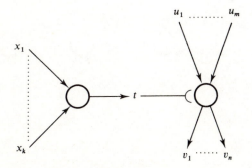

Figure 2.14   A relation for a conditional statement.

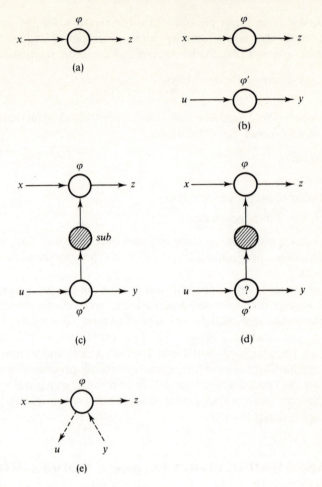

Figure 2.15   A relation with a subproblem.

If we assume that the function for computing y from u is fixed for ever, then we get a relation binding x and z (Figure 2.15(a)). If we also want to express the dependence of y on u, we have two relations (both containing single operators) (Figure 2.15(b)). But the latter model omits the important fact that the relation φ depends on the relation φ'. This fact can be described by means of control *sub*, as shown in Figure 2.15(c).

Let us extend computational models as semantic networks with one more element – with a node which represents a problem. On a model M we shall represent a problem $(M \vdash u \rightarrow y)$ by a node marked with a question mark "?". This node can be regarded as a still unknown relation which has u and y as input and output variables (Figure 2.15(d)). The meaning of the control *sub* is that the relation can be applied only if its subproblem, i.e. the problem $(M \vdash u \rightarrow y)$, is solvable, and then the program for solving this

problem serves as an input parameter for the relation (for the operator φ). Again, we shall also use a simpler form of graphical representation of relations with subproblems. Such a representation of the relation for integral $z = \int_0^x y \, du$ is shown in Figure 2.15(e).

Note Computational models which contain control *sub*, structural relations and only the following types of relations:

- constant 0;
- plus 1;
- operator of primitive recursion;
- operator of minimization;

are general enough for representing any recursive function. For any general recursive function a program which computes the function can be synthesized automatically.

We shall not investigate algorithms for the automatic synthesis of programs here. Instead of this we shall describe in the next section a correspondence between computational models and sets of axioms of structural synthesis, which were described in Section 1.3.1. This correspondence enables us to transform a computational model into a set of axioms and to use structural synthesis methods for automatic construction of programs which solve problems on the computational model. In particular, structural synthesis is needed when we use computational models with subproblems instead of simple computational models.

2.3.6 TRANSFORMING COMPUTATIONAL MODELS INTO AXIOMS

Let us consider an operator

$$\varphi = \{y_i := f_i(x_1, \ldots, x_m) \mid i = 1, 2, \ldots, n\}$$

in a computational model. First of all, we can transform it into a set of operators, each of which computes only one output variable. For this purpose we introduce a new variable y and a structural relation

$$y = (y_1, \ldots, y_n).$$

The set of operators is:

$$y_i := select_i(y), \qquad i = 1, 2, \ldots, n$$
$$y := constr(f_1(x_1, \ldots, x_m), \ldots, f_n(x_1, \ldots, x_m)).$$

Any operator with a single output variable $y := f(x_1, \ldots, x_m)$ can be represented in the form of a computability statement as follows:

$$X_1, \ldots, X_m \to Y,$$

where $X_1, \ldots, X_m, Y$ are propositional variables. Applying this transformation to every operator of a simple computational model M, we can build a set S of computability statements which represent computability on this model.

As an example, we represent the computational model of percentages from Section 2.3.2 as a set of computability statements. Again, for any variable x we use the capital letter X to denote the proposition 'x is computable.' The three equations from the computational model of percents give us the following axioms:

$$W \& P \to R$$
$$W \& R \to P$$
$$P \& R \to W$$
$$P \& W \to C$$
$$P \& C \to W$$
$$W \& C \to P$$
$$P \& R \to C$$
$$P \& C \to R$$
$$R \& C \to P$$

We can see that the number of axioms is much larger than the number of relations. Practically it is more convenient to represent computational models as semantic networks. But equivalent logical representation is useful for theoretical investigations.

It can be proved that using inference rules SSR described earlier we can prove the sequent $(S \vdash X_1 \& \ldots \& X_n \to Y)$ if the problem $(M \vdash x_1, \ldots, x_m \to y)$ is solvable. A problem $(M \vdash x_1, \ldots, x_m \to y_1, \ldots, y_n)$ can be divided into smaller problems $(M \vdash x_1, \ldots, x_m \to y_i)$ $i = 1, 2, \ldots, n$.

Solvability of $(M \vdash x_1, \ldots, x_m \to y_1, \ldots, y_n)$ follows from the solvability of all problems $(M \vdash x_1, \ldots, x_m \to y_i)$, $i = 1, 2, \ldots, n$.

An operator φ, with $in(\varphi) = \{x_1, \ldots, x_m\}$, $out(\varphi) = \{y_1, \ldots, y_n\}$ bound by the control sub, with a subproblem with input $u_1, \ldots, u_k$ and output $v_1, \ldots, v_l$ can be represented by computability statements:

$$(U_1 \& \ldots \& U_k \to V_1) \& \ldots \& (U_1 \& \ldots \& U_k \to V_l) \to (X_1, \& \ldots \&, X_m \to Y_1)$$
$$\vdots$$
$$(U_1 \& \ldots \& U_k \to V_1) \& \ldots \& (U_1 \& \ldots \& U_k \to V_l) \to (X_1 \& \ldots \& X_m \to Y_n).$$

Applying these transformations to all operators of a computational model M with control sub we can transform the model into a set of axioms S for structural synthesis. Again, the sequent $(S \vdash X_1 \& \ldots \& X_m \to Y)$ is

derivable if and only if the problem $(M \vdash x_1, \ldots, x_m \rightarrow y)$ is solvable. This allows us to use structural synthesis of programs for solving problems on computational models with the control *sub*.

2.3.7 COMPUTATIONAL MODELS AND DATA FLOW

Looking at the graphical representation of a simple computational model it is easy to see that it can be considered as a data-flow schema. In particular, we can denote known values of variables by distinguished nodes, and propagate the values along the network in accordance with the rules for the application of operators. In Figure 2.16 three successive steps of computation – application of operators *a*, *b* and *c* – are shown. This computational model demonstrates that some operators can be applied in different order: for instance, instead of *b* the operator *c* could be applied, to be followed by *b*. Some operators can be applied in parallel: for instance, the operators *b* and *c*. The analogy to data flow shows us an efficient algorithm for finding a sequence of operators which solves a problem on a simple computational model.

Let us assume that a counter is associated with every operator, which shows how many input variables of the operator still have unknown values. The algorithm keeps a track of variables whose values have become known, but which have not been checked to find whether they can be used for computations. Let us denote the set of such variables by N. At the beginning N is the set of input variables of the problem. The algorithm stops when N is empty. The main action of the algorithm is taking a variable, let us say x,

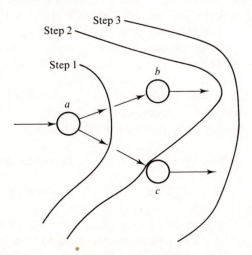

Figure 2.16   Propagating values on a computational model.

from N and applying it to computations. This is done as follows:

1.   If there is no arrow coming out of the node of the variable x (the variable does not belong to input of any operator) then the variable is deleted from N and its application is over.

2.   If there is still an outcoming arrow, then an operator to which the arrow leads is checked and the arrow itself is deleted (or marked as inaccessible). If the value of the counter of the operator is greater than 1, it is decreased by 1. If the value of the counter of the operator is exactly 1, then the variable x is the last needed for applying the operator. In this case the operator is applied, and its output variables, the values of which were computed for the first time, are added to the set N. All arrows coming out from the node of the variable x are processed this way, and then x is deleted from N.

3.   This process is repeated for every variable in the set N.

From the description of this algorithm we see that every arrow in the network is checked only once. Also every variable and every operator is used only once. Consequently, the time needed by this algorithm for finding out if a problem is solvable and for building a sequence of operators for a solvable problem is proportional to the size of the network. That means that the time complexity of the algorithm is linear and the algorithm is very fast! This algorithm is described in details for simple computational models in Dikovski (1985).

Also computational models with subproblems can be considered as data-flow schemas. But, in this case, data flow for a subproblem along arrows for any subproblem can be repeated many times. For instance, in our example of integration, y is computed from u many times to find z from x (see Figure 2.17). Unfortunately, any algorithm which checks solvability of an arbitrary problem on an arbitrary computational model with subproblems may work very slowly. Checking solvability on such a model is equivalent to theorem proving in intuitionistic propositional calculus, and this is a P-space complete problem (Volozh $et\ al.$, 1982).

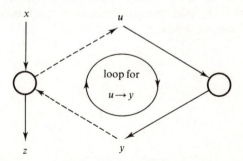

Figure 2.17   Data flow of a subproblem.

2.4 Comments and references

Semantic networks appeared in artificial intelligence works in the middle of the 1960s. Minsky gathered a number of Ph.D. theses into a book (Minsky, 1968) through which the work became well known among AI researchers. Particular kinds of semantic networks – computational models – were applied to specify problem conditions in the beginning of the 1970s (Tyugu, 1970). A practical problem solver built on the basis of computational models was used for implementing a number of small intelligent software packages and databases for computer aided design (Tyugu, 1972). This problem solver became a prototype for programming systems with automatic program synthesis (Kahro *et al.*, 1981; Tyugu, 1977).

Networks were applied to express the meaning of natural language texts by Fillmore in the form of case grammars (Fillmore, 1965). Representation of the meaning of texts in the form of semantic networks was widely practically used, in particular, by Apresian in his automatic translation system (Apresian, 1978).

In 1975 Minsky introduced the concept of a frame as a knowledge module (Minsky, 1975). A number of works in knowledge representation followed. Knowledge-representation languages and frame-representation languages appeared: φ-language (Briabrin, 1978), RX-codes (Pospelov, 1974), KRL† (Bobrow and Winograd, 1970) and FRL (Roberts and Goldstein, 1978).

In the Soviet Union, two large projects existed – 'Dialogue' and 'Situation' – which united researchers from various institutes where AI methods were developed mainly for application purposes. These investigations resulted in several systems for natural language understanding and problem solving: DILOS (Briabrin, 1978), DISPUT (Mikulich, 1982), POET (Popov, 1982), and so on.

AI is still exerting little influence on programming languages. But abstract data types in programming are already quite close to the abstract concepts represented by frames. A small step remaining is to implement in the Ada‡ language automatic usage of external specifications of procedures. Input–output roles of procedure parameters could be used in Ada packages for automatic planning of computations, if some changes in semantics of packages were made. In this case, the packages really become modules of knowledge about computability.

---

† KRL is a trademark of Xerox Corporation.
‡ Ada is a trademark of the US Department of Defense.

Chapter 3

The Language of Knowledge-Based Programming

3.1 General features of the language

3.1.1 GOALS OF THE LANGUAGE DESIGN

In previous chapters we considered two different forms of knowledge representation – formal theories and semantic networks. These forms are equivalent to each other in the sense that knowledge represented in either of them can be transformed into the other form without loss of information. Both forms are suitable for automatic program construction in a computer. But unfortunately neither of these forms is suitable for knowledge representation for humans. For this purpose we need a much more convenient language. Up to now, no natural language has been applicable as an input language for computers. We must therefore introduce a formal language for describing knowledge for solving problems. We shall call this language a programming language, though it is quite different from the usual programming languages such as FORTRAN, Pascal or BASIC.

Designing the language, we shall keep in mind that the goal of a user of the language is solving problems, and not just writing programs which put a computer into action. First we shall aim for a language convenient for the user and perhaps not very efficient for implementation. Afterwards, in order to achieve acceptable performance for programs written in the language, we must make some concessions and take into consideration practical restrictions.

From the point of view of a user who is programming his problem on a computer the ideal situation is when a computer 'understands' every word. In this case, a program may contain a single word meaning just the job which must be done. Such systems, called turnkey systems, actually exist, and they are quite popular among users. But these systems are very specialized, and we cannot say that we are programming them when pushing a button, or typing a single command.

In the first chapter we represented a problem by a single statement – a

problem statement. The computer must transform this statement into a more detailed program using some additional knowledge. This approach is still too close to the ideal case and cannot be used in general. Knowledge about a particular problem must be supplied together with the problem statement. At least, the problem statement must contain a reference to the knowledge (the name of the data representing the knowledge).

There are also cases where it is easier to describe explicitly the actions needed to achieve the result, and not to try to specify problem conditions in detail for automatic planning of actions. This may be true even if the performer (the problem solver) is human. For example, if a performer is incompetent, then it is easier to give him orders telling him what to do, rather than explaining the problem in detail and then relying on his understanding of problem conditions and taking the right actions. This is the reason why we shall introduce procedural statements into our language. Unlike the usual programming languages, we shall divide the procedural statements into action statements and control statements.

The following kinds of statements will be included in the language:

- a problem statement, where it is said what is given and what must be found;

- specifications for representing knowledge about problem conditions;

- action statements for describing actions needed in the process of problem solving;

- control statements for combining actions into larger parts of programs.

Our main objective is convenience of language usage, and efficiency is not considered crucial, so we postulate the following principle of design:

> The system must remember and use automatically everything that has been said to it at any time.

This principle can be easily applied to knowledge represented in the form of computational models. But it is difficult to apply it to programs stored in a computer, because it contradicts modularity – it means that even local specifications in a program must be available from outside the program. For programs we postulate the following principle:

> Programs are indivisible entities of knowledge showing how to perform some kinds of actions. They can be programmed in any language supported by the computational environment.

We assume that the language we are designing will be used in a computational environment which supports modularity of programs and contains conventional programming languages. In particular, one version of

the system with our language is running in the environment of **IBM** operating systems and uses their modularity. The modules are object modules translated from FORTRAN, COBOL, PL/1, Algol or Assembler language.

The second principle has the consequences that

- the programs are interconnected only through parameters;
- no side effects are allowed;
- synchronization variables for parallel processes are also parameters of programs;
- final type checking must be done at the level of programs and not at the level of knowledge representation.

The name of the language we are going to describe is UTOPIST. This name was introduced in 1970 for a compiler of a very primitive specification language which was developed further in 1974 and which obtained more or less final shape in 1977 (Tyugu, 1977; 1979).

3.1.2 OBJECTS

The UTOPIST language is intended for representing problem conditions as a set of specifications each of which describes an abstract object. The abstract object is an abstraction of some situation, object, relation or action. It is represented as a computational model in a computer. Problems can be specified and solved on computational models, as described in the previous chapter. We can say that an abstract object can be anything that can be represented as a

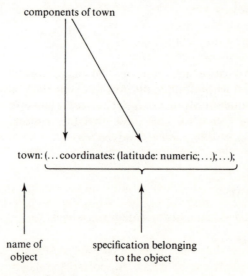

Figure 3.1   The structure of an abstract object.

computational model. Some are very simple, for example:

> *velocity*: **numeric**;

but most abstract objects and their specifications have a complicated form. Figure 3.1 shows the structure of an abstract object which represents a town. All that is needed for the description of the abstract object is given in parentheses after its name and a colon. In particular, there can again be specifications of abstract objects which are in this case its components. In Figure 3.1 the objects *coordinates* and *latitude* are components of the object *town*.

Let us consider once more the examples about percentages and motion which were described in Chapter 2. Complete specifications of these concepts in UTOPIST are as follows:

> *motion*: $(t_1, t_2, Dt, v_1, v_2, Dv, v, Ds, f, a, m,$
> $\qquad\quad E_1, E_2, DE$: **numeric**;
> $\qquad Dt = t_2 - t_1;$
> $\qquad Dv = v_2 - v_1;$
> $\qquad v = (v_1 + v_2)/2$
> $\qquad DE = E_2 - E_1;$
> $\qquad E_1 = m * v_1 \wedge 2/2;$
> $\qquad E_2 = m * v_2 \wedge 2/2;$
> $\qquad f = m * a;$
> $\qquad Dv = a * Dt;$
> $\qquad Ds = v * Dt;);$
> *percents*: $(w, p, r, c :$ **numeric**;
> $\qquad w = p + r;$
> $\qquad p/w = c/100;$
> $\qquad p/r = c/(100 - c););$

These texts in UTOPIST, which is a formal language, are still quite natural and can be understood without difficulty. We have changed the Greek letter Δ to D and have introduced only one redundant word – **numeric** – which shows the type of variables. Now we call these variables objects (!) and they are components of the objects *percents* and *motion*.

3.1.3 PROGRAMS

A program in UTOPIST consists of statements which are

- specifications;
- actions;
- commands.

A program starts with a heading of the form

> **program** ⟨program name⟩;

and ends with the line

> **end**;

It is convenient to put specifications at the beginning of a program and then to write an action part which is quite often only one statement – a problem statement. The usual structure of a program is shown in Figure 3.2.

Here is an example of a UTOPIST program which can be easily understood:

> **program** *firstprogram*;
> **let** X, Y, Z: **numeric**;
> $X + Y = 2.5$;
> $Z = X - Y$;
>
> **actions** ⊢ $X \rightarrow Z$;
> **end**;

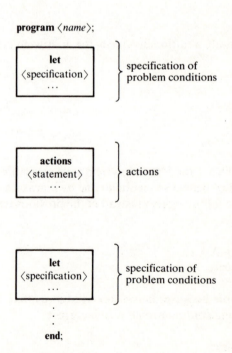

program ⟨*name*⟩;

> **let**
> ⟨specification⟩
> ...
$\left.\right\}$ specification of problem conditions

> **actions**
> ⟨statement⟩
> ...
$\left.\right\}$ actions

> **let**
> ⟨specification⟩
> ...
$\left.\right\}$ specification of problem conditions

.
.
.

end;

Figure 3.2   The structure of a program.

Two equations of the program represent relations which can be used for computations. The only action statement is

$$\vdash X \to Z;$$

which means that Z must be computed from X. This program is equivalent to the following two assignments:

$$Y := 2.5 - X;$$
$$Z := X - Y;$$

Instead of the line

end;

we can continue the program as follows:

let W : **numeric**
$\quad W = Z + X * Y;$
$\quad X = 0.5;$
actions
$\quad \vdash W;$
end;

In this case we shall additionally have the following fragment of object program:

$$X := 0.5;$$
$$Y := 2.5 - X;$$
$$Z := X - Y;$$
$$W := Z + X * Y;$$

Let us recall that the UTOPIST system uses everything that it has been told, but it processes the text sequentially line by line as it is typed. Therefore, if we try to type the following text instead of the previous text,

let $X = 0.5;$
$\quad W = Z + X * Y;$
$\quad W$: **numeric**;

we will be in trouble because the system will tell us that W is an unknown object. The following continuation is also incorrect:

let W : **numeric**;
$\quad W = Z + X * Y;$

```
   actions
      ⊢ W;
   end;
```

because W cannot be computed if the value of X is not given. The difference from the first example is that in the first case it was specified that X is an input variable of the problem (the problem statement was $\vdash X \rightarrow Z$).

Real features of a language can be demonstrated only on notably more complicated examples which contain complicated abstract objects. Up to now we have specified only *motion* and *percents*. Let us use them to specify a problem which was considered in Section 2.3.4:

```
   program secondprogram;

   let firstly : motion;
       afterwards : motion v1 = firstly.v2,m = firstly.m;
       relation : percents p = firstly.Dt,
                           r = afterwards.Dt;
       s : numeric;
       s = firstly.Ds + afterwards.Ds;
   actions
       ⊢ firstly.m, firstly.F, firstly.v1,
       relation.c, afterwards.F, relation.w → s;
   end;
```

The words *firstly*, *afterwards* and *relation* are identifiers, chosen freely to denote three abstract objects (*motion* and *percents*).

3.1.4 SYNTACTIC NOTATIONS

UTOPIST statements are built of the following elements:

- reserved words the meaning of which is understood by the system (such as **let**, **end**, etc.);
- identifiers for naming different entities;
- constants (numbers, logical constants and texts);
- delimiters;
- comments which are ignored by the system but are useful for users.

The language has only a small number of reserved words. In this book these words are printed in bold font for better readability. The reserved words are:

all, actions, and, apply, boolean, copy, delete, do, else, end, exit, false, fi, fun, help, if, insert, is, let, macro, next, not, numeric, program, od, or, run, space, text, then, true, undefined, virtual, while.

Also the names of primitive functions are printed in bold font:

abs, arctg, cos, exp, ln, log, sin, sqrt, tg.

Identifiers are built as usual of letters and digits, and begin with a letter. We shall also allow the characters # and _ in identifiers, for instance, FILE_IN, FILE_OUT, RECORD # 12.

Constants are numbers, texts and logical values. Numbers are represented either in the usual way or in the form of scientific representation, for example:

$$- 5, 21.0001, 3.6E - 9.$$

Logical values are

true, false.

Textual constants are placed in quotes: for example,

'Tom Higgins'
'blue'.

The following delimiters are used in the language:

$$: ; , ( ) + - * / \wedge = := \ldots . < > \leqslant \geqslant \equiv \neq \rightarrow \vdash$$

A comment is any line which begins with an asterisk.

We shall use the following syntactic notations for language description:

- Names of syntactic constructions are placed in angled brackets ($\langle \ \rangle$). We already know the following constructions:

  - $\langle$number$\rangle$,
  - $\langle$boolean constant$\rangle$,
  - $\langle$textual constant$\rangle$,
  - $\langle$constant$\rangle$,
  - $\langle$identifier$\rangle$,
  - $\langle$comment$\rangle$.

- If some position of a language construction can contain one of several alternatives, let us say, A, B or C, it can be designated by means of { } as follows:

$$\{A \mid B \mid C\} \quad \text{or} \quad \left\{ \begin{array}{c} A \\ B \\ C \end{array} \right\}$$

- Placing a construction inside square brackets ([ ]) means that this construction can be omitted in this position, for instance,

$$[A]B \qquad \text{and} \qquad \{B \,|\, AB\}$$

have one and the same meaning.

- $A \ldots$ means that A can be repeated one or more times in this position.
- $A, \ldots$ means exactly the same as $A \,[,A] \ldots$
- $A; \ldots$ means exactly the same as $A \,[;A] \ldots$
- The symbol ::= means 'is defined as'.

The following definition of program is an example of a syntactic definition:

$$\langle program \rangle ::= \textbf{program} \; \langle identifier \rangle; \; \begin{cases} \textbf{let} \; \langle specification \rangle \ldots \\ \\ \textbf{actions} \; \langle action \rangle \ldots \\ \qquad \langle command \rangle \end{cases} \textbf{end};$$

This formula specifies the structure of a UTOPIST program already known to us.

3.1.5 INTUITIVE SEMANTICS

In setting out to define a language we must agree how to represent the meaning of the language. There are several ways to represent the semantics of a programming language: denotational semantics, which is based on a sound mathematical basis; axiomatic semantics, which uses formal logic; and operational semantics, which more or less appeals to the intuitive meaning of computations. Operational semantics is represented by means of an abstract machine and rules for translation of the language into the language of that machine. The abstract machine must be so simple that no doubts can occur about the correctness of its definition even if it is given fairly informally. The definition of a machine must determine its behaviour for any program written in the language of the machine. Specification of this language can be considered either as a part of the specification of the abstract machine or as a specification of another language – the semantic language whose semantics is directly represented in terms of operations of the abstract machine. A special case of this approach is the definition of a machine which directly executes the statements of the programming language whose semantics is being described. But in this case we cannot hope that the machine will be simple enough.

In spite of the primitive nature of operational semantics we choose this method for describing the meaning of texts written in UTOPIST. The reasons for this are

- the similarity of this approach to intuitive concepts of computations;

- the possibility of using computational models directly as specifications in a semantic language;
- the flexibility of the notion of the semantic machine, which enables us to ignore the meaning of primitive operations.

The last feature is especially important because, in the case of the structural synthesis of programs, the properties of operations are not taken into account, and the set of primitive operations is potentially infinite – it can be changed from program to program.

Let us start with the specification of semantic language. A program in semantic language consists of two parts:

- a program model;
- a control tree.

The program model contains all variables of the program and all its primitive operators. The types of variables and operators acceptable in a program model are determined by the semantic machine – it must be able to apply operators and to compute values of variables. The program model is a computational model every relation of which contains only one operator.

The control tree determines an order of execution for the operators and the structure of the program. Every node of the control tree represents a part of the program containing the operators which are descendants of this node. The root of the control tree represents the whole program, and terminal nodes represent primitive operators which can be directly executed by the abstract machine. Therefore, the operators in the terminal nodes of the control tree must be present in the program model.

Let us consider an arbitrary nonterminal node f in a control tree. Let $f1, f2, \ldots, fk$ be the sons (the immediate descendants) of the node f, represented in the same order as they appear in the tree. (In general, this order is essential, so that any alteration of this order may change the program.) The node f has a type of control assigned to it, which we denote $control(f)$. Depending on the control type, it can also have a tuple of control variables $t1, t2, \ldots, tm$ which must be variables of the program model. The admissible control types are determined by the abstract machine.

Thus we have described the whole semantic language, i.e. the language of programs of the abstract machine. As we can see, it is indeed a very abstract language. A program in this language is represented in the form of two graphs. One of them is a special kind of semantic network – a computational model. It determines the operators which can be executed and possible data-flow paths. We can say that it represents an operational part of a program. The other graph is a tree which represents the overall structure of the program as well as the sequence of execution of its parts. Further concretization of the programming language is related to the abstract machine.

The abstract machine has a memory where values of all the variables of

the program model can be stored. It also has a processor able to execute any operator of the program model. The sequence of execution of operators is determined by the control tree of a program as follows:

1. Every node of the control tree represents a program which can be executed.

2. Execution of a terminal node of the control tree consists of the execution of its operator (which must be an operator of the program model).

3. Execution of a nonterminal node of the control tree consists of the execution of all its sons in a way prescribed by the control type associated with this node.

4. Execution of a program is execution of the root of its control tree.

Let us notice that we do not assume that the computations (i.e. the execution of operators) must be done sequentially. Hence, we can introduce control types for parallel computations. Let f be a nonterminal node with a control type, control variables $t1, t2, \ldots, tm, m \geqslant 0$, and sons $f1, f2, \ldots, fk$ in a control tree.

1. *seq* is the control type for sequential execution of the nodes $f1$, $f2, \ldots, fk$. We shall denote it also by $f = (f1; f2; \ldots; fk)$.

2. *par* is the control type for parallel execution of the nodes. It means that $f1, f2, \ldots, fk$ can be executed in an arbitrary order (maybe in parallel). We shall denote it also $f = (f1, f2, \ldots, fk)$.

3. *case* is the control type for executing one of the sons of the node depending on the values of $t1, t2, \ldots, tm$. In this case $m = k$, and control variables must be of boolean type. The variables $t1, t2, \ldots, tk$ are checked from left to right and for the first variable ti which has the value **true** the operator fi is executed. We shall denote such a node also by $f = case((t1, t2, \ldots, tk)(f1, f2, \ldots, fk))$.

4. *iter* is the control type for iteration. In this case the node f must have exactly one son $f1$ and one control variable $t1$. The son $f1$ is executed until $t1$ takes the value **false**. We denote this node also $f = iter(t1, f1)$.

Notes

1. The control types *seq*, *case* and *iter* constitute the set of conventional control types of structured programming.

2. We have introduced a textual representation of the control part of programs. The tree structure is denoted by means of parentheses, and control types are written immediately before the opening parentheses.

3. If we introduce a textual representation also for primitive operators, then we obtain a programming language. But this language will not contain data specifications, which must still be given in the program model.

4.   Adding new variables and operators into the model of a correct program does not change the meaning of the program. Indeed, a program model can contain any number of operators and variables which are not referred to in the control tree of the program. Any finite set of programs can have a common program model which is a correct model for every program of this set.

As a consequence of this last remark, an abstract machine together with a computational model can be considered as a semantic machine for a set of programs, the operators and data-flow conditions of which are represented by the model. This is a highly specialized machine which can be very efficient for representing the semantics of this particular set of programs. In the following chapters we shall describe some machines of that kind by building the computational models of these machines.

From another point of view, even the semantic language which we have described here is, in some sense, a specialized language, because we have fixed the set of admissible control types. Let us try to remove this restriction. For this purpose we have to extend the notion of a program model and to include relations with subproblems into it. A partial relation with subproblems (containing a single operator) can express any control type – it can be just a program which uses the programs of subproblems in a proper way. Now we can change the definition of a control tree in the following way. A control tree is a tree with some operator of a program model associated with each of its nodes. A node of this tree has sons if and only if its associated operator has subproblems, and in this case every subproblem corresponds to one of its sons. The definition of the abstract machine remains practically unchanged. Execution of a program is execution of the root of its control tree. Execution of any node of the control tree is application of its associated operator. The control types: *seq, case, par, iter* can be represented by preprogrammed operators which have subproblems.

3.2 Specifications

3.2.1 THE MEANING OF SPECIFICATIONS

Specifications have the following syntax:

$$\langle \text{specification} \rangle ::= \langle \text{id} \rangle, \dots : \langle \text{type specifier} \rangle;$$

The meaning of specifications is determined by type specifiers, which can be of great variety. A type specifier can be primitive, structured, class, undefined or sequence:

$$\langle \text{type specifier} \rangle ::= \left\{ \begin{array}{l} \langle \text{primitive specifier} \rangle \\ \langle \text{structured specifier} \rangle \\ \langle \text{class specifier} \rangle \\ \langle \text{undefined} \rangle \\ (\langle \text{sequence specifier} \rangle) \end{array} \right\}$$

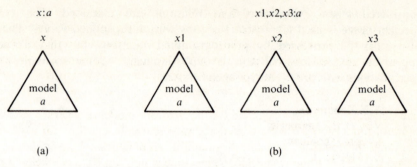

$x : a$ $x1, x2, x3 : a$

x $x1$ $x2$ $x3$

(a)   (b)

Figure 3.3   Computational models of specifications.

Let x be an identifier and a be a type specifier. The meaning of the specification

$$x : a;$$

is that a new abstract object is created which gets the name x and obtains all properties specified by a. These properties are represented by means of a computational model which is built from the type specifier a (Figure 3.3(a)).

Let $x1, x2, \ldots, xk$ be identifiers and a be a type specifier. The meaning of the specification

$$x1, x2, \ldots, xk : a;$$

is the same as the meaning of the following sequence of specifications:

$$x1 : a; x2 : a; \ldots; xk : a; \qquad \text{(see Figure 3.3(b))}.$$

3.2.2 PRIMITIVE TYPES

Syntax:

$$\langle\text{primitive specifier}\rangle ::= \left\{ \begin{array}{l} \textbf{numeric} \\ \textbf{boolean} \\ \textbf{text} \\ \textbf{space} \end{array} \right\}$$

The meaning of primitive types is determined as follows. A specification

$$\langle\text{id}\rangle : \langle\text{primitive specifier}\rangle$$

generates an abstract object – a variable of the given type. Further on, this variable can be bound with relations. Variables of the types **numeric**, **boolean** and **text** can be used in expressions and values can be assigned to them in assignment statements. This part of the semantics of variables will be

considered when expressions and relations are discussed. The type specifier **space** is used for abstract objects with encapsulated values. These values can be processed by preprogrammed functions, but they cannot appear in expressions of the UTOPIST language. Some examples of specifications with primitive type specifiers are:

> X,Y,Z : **numeric**;
> $NUMBER$: **numeric**;
> *accepted* : **boolean**;
> $NAME$: **text**;
> $TABLE$: **space**;

3.2.3 STRUCTURED TYPES

Syntax:

$$\langle \text{structured specifier} \rangle ::= (\left\{ \begin{array}{l} \langle \text{specification} \rangle \dots \\ \textbf{virtual} \langle \text{specification} \rangle \dots \\ \langle \text{relation} \rangle \dots \end{array} \right\} \dots)$$

A structured specifier defines a structured object that has components defined by the specifications given in parentheses. Components are abstract objects whose values constitute the value of the object defined by the structured specifier. Specifications after the word **virtual** define virtual components of the structured object. Virtual components can be used in computations automatically, but their values are not contained in the value of the structured object. A simple example of a structured object is

> *point* : (x : **numeric**;
> y : **numeric**;);

The following specification represents also a structured object with two components:

> *compl* : (*re,im*: **numeric**;
>   **virtual**
>   *mod,arg*: **numeric**;);

but this object has, in addition, two virtual components *mod* and *arg*.

Specifying a structured object, one must be careful not to give the same name to its different components or virtual components. This means, for instance, that the following specification is incorrect:

> x: (y: **numeric**;
>   **virtual** y: **numeric**;);

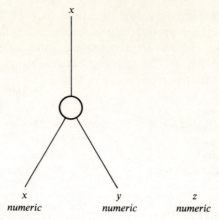

Figure 3.4   A model with a virtual variable.

but the specification

> x: (x, y : **numeric**;
> *virtual* z : **numeric**;));

is correct. The computational model for the abstract object x represented by the last specification contains

1. one variable for x itself;
2. two variables for its components x and y;
3. a structural relation binding structured x with its components x and y;
4. a variable for the virtual component z of the structured object x.

This computational model is shown in Figure 3.4.

A more complicated example is the following specification of a person:

> *PERSON*:
>   (*NAME*:
>   (*FAMILYNAME* : **text**;
>   *FIRSTNAME*   : **text**;
>   *PATRONYMIC* : **text**;));
>   *BIRTHDATE*   :
>   (*DAY*   : **numeric**;
>   *MONTH*   : **numeric**;
>   *YEAR*   : **numeric**;));
>   *SEX* : **text**;));

This specification is almost in the style of COBOL. And, indeed, it is the specification of a record.

The computational model of a structured object is built of models of its

Specification: Computational model:

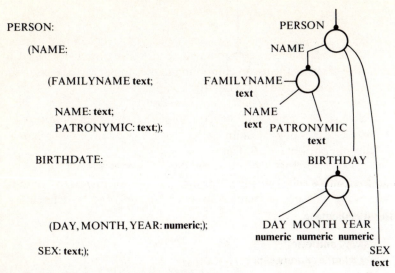

PERSON: PERSON

    (NAME: NAME

        (FAMILYNAME text;   FAMILYNAME
                                                            text

        NAME: text;   NAME
        PATRONYMIC: text;);   text PATRONYMIC
                                                               text

    BIRTHDATE: BIRTHDAY

        (DAY, MONTH, YEAR: numeric;);   DAY MONTH YEAR
                                             numeric numeric numeric

    SEX: text;);   SEX
                                                                  text

Figure 3.5   Building a model of *PERSON*.

components. Figure 3.5 shows the step-by-step construction of the model of *PERSON*. Computational models of structured objects can be very large and complicated. We therefore introduce an abbreviated form for the graphical representation of models as shown in Figure 3.6. The representation in Figure

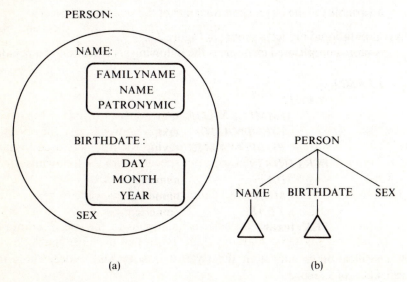

(a)   (b)

Figure 3.6   Granular models.

3.6(a) is similar to the representation of frames; the other representation (Figure 3.6(b)) shows explicitly the tree structure of the structured object.

3.2.4 COMPOUND NAMES

According to the principle: 'the system remembers everything that has been said to it', it is possible at any moment to use any object described to the system. This requires the use of compound names to refer to objects described within other objects. The following rule is valid:

> Any component *A* of an object *B* is called *B.A* outside of *B*. If *B* in its turn is a component of an object *C*, then outside of *C* the name of the inner object is *C.B.A*, etc.

According to this rule, outside of the specification of *PERSON* we must use the following compound names to refer to the objects defined by this specification:

> *PERSON.NAME*
> *PERSON.NAME.FAMILYNAME*
> *PERSON.NAME.FIRSTNAME*
> *PERSON.NAME.PATRONYMIC*
> *PERSON.BIRTHDATE*
> *PERSON.BIRTHDATE.DAY*
> *PERSON.BIRTHDATE.MONTH*
> *PERSON.BIRTHDATE.YEAR*
> *PERSON.SEX*

If, in its turn, *PERSON* is a component of *PEOPLE*, then we must sometimes add the prefix *PEOPLE* to these names, for instance, *PEOPLE.PERSON.SEX*.

3.2.5 SEQUENCES

If an object contains many similar components, it is sometimes inconvenient and unnecessary to give an explicit name to every component of the object. In this case the components can be numbered and the numbers used to name them. This is done by means of a sequence specifier with the following syntax:

> ⟨sequence specifier⟩ ::= 1 .. [⟨number⟩] : ⟨type specifier⟩

The semantics of a sequence specifier is analogous to the specification of a row of objects with one and the same type. Let us have the following specification:

> *X1, X2, X3* : **numeric**;

This specification defines three objects: *X1*, *X2*, *X3*. Similar objects can be specified as follows:

>   1 .. 3 : **numeric**;

But in this case the names of the objects will be # *1*, # *2*, # *3*. This is the only difference between the two specifications.

Another example of specification of the sequence is

>   *MATRIX* : (1 .. 15 : (1 .. 29 : (*re,im* : **numeric**;);););

This *MATRIX* has components for rows: # *1*, # *2*, ..., # *15*; and components for elements in rows: # *1.* # *1*, # *1.* # *2*, ..., # *15.* # *29*.

The number in a sequence specifier shows the number of components of the sequence. If the number is absent, then an infinite sequence is specified. (It is possible to specify infinite sequences in abstract objects, but obviously it is not possible to compute the value of an infinite sequence as a whole.)

Note that a sequence essentially differs from an array, although at first glance they may seem similar. An array is a data structure, and operations such as reading a value or writing a new value of an element determined by its indices are always applicable. But one cannot compute names of elements of a sequence (there are no such constructs in the language as # (*i*) or # (*i* + 1)).

3.2.6 NAME PATTERNS

A compound name can contain the word **all**. It is equivalent to a list of names. A name *x*.**all**.*y*, denotes all objects which have names *x*.⟨id⟩.*y*. The construction *x*.**all**.*y* is a name pattern which can be used anywhere instead of a list of names *x.a.y*, ..., *x.b.y*, where *a*, ..., *b* is a list of identifiers, and it contains all names of components of *x* that match the pattern. The word **all** can appear in a name pattern several times. The name pattern *MATRIX*.**all**.**all**.*re* denotes real components of all elements of the matrix specified in Section 3.2.5.

3.2.7 COPIES

The specification of a structured object can be used as a part of the specification of a new structured object.

Syntax:

>   ⟨copy⟩ ::= **copy** ⟨name⟩

Let *A* be the name of a structured object. Then

>   **copy** *A*;

in a specification is equivalent to the text contained in parentheses of the type specifier of the abstract object *A*. For example, having a specification of *PERSON* (see Section 3.2.3), we can define an *EMPLOYEE* as follows:

> *EMPLOYEE*: (**copy** PERSON;
>   *NUMBER*: **numeric**;
>   *DEPARTMENT*: **text**;);

this specification has exactly the same meaning as

> *EMPLOYEE*: (
>   *NAME*: (*FAMILYNAME*: **text**;
>   *FIRSTNAME*: **text**;
>   *PATRONYMIC*: **text**;);
>   *BIRTHDATE*: (*DAY*: **numeric**;
>   *MONTH*: **numeric**;
>   *YEAR*: **numeric**;);
>   *SEX*: **text**;
>   *NUMBER*: **numeric**;
>   *DEPARTMENT*: **text**;);

One must be careful when using **copy** *x*; because this specification introduces implicitly a number of names – the names of all components of *x*.

3.2.8 TYPES OF OBJECTS

Any abstract object can be used as a type specifier. This has a consequence that we can create infinitely many types (as many as there are different abstract objects which can be specified in UTOPIST). Making amendments, any structured object can be used to build a variety of new types. For example, the following specification can be used to create numeric types with various numbers of decimal digits in the fractional part of the external representation of a number:

> *NUMERIC*: (*val*: **numeric**;
>   **virtual**
>   *representation*: 1 ..: **numeric**;

> * it is assumed here that every element of the representation is
> * one of the numbers: 0,1,...,9, i.e. it is a decimal digit.

> *fractiondigits*: **numeric**;
> *F1*: *representation*, *fractiondigits* → *value* (M1);
> *F2*: *value*, *fractiondigits* → *representation* (M2););

Examples of usage of this type are

> X: *NUMERIC fractiondigits* = 5;
> Y: *NUMERIC fractiondigits* = 3;

The following continuation of the example is correct due to the coercion of types, which will be discussed later in this section:

> $X = 110.33566;$
> $X = Y;$

and if we ask for the value of Y, we shall get 110.336.

The principle applied to the types in UTOPIST is

> The type of an object is uniquely determined by the computational model of the object.

Any abstract object in the UTOPIST language possesses a unique type. Many of the types are quite similar, and we use various equivalence relations on the set of types. Here we say for brevity 'equivalent objects' instead of 'objects which have equivalent types'.

Primary equivalence   Equivalent objects have one and the same primitive type or are specified by inheritance from the same primitive type. All objects which are not equivalent to any object of primitive type are equivalent with each other. So we have classes of primary equivalence corresponding to the specifiers: **numeric, text, boolean, space** and one class for all other objects.

Weak structural equivalence   Objects with identical structure and identical types of primitive components are equivalent. (Names of components are not taken into account.)

Strong structural equivalence   Objects with identical structure, identical names of components and identical types of primitive components are equivalent.

Partial structural equivalence   If a specification of an object can be obtained from a specification on some other object by

1.   deleting its tail starting from some construction and
2.   completing the remaining part with parentheses,

then the object is called the initial part of this other object.

Two objects are partially structurally equivalent if one of them is weakly structurally equivalent to an initial part of the other object.

3.3 Relations

Relations in the UTOPIST language can be represented explicitly in the form of equations or in the form of programs which are in a program library. Besides that, relations can be defined implicitly. In particular, structural relations are presented implicitly in specifications of structured objects (see Section 3.2.3).

Representing relations by means of programs is a general case in a sense that the other representations can be transformed into this form. But equations are often much more convenient, and also using parentheses is a common way of expressing the structure of an object. Therefore we have also introduced these forms of representation of relations into UTOPIST.

3.3.1 EXPRESSIONS

Syntax:

$$\langle \text{expression}\rangle ::= \left\{ \begin{array}{l} \langle \text{name}\rangle \\ \langle \text{value}\rangle \\ \langle \text{arithmetic expression}\rangle \\ \langle \text{logical expression}\rangle \end{array} \right\}$$

Any value is an expression. We have primitive values: numbers, boolean values (**true** and **false**) and texts. The latter are strings of characters placed in quotes and containing no quotes within themselves. Other values are built from primitive values by means of parentheses and commas: for example,

$$(-5.1, -1.5)$$
$$((\text{'Johnson','Peter','Paul'}),(15,04,1932),\text{'male'})$$

The latter value has the exact structure of a person.

Syntax of value:

$$\langle \text{value}\rangle ::= \left\{ \begin{array}{l} \langle \text{primitive value}\rangle \\ \\ (\langle \text{value}\rangle,\ldots) \end{array} \right\}$$

Arithmetic expressions are built up from names of objects and numbers by means of arithmetic operations, parentheses and functions as usual. Objects in arithmetic expressions must either have numeric type or contain only one nonvirtual component, and this component must have numeric type.

Arithmetic operations are:

+   addition,
−   subtraction,

*   multiplication,
/   division,
∧   exponentiation.

Primitive functions are:

abs, arctg, cos, exp, ln, log, sin, sqrt, tg.

Some examples are:

sqrt$(A + \textbf{sin}(Q/1 - 13.5 * R))$.

Names of relations can be used as functions, but this will be discussed later.

Logical expressions are constructed from the boolean values **true** and **false**, names of objects, and predicates, by means of parentheses and the logical operations

and, or, not.

Objects in logical expressions must either have boolean type or contain only one nonvirtual component, which must be of boolean type.

Predicates are built up from expressions by means of relation symbols:

≡   equal,
≠   not equal,
<   less than,
≤   less or equal,
>   greater than,
≥   greater or equal.

The first predicate symbol (≡) can be used for any type of expression. All other predicate symbols are applicable only for arithmetic expressions. Some examples are:

$MATRIX1 \equiv MATRIX2$
$q \neq 0$
$\textbf{ln}(x+1) < \textbf{sqrt}(Z - 1)$
not$(X.o$ **or** $A.B)$

3.3.2 EQUATIONS

Syntax:

⟨equation⟩ ::= ⟨expression⟩ = ⟨expression⟩

In the case of structured objects that have more than one nonvirtual component an equation can have only the form $x = y$ or $x = c$ where x, y are names of objects, and c is a value. In these equations x and y or x and c must have partially equivalent types. These equations induce equations $x.a = y.a$ between all the corresponding components $x.a, y.a$ of the objects x and y or equations $x.a = c_a$ between components of x and corresponding components of the value c.

For instance, the equation

$$PERSON = EMPLOYEE$$

means that

$$PERSON.NAME = EMPLOYEE.NAME$$
$$PERSON.NAME.FAMILYNAME =$$
$$EMPLOYEE.NAME.FAMILYNAME \text{ etc.}$$

The only components of *EMPLOYEE* that do not match and so will not be bound by equations, are *EMPLOYEE.NUMBER* and *EMPLOYEE.DEPARTMENT.*

Finally, every equation of the form $x = y$ is replaced by two operators: $x \rightarrow y$ and $y \rightarrow x$. And every equation of the form $x = c$, where c is a constant, is replaced by one operator $\rightarrow x$.

In the case where one of the expressions is neither a name nor a value, the type of expressions can be only logical or arithmetic. In both cases the equation is considered to be a symmetric relation with the rank equal to 1. Let us look at some simple examples. The equation

$$x = 2 * x + 1$$

determines a relation with a single variable x which is the output variable of the relation. It enables us to evaluate x and the value of x will be -1. Let us recall that in some programming languages the statement

$$x = 2 * x + 1$$

means that the value of x must be multiplied by 2 then 1 must be added and the result must be assigned to x as its new value.

In the latter equation x is not necessarily of the numeric type. It can also be a structured object with one nonvirtual component which is numeric. In this case the value of x is also numeric (it contains only the values of its nonvirtual components). This feature is very useful for handling physical entities with various units, as will be shown in Section 4.4.1.

The equation $A = \textbf{not } B$ determines a symmetric relation with two

weakly bound variables A and B. It is obvious that it is not possible to solve every logical equation for every variable contained in it. The same applies to arithmetic equations. Let us consider an arithmetic equation in general form:

$$f(x_1, \ldots, x_n) = 0,$$

where the function f is represented by an arithmetic expression, containing variables $x_1, \ldots, x_n$. Trying to solve the equation for a variable x_i, $1 \leqslant i \leqslant n$, we have one of the following situations:

1.   the equation is solvable and there exists a unique solution for x_i;
2.   the equation is not solvable uniquely for x_i;
3.   the equation is uniquely solvable for x_i only in a restricted domain of $(x_1, \ldots, x_{i-1}, x_{i+1}, \ldots, x_n)$.

   In the first case the partial relation specified by the equation contains an operator

$$x_i := \varphi(x_1, \ldots, x_{i-1}, x_{i+1}, \ldots, x_n)$$

which is applicable for any values of $x_1, \ldots, x_{i-1}, x_{i+1}, \ldots, x_n$.

   In the second case the relation does not contain operators with the output variable x_i.

   In the third case the relation contains a partial operator

$$x_i := \varphi(x_1, \ldots, x_{i-1}, x_{i+1}, \ldots, x_n).$$

Automatic investigation of the solvability of equations is very complicated; therefore, the compiler of UTOPIST represents any equation as a completely symmetric relation with the rank 1.

   The investigation of real properties of equations is postponed to the computation stage, and it is then done interactively with the help of a user. It is safe to specify only equations in which every variable can be evaluated uniquely.

   We have already used equations for specifying the concepts *motion* and *percents* in Section 3.1.2. Here we merely give in addition an example of a specification with equations.

   line: $(P, Q: (x, y:$ **numeric**;);
       angle, length: **numeric**;
       length $*$ **cos** *angle* $= Q.x - P.x$;
       length $\wedge 2 = (Q.x - P.x) \wedge 2 + (Q.y - P.y) \wedge 2$;);

This description contains practically everything that can be said about an interval of a straight line in general – two points P and Q which are ends of the

line, their coordinates *P.x*, *P.y*, *Q.x*, *Q.y*, as well as *length* and *angle* of inclination of the line bound to the coordinates of its ends.

3.3.3 PREPROGRAMMED RELATIONS

$$\left\{ \begin{array}{l} \text{Syntax:} \\ \quad \langle \text{preprogrammed relation} \rangle ::= \\ \quad\quad \left[\left\{ \begin{array}{l} \langle \text{name} \rangle \\ \langle \text{subproblem} \rangle \\ \textbf{rank } \langle \text{number} \rangle \langle \text{name} \rangle, \dots \end{array} \right\} \right], \dots \rightarrow \langle \text{name} \rangle, \dots \right\} (\langle \text{implementation} \rangle); \end{array} \right.$$

$\langle \text{subproblem} \rangle ::= (\langle \text{name} \rangle, \dots \rightarrow \langle \text{name} \rangle, \dots)$

$\langle \text{implementation} \rangle ::= \left\{ \begin{array}{l} \langle \text{program name} \rangle \\ \textbf{macro } \langle \text{macro name} \rangle \end{array} \right\}$

For example,

$$MATRIX \rightarrow MATRIX1 \text{ (TRANSPON)};$$

specifies a relation with an input variable *MATRIX* and an output variable *MATRIX1* represented by a program *TRANSPON*. The types of the variables *MATRIX* and *MATRIX1* are not specified here, but naturally these types must match the types of the parameters of the program *TRANSPON*.

Let us describe the meaning of each part of this specification. To the left of the arrow we put the input variables of the relation and to the right its output variables. A relation can have subproblems; they are taken into parentheses. Again, to the left of the arrow are written arguments of the subproblem and to the right its results. The relation beginning with **rank** is a completely symmetric relation with the rank equal to the number given in the specification. This form of relation is only an abbreviation enabling us to represent several preprogrammed operators as a single relation. Its usage is illustrated in Section 5.3.3.

Preprogrammed relations can be implemented either as a program or as a macro definition. In the first case we use only the name of the program and in the second case the word **macro**, followed by the macro name which allows us to find the implementation from a library. The specification of a preprogrammed relation can be regarded as an external view of a program, which shows only computational possibilities presented by the program. Neither the types of bound variables nor the function that the program performs are specified.

Comparing the specifications of preprogrammed relations and the computability statements introduced in the previous chapter, we can see a complete analogy between them. For instance, the specification

$$x \rightarrow y(F);$$

corresponds to the computability statement

$$x \underset{F}{\rightarrow} y.$$

Actually, these are two different representations of one and the same fact – the computability of y from x by means of F.

Preprogrammed relations can be used for specifying large modular programs. A computational model which contains such relations is actually a schema for assembling a modular program. The following is an example of specification of a programming system:

> **let** *progsyst*:
>   (*fortran, assembler, message, object, load, code,*
>   *listing*: **space**;
>   *libname*: **text**;
>   *loadaddr*: **numeric**;
>   *FORTRAN*: *fortran* → *object, message* (FCOMP);
>   *ASM*: *assembler* → *object, message* (ASM);
>   *LEDIT*: *object, libname* → *load* (LKD);
>   *LOAD*: *load, loadaddr* → *code* (LOADER);
>   *PRINT*: *message* → *listing* (WRITER););

The computational model of this programming system is presented in Figure 3.7.

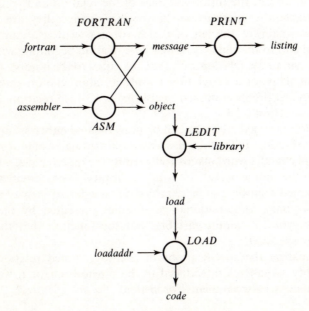

Figure 3.7   A computational model of a programming system.

3.3.4 CONDITIONAL RELATIONS

Syntax:

$\langle$relation$\rangle ::= [\langle$id$\rangle :][$**if**$\langle$logical expression$\rangle$ **then**$]$

$$\left\{\begin{matrix}\langle\text{equation}\rangle \\ \langle\text{preprogrammed relation}\rangle, \end{matrix}\right\};$$

Here we gave the complete syntax of the relation. The identifier is the name of the relation. It can be absent. A relation, represented as an equation or a preprogrammed relation, can be preceded by a condition that determines the applicability of the relation. A conditional relation is applicable only if the logical expression in the condition can be evaluated and its value is true.

Let us consider the specification of a diode as an example where conditional relations are used. This specification contains variables for electrical current I through the diode, for voltage U on it and for two resistances: direct resistance Rd (which is very small) and inverse resistance Ri (which must be big). The applicability of relations here depends on the direction of the current I (on its sign).

$DIODE$: $(U, I, Rd, Ri$: **numeric**;
if $I > 0$ then $U = I * Rd$;
if $I < 0$ then $U = I * Ri$;
if $U > 0$ then $U = I * Rd$;
if $U < 0$ then $U = I * Ri$;);

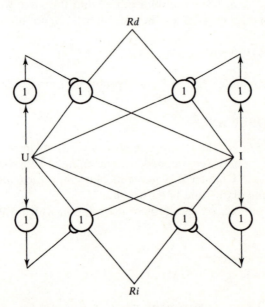

Figure 3.8 A model of $DIODE$.

It may seem that we have put too many relations into this specification, but the first two relations cannot be used for finding current from a given voltage and resistance, because the conditions of these relations depend on current, and the last two are not applicable for finding voltage, because the conditions of these relations depend on voltage.

A conditional statement defines implicitly a boolean variable which is the control variable of the relation (see Section 2.3.5). Figure 3.8 shows the computational model of the concept *DIODE*.

We introduce the following two abbreviations for conditional statements.

1.   If several relations $a_1, \ldots, a_n$ have one and the same condition, we can write them in parentheses after the condition, which is written only once:

   if b **then** $(a_1; \ldots; a_k)$;

2.   If the conditional relations

   if b_1 **then** a_1;
   if b_2 **then** a_2;
   . . .
   if b_k **then** a_k;

are such that $b_1 \vee b_2 \vee \cdots \vee b_k$ is true for any values of variables and the relations $a_1, a_2, \ldots, a_k$ bind variables in one and the same way, i.e. have the same input and output variables, then we can use the notation

$$(b_1 \rightarrow a_1 \,|\, b_2 \rightarrow a_2 \,|\ldots|\, b_k \rightarrow a_k);$$

This notation facilitates the synthesis of programs from conditional relations.

3.3.5 SUBPROBLEMS

We have already considered subproblems of relations in Section 2.3, where computational models were defined. The meaning of subproblems is exactly the same here as in Chapter 2. Arguments of a subproblem are written to the left and its results to the right of the arrow.

As an example, we specify here the relation which was considered in Section 2.3.5.

   let x,y,u,z: **numeric**;
      $(u \rightarrow v), x \rightarrow z \,(SIMPSON)$;

where $SIMPSON$ is the name of the integration program.

3.3.6 RELATIONS IN SEQUENCES

Let us consider a sequence $1..:(X,Y,Z:$ **numeric**$;)$. The objects $\#1, \#2, \ldots$ may actually have complicated internal structures. But we are interested only in the ways of binding components of these objects with each other, and we therefore start with simple examples.

First, we can specify a relation that does not belong to any of the objects $\#1, \#2, \ldots$ but which binds some of their components:

$$\#1.X = \#2.X + 2.5;$$

Second, in any of these objects we can specify relations which bind their components with some outer objects:

$T:$ **numeric**;
$1..:(X,Y,Z:$ **numeric**; $X + Y = T;);$

Third, when specifying a relation that does not belong to the objects of the sequence, we can use name patterns to bind components of all objects with the relation:

$Y:$ **numeric**;
$ROW:(1 \ldots 100:(X,Y,Z:$ **numeric**$;););ROW$.**all**.$Y \rightarrow Y(CONSTR);$

Finally, in the specification of an element of the row we can use the name **next** to denote the successor of the element.

Putting all these specifications together we have

$T:$ **numeric**;
$ROW:(1 \ldots 100:(X,Y,Z:$ **numeric**;
   $X + Y = T;$
   next.$Z = Z + 1;$);
   $\#1.X = \#2.X + 2.5;);$
   $Y:$ **numeric**;
   ROW.**all**.$Y \rightarrow Y(CONSTR);$

Figure 3.9 shows the computational model which corresponds to this specification.

The question arises of what to do if we wish to bind components of non-neighbouring elements of a sequence. In this case we have to introduce additional components of elements and use these components as some temporary memory space for transferring values along the sequence.

As an example, let us specify the sequence of Fibonacci numbers

$$1,1,2,3,5,8,13,\ldots$$

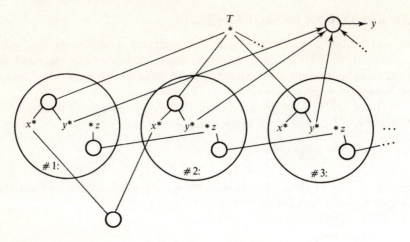

Figure 3.9   A model of a sequence.

which is defined by the equations

$$f_{i+2} = f_i + f_{i+1}, \qquad f_1 = f_2 = 1.$$

In order to represent it in UTOPIST, we transform the first equation into the form

$$f_{i+1} = f_{i-1} + f_i,$$

and use an additional variable x for storing f_{i-1}, so that we shall have

$$f_{i+1} = x + f_i,$$

where $x = f_{i-1}$. The complete specification is:

Fib: $(1 .. : (f, x: \textbf{numeric}; \textbf{next}.f = f + x; \textbf{next}.x = f;);$
$\qquad \# 1.f = 1; \# 2.f = 1;);$

Sequences enable us to specify some interesting concepts which demonstrate that structural synthesis can be used not only for building programs from complicated preprogrammed functions, but also for synthesizing programs from a very simple basis. We show how to specify addition of natural numbers, using only the constant 1 and the operation + 1. (In order to do this, we are not allowed to use equations in general form.) First of all, natural numbers can be defined as

$1 .. : (value: \textbf{numeric};$
$\qquad \textbf{next}.value = value + 1;);$
$\qquad \# 1.value = 0;$

Addition of natural numbers is defined as

> *plus*: (*x,y,z*: **numeric**;
>
> * *z* is the sum of *x* and *y*.
>
> 1 .. : (*u,v*: **numeric**;
>   **next**.*u* = *u* + 1;
>   **next**.*v* = *v* + 1;
>   **if** *u* = *y* **then** *z* = *v*;)
>   #*1.u* = 0;
>   #*1.v* = *x*;);

3.4 The inheritance specifier

Now we are going to discuss one of the most interesting constructions of the UTOPIST language.

Syntax:

> ⟨inheritance specifier⟩ ::= ⟨name⟩ [⟨amendments⟩].

The name of any object can be used as a specifier in a specification. In this case the new object which is specified will inherit all properties of the object the name of which is used as the specifier. For example,

> *X* : **numeric**;
> *Y* : *X*;

means exactly the same as

> *X* : **numeric**;
> *Y* : **numeric**;

3.4.1 SIMPLE INHERITANCE

If no amendments are shown in the specification, then we have the case of simple inheritance. In this case the computational model of the new object is an exact copy of the model of the object from which it is inherited. Only full names of components are changed. In the computational model of the specification

> *y*: *x*

any object which had the name *x.a* will get the name *y.a*. For example, we can use objects *point* and *PERSON*, which we have specified already, to specify

new objects:

> *T*: *point*;
> *TOM*: *PERSON*;

Remembering that *point* had components *x* and *y* with full names *point.x*, *point.y*, we get full names *T.x* and *T.y* for components of *T*. Analogously, as components of *PERSON* had the names *PERSON.NAME*, *PERSON.NAME.FAMILYNAME*, etc., so the components of *TOM* will get the names *TOM.NAME*, *TOM.NAME.FAMILYNAME*, etc.

Specifications by inheritance are very powerful linguistic tools, especially when they can be used as freely as in UTOPIST. We can use any abstract object as a prototype of a new object, i.e. all that has been specified is immediately applicable for further specifications. Up to now it has been practically feasible to build a graphical representation of the computational model of any specification because all variables and almost all relations were explicitly represented in the specification. When inheritance is used, it becomes practically impossible to visualize a computational model in detail. This means that specifications become more meaningful. Let us recall once again that a computational model is a description of an abstract object, and therefore there is no need to store it in extended form in the memory of a computer. Hence, the size of a computational model is not directly connected with the memory size needed to store a specification.

Inheritance can be used for specifying complicated objects in a bottom-up manner very compactly, starting from details and small pieces and then putting them together. Using inheritance, we can avoid nested specifications which are hard to understand. For example, a specification of the staff of a company can be given step by step as follows:

> *ADDRESS*: (*APARTMENT*: **numeric**;
>   *HOUSE*: **numeric**;
>   *STREET*: **text**;
>   *TOWN*: **text**;
>   *ZIPCODE*: **text**;);
> *DATE*: (*DAY, MONTH, YEAR*: **numeric**;);

*the following is a general description of a person:

> *PERSON*: (*NAME*: (*FAMILYNAME*,
>   *FIRSTNAME*,
>   *PATRONYMIC*: **text**;);
>   *HOMEADDRESS*: *ADDRESS*;
>   *WORKINGADDRESS*: *ADDRESS*;
>   *SEX*: **text**;
>   *BIRTHDATE*: *DATE*;);

*the specification of an employee is as follows:

EMPLOYEE: (*CODE*: **text**;
            PERSONALITY: *PERSON*;
            SALARY: **numeric**;
            DEPARTMENT: **text**;);

*the specification of a department is as follows:

DEPARTMENT: (*CODE*: **text**;
              HEAD: *EMPLOYEE*;
              HEAD.DEPARTMENT = *CODE*;
              STAFF: (1 ..: *EMPLOYEE*););

If we intend to select employees of departments one by one, then it is useful to specify some relations and to extend the specification of *STAFF* as follows:

STAFF: (1 ..:
         (*EMPLOYEE:EMPLOYEE*;
         virtual
         LASTEMPLOYEE: **bool**;
         LAST: → *LASTEMPLOYEE* (TESTLAST);
         if not fun *LAST* **then**
         NEXT: *EMPLOYEE* → **next**. *EMPLOYEE* (NEXTEMP);

* we can also add a relation for finding the first
* employee of the department,
* who is the head of the department.

STAFF.#1 = *DEPARTMENT.HEAD*;);

Let us note that *STAFF*.#i = *STAFF*.#i.*EMPLOYEE*, because the virtual component *LASTEMPLOYEE* is not contained in the elements of *STAFF*.

3.4.2 INHERITANCE WITH FIXED VALUES OF COMPONENTS

In the simplest case, an amendment has the form

⟨name⟩ = ⟨value⟩

where ⟨name⟩ is the name of a component of the prototype object. The specification

$X:YZ = $ ⟨value⟩;

has the same meaning as

$$X:Y;$$
$$X.Z = \langle value \rangle;$$

If an inheritance specifier contains several amendments they are processed independently of each other in an arbitrary order. For example, the specification

$$X:Y\, Z1 = v_1, Z2 = v_2;$$

where v_1 and v_2 are constants, can be changed to

$$X:Y;$$
$$X.Z1 = v_1;$$
$$X.Z2 = v_2;$$

as well as to

$$X:Y;$$
$$X.Z2 = v_2;$$
$$X.Z1 = v_1;$$

In any amendment $Z = v$ object Z and value v must have weakly structurally equivalent types. Some examples are:

$$T: point\ x = 0.5;$$
$$BOB: PERSON$$
$$NAME = (`JOHNS', `ROBERT'),$$
$$BIRTHDATE = (13, 5, 1930);$$

3.4.3 AMENDMENTS WITH ADDITIONAL RELATIONS

A more general form of amendments is

$$\langle name \rangle = \langle expression \rangle,$$

where the expression does not contain the name from the left-hand side of the amendment. A specification

$$X:Y \quad Z = V;$$

where V is an expression, is equivalent to

$$X:Y;$$
$$X.Z = V;$$

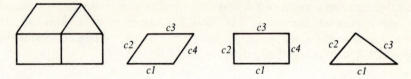

Figure 3.10   A compound object.

Some examples are:

> $T1$, $T2$: *point*;
> $T3$: *point* $x = T1.x$, $y = T1.y - T2.y$;

Using amendments, it is easy to specify a situation where several objects have common parts. For example, a house, shown in Figure 3.10, can be specified by means of objects *rectangle*, *parallelogram* and *triangle* as follows:

> $HOUSE$: ($WALL1$: *rectangle*;
> $WALL2$: *rectangle* $c2 = WALL1.c4$;
> $ROOF$: *parallelogram* $c1 = WALL2.c3$,
> $c2 = ROOF.c4$;
> $ROOF1$: *triangle* $c1 = WALL2.c3, c2 = ROOF.c4$;);

3.4.4 EXPLICIT AND IMPLICIT BINDING IN AMENDMENTS

Any amendment binds a component of the new object. This component can be determined explicitly by its name as we have done up to now. But it can also be determined implicitly – positionally. In this case the amendment does not contain the name of a component which must be bound, and has the form

$$\langle \text{amendment} \rangle ::= \begin{Bmatrix} \langle \text{value} \rangle \\ \langle \text{name} \rangle \end{Bmatrix}$$

The following rules are valid:

1. If the first amendment in an inheritance specifier does not contain the name of a component, then the first component is bound by this amendment.
2. If an amendment does not contain the name of a component and it is preceded by another amendment, then the component following the component of the preceding amendment is bound.

We see that something must be known about the internal structure of the prototype object – the order of components which are being bound or their names must be known.

If the number of amendments is small, then it is easier and more reliable to determine components by their names. But in the case of numerous

amendments, and especially if it is unimportant which component is bound by any particular amendment, implicit binding is more convenient. In particular, it is useful for specification of input–output. Let us consider the objects *PERSON* as specified earlier and

$$DESCRIBE: (1 \ldots : PERSON; \rightarrow \textbf{all} (INPUTALL););$$

Now we can use positional binding in the following inheritance specification:

$$INPUT: DESCRIBE \ BOB, TOM, JULIA;$$

as soon as we have specified

$$BOB, TOM, JULIA: PERSON;$$

3.4.5 UNDEFINED COMPONENTS

The last case of type specifier we are now going to discuss is an undefined specifier:

$$\langle \text{undefined specifier} \rangle ::= \textbf{undefined}$$

A specification

$$x: \textbf{undefined};$$

where x is any identifier, can be used only for specifying a component of some other object y. It describes an abstract object $y.x$ with unknown properties. The properties of this object must be specified later, when the object y is used as a prototype in an inheritance specification. Objects with unknown components are frames, similar, for instance to frames in the FRL language (Roberts and Goldstein, 1978). Components of undefined type are slots in the frames.

An undefined object x has the property that any name $x.z$, where z is an identifier, can be a name of its component, and therefore, any construction $x.\langle id \rangle$ is accepted as a legal name of the component of the object x. For example, having specified

$$TOWN: \textbf{undefined};$$

we can immediately use the names: *TOWN.INHABITANTS*, *TOWN.* *TRANSPORT.CARS*, *TOWN.CHILDREN*, *TOWN.DISTRICT.#1* etc. Moreover, it is assumed that the types of these objects (which, actually, are also undefined) always match the types needed in constructions where they

are used. Therefore, we can specify relations

$$TOWN.TRANSPORT.CARS = k1 * TOWN.INHABITANTS;$$
$$TOWN.CHILDREN = k2 * TOWN.INHABITANTS;$$

where *k1* and *k2* are numeric objects. Objects with undefined components can express general laws which are valid for objects of different structure. Let us describe, for instance, a balance between consuming and supplying:

> *BALANCE*:
>   (*consumers*: **undefined**;
>
> * contains *consumers* which have a component
> * *amount* for the consumed amount
>
>   *suppliers*: **undefined**;
>
> * contains suppliers which have a component
> * *amount* for the supplied amount
>
>   *difference, consumed, supplied*: **numeric**;
>   *consumers*.**all**.*amount* → *consumed* (SUM);
>   *suppliers*.**all**.*amount* → *supplied* (SUM);
>   *difference = supplied − consumed*;);

The abstract object *BALANCE* describes properly any balance between consuming and supplying something (electric power, food, etc.) the measure of which is called *amount*.

    This example shows us that names of components of undefined objects must be used in accordance with some agreements about the internal structure (and about the names) of the objects which can be substituted for the undefined object. It is always useful to represent these agreements as comments.

3.4.6 EXTENDING AN INHERITED SPECIFICATION

Let us take the following specifications

> $X:(\ldots);$
> $Y:(\ldots; Z: \textbf{undefined}; \ldots);$

Then the specification

> $A:Y \quad Z = X;$

represents an object *A* which differs from the prototype object *Y* in the

following ways:

1.   its component *Z* has the same specification as *X* has;
2.   the objects *X* and *A.Z* are bound by the equation *X* = *A.Z*.

Let us note that objects with undefined components are similar to parameterized types (generic types). For instance, we can specify a stack with an undefined type of element:

   stack: (. . . ; *element:* **undefined**; . . .);

and then use this for building stacks for different types of elements:

   e1: **numeric**;
   m1: stack element = *e1*;
   request: (*number:* **numeric**;
               resource: **text**;
               asks: **text**;
               amount: **numeric**;);
   m2: stack element = *request*;

It is also possible to specify the type of an undefined component in amendments without binding it with an equation. This is done using the word **is** instead of the equals sign in the amendment:

   m3: stack element **is numeric**;
   m4: stack element **is request**;

In the case of specification

   A:Y   Z **is** *X*

A inherits everything from *Y*, and *Z* receives the type of *X*, but the equation *Z* = *X* is not added to the computational model of *A*.

An undefined component can be bound in an amendment with any other object, even with the object in the specification of which the amendment is written. This enables us to build recursive specifications. For instance, let us specify a person as follows:

   PERSON: (*name:* **text**;
               age: **numeric**;
               address: **text**;
               sex: **text**;
               father, mother: **undefined**;);

Having specified

PEOPLE: PERSON;

(i.e. *PEOPLE* and *PERSON* are synonymous) and

Ivan, Maria: PEOPLE;

we can already specify their child:

Sergei: PERSON father = Ivan, mother = Maria;

3.5 Action statements

UTOPIST includes four types of statements for specifying actions:

- problem statements;
- assignment;
- procedure call;
- application of relation.

Statements differ from specifications – they are executed, whereby specifications are taken into account for doing something, e.g. for executing a problem statement. Any statement prescribes actions which must be performed when the statement is executed.

3.5.1 PROBLEM STATEMENT

Syntax:

$\langle$problem statement$\rangle ::= [\langle$name$\rangle] \vdash [\langle$name$\rangle, \ldots \rightarrow] \langle$name$\rangle, \ldots$

Let us consider the statement

$$M \vdash X_1, \ldots, X_k \rightarrow Y_1, \ldots, Y_n,$$

where $M, X_1, \ldots, X_k, Y_1, \ldots, Y_n$ are the names of abstract objects, M must be the name of an object given in the specification part of program, $X_1, \ldots, X_k$, $Y_1, \ldots, Y_n$ are the names of the components of this object. The problem statement is semantically correct if it represents a problem solvable by means of the structural synthesis of programs, as described in the first two chapters.

A semantically correct problem statement is equivalent to a program for solving the problem in the sense that it can be replaced by this program without changing the meaning of the program at the point where the problem statement occurs.

The effect of execution of the problem statement

$$M \vdash X_1, \ldots, X_k \rightarrow Y_1, \ldots, Y_n;$$

is the evaluation of variables $Y_1, \ldots, Y_n$. The subroutines that are used for computing these values can have side effects: in particular, they can influence the computational environment by reading from files and writing into files. But execution of the problem statement cannot influence other variables of the program except its output variables. If the problem statement has the form

$$\vdash X_1, \ldots, X_k \rightarrow Y_1, \ldots, Y_n;$$

all specifications written in the program can be used for solving this problem.
   Input variables can be also absent in a problem statement –

$$M \vdash Y_1, \ldots, Y_n;$$

A problem without input variables can be solvable only if its model contains relations which do not have input variables. For instance, after adding to M new relations

$$X_1 = c_1; X_2 = c_2; \ldots; X_k = c_k$$

where $c_1, \ldots, c_k$ are input values for $X_1, \ldots, X_k$, we can use the problem statement

$$M \vdash Y_1, \ldots, Y_n;$$

instead of its general form

$$M \vdash X_1, \ldots, X_k \rightarrow Y_1, \ldots, Y_n;$$

3.5.2 ASSIGNMENT

Syntax:

$$\langle \text{assignment} \rangle ::= \langle \text{name} \rangle := \langle \text{expression} \rangle;$$

Expression is defined as in the specifications. All names of objects must be defined in the specification part of the program. The type of the object in the left-hand part of the assignment must be weakly structurally equivalent to the type of the expression in the right-hand part. Execution of an assignment is evaluation of the expression and assigning its value to the object whose name is written in the left-hand part of the statement.

Some examples are as follows:

$DATE := (20,11,1950);$
$P.O := R.S;$
$b := amount < 10$ **and** $amount \neq 0;$

3.5.3 PROCEDURE CALL

Syntax:

⟨procedure call⟩ ::=
  call ⟨identifier⟩ [(⟨expression⟩,...)];

Identifier in the procedure call must be the name of a procedure which is accessible for the system. Expressions are actual parameters of the procedure. Parameters are called by value. Expressions are defined in the same way as in specifications.

Execution of a procedure call is performed as follows:

1. all expressions are evaluated;
2. the values of expressions are substituted for formal parameters of the procedure;
3. the procedure is executed;
4. new values are assigned to those actual parameters which are the names of objects.

3.5.4 APPLICATION OF A RELATION

Syntax:

⟨application of relation⟩ ::=
  apply ⟨name⟩ [(⟨expression⟩,...)];
  fun ⟨name⟩ [(⟨expression⟩,...)]

The name next to **apply** or **fun** is that of the relation which must be applied. Expressions are defined as in specifications. A relation used in this statement must be specified as a preprogrammed relation, and it cannot have subproblems. Expressions written in parentheses after the relation name are actual parameters which correspond positionally to bound variables of the relation. The actual parameters can be fewer in number than the bound variables of the relation.

The application of a relation differs essentially from a procedure call. It is performed as follows:

1. All expressions which are actual parameters are evaluated.

2. The values of expressions are passed into the computational model and used as values of bound variables of the relation.

3. Then the relation is applied, using new values of the bound variables for these input variables of the relation for which they were given in the statement.

4. New values of the bound variables of the relation are stored in the computational model.

5. If the statement begins with the word **apply**, then new values of the bound variables are passed into the program as values of actual parameters.

6. If the statement begins with the word **fun** then the statement is a function call, and values of output variables of the relation constitute a new value which is passed into the program as the value of the function.

Let us consider an example of the use of a stack:

```
stack: (length: numeric;
         state: space;
         virtual elem: undefined;
         create: length → state (M1);
         push: elem, state → state (M2);
         pop: state → elem, state (M3););
```

Now we specify stacks for different types of elements:

```
pointer: numeric;
m1: stack elem = pointer,
         length = 50;
lexeme: (code: numeric;
          addr: numeric;);
m2: stack elem = lexeme;
```

Both stacks can be used in statements of applications of the relation. We must start by creating actual stacks:

```
apply m1.create;
apply m2.create(2000);
```

thereafter we can store something

```
apply m1.push (13);
apply m2.push ((66,13));
```

and read it again

> **apply** *m1*.*pop*(*pointer*);

Statements **apply** and **fun** enable us to use abstract objects as abstract data types. An abstract data type T with components (subtypes) $x_1, \ldots, x_m$ and operations $f_1, \ldots, f_n$ can be specified as an abstract object

$$T: (x_1: \ldots;$$
$$\quad x_m: \ldots;$$
$$\quad f_1: \ldots;$$
$$\quad f_n: \ldots;);$$

The object T as well as any object $K:T$ specified by inheritance from T can be used as an actual object in a UTOPIST program. The functions of these objects are $T.f_1, \ldots, T.f_n$, $K.f_1, \ldots, K.f_n$. They can be used in constructions **apply** $T.f_i$; **apply** $K.f_i$, as well as in **fun** $T.f_i$ and **fun** $K.f_i$.

3.6 Control statements

The order in which action statements are executed is prescribed by control statements:

- compound statement;
- conditional statement;
- loop statement;
- exit statement.

These are well-known statements of conventional structured programming languages. We decided to separate them from the action statements, because they do not define new functions, but represent rules of combining functions into larger pieces of programs. They are schemes which prescribe the order of execution of statements. The semantics of the control statements has been described already in Section 3.1.5, where the control tree of a program was defined.

3.6.1 COMPOUND STATEMENT

Syntax:

> ⟨compound statement⟩ ::=
> [⟨identifier⟩:] (⟨statement⟩...);
>
> $\langle \text{statement} \rangle ::= \begin{Bmatrix} \langle \text{action statement} \rangle \\ \langle \text{control statement} \rangle \end{Bmatrix}$

Execution of the compound statement is sequential execution of the statements placed in braces. The identifier before the parentheses is a label. An example is:

$$L: (X := 1; \textbf{call } Q(X,Y); A := Y;);$$

The semantics of a compound statement can be represented in the semantic language described in Section 3.1.5 by the following construction:

$$(\varphi_1; \ldots; \varphi_k);$$

where $\varphi_1, \ldots, \varphi_k$ are operators which represent statements.

3.6.2 CONDITIONAL STATEMENT

Syntax:

> $\langle$conditional statement$\rangle ::=$
> **if** $\langle$boolean expression$\rangle$ **then** $\langle$statement$\rangle$
> [**else** $\langle$statement$\rangle$]**fi**;

The boolean expression is defined in the same way as in specifications. Execution of a conditional statement is performed as follows. Firstly, the boolean expression is evaluated. If its value is **true** then the first statement is executed. If the value of the boolean expression is **false**, then the second statement is executed, if it is given in the conditional statement. In semantic language, the semantics of the conditional statement **if** B **then** φ_1 **else** φ_2 **fi** is presented by the construction

$$(\varphi_0; \textbf{cond } (t_1, t_2)(\varphi_1, \varphi_2)),$$

where φ_0 is an operator which performs the following two assignments:

$$t_1 := B; t_2 := \textbf{not } B;$$

3.6.3 LOOP STATEMENT

Syntax:

> $\langle$loop$\rangle ::=$ **while** $\langle$boolean expression$\rangle$
> **do** $\langle$statement$\rangle$
> **od**;

A loop statement is executed as follows. The boolean expression is evaluated. If its value is **false**, then execution of the loop statement is finished.

If it is **true**, then the statement between **do** and **od** is executed and the whole executions process is repeated, beginning with the evaluation of the boolean expression. In semantic language, the meaning of the loop statement

while B **do** φ **od**;

is expressed as follows:

$(\varphi_0; \mathbf{iter}(t,(\varphi;\varphi_0)))$,

where φ_0 is an operator which computes $t := B$.

3.6.4 EXIT STATEMENT

Syntax:

$\langle \text{exit} \rangle ::= \textbf{exit} \langle \text{identifier} \rangle;$

The identifier in the exit statement must be a label of a statement into which the exit statement is included. Execution of the exit statement means an unconditional jump to the statement following the statement with the label written in the exit statement.

For example:

```
x := 1;
L: (while X < 10 do
        P: (call A1;
            if C > 1 then exit L fi;
            call A2;
            if C = 0 then exit P fi;
            call A3;);
        od;);
```

An exit statement

$L: (\dots(\dots \textbf{exit } L;\dots)\dots)$

can be replaced by the following operators:

$T := \textbf{true};$
$T := \textbf{false};$

The first operator must be placed at the beginning of the statement with the label L, and the second operator must be substituted for exit L. Besides that, all statements φ following **exit** L; must be changed to conditional statements **if** T **then** φ**fi**;.

3.7 Structure and semantics of programs

Now we have described all the statements of UTOPIST, and we can observe how a program as a whole will be translated into semantic language which we presented in Section 3.1.5.

A program in semantic language is represented by a program model and a control tree. The bulk of the program model is obtained from specifications, but action statements also contribute operators and variables to the program model.

The upper levels of the control tree describe the general course of solving a problem and are derived from control statements of the program. During the translation process, the control tree becomes more detailed, and the program model can be often simplified. In order to follow these processes we shall consider three phases of the semantic representation of a UTOPIST program:

- source program;
- result of translation (program with synthesized parts);
- executable code.

A user of the UTOPIST language usually has to know only the upper semantic level – the meaning of a source program. For debugging, however, sometimes the intermediate level must also be known. It is assumed that the code of the whole program is never needed.

3.7.1 SOURCE PROGRAM

The structure of the source program is

> **program** ⟨name of program⟩;
> ⟨specifications⟩
> ⟨statements⟩
> **end**;

Specifications include constructions of two kinds: specifications of abstract objects and relations which bind these objects. The semantics of an abstract object is represented by a computational model. The specifications of a program all taken together also represent a computational model which describes the whole situation (problem conditions) in which the problem must be solved. This abstract object has ⟨name of program⟩ as its name. During the program synthesis a program model is built from the computational model of this abstract object.

Specifications may contain more objects and relations than needed for building a program model. This does not cause any significant inefficiency,

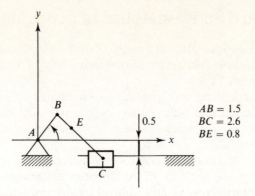

Figure 3.11   A crank mechanism.

because this redundancy can be diminished before the executable code is generated.

Let us consider the analysis of a crank mechanism shown in Figure 3.11 as an example of writing a program in UTOPIST. We are interested in the dependence of the coordinates of point E on the angle of the bar AB when the angle changes from 0 to 180° in steps of 10°.

It is easy to see that this problem can be specified in terms of intervals of straight lines (we call them bars) using some basic knowledge from analytical geometry. Actually, we need only the concepts *point* and *bar*, which we specify at the beginning of our program:

> **program** *mech*;
>   **let** *point*: $(x,y$: **numeric**);
>   *bar*: $(P,Q$: *point*;
>   **virtual** *l,alpha*: **numeric**;
> $l \wedge 2 = (P.x - Q.x) \wedge 2 + (P.y - Q.y) \wedge 2$;
> $l * cos(alpha) = Q.x - P.x;$);

Now we can use the abstract objects *point* and *bar* to specify the whole mechanism:

> M: (AB: *bar* $P = (0,0), l = 1.5$;
> BC: *bar* $P = AB.Q, l = 2.6, Q.y = -0.5$;
> BE: *bar* $P = BC.P, l = 0.8, alpha = BC.alpha;$);

The abstract object M represents problem conditions for computing the coordinates of point E from the given angle $AB.alpha$, but we have specified more objects, and the general structure of the whole problem specification is represented in Figure 3.12(a).

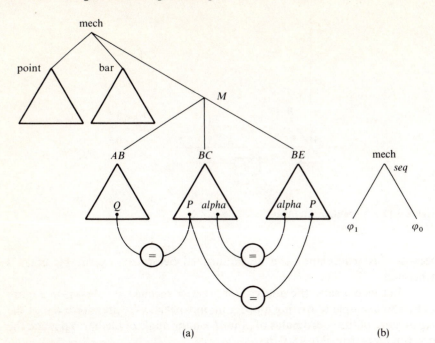

(a)   (b)

Figure 3.12   A model of problem conditions.

Now we have to write a procedural part of our program where we give an initial value for *AB.alpha* and write a loop to compute and print a table of results:

```
actions
    AB.alpha = 0;
    while AB.alpha < 180
    do (M⊢ AB.alpha → BE.Q;
        call print (AB.alpha, BE.Q.x, BE.Q.y););
    od;
end;
```

The statements of the source program are translated into a control tree (Figure 3.12(b)). The root of the tree represents the whole program called *mech*, its descendants are nodes for assignment and loop. But the loop contains, in its turn, a problem statement, a procedure call and an assignment. Besides that, the looping condition is transformed into an assignment to a boolean variable. So we get additional operators. Taking into account the semantics of the loop we get the control tree shown in Figure 3.13(b).

The procedural part of the source program contributes, in addition to the control tree, some new operators and variables to the program model. Only those objects whose names are present in the procedural part of the

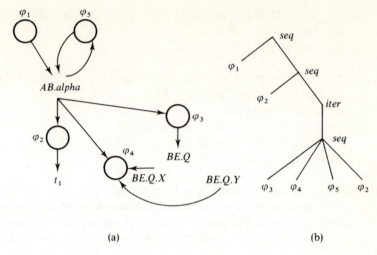

(a)   (b)

Figure 3.13   The program model and control tree.

source program are initially included in the program model. Also included in the program model are the operators explicitly represented by statements of the source program. The problem statement is represented in the program model by a single operator at this stage (Figure 3.13(a)).

A semantic machine for implementing this language must still be quite powerful – it has to synthesize programs for problem statements. At this stage a whole program is represented in three parts:

- a program model;
- a control tree;
- a computational model of all specifications needed for program synthesis.

3.7.2 RESULTS OF PROGRAM SYNTHESIS

Quite often, the procedural part of a program contains a single problem statement and nothing else. In this case the control tree obtained after translation of the source program is trivial. The building of the actual control tree takes place only while programs for problems statements are synthesized. Even in our case 11 new operators are added to the control tree during the program synthesis phase. For the problem statement

$$M \vdash AB.alpha \rightarrow BE.Q;$$

the following program is synthesized:

$$\varphi_6\colon AB.Q.x := AB.l * \cos{(AB.alpha)} + AB.P.x;$$

φ_7: $AB.Q.y := AB.P.y + \mathbf{sqrt}\,(AB.l \wedge 2 - (AB.P.x - AB.Q.x) \wedge 2)$;
φ_8: $AB.Q := (AB.Q.x, AB.Q.y)$;
φ_9: $BC.P := AB.Q$;
φ_{10}: $BE.P := BC.P$;
φ_{11}: $BC.Q.x := BC.P.x + \mathbf{sqrt}\,(BC.l \wedge 2 - (BC.P.y - BC.Q.y) \wedge 2)$;
φ_{12}: $BC.alpha := \mathbf{arccos}\,((BC.Q.x - BC.P.x)/BC.l)$;
φ_{13}: $BE.alpha := BC.alpha$;
φ_{14}: $BE.Q.x := BE.l * \mathbf{cos}\,(BE.alpha) + BE.P.x$;
φ_{15}: $BE.Q.y := BE.P.y + \mathbf{sqrt}\,(BE.l \wedge 2 - (BE.P.x - BE.Q.x) \wedge 2)$;
φ_{16}: $BE.Q := (BE.Q.x, BE.Q.y)$;

This is one of the programs which can be obtained by means of structural synthesis on the computational model of the abstract object M. This program is a sequence of operators. Therefore, the node of the problem statement in the control tree is replaced by a control node for sequence and nodes for operators $\varphi_6, \ldots, \varphi_{16}$.

This gives the control tree of our program in its final form (Figure 3.14).

All operators that are added to the control tree at the program-synthesis stage come from the computational model of the program specifications. These operators (and only these) must be added to the program model. In general, as a result of synthesis of programs for all problem statements, we get an extended control tree and a program model which contain exactly the operators needed for computations. The operators are assignments and procedure calls of the source program and operators of the computational models of abstract objects used in specifications. The semantic machine for performing computations need only be able to execute these operators. A computational model for all specifications is no longer needed.

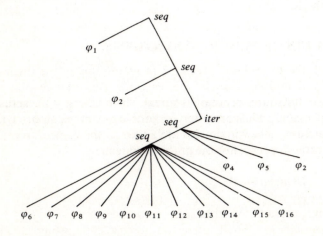

Figure 3.14   The extended control tree.

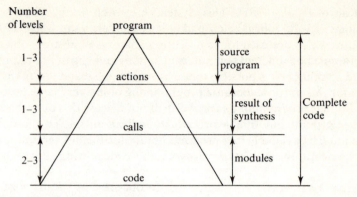

Figure 3.15   The size of a program.

3.7.3 PROGRAM SIZE

Proportions of programs at different levels are shown in Figure 3.15. Only a small proportion of the actions is specified explicitly in a source program written in the UTOPIST language. This is at the top of a pyramid of actions included in the program. The next layer of actions is added automatically by means of program synthesis. The most complicated and the largest layer consists of preprogrammed procedures which, once programmed, are used many times.

To estimate the size of a program, let us make some assumptions about its structure. We assume that nonterminal nodes of the control tree have four descendants on average. This is a rough estimate, but it seems quite realistic. Then we estimate the size of the three layers of the program as follows:

1.   The depth of nested constructions of a source program is from 1 to 3.

2.   Automatic synthesis of programs gives us also the nesting depth from 1 to 3. It means that we use at most two levels of subproblems. Double integration, minimax problems and algorithms over matrices have this depth.

3.   Preprogrammed modules can have a nesting depth from 2 to 3, i.e. the number of commands in modules varies from 16 to 64.

In this case the overall depth of program varies from 4 to 9. And, bearing in mind that every node has 4 descendants on average, we get the size of programs from $2^8 = 256$ to $2^{18} \simeq 250\,000$ commands. Using automatic synthesis gives us programs of a considerable size!

3.8 Environment and language extensions

Here we consider very briefly some additional facilities which are more or less common to different versions of the knowledge-based programming system

PRIZ (Kahro *et al.*, 1981). This system has been installed on various mainframes (Ryad, Elbrus, etc.) and minicomputers (Nord-100, PDP-11). Procedures which are used for representing relations of abstract objects can be programmed on different computers in various languages. For example, on the Ryad computers it is possible to use assembler language, FORTRAN, COBOL and PL/1 for this purpose. Because programming of not very large procedures is a traditional programming task, we shall not discuss this question here at all. We just point out that a procedure used as an implementation of a relation must be available in a program library for the linkage editor (or for the interpreter) at the moment when executable code is being built (or loaded).

3.8.1 KNOWLEDGE BASE

One of the basic principles of conceptual programming is that the conceptual programming system remembers everything that it has been taught, and this knowledge is easily accessible. This principle is realized in PRIZ by means of a knowledge base in virtual memory. The knowledge base is handled by means of three commands:

- **insert**,
- **delete**,
- **from**.

The command

    insert X;

stores specification of the abstract object X into the knowledge base. This specification remains in the knowledge base after the program ends, and it can be used at any time in the future.

The objects stored in the knowledge base by means of the command **insert** differ from the abstract object of a program – they are not connected by relations with other objects. The purpose of these objects is different – they are always used in inheritance specifications to describe other objects. We shall call them **concepts**, because they are applied as concepts known to a computer.

If a compound object is stored as a concept in the knowledge base, then its components are also applicable as concepts. For instance, if the command

    insert *mech*;

had been executed for the *mech* that was specified in Section 3.7.1, then, besides the concepts *mech*, we could use also concepts *mech.point*, *mech.bar*, *mech.M*, etc.

Executing the command **insert** X; extends the UTOPIST language with a

new specifier X, and in the case when X is a compound object, then also with specifiers $X.X1,\ldots,X.Xk$, which are the names of its components.

Primitive specifiers **numeric**, **text**, **boolean**, **space** can be regarded as names of objects inserted into the knowledge base when the system was generated. If somebody wishes to specify an item of data called $STRING$ which has the same properties as **text**, then it can be done as follows:

> $STRING$: **text**;
> **insert** $STRING$;

Thereafter it is permissible to write

> S: $STRING$;

instead of

> S: **text**;

The command insert has also another form:

> **insert** ⟨name⟩ **into** ⟨name⟩;

where the second name belongs to an object from the knowledge base, i.e. it is the name of concept. The first name denotes the object to be inserted into the knowledge base.

For example, if we have given a command **insert** $GEOMETRY$; then we can continue

> $POINT$: $(x,y$: **numeric**;);

and insert this specification into the knowledge base into the concept of geometry:

> **insert** $POINT$ **into** $GEOMETRY$;

As a result of the second command, we shall have

1. an object $GEOMETRY.POINT$ in the knowledge base, and
2. a new specification of $GEOMETRY$ which contains $POINT$ as a component.

The command

> **delete** ⟨name⟩;

is for deleting a concept from the knowledge base. The name can be a

compound name, so it is possible to delete components of objects. In this case it is checked if the component is bound by any relation. If so, then it cannot be deleted, because its deletion would destroy the consistency of the specification.

The command

from ⟨name⟩;

restricts access to the semantic memory and enables us to use short names instead of full compound names. The effect of the command

from X;

where X is the name of an object from the knowledge base, is that the only objects which remain accessible are those which have names X . Y (Y is the name of any component of X), and instead of X . Y the name Y can be used. For example, after using the command

from $GEOMETRY$;

we can write

$T1,T2$: $POINT$;

instead of

$T1,T2$: $GEOMETRY.POINT$;

3.8.2 THE MACROPROCESSOR

The PRIZ system contains its own macroprocessor for defining macros and for extending source text using these macro definitions.

The macroprocessor can be switched off, and then the PRIZ system accepts the source text in pure UTOPIST. If the macrosystem is switched on, then a source program is handled, first of all, by the macroprocessor and only after that by the UTOPIST compiler.

Any macro definition determines a new construction (a sentence, a specification) which becomes applicable as soon as the macro definition is presented to the system. The form of the construction is determined by a pattern which is a part of the macro definition. The pattern is followed by the macro body. This is a text which will be substituted instead of the macro in a source text.

The form of a macro definition is as follows

macro
⟨pattern⟩

```
    mbegin
⟨macro body⟩
    mend;
```

The pattern must contain the macro name – a sequence of symbols between ampersands – for example,

&BEGIN&

&FIND&

If a pattern consists only of a macro name, then the name itself becomes a new construction accepted in a source text.

Some examples are:

macro
&BEGIN&
mbegin
program *ONE*;
   let *a,b,c,x,y,z*: **numeric**;
mend;
macro
&FINDS&
mbegin
actions
   ONE ⊢
mend

Having these simple definitions we can shorten some programs which contain only *a,b,c,x,y,z* of **numeric** type: for example,

BEGIN
x = 0.1;
x ∗ *y* = 3.5;
FIND y;
end

It is easy to see that after replacing *BEGIN* and *FIND* by texts given in macro definitions we obtain correct programs in UTOPIST. A pattern can contain arbitrary text besides the macro name. And it can also contain parameters – identifiers preceded by an ampersand. For example,

&FIND& SUCH &P FROM &R FOR WHICH &Q

In this pattern, besides the name *&FIND&* three parameters *&P, &R, &Q* are included. The pattern matches any sentence which differs from the pattern

only in having, instead of the parameters *&P*, *&R* and *&Q*, any text that does not contain the delimiter which follows the parameters. (In this example the delimiter is a space.)

If a parameter occurs in a macro body, then it is replaced by the same text which has been written in its place in the source text where macro is used.

For example, we can rewrite once more the macro *FIND*:

macro
&FIND& &P;
mbegin
actions
    ONE ⊢ *&P;*
end;
mend;

This allows us to write the example program one line shorter:

BEGIN
$x = 0.1;$
$x * y = 3.5;$
FIND y;

Macrosystems are especially useful in cases when a user is not happy with the syntax of UTOPIST and likes additional syntactic sugar in his programs. For example, having defined an abstract object *usefulfunctions* with relations $f1, \ldots, fn$, it is possible to use these relations in application statements, by writing **apply**$usefulfunctions.f1(\ldots)$, etc. The words **apply**$usefulfunctions$ are superfluous for a user, and he can define macros

macro
&f1& (&P1)
mbegin
apply$usefulfunctions.f1(\&P1)$
mend

macro
&fn & (&P1)
mbegin
apply$usefulfunctions. fn(\&P1)$
mend

which enable the user to write simply $f1(\ldots)$, $fn(\ldots)$ for function calls.

3.8.3 OTHER COMMANDS

There are several other useful commands available:

help;
options;
run;

help is for asking help from the system when a user does not know how to proceed. By using **options** the user is able to change system options, for example to choose the compilation or interpretation mode of execution of the source program. **run** is for executing any program which is in library, and has one parameter – the name of the program to be executed.

Using the command **run** and a macroprocessor it is possible to add new commands in the form chosen by the user.

3.9 A small knowledge-based programming system

Before closing this chapter we shall describe briefly a knowledge-based programming system for personal computers. The system called MICROPRIZ is running on IBM personal computers and also under the operating system CPM/86 (see Kypp, 1986). Its input language is syntactically simpler than UTOPIST, because it has been designed for use on personal computers. The keywords like **program**, **actions**, **let**, **end** etc. are abandoned. Specifications of numeric objects can be omitted and semicolons at the end of sentences are not needed. Nevertheless, this language possesses all the principal features of a conceptual programming language, including inheritance, preprogrammed relations with subproblems and problem statement.

MICROPRIZ is just a program that runs on an IBM PC. It understands a larger set of commands than PRIZ, and it is quite simple to use. From a user's point of view it is a problem solver with an easily extensible knowledge base.

To use MICROPRIZ, a user must be familiar with the notions of *object* and *concept*, as defined in this chapter. The *knowledge base* of MICROPRIZ is just a set of concepts stored in a file. Text in the input language of MICROPRIZ is a *problem specification*. A user can ask to see the *problem model*, which is an extended representation of a problem specification where all objects and relations are represented explicitly. A *command* is a line beginning with '!' or '?'. Any command is immediately executed by MICROPRIZ. There is no procedural part of the input language except commands. First of all, we can use MICROPRIZ for solving equations. Assuming that we want to solve the equations

$$X + Y = 1$$
$$2 * X = 10$$

we just type the equations and therefore ask for the values of X and Y by typing the command

$$? X, Y$$

The answer will be displayed as follows:

$$\rightarrow X = 5.00000$$
$$\rightarrow Y = -4.00000$$

As we can see, no specifications are needed for numeric objects (for X and Y in this example). In UTOPIST, the same problem had to be specified as follows:

program X Y;
   let X, Y: **numeric**;
      X + Y = 1;
      2 * X = 10;
   actions
      ⊢ X, Y;
  end;

To define and edit new concepts there is a command !*e*. In the simplest case concepts are sets of equations. The concept of motion familiar to us can be specified in MICROPRIZ by typing

!E MOTION
    DT = T2 − T1
    DV = V2 − V1
    V = (V1 + V2)/2
    DE = E2 − E1
    E1 = M * V1 ∧ 2/2
    E2 = M * V2 ∧ 2/2
    F = M * A
    DV = A * DT
    DS = V * DT
!A (accept and save the concept)

More interesting concepts can be specified when programs are used to represent relations. A useful concept is *TABLE*, for tabulating values of the object called *FUN* depending on values of the object *ARG*. The latter takes values in the interval (*FROM, TO*). The component *STEP* shows how the value of *ARG* is changed after every iteration:

!E TABLE
   ARG : NUMERIC
   FUN : UNDEFINED
   FROM : NUMERIC
   TO : NUMERIC
   STEP : NUMERIC
   RESULT : NUMERIC
   (ARG → FUN), FROM, TO, STEP → RESULT(TABLE)
!A

We can see that the component *FUN* is specified as an undefined object. This enables us to generate different tables by binding *FUN* with objects that have

the structure of a row of the table. To tabulate the squares of integers from 1 to 10 we now write

$Y = X \wedge 2$
ROW: (X Y)

this specifies the structure of row

T:TABLE FROM = 1 TO 10 STEP = 1 ARG = X FUN = ROW
?T.RESULT

The specification

ROW: (X Y)

represents a structure which had to be written in UTOPIST as follows:

ROW: (X, Y: **numeric;**);
ROW.X = X;
ROW.Y = Y;

We have used MICROPRIZ for solving physics problems given to students at a technical university during the first semester of physics studies. We followed the course given in Tallinn Technical University and specified the concepts in MICROPRIZ. We observed that in order to solve the problems in physics a student had to learn from one to three new concepts in a week. The typical concepts were, for instance, motion, rotation, etc.

Having, for instance, the concept of motion, we can already specify the following problem:

Find the force applied to a pole by a falling mass 700 kg that falls from a height of 3.5 m and pushes the pole 5 cm into the ground.

The specification of this problem in MICROPRIZ is:

X1: MOTION M = 700   S = 3.5   A = 9.81   V1 = 0
X2: MOTION M = 700   S = 0.05   V1 = X1.V2   V2 = 0
?X2.F

All the problems given to physics students during the first semester were approximately of the same complexity and each of them was programmed in several lines. The total number of concepts needed for solving these problems was about 30. This experiment shows us that knowledge bases in physics, geometry and some other fields can already be made as software packages for general use. The next chapter is devoted to representing this kind of knowledge in the UTOPIST language.

One more difference between MICROPRIZ and PRIZ is the option of symbolic computations. If no preprogrammed relations are included in an algorithm synthesized for solving a problem in MICROPRIZ, then it is possible to ask for a solution of the problem in symbolic form. In this case equations are solved symbolically and the expressions found for variables are passed on and substituted into new equations until the result is expressed in terms of the input variables only.

As an example, we find binomial coefficients by calculating various powers of $a + b$. In order to do this we type

$$x = a + b$$
$$x0 = x \wedge 0$$
$$x1 = x \wedge 1$$
$$x2 = x \wedge 2$$
$$x3 = x \wedge 3$$
$$x4 = x \wedge 4$$

and find the answers using the command

$$?a, b \rightarrow x0, x1, x2, x3, x4.$$

The answer will be:

$$\rightarrow x0 = 1$$
$$\rightarrow x1 = x + y$$
$$\rightarrow x2 = x \wedge 2 + 2 * x * y + y \wedge 2$$
$$\rightarrow x3 = x \wedge 3 + 2 * x \wedge 2 * y + 3 * x * y \wedge 2 + y \wedge 3$$
$$\rightarrow x4 = x \wedge 4 + 4 * x \wedge 3 * y + 6 * x \wedge 2 * y \wedge 2 + 4 * x * y \wedge 3 +$$
$$y \wedge 4.$$

We can also ask for an explanation of the method of solving a problem. The explanation given by MICROPRIZ is actually a proof of the solvability of the problem. For the problem of binomial coefficients the explanation is the following:

$$a, b \rightarrow x$$
$$x \rightarrow x0$$
$$x \rightarrow x1$$
$$x \rightarrow x2$$
$$x \rightarrow x3$$
$$x \rightarrow x4.$$

This can be read as

'a, b give x'
'x gives x0'

'x gives x1'
'x gives x2'
'x gives x3'
'x gives x4'.

An explanation can be asked also for numerically solved problems. In this sense MICROPRIZ behaves like an expert system, not only solving problems but explaining how the solution is found as well.

Chapter 4

Representation of Basic Knowledge in Mathematics and Physics

In this chapter we consider concepts and problems from high-school mathematics and physics. Naturally, we are not interested in the conventional programming of these problems. The question is which concepts are needed for specifications of problems solved in mathematics and physics by students. Our goal is to teach a computer to solve problems from students' textbooks. To enable a computer to solve problems represented in the same form as to students (or in a form close to that), we must supply the computer with a considerable amount of knowledge in physics and mathematics.

The results of this activity have a practical value. For example, a design engineer has to solve a number of simple computational geometric problems during a design process. It is difficult or, at least, inconvenient for him to program these computations in FORTRAN. As a result, the engineer performs many simple geometric computations manually. But, if it were sufficient only to describe the problem in order to obtain an answer from a computer, then obviously it would be more convenient to use the computer for solving problems. It is essential that a computer graduates from being a calculating device to becoming a problem solver.

The same goal can be achieved by building intelligent software packages and expert systems. These are highly specialized systems capable of solving problems on the human expert level. In this chapter we consider a quite different approach to problem solving – instead of specialized software we supply a computer with general knowledge taught to children in a secondary school. This is also the difference between our system and former problem solvers: for instance, the programs of Raphael and Bobrow (see Minsky, 1968). These problem solvers were specialized in a particular class of problems, and demonstrated the principal possibilities of text understanding and automated problem solving. But they did not use an extensible knowledge base in the sense understood today. A problem solver must have two particular features: know-how for problem solving and knowledge of the problem domain. Here we assume that the system possesses the know-how already.

120

This know-how, in the form of understanding a specification language and the ability to synthesize programs for solving problems, has been presented in previous chapters. Besides that, the problems considered in this chapter are so simple that it is sufficient to know how to solve problems as taught by G. Polya in his famous book (Polya, 1946). In our terminology it means that in this chapter we use mostly solution planning on simple computational models.

Many people agree that programming can be considered as akin to teaching a computer. Conventional programming corresponds to teaching a computer to solve a particular problem or a very restricted class of problems which differ from one another by input values. Conceptual programming is teaching a computer to understand new concepts that are useful for describing various problems. Let us point out once more that the concepts are not useful *per se*, but only in the case when the solver already has the know-how needed for using the concepts for problem solving.

4.1 How to define new concepts

4.1.1 CONCEPTS AND SUBCONCEPTS

We shall define concepts in the UTOPIST language. A concept is presented in UTOPIST as an abstract object. Usually, in a definition of a concept other concepts are used to specify components of the abstract object. Only a small number of basic concepts are defined directly, using only primitive data types. Such concepts are, for example, physical entities: length, area, time etc.

> *length* **numeric**;
> *area* **numeric**;
> *time* **numeric**;

The concept of point is defined by coordinates which represent lengths:

> *POINT*: (*x,y,z*: *length*;);

or by coordinates which represent length and angles:

> *POINT*: (*r*: *length*;
> *phi,lambda*: *angle*;);

The components *x*, *y* and *z* of the abstract object *POINT* are subconcepts which belong to the concept of point. So are the components *r,phi,lambda* in the second specification of *POINT*.

We can define as many subconcepts of a concept as we like, and it may even be useful to build in redundancy in this case. A point can be specified so

that it has Cartesian coordinates as well as polar coordinates. Also relations between these two systems of coordinates can be presented in the specification:

> *point*: $(x,y,z$: *length*;
> **virtual**
> r: *length*;
> *phi,lambda*: *angle*;
> $r \wedge 2 = x \wedge 2 + y \wedge 2 + z \wedge 2;$
> $r * \sin(lambda) = z;$
> $r * \cos(phi) = x;)$;

We decided to represent here the value of *point* in Cartesian coordinates, and therefore we presented polar coordinates as virtual components of *point*. Also relations can be added quite freely, because there are no restrictions on redundancy. For instance, if we should like a more symmetric definition of *point* we can add an equation which binds *y* with *phi* and *r*:

> $r * \sin(phi) = y;$

If inheritance is used, then a specification of a concept may contain a lot of implicit information about it. For instance, the following specification of *line* depends on the properties of the point:

> *line*: $(P,Q$: *point*;
> **virtual**
> l: *length*;
> *inclination*: *angle*;
> $\sin(inclination) * l = Q.z - P.z;$
> $l \wedge 2 = (P.x - Q.x) \wedge 2 + (P.y - Q.y) \wedge 2 + (P.z - Q.z) \wedge 2;)$;

And the specification of *family* depends on the properties of *PERSON*:

> *family*: (*father, mother*: *PERSON*;
> *children*: $(1..$: *PERSON*
> *PATRONYMIC* = *father.FIRSTNAME*;$);$
> $);$

This enables us to specify new concepts very economically, using existing concepts as prototypes, if we define the concepts in a proper order.

4.1.2 SELECTING USEFUL CONCEPTS

We must not be deceived by the apparent simplicity of specifying new concepts in UTOPIST. This is only a technical aspect of the task – a knowledge representation. A significantly more complicated task is the knowledge

acquisition which is an essential part of the process of defining concepts. First of all, we must distinguish the selection and specification of general concepts from the specification of specific concepts for a restricted problem domain. In this chapter we are interested in general concepts. Introducing general concepts aims to give the computer general education in mathematics and in physics. In this particular case the selection of useful concepts is easier, because we can use the experience of teaching children in school.

In this chapter we define well-known concepts. We must select them carefully – too many concepts would be difficult to use because of the necessity to remember them and their components when used explicitly in problem specification. The definition of a number of specific concepts for particular problem domains will be discussed in the following chapters.

4.1.3 SIMPLE GEOMETRIC FIGURES AND BODIES

The specification of geometric figures and bodies is a good subject for demonstrating conceptual programming technique. Basic knowledge about geometric figures and bodies is available in numerous handbooks and has an essentially computational nature. However, we must take into account that these concepts were formed gradually starting from an ancient science. Consequently, we shall meet some classical knowledge which cannot be represented in the form of computational models. Here we meet the restrictions of our approach – we can represent only the knowledge about computability.

Setting out to represent geometric knowledge, we start with the basic concepts which will be used later as parts of various definitions:

> *area*: **numeric**;
> *volume*: **numeric**;
> *height*: **numeric**;
> *perimeter*: **numeric**;
> *side*: **numeric**;
> *diagonal*: **numeric**;
> *radius*: **numeric**;
> *angle*: **numeric**;
> *diameter*: **numeric**;
> *pi*: (*val*: **numeric**;
>   *val* = 3.14159;));

The following specifications of figures can pass without comment:

> *circle*: (*r*: *radius*;
>   *s*: *area*;
>   *p*: *perimeter*;
>   *d*: *diameter*;
>   *d* = 2 * *r*;

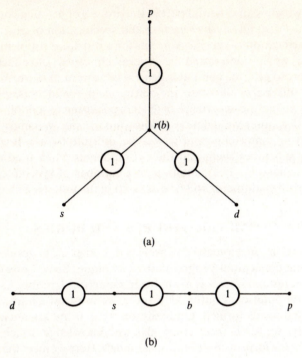

Figure 4.1 Two models of a square.

$$s = pi * r \wedge 2;$$
$$p = 2 * pi * r;);$$
square: (b: side;
   d: diagonal;
   s: area;
   p: perimeter;
   $s = b \wedge 2;$
   $d \wedge 2 = 2 * b \wedge 2;$
   $p = 4 * b;);$

Computational facilities which result from these specifications can be seen in Figure 4.1(a), which represents the scheme of the computational model of the circle and also of the square. The only difference between the schemes is in the notation for the radius of the circle and the side of the square.

   Equivalent computational facilities can be presented by computational models with the scheme shown in Figure 4.1(b). The relations of the square will be in this case

$$s = b \wedge 2;$$
$$d \wedge 2 = 2 * s;$$
$$p = 4 * b;$$

and for the circle

$$s = pi * r \wedge 2;$$
$$s = pi * d \wedge 2/4;$$
$$p = 2 * pi * r;$$

The solvability of problems can be determined easily in this case. If the value of a variable contained in the computational model is known, then values of all other variables can be computed. In other words a square or a circle is completely determined as soon as one value of its parameters is given.

Some symmetric bodies also have such specifications, which allow all variables to be computed from a given value of any variable.

$sphere$: (r: $radius$;
   d: $diameter$;
   s: $area$;
   v: $volume$;
   $d = 2 * r$;
   $s = 4 * pi * r \wedge 2$;
   $v = 4 * pi * r \wedge 3/3$;);
$cube$: (b: $side$;
   d: $diagonal$;
   s: $area$;
   v: $volume$;
   $d \wedge 2 = 3 * b \wedge 2$;
   $v = b \wedge 3$;);
$tetrahedron$: (b: $side$;
   s: $area$;
   v: $volume$;
   $s = b \wedge 2 *$ **sqrt**(3);
   $v = b \wedge 3 *$ **sqrt**(2)/12;);

A computational model which has a star-like schema gives on average shorter programs for solving problems than a model with a schema in the form of a sequence of relations (compare Figures 4.1(a) and 4.1(b)). If in a simple computational model all variables can be computed from any given variable and all relations have the rank $n-1$, where n is the number of bound variables of the relation, then the schema of such a computational model is a tree or the computational model can be transformed into a model with a tree-like schema so that the number of solvable problems will not decrease. Indeed, due to the computability of y from x, for any variables x and y of the model there exists a path from x to y. From the fact that all relations are symmetric and are applicable as soon as one of the bound variables is given, the inverse statement can be deduced: if there is a path from x to y, then y can be computed from x. In this particular case computability coincides with the

reachability of vertices of the graph, which is the schema of the computational model.

Let us specify a rectangle now.

rectangle: (*b1, b2*: *side*;
　　　　　d: *diagonal*;
　　　　　s: *area*;
　　　　　p: *perimeter*;
　　　　　$s = b1 * b2$;
　　　　　$p = 2 * (b1 + b2)$;
　　　　　$d \wedge 2 = b1 \wedge 2 + b2 \wedge 2$;);

The rectangle is completely determined only in the case when two of its elements are given and one of these elements is a side (*b1* or *b2*). We should like to find all its elements from given values of any two of them. As the sides *b1* and *b2* are bound symmetrically we shall have in some cases freedom to choose arbitrarily which of the values belongs to side *b1* and which belongs to *b2*.

Speaking in terms of computational models, we wish to extend the set of solvable problems for the rectangle so that we can solve any problem with two input variables. The only way to do this is by adding new relations. Obviously, we must add equations which enable us to find something new if one of the following pairs of variables is given: $(d, s), (d, p), (s, p)$. The schema of the computational model for a rectangle allowing us to solve all problems with two input variables is fairly symmetric and is shown in Figure 4.2. This model has the following specification:

rectangle: (*b1, b2*: *side*;
　　　　　d: *diagonal*;
　　　　　s: *area*;
　　　　　p: *perimeter*;
　　　$s = b1 * (p/2 - b1)$;
　　　$s = b2 * \mathbf{sqrt}(d \wedge 2 - b2 \wedge 2)$;
　　　$d \wedge 2 = b1 \wedge 2 + b2 \wedge 2$;
　　　$p = 2 * (b1 + \mathbf{sqrt}(d \wedge 2 - b1 \wedge 2))$;
　　　$s = b2 * (p/2 - b2)$;);

We can use another way of solving any problem with two input variables for a rectangle. In the PRIZ system we can use a special mode for program synthesis where relations are considered as equations which constitute a system of simultaneously solvable equations (see Section 1.3.6). Having observed that there are five variables and three equations in the computational model of the rectangle, we can assume that the system of equations can be solved as soon as any two variables have determined values. Actually, we have also to check that the set of equations has a proper structure, this question is discussed thoroughly in Karzanov and Faradjev (1975).

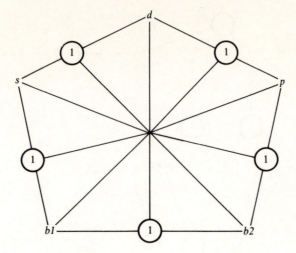

Figure 4.2   A model of a rectangle.

A number of geometric figures can be specified in an easier way, if it is possible to solve systems of equations. We present here specifications for a rhombus, which is complete only for the case when systems of equations can be solved.

> *rhombus*: (*b*: *side*;
>   *d1*, *d2*: *diagonal*;
>   *s*: *area*;
>   *p*: *perimeter*;
>   *alpha1*, *alpha2*: *angle*;
>   *h*: *height*;
> $alpha1 + alpha2 = 90$;
> $\cos(alpha2/2) * d1 = h$;
> $s = d1 * d2/2$;
> $p = 4 * b$;
> $s = b * h$;
> $\cos(alpha1/2)/(2 * b) = d2$;);

In representing a rhombus we meet a new difficulty – a rhombus cannot be determined by every pair of its elements listed in the specification above. For example, two diagonals *d1* and *d2* determine a rhombus uniquely, but the pairs of element *alpha1*, *alpha2* or *b*, *p* do not. This fact can be seen from the schema of the computational model (Figure 4.3).

Let us return once again to the concept of circle. Concepts of sector and segment are bound with it, and we can specify them as subconcepts of circle. But it seems more useful to specify these two concepts, making the circle their subconcept. The reason for this is that a circle is often used

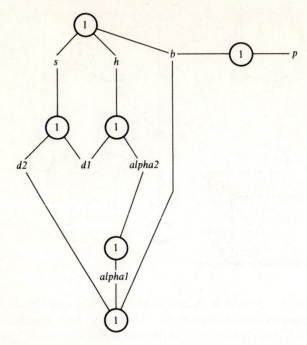

Figure 4.3   A model of a rhombus.

independently, but sector and segment are mostly used as parts of a circle, i.e.
a circle is also referred to when a sector or a segment is used:

> *sector*: (*r*: *radius*;
>   *alpha*: *angle*;
>   *s*: *area*;
>   **virtual**
>   *in*: *circle*;
>   *r = in.r*;
>   *s = in.s ∗ alpha*/360;);

> *segment*: (*arc*: *numeric*;
>   *chord*: *numeric*;
>   *alpha*: *angle*;
>   *s*: *area*;
>   *in*: *circle*;
>   *arc = alpha ∗ in.p*/360;
>   *s* = 0.5 ∗ *in.r* ∧ 2 ∗ (*alpha* ∗ *pi*/180 − **sin**(*alpha*));
>   *h = in.r* − 0.5 ∗ **sqrt**(4 ∗ *in.r* ∧ 2 − *chord* ∧ 2);
>   *chord* = 2 ∗ **sqrt**(2 ∗ *chord* ∗ *in.r* − *chord* ∧ 2);););

At this point we will stop specifying geometric figures and suggest that
the reader may like to specify some concepts like trapezoid, cylinder,
cone, etc.

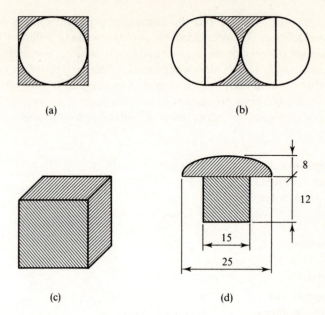

(a) (b)

(c) (d)

Figure 4.4 Combinations of figures.

4.1.4 PUTTING FIGURES TOGETHER

In Figure 4.4 a number of pictures are presented which are combinations of simpler figures known to us. We are asked to compute the total value of the shaded area for every picture. Having the specifications from Section 4.1.3 we can immediately write programs to solve these problems.

```
program #1;
    let x,s: numeric;
        k: square b = x;
        c: circle d = k.b;
        s = k.s − c.s;
    actions
        #1 ⊢ x → s;
    end;
program #2;
    let x,s: numeric;
        k: square b = x;
        c1,c2: circle d = k.b;
        s = k.s − c1.s/2 − c2.s/2;
    actions
        #2 ⊢ x → s;
    end;
```

Program $#2$ gives the same result as program $#1$ if the value of x is the

same. This is quite obvious, but the automatic program synthesizer cannot guess it. We deliberately specified these two problems in different ways. The usual approach of conceptual programming is to make a specification which exactly corresponds to problem conditions. Changing problem conditions, like any other manual activity, is a source of errors, and it must be done only if it gives us significant improvement in the efficiency of programs. Naturally, this does not diminish the importance of understanding problem conditions properly.

```
program # 3;
   let x,s: numeric;
        k: square b = x;
        r1,r2: rhombus b = k.b,alpha = 45;
        s = k.s + r1.s + r2.s;
   actions
        # 3 ⊢ x → s;
   end;
program # 4;
   let s: numeric;
        p: rectangle b1 = 15, b2 = 12;
        s1: segment h = 8, chord = 25;
        s = p.s + s1.s;
   actions
        # 4 ⊢ s;
   end;
```

These four programs are so simple that they need no comments. They can be abbreviated even more if we use the macros *BEGIN* and *FIND* specified in Section 3.8.2. For example, instead of the fourth program we can write

```
BEGIN
   p: rectangle b1 = 15, b2 = 12;
   s1: segment h = 8, chord = 25;
   z = p.s + s1.s;
FIND z;
```

This program contains no redundant words. Thus, the program is still quite comprehensible to everyone who

1. understands the notation '*p: rectangle*' as '*p* is a *rectangle*';

2. knows that *p.s* and *s1.s* denote '*s* of *p*' and '*s* of *s1*';

3. knows about rectangles and segments in that a rectangle has sides *b1*, *b2* and area *s*, a segment has height *h*, area *s* and a *chord*.

Introducing some macro definitions we can change the form of

programs and bring our programming language very close to natural language: for example,

> *Begin*
> k is a rectangle, *side1* = 15, *side2* = 12.
> *s1* is a segment, *height* = 8, *chord* = 25.
> It is known that s equals the area of p plus the area of *s1*. Find s.

But we are not especially interested in programming in natural language, because this makes the texts of programs longer and often also induces ambiguities.

4.2 Trigonometry

UTOPIST is directly applicable to trigonometry only when programming computational problems. It does not contain facilities for intricate symbolic computations and, if needed, these facilities must be programmed separately. But the computational model of a triangle is interesting in itself. Therefore, we shall consider several versions of computational models of a triangle which represent this concept with different degrees of exactness.

4.2.1 SIDES AND ANGLES OF A TRIANGLE

Let us denote the angles of a triangle *alpha*, *beta*, *gamma* and the opposite sides of the angles *a*, *b*, *c* respectively. Here we present a commented computational model of a triangle:

> *triangle*:
> (a, b, c: **numeric**;
>
> ∗*a,b* and *c* are sides of the triangle.
>
>   *alpha*, *beta*, *gamma*: **numeric**;
>
> ∗ *alpha*, *beta*, *gamma* are the angles of the triangle
> ∗ opposite to *a*, *b*, *c* respectively.
> ∗ the relations are
> ∗ 1. sum of angles:
>
>   *alpha* + *beta* + *gamma* = 180;
>
> ∗ 2. theorem of sines:
>
> a/**sin**(*alpha*) = b/**sin**(*beta*);
> b/**sin**(*beta*) = c/**sin**(*gamma*);
> c/**sin**(*gamma*) = a/**sin**(*alpha*);

* 3. theorem of cosines:

$$a \wedge 2 = b \wedge 2 + c \wedge 2 - 2 * b * c * \textbf{cos}(alpha);$$
$$b \wedge 2 = c \wedge 2 + a \wedge 2 - 2 * c * a * \textbf{cos}(beta);$$
$$c \wedge 2 = a \wedge 2 + b \wedge 2 - 2 * a * b * \textbf{cos}(gamma);$$

* end of specification.

);

Looking at the relations we can see that three of them are quadratic equations for the sides of the triangle and, consequently, they can have two different solutions. Indeed, if two sides and an angle opposite to one of the sides are given, then two triangles can be constructed which satisfy the specification. Representing the relations by means of programs, we can modify the specification. For instance, we can agree on always taking the triangle which has the shorter side. As a result, we shall have a restricted specification of a triangle.

The schema of the computational model of the triangle we have specified is shown in Figure 4.5(a). It is symmetric with respect to sides and angles. It would be nice to represent this schema by a single symmetric relation. But that is impossible, because nothing can be computed from three given angles, whereas any other three elements of a triangle are sufficient to compute all the other elements.

Let us generalize the concept of symmetric relation in such a way that it will be applicable for specifying the relation between angles and sides of a triangle. We associate a weight with every variable of the computational model. The weights are natural numbers. (Hitherto a symmetric relation has been defined, so that the weights of all variables have been equal to 1.) Let us agree that the rank of a generalized symmetric relation is the sum of the

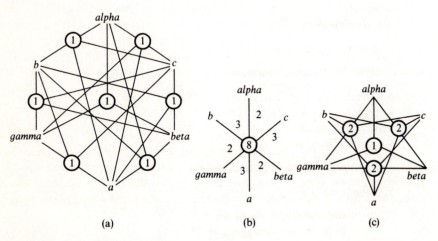

(a)   (b)   (c)

Figure 4.5   A model of a triangle.

weights of the variables which can be computed from the relation. This enables us also to represent relations such as that between the angles and sides of a triangle as a generalized symmetric relation.

We associate weight 2 with every angle of a triangle and weight 3 with every side. Now we can represent a computational model of a triangle as a single generalized symmetric relation with rank 8. Indeed, the sum of weights of three sides is 9, and the relation is not applicable. The sum of weights of any other three elements is at most 8, and the relation is applicable. The schema of this computational model is shown in Figure 4.5(b).

A different schema for a computational model of the triangle is shown in Figure 4.5(c). In this model, there are three relations any of which binds three sides and two angles. They can be, for example, the following:

1st relation:
$$a/\sin(alpha) = b/\sin(beta)$$
$$a \wedge 2 = b \wedge 2 + c \wedge 2 - 2 * b * c * \cos(alpha)$$

2nd relation:
$$b/\sin(beta) = c/\sin(gamma)$$
$$b \wedge 2 = c \wedge 2 + a \wedge 2 - 2 * c * a * \cos(beta)$$

3rd relation:
$$c/\sin(gamma) = a/\sin(alpha)$$
$$c \wedge 2 = a \wedge 2 + b \wedge 2 - 2 * a * b * \cos(gamma).$$

Besides these three relations the model contains the relation for the sum of angles:

$$alpha + beta + gamma = 180.$$

It is easy to compute the number of problems solvable on this computational model. There are $C_3^6 - 1 = 19$ maximal solvable problems with three variables, and 3 solvable problems with two given variables (two angles are given). For each of the 19 problems there exist 6 smaller solvable problems where only one or two variables are asked. The total number of solvable problems for one triangle is

$$19 + 3 + 19 * 6 = 136.$$

Only one of the problems – computing three angles from given three sides – does not have analogous symmetric problems. Every other solvable problem has two symmetrical problems which differ only in the notation of sides and angles. Taking into account the symmetry, the number of different solvable problems is reduced:

$$135/3 + 1 = 46.$$

The only essentially different problems are the maximal solvable problems, because by solving them we can obtain answers for any solvable problem. The number of such problems is 8. These are the problems which are taught to students in secondary school. The total number of problems which can be specified on a triangle is $2^{2\times6} = 4096$, so the percentage of solvable problems is approximately 3.3%.

Our approach to problem solving effectively means that it is easier to solve a problem directly than to try to find an analogous solvable problem and reduce the problem to it. Hence, we have indeed 136 different solvable problems which must be solved independently. The number of different problems can be decreased if only maximal solvable problems are being solved. But in general this leads to excessive use of memory and excessive computations.

4.2.2 THE COMPLETE MODEL OF A TRIANGLE

We can extend the concept of triangle with the following subconcepts:

> s – area,
> p – half the perimeter,
> r – radius of a circle inscribed in the triangle,
> ha, hb, hc – heights to sides a, b, c.

The new specification is

> $triangle$: (**copy** $triangle$;

> *additional components:

>> s: **numeric**;
>> p: **numeric**;
>> r: **numeric**;
>> ha, hb, hc: **numeric**;

> *additional relations:

>> $2 * p = a + b + c$;

> *formula of Heron:

>> $s = \textbf{sqrt}(p * (p - a) * (p - b) * (p - c))$;

> *formulae for area:

>> $s = a * ha/2$;
>> $s = b * hb/2$;
>> $s = c * hc/2$;
>> $s = p * r$;

> *end of specification.

>);

We have added 6 new variables to the model of the triangle and increased the total number of problems on this model to 2^{24}. The number of solvable problems has also increased. If we assume that the systems of equations are solvable (see Section 1.3.6), then a lot of problems with three input variables are solvable. But there are still problems with three input variables which are unsolvable. Nothing can be computed from any of the following triplets: (*alpha*, *beta*, *gamma*), (*s*, *p*, *r*), (*a*, *ha*, *s*), (*b*, *hb*, *s*) and (*c*, *hc*, *s*). The number of maximal solvable problems with three input variables is

$$C_3^{12} - 5 = 215.$$

Every maximal solvable problem also has smaller solvable problems with the same input and a smaller number of output variables. The number of smaller solvable problems which correspond to a maximal solvable problem is $2^9 - 2$. So the total number of solvable problems with three input variables is $215 * (2^9 - 1) = 109\ 865$. We must add to this 15 solvable problems with two input variables (three for each of the sets (*alpha*, *beta*, *gamma*), (*s*, *ha*, *a*), (*s*, *hb*, *b*), (*s*, *hc*, *c*), (*s*, *p*, *r*)). Though the amount of solvable problems is considerable, the percentage of solvable problems in the total number of problems has decreased.

We have discussed problems solvable on a triangle as thoroughly as this in order to demonstrate how the specification of a concept is developed. It was quite easy to build a specification of a triangle. But thereafter we had to analyse the possibilities of problem solving given by this specification. It took us more time. We have not obtained a complete answer to the question: 'What can a computer do with the concept of a triangle?' Indeed, this concept can be used in a combination with other concepts, and this adds many new possibilities of problem solving. But at least we have demonstrated that no conventional programming of 'variants of problems on a triangle' can give us the generality obtained by specifying a triangle in UTOPIST.

A question may arise whether it is reasonable at all to supply a computer with knowledge for solving such simple problems. Indeed, anyone who has learned a little trigonometry can solve these problems without any difficulties, and perhaps can program the computations on a computer, if needed. However, conceptual programming includes automation of simple and routine tasks which can be performed by a computer much faster and more efficiently than by a man. This has a considerable effect on computer users, because it enables them to concentrate on more intelligent tasks. We can say that a computer changes from a programmable calculating machine to an intelligent partner in problem-solving tasks – a partner that knows mathematics and physics at the secondary-school level. In this section we have demonstrated that the concept of a triangle is indeed comprehensible to our system, because the latter can solve all the computational problems on a triangle which can be solved by man.

4.2.3 SPECIAL KINDS OF TRIANGLES

We have demonstrated how to extend the specification of a triangle, adding new subconcepts and relations that bind them. Now we are going to discuss how to define particular triangles using constraints on their elements. We shall define concepts of a right-angled triangle, equilateral triangle and isosceles triangle using the concept of triangle specified in Section 4.2.2 as a superconcept, i.e. a concept which is more general than the one which is being specified.

Conceptual programming gives us a convenient means for specifying new concepts using superconcepts. This is inheritance specification with amendments. To define a right-angled triangle it is enough to write

righttriangle: triangle gamma = 90;

But sometimes amendments are not sufficient for making changes needed in the new specification. For instance, for specifying an isosceles triangle we have to add a relation which binds two sides of the triangle. In this case it is easier to use copying:

isosceles_triangle: (**copy** *triangle*;
$a = b$;
alpha = *beta*;
gamma = 180 − 2 ∗ *beta*;);

The last equation is obviously redundant − it can be deduced from the equations *alpha* = *beta* and *alpha* + *beta* + *gamma* = 180. Nevertheless, we add this equation to avoid the need for solving a system of equations when the concept is used. If we did not add the equation *gamma* = 180 − 2 ∗ *beta*, then even computing *beta* from *gamma*, for example, could be done only by solving the system of equations:

alpha = *beta*;
alpha + *beta* + *gamma* = 180;

The difficulty here lies not in solving this system but in finding it among many other equations in a computational model of a problem where the concept of triangle has been used and in understanding that it is solvable.

Using the construction **copy** *X*; we must know exactly the names of the components of *X*, because these components are introduced into the specification where **copy** *X*; is used. We can avoid this situation and use undefined components of related concepts. Let us have several concepts which have some similar components. For example, we can define various triangles which all have sides *a*, *b*, *c* and angles *alpha*, *beta*, *gamma*. If the components

which must be explicitly used in specifications have identical names in different versions of the concept, then we can use undefined specifications.

> rightangled: (triangle: **undefined**;
> triangle.gamma $= 90$;
> triangle.c $\land$ 2 $=$ triangle.a $\land$ 2 $+$ triangle.b $\land$ 2;
> triangle.c $*$ **sin**(triangle.alpha) $=$ triangle.a;
> triangle.c $*$ **sin**(triangle.beta) $=$ triangle.b;

$*$ f and g are projections of legs a and b respectively.

> f, g: **numeric**;
> $f =$ triangle.a $*$ **sin**(alpha);
> $g =$ triangle.b $*$ **sin**(beta););

In this specification we can doubtless use notations f and g for projections of legs because all other variables have a prefix *triangle*. This concept can be used in combination with any other triangle. It bears all the properties of a right-angled triangle. Actually, it represents the property of a triangle: 'to be a right-angled triangle'. An example is

> T: triangle;
>
> RCT: rightangled T;

We can construct specifications for other properties of triangles in a similar way.

Different kinds of triangles can be represented as subconcepts of a single concept of the triangle. In this case any particular triangle can be represented as follows:

> T1: triangle.rightangled;
>
> T2: triangle.isosceles;

There is still one more way for representing different kinds of triangles by one concept. We can introduce an additional variable which shows the type of triangle. This allows us to use conditional relations which are applicable only for a particular type of the triangle. The following specification contains the component

> type: **text**;

which can have one of the following values: 'right-angled', 'equilateral', 'isosceles'

> triangle: (type:**text**;
> **copy** triangle;

* relations for a right-angled triangle:

if *type* ≡ '*rightangled*' **then**
  (*gamma* = 90;
  $c \wedge 2 = a \wedge 2 + b \wedge 2$;
  sin(*alpha*) ∗ c = a;
  sin(*beta*) ∗ c = b;);

* relations for an isosceles triangle:

if *type* ≡ '*isosceles*' **then**
  (*a* = *b*:
  alpha = *beta*;
  beta = 180 − 2 ∗ beta;);

* relations for an equilateral triangle:

if *type* ≡ '*equilateral*' **then**
  (*a* = *b*:
  b = *c*;
  alpha = 60;
  beta = 60;
  gamma = 60;);

* end of specification.

  );

This specification represents properties of various triangles and can be used for defining particular triangles with these properties. In general, it can be used as follows:

  T: *triangle*;

For special triangles the usage is

  T1: *triangle* '*rightangled*';
  T2: *triangle* '*equilateral*';
  T3: *triangle* '*isosceles*';

Using a triangle as an example, we have discussed here various ways of extending and enriching specifications, and defining restricted concepts using the general concept of a triangle as a superconcept. Which of these possibilities to use depends on the goal that must be achieved – a user may wish to specify a concept for many projected applications or he may intend to use the concept only to write one particular program. In the latter case there is no need to specify all the variants of a concept: in particular it is unnecessary to use components *type*: **text**; or *triangle*: **undefined**; in the specification.

4.2.4 EXAMPLES OF PROBLEMS

Any computational problem on a single triangle can be specified by means of one inheritance statement and one problem statement: for example,

> **program** #5;
>   **let** T: *triangle alpha* = 62, *beta* = 89, c = 35.9;
>   **actions** T ⊢ a,b,s;
>   **end**;

Additional restrictions can be represented as equations:

> **program** #6;
>   **let**
>   T: *triangle alpha* = 42, c = 35.9;
>   T.*beta* = 2 * T.*alpha*;
>   **actions**
>   #6 ⊢ T.a, T.b, T.s;
>   **end**;

In the latter case we must be careful when writing the problem statement. The problem can no longer be solved on the triangle T (the problem T ⊢ a,b,s is unsolvable), because an additional relation is given separately as an equation. Now we must use the name #6 of the whole program in the problem statement, and, consequently we must add prefix T to variables a, b, s, so we write:

> #6 ⊢ T.a, T.b, T.s;

in the problem statement.

Let us consider examples where several triangles are combined with each other. Figure 4.6(a) shows a situation when a distance between the

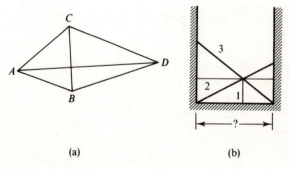

(a)   (b)

Figure 4.6   Examples of problems on triangles.

points *A* and *D* must be calculated from a known distance between the points *B* and *C*. Angles *CBA*, *BCA*, *BCD*, *CBD* are also given. The program for solving this problem is as follows:

> **program** #7;
>   **let**
>   *BC, CBA, BCA, BCD, CBD, AD*: **numeric**;
>   *ABC*: *triangle b = BC,*
>   *alpha = CBA,*
>   *gamma = BCA;*
>   *BCD*: *triangle a = BC,*
>   *beta = CBD,*
>   *gamma = BCD;*
>   *ACD*: *triangle a = ABC.a,*
>   *b = BCD.b,*
>   *c = AD;*
>
>   * in addition to this we must specify an equation which binds
>   * *ACD.gamma* with angles of other triangles:
>
>   *ACD.gamma = BCA + BCD;*
>   **actions**
>   #7 ⊢ *BC, CBA, BCA, BCD, CBD* → *AD;*
>   **end;**

Figure 4.6(b) shows a problem of finding the width of a well at the bottom of it. It is known that the Egyptian priests could solve this problem using the properties of triangles. Our program for solving the problem is as follows:

> **program** #8;
>   **let**
>   *x*: **numeric**;
>   *T1*: *triangle* 'rightangled',
>   *c = 3,*
>   *a = x;*
>   *T2*: *triangle* 'rightangled',
>   *c = 2,*
>   *b = x;*
>   *T3*: *triangle c = x,*
>   *hc = 1,*
>   *alpha = T1.beta,*
>   *beta = T2.alpha;*
>   **actions**
>   #8 ⊢ *x;*
>   **end;**

To solve this problem the synthesizer must find a solvable system of equations and solve it. Here a system of equations has appeared as a result of binding several computational models into one model (the variable x which we must calculate is included in all three triangles and it can be calculated only by solving a system of equations).

4.3 Other concepts

Analogously to concepts of geometry, concepts of other branches of mathematics can be specified. It would be very interesting to represent a full course in mathematics for a computer. But this is a much larger undertaking than writing a book on artificial intelligence methods. Therefore, we shall specify here only a small number of well-known concepts from mathematics.

4.3.1 PERCENTAGE

We extend here the concept of percentages we used in previous chapters.

> *percents*: (*part, whole, rest, percent*: **numeric**;
> $whole = part + rest$;
> $part = whole * percent/100$;
> $part/rest = percent/(100 - percent)$;

* the new part of the specification begins here. It represents
* calculations of interests.

> *sum, interests, initsum*: **numeric**;
> *years*: **numeric**;
> $initsum = whole$;

* *initsum* is another name for the whole sum for calculating
* interests.

$sum = (1 + percent/100) \wedge years *$ initsum;
$interests = sum - initsum$;);

4.3.2 DIVISIBILITY

We describe a concept of divisibility which includes the idea of division with a remainder as well as the criterion of divisibility.

> *division*:
> (*dividend, divisor, quotient, remainder, lastdigit*: **numeric**;
> **if** *divisor* $\neq 0$ **then**
> *dividend, divisor* $\rightarrow$ *quotient, remainder* (DIV);

* in this case it makes sense to represent a relation

* *dividend* = *divisor* * *quotient* + *remainder* in the form
* of a program DIV.
* divisibility is defined also by means of a program:

divisibility: **boolean**;
    dividend, divisor → *divisibility* (DIV1);

* knowing the last decimal digit of a divisor, we can recognize
* divisibility by 5:

if *lastdigit* = 0 **or** *lastdigit* = 5
    and *divisor* = 5 **then**
        divisibility = **true**;
if *lastdigit* ≠ 0 **and** *lastdigit* ≠ 5 **and**
    divisor = 5 **then**
        divisibility = **false**;

* end of specification.
    );

Naturally, divisibility by 5 is represented here only as an example. Any
other knowledge of the same kind can be added to this concept. The relation
represented by program DIV1 finds the divisibility for any integers. Besides
that, divisibility can be found from the condition

remainder = 0.

Let us now specify the concept of the greatest common divisor, which
has become almost a standard exercise of program construction in the
literature.

gcd: (*x,y, result*: **numeric**;
        1 .. : (*x,y*: **numeric**;
            if *x* > *y* **and** *y* ≠ 0 **then**
                (**next**.*x* = *x* − *y*;
                 next.*y* = *y*;);
            if *y* > *x* **and** *x* ≠ 0 **then**
                (**next**.*y* = *y* − *x*;
                 next.*x* = *x*;);
            if *x* = *y* **then**
                result = *x*;);););

* we can add a message for the case when *x* < 0 or *y* < 0 or
* *x* * *y* is not an integer:

solvable: **boolean**;
if *x* < 0 **or** *y* < 0 **or not** int (*x*) **or not** int (*y*) **then**
    solvable = **false**;

if $x > 0$ **and** $y > 0$ **and int** (x) **and int** (y) **then**
   solvable = **true**;);

The program for computing the greatest common divisor is as follows:

```
program gcd;
  let
    gcd: gcd;
  actions
    gcd ⊢ x,y → result;
  end;
```

Here we have deliberately used the identifier *gcd* in various positions (to denote different objects):

1. as the name of the program;
2. as the name of an abstract object;
3. as the name of a prototype object;
4. as the name of an abstract object which represents problem conditions.

This program is correct, but only the third occurrence of *gcd* in it is obligatory. The other occurrences can be changed to other names and for the sake of clarity it is better to do so.

    The name in the problem statement of this program can be the name of the program as well as the name of the object specified as *gcd*. If these names coincide, then the semantics of the language says that it is the name of the object. The following program for computing *gcd* is more reliable and easier to understand:

```
program #9;
  let q: gcd;
  actions
    q ⊢ x,y → solvable;
    if q.solvable then
      q ⊢ x,y → result;
  end;
```

4.3.3 SIMILARITY OF FIGURES

In order to discuss the similarity of two figures we have to relate the sides and angles of one figure to the sides and angles of the other figure. A straightforward way is to use the same names for corresponding elements of different figures. Actually we applied this approach when we specified triangles. All of them had the sides *a,b,c* and angles *alpha,beta,gamma*. Let us

use this for defining the similarity of triangles now:

> *similar*: (*T1*, *T2*: **undefined**;

> * *T1* and *T2* must be some kind of triangles.

>> *k*: **numeric**;

> * *k* is the ratio of similarity.

>> *T1.alpha* = *T2.alpha*;
>> *T1.beta* = *T2.beta*;
>> *T1.gamma* = *T2.gamma*;
>> *T1.a* = *k* ∗ *T2.a*;
>> *T1.b* = *k* ∗ *T2.b*;
>> *T1.c* = *k* ∗ *T2.c*;);

This concept of similarity can be used only for triangles where sides and angles are properly denoted. Another way of establishing the correspondence between elements of different figures is to use the position of their components. We give now a more general definition of similarity which is applicable to all polygons which have computational models satisfying the following constraints:

1. All linear elements (sides, diagonals etc.) have a component *length*.
2. All angles have a component *angle*, which represents the value of the angle.
3. In polygons of one and the same type all elements are positionally ordered in one and the same way. The concept is

> *polysimilar*: (*F 1*, *F 2*: **undefined**;

> * *F 1* and *F 2* are the polygons which have models satisfying the
> * restrictions 1, 2 and 3.

>> *k*, *l*: **numeric**

> * *k*, *l* are the ratios of similarity.

>> *k* ∗ *l* = 1;
>> *F 1*.**all**.*angle* → *F2*.**all**.*angle* (EQUAL);
>> *F2*.**all**.*angle* → *F1*.**all**.*angle* (EQUAL);

> * the program EQUAL assigns the value of the
> * *i*th input variable
> * to the *i*th output variable *i* = 1, 2, …, *m*, where *m* is the
> * number of input (output) variables, i.e. the number of angles
> * in *F 1* and *F 2*.

>> *k*, *F 1*.**all**.*length* → *F 2*.**all**.*length* (TIMES);
>> *l*, *F 2*.**all**.*length* → *F 1*.**all**.*length* (TIMES);

∗ the program TIMES multiplies the value of $(i + 1)$st input
∗ variable to the value of the first input variable and assigns
∗ the result to the ith output variable, $i = 1, 2, \ldots, n$, where
∗ n is the number of linear elements in Figure $F\,1$ and in $F\,2$.
∗ end of specification.

   );

4.3.4 FUNCTION, ITS MAXIMUM AND MINIMUM

Let us specify the concept of a numeric function. We introduce the following subconcepts:

● *argument* of the function;
● *value* of the function for a given value of an argument;
● *domain*.

We also define maximum and minimum of the function and specify the precision of finding the points where the function takes its maximal and minimal value. This is represented by the maximal error of the argument – *maxerr*.

function:
  (*argument, value*: **numeric**;
   domain: (*from, to*: **numeric**;));

∗ *domain. from* and *domain.to* are the end points of an interval
∗ which is the domain of the function.

  minimum, maximum: **numeric**;

∗ these are minimal and maximal values of the function.

  argmin, argmax: **numeric**;

∗ *argmin* and *argmax* are the values of the argument where the
∗ function takes its minimal and maximal value.

  maxerr: **numeric**;
  domain,maxerr,(*argument* $\longrightarrow$ *value*) $\longrightarrow$ *argmin,minimum*(MIN);

∗ the program MIN calculates the minimal value of the function
∗ and the value of the corresponding argument. In order to do this, the
∗ value of the function is repeatedly
∗ calculated for various values of the argument.

  domain,maxerr,(*argument* $\longrightarrow$ *value*) $\longrightarrow$ *argmax,maximum*(MAX);

* the program MAX works analogously to MIN and
* finds the maximum.

    $\rightarrow$ *maxerr* (DEFAULTERR);

* the program DEFAULTERR assigns a default value to the
* variable *maxerr*. This relation is applied only when the value
* of *maxerr* is not given otherwise.
* end of specification.

    );

The concept of function can be used, for instance, as follows:

    R: (FF: *function domain* $= (0, 1)$;

* we have defined a function FF with the domain from 0 to 1.

    $FF.value = FF.argument \wedge 3$;

* now the function FF is defined completely.

    GF: *function domain. from* $= 0$, *domain.to* $= 1$;
    $GF.argument, FF.maximum \rightarrow GF.value(Q)$;);

The function GF depends on the maximal value of the function FF. However, the maximal value of FF is a constant and the maximum of GF can be computed by varying only the variable $GF.argument$. The problem

    $R \vdash GF.maximum$

is solvable.

    Let us use the concept of function to solve the problem shown in Figure 4.7. An interval of a straight line AB is given. Its length is 50. A point C

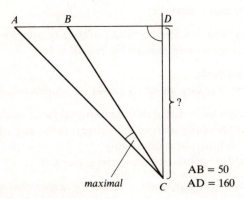

Figure 4.7 An optimization problem.

is moving along a straight line which is perpendicular to the line AB and which intersects it in the point D. The distance AD is 160. What is the distance CD when the interval AB is visible from the point C at the biggest angle, and what is this angle?

Figure 4.7 shows us that the interval CD and the angle ACB can be bound through the triangles ABC and ADC. Both of the triangles have one side given. They have a common angle CAB. Finally, using our concept of function, we shall specify the maximum of ACB depending on CD. In UTOPIST this is written as follows:

```
program #10;
  let x: numeric;
    ABC,ADC: triangle
    ABC.beta = ADC.beta;
      ADC.b = x;
      ABC.b = ADC.c;
      ABC.a = 50;
      ADC.a = 160;
      ADC.gamma = 90;
    F: function domain = (0, 1000),
              argument = x,
              value = ABC.alpha;
```

* we have taken for the domain of the function an interval which
* obviously contains the needed value.

```
  actions
    #10 ⊢ F.argmax, F.max;
  end;
```

4.3.5 SEQUENCES

UTOPIST contains the means for representing sequences. We have already used these means for defining Fibonacci numbers in Section 3.3.6. In general, a specification of a numeric sequence is as follows:

```
sequence: (1 .. : (e, S: numeric;
          next.e = f(e);
```

* e is the element and S is the sum of a sequence. For any
* particular sequence the function f as well as the constant g
* must be represented as expressions.

```
          next.S = S + e;);
            # 1.S = 0;
            # 1.e = g;);
```

#n.e and *#n.S* are names of the *n*th element and of the sum of the first *n* elements of a sequence. For instance, an arithmetic progression can be specified as follows:

$$arprogr: (1 ..: (e, S, d, a1: \textbf{numeric};$$
$$\textbf{next}.e = e + d;$$
$$\textbf{next}.S = S + e;);$$
$$\#1.S = 0;$$
$$\#1.e = a1;);$$

where *a1* is the first element of the progression, and *d* is increment of the progression.

Arithmetic progression can also be specified in more detail, taking into account the well-known relations, where *an* is the *n*th element of the progression,

$$an = a1 + (n - 1) * d$$
$$S = (a1 + an) * n/2$$
$$S = (2 * a1 + (n - 1) * d) * n/2.$$
$$arprogression: (a1, an, S, d, n: \textbf{numeric};$$
$$an = a1 + (n - 1) * d;$$
$$S = (a1 + an) * n/2;$$
$$S = (2 * a1 + (n - 1) * d) * n/2;);$$

Analogously, we can specify the geometric progression:

$$geomprogression: (a1, an, S, k, n: \textbf{numeric};$$
$$an = a1 * k \land (n - 1);$$
$$\textbf{if } k \neq 1 \textbf{ then}$$
$$S = (an * k - a1)/(k - 1););$$

4.3.6 A TYPICAL PROBLEM

An abstract object in UTOPIST can represent a situation or a class of situations which are close to each other. This allows us to represent typical problem conditions as abstract objects, i.e. to give specifications of classes of problems directly in UTOPIST. In this case, it is convenient to speak about an abstract object as a frame of the situation which corresponds to the problem conditions.

Let us consider the following class of problems. During a time interval *T* a quantity *Q* of a substance is obtained. More precisely, there exist simultaneously two processes: adding the substance with a speed *v1* and taking away the substance with a speed *v2*. We assume that $v1 > v2$. If, on the contrary, $v2 > v1$, then the quantity *Q* is lost during the time interval *T*. In addition, the situation can be described by *Q1* – the quantity which is added in the time interval *T*, and *Q2* – the quantity which is taken away at the same

time. The difference of speeds $v1$ and $v2$ we denote as dv, the initial amount of material we denote by Q_0 and the final amount by Q_f.

accumulation: (time, T: **numeric**;
        quantity, Q: **numeric**;
            v1: **numeric**;
            v2: **numeric**;
            Q1,Q2: **numeric**;
            dv: **numeric**;
            Q_0,Q_f: **numeric**;
        time = T; quantity = Q;

* here we have introduced synonyms for the names of some
* entities. This is convenient for various users who may use
* different names for the entities.

$Q = Q1 - Q2$;
$Q1 = v1 * T$;
$Q2 = v2 * T$;
$dv = v1 - v2$;
$Q = dv * T$;
$Q = Q_f - Q_0$;);

Having specified the concept *accumulation*, we have provided knowledge for solving quite a number of various problems. These are, for instance, problems about the accumulation of liquid in tanks, problems concerning the balance in a situation when two contradicting processes are performed, etc. It also represents a situation where there are two motions with the speeds $v1$ and $v2$ in one and the same direction. Then $Q1$ and $Q2$ are distances. Here we have acted in a way which is not allowed at school when teaching children: we have merely written some equations which specify the situation. Examples of problems of this kind are used for teaching children to understand problem conditions, to choose a way of solving the problem, and finally to put together equations. We cannot put this intellectual task to a computer – it must be done by the user. He must understand the problem, find proper concepts for formalizing it and write the specification of the problem. In our example the user must understand that the concept of accumulation is applicable and he must choose the right terms (*time, quantity, T, Q,*...) to specify the given situation.

4.4 Elementary physics

4.4.1 UNITS AND DIMENSIONS

We start our presentation of physical concepts with a discussion of basic physical entities and units for measuring these entities. The technique suggested here for representing physical entities and for automatic coercion

Table 4.1   Physical units.

Entity	Units		
	Name	*Abbreviation*	*Notation in* UTOPIST
length	metre	m	[m]
mass	kilogram	kg	[kg]
time	second	s	[s]
electric current	ampere	A	[A]
temperature	kelvin	K	[K]
amount of substance	mole	mol	[mol]
area	square metre	m^2	[m ∧ 2]
volume	cubic metre	m^3	[m ∧ 3]
angular velocity	radian per second	rad/s	[rad/s]
angular acceleration	radian per second squared	rad/s^2	[rad/s ∧ 2]
velocity	metre per second	m/s	[m/s]
acceleration	metre per second squared	m/s^2	[m/s ∧ 2]
force	newton	N	[N]
moment of inertia		$kg\,m^2$	[kg m ∧ 2]
moment of force		$N\,m^2$	[N m ∧ 2]
energy	joule	J	[J]
power	watt	W	[W]
quantity of electricity	coulomb	C	[C]
electric conductivity	ampere per volt-metre	A/V m	[A/Vm]
electromotive force	volt	V	[V]
electric field strength	volt per metre	V/m	[V/m]
electric capacitance	farad	F	[F]
magnetomotive force (electric current)	ampere	A	[A]
electric resistance	ohm	Ω	[Ohm]
specific resistance		Ω/m	[Ohm/m]
pressure	pascal	Pa	[Pa]
density	kilogram per cubic metre	kg/m^3	[kg/m ∧ 3]

of units is applicable also for the geometric problems discussed in the previous section without taking units into account.

We represent all relations between physical entities in one and the same system of units – let us use the international SI system. Table 4.1 represents the physical entities we shall use in this chapter, with their dimensions and notations. We apply here an extension to the syntax of identifiers that proved to be convenient in the MICROPRIZ system. The identifiers can be taken into brackets [ ] and the identifier in brackets can contain characters /, * and ∧. This enables us to denote units almost in the usual way. For instance, we can write [m ∧ 3] for cubic metres, [cm/s ∧ 2] for acceleration given in cm/s², etc.

A specification of a physical entity includes a component for its value in SI units and can also contain a number of virtual components for values represented in other units. The relations which bind the values measured in various units are also included in the specification. Let us start with a specification of length:

> *length*: ([*m*]: **numeric**;
>   **virtual**
>   [*mm*], [*cm*], [*dm*], [*km*]: **numeric**;
>   *inches, feet, yards, miles*: **numeric**;

* [*mm*], *inches* etc. represent the values of length measured in
* millimetres, inches etc.

[*mm*] $= 1000 * [m]$;
[*cm*] $= 100 * [m]$;
[*dm*] $= 10 * [m]$;
[*m*] $= 1000 * [km]$;
inches $= 39.37 * [m]$;
feet $= 3.28 * [m]$;
yards $= 1.09 * [m]$;
miles $= 0.000621 * [m]$;);

We have specified here a computational model with a star-like schema (see Section 4.1.3). It has a variable [*m*] in the centre. Therefore, transformation of length measured in any given units into any other units takes at most two steps. (There are 36 different possible transformations.)

The concept of time is specified analogously:

> *time*: ([s] : **numeric**;
>   **virtual**
>   *nanoseconds, microseconds, milliseconds,*
>   *minutes, hours, days*: **numeric**;
>   *nanoseconds* $= 1E9 * [s]$;
>   *microseconds* $= 1E6 * [s]$;

$$milliseconds = 1000 * [s];$$
$$[s] = 60 * minutes;$$
$$[s] = 3600 * hours;$$
$$[s] = 24 * 3600 * days;);$$

A reader may be dissatisfied with the fact that specifications written in UTOPIST do not represent the whole meaning of concepts. Indeed, they reflect only the computational side of concepts. This is especially obvious when physical processes are considered. Actually, we specify only computational facilities, associated with various objects, processes and situations. But let us recall that we are considering here a new programming technique, and not the general way of representing knowledge about the world around us. The goal of the present section is to show how we can detect and specify a number of concepts which allow us to program many problems in such a complicated and profoundly investigated field as physics.

We assume that all physical entities we need are already specified in the manner used for length and time. In this case, any entity contained in a problem specification can be represented by means of an inheritance specification. For example:

$$F: force\ pounds = S;$$
$$L: length\ [cm] = 100;$$
$$E1, E2: energy;$$
$$T: time\ [s] = 30;$$

We have designed specifications of physical entities in such a way that we can use them (i.e. $F, L, E1, T$) immediately in arithmetic expressions, because they contain only one nonvirtual component – the value of the entity represented in the SI system. In this case the coercion of units is done automatically as shown in Section 3.3.2. For instance, we can write

$$E1 - E2 = F * L;$$

showing that the difference of energies $E1$ and $E2$ is the work done by force F along the path with length L. And this equation is correct because nonvirtual components of $E1, E2, F, L$ are all in the SI system.

Let us construct a program for the following problem: 'An aircraft has a velocity of 800 km/h. How many centimetres will it cover in 5 seconds?' First of all, we have to specify explicitly all entities referred to in the text of the problem. Thereafter we can write the equations which are needed (one equation in this particular case).

program #11;
  let
    $v: velocity\ [km/h] = 800;$

T: *time* [*s*] = 5;
L: *length*;
   L = *v* * *T*;
actions
   #*11* ⊢ *L*.[*cm*];
end;

We can observe once again that a program in UTOPIST does not contain any redundant information. This is exactly the style of conceptual programming – we have represented the entities involved in the problem and specified the relation which binds them.

4.4.2 MECHANICS

Let us regard statics in the two-dimensional world now. First of all, we introduce the force vector:

fvector: (**copy** *force*;
        px, *py*: *force*;
        [*N*] $\wedge$ 2 = *px* $\wedge$ 2 + *py* $\wedge$ 2;);

This vector can be used for specifying the equilibrium of a body.
   The basic law of statics is:

a body is in a state of equilibrium if the sum of force vectors and the sum of moments which influence it are equal to zero. (It is assumed that all moments are reduced to one and the same centre of rotation.)

   In the general case of two-dimensional statics we have n force vectors p_i which are represented through their components px_i, py_i, $i = 1, 2, \ldots, n$, and m moments $M_1, \ldots, M_m$. Equations representing the basic law of statics are

$$px = px_1 + px_2 + \ldots + px_n = 0$$

$$py = py_1 + py_2 + \ldots + py_n = 0$$

$$M = M_1 + M_2 + \ldots + M_n = 0$$

We have already used a program SUM for calculating the sum of components of an object in Section 3.4.5. Let us use the same program here.

equilibrium:(
        load: **undefined**;

* it is assumed that all forces and momentums are the components
* of load.

p: force;
M: moment;

* *p* and *M* are the sums of forces and momentums influencing a
* body.

*load.**all**.px* → *px*(SUM);
*load.**all**.py* → *py*(SUM););
*load.**all**.M* → *M* (SUM);
p.px = 0;
p.py = 0;
M = 0;

* the three equations presented above express the basic law of
* statics.

);

Now we describe the dynamics of a mass point for two special cases:

1.   translatory movement;
2.   rotatory movement.

The first case was discussed in Section 2.3.2. We therefore present its specification here without comment. The difference from the specification given in Section 2.3.2 is that here we use basic physical entities with dimensions. This means, in particular, that equations like

$$DT = T2 - T1;$$
$$Dv = v2 - v1;$$

have the same meaning as

$$DT.[s] = T2.[s] - T1.[s];$$
$$Dv.[m/s] = v2.[m/s] - v1.[m/s];$$

(According to our agreement any physical entity is defined so that its only nonvirtual component is its value in SI units.)

translatory_movement:
  (*T1, T2, DT: time*;
  $DT = T2 - T1;$
  v, v1, v2: velocity;
  $Dv = v2 - v1;$
  $v = (v1 + v2)/2;$

E1, E2, DE: *energy*;
DE = E2 − E1;
L1, L2, DL: *distance*;
DL = L2 − L1;
a: *acceleration*;
m: *mass*;
F: *force*;
F = m ∗ a;
E1 = m ∗ v1 ∧ 2/2;
E2 = m ∗ v2 ∧ 2/2;
Dv = DT ∗ a;
DL = v ∗ DT;);

The laws of dynamics can be represented in vector form analogously to the way in which we have specified statics. In order to do this, the vectors of velocity, acceleration and shift must be specified in addition to the vector of force. We leave this as an exercise to the reader.

The specification of rotation differs from the specification of translatory movement mainly in the names of its components. Angle (*alpha*), angular speed (*omega*), angular acceleration (*epsilon*), moment (*M*) and moment of inertia (*I*) are used in the place of distance, velocity, acceleration, force and mass. Radius of trajectory (*R*) is a new component. It is also useful to add radial (*ar*) and tangential (*at*) component of acceleration and linear velocity (*v*).

rotation:
(alpha1,alpha2, Dalpha : *angle*;
Dalpha = alpha2 − alpha1;
omega,omega1,omega2, Domega : *angular_velocity*;
Domega = omega2 − omega1;
omega = (omega2 + omega1)/2;
E1, E2, DE: *energy*;
DE = E2 − E1;
T1, T2, DT: *time*;
DT = T2 − T1;
epsilon: *angular_acceleration*;
I: *momentum_of_inertia*;
M: *moment*;
m: *mass*;
L: *distance*;
F: *force*;
v: *velocity*;
at, ar: *acceleration*;
R: *length*;
F = m ∗ a;
E1 = m ∗ v1 ∧ 2/2;

$$E2 = m * v2 \wedge 2/2;$$
$$Dv = DT * a;$$
$$DL = v * DT;$$

* m, F, v, at and ar are related to the characteristic
* parameters of rotation as follows:

$$I = m * R \wedge 2;$$
$$M = F * R;$$
$$omega = v/R;$$
$$epsilon = at/R;$$
$$ar = omega \wedge 2 * R;$$

* end of specification.

);

Both specifications of movement can be put together as follows:

movement: (*translatory* : *translatory_movement*;
        rotatory: *rotation*;);

A considerable amount of knowledge in physics is represented in the form of specifications of typical situations. For example, a typical situation is represented in Figure 4.8, where a body on an inclined plane is shown. It is useful to equip a computer with the same kind of knowledge. Such knowledge can be easily represented in the form of computational frames, which contain the concepts typical to the situation described bound by some relations.

A verbal description of the situation shown in Figure 4.8 goes as follows:

A solid body lies on a plane which is inclined at the angle *inclination*. The body has mass *m*. The coefficient of friction between the body and the plane is *k*, and the angle of friction is *psi*. The body is at a standstill if *inclination* is not bigger than *psi*. It moves according to the laws of translatory movement if *inclination* is bigger than *psi*.

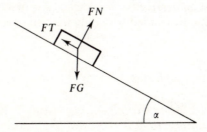

Figure 4.8   A body on an inclined surface.

The body is influenced by forces FG (its weight), FN (the normal component of the reaction of the plane), and FT (the tangential component of the reaction of the plane).

The specification of the situation in UTOPIST goes as follows:

incl: (*inclination* : *angle*;
     friction_coefficient, k: **numeric:**
     friction_coefficient = k;
     friction_angle,psi: *angle*;
     friction_angle = psi;
     mass, m: *mass*;
     mass = m;
     FG, FN, FT: *force*;
     sliding: *movement.translatory m = mass*;
     $k = $ **tg**(*psi*);
     $FN = FG * $**cos**(*psi*);
     $FT = FG * $**sin**(*psi*);
  if *inclination* $\leqslant$ *psi* **then**
    sliding.F $= 0$;
  if *inclination* $>$ *psi* **then**
    sliding.F $= FT - FN * k$;);

Now it is time to put our concepts in physics into proper order. To do this, we create a specification of physics in the knowledge base and include the mechanics into it for a start. Later we shall expand the physics specification by appending new parts representing electricity, etc. It is also useful to have direct definitions of all physical entities in the specification of physics. We therefore begin the specification of physics with specifications of length, time and other entities.

    program *housekeeping*;
      let *physics*:
         (*length, distance*: *length*;
          time: *time*;

    * this text must be completed by specification of all basic
    * entities. We have included here only the two concepts
    * specified above.

        mechanics:
          (*statics*: *equilibrium*;
         movement:
            (*translatory*:*translatory_movement*;
            rotatory: *rotation*;
            sliding: *incl*;);););

* this specification can be immediately included into the knowledge
* base:

    insert *physics*;
end;

4.4.3 ELECTRICITY

Let us assume that the basic electrical entities have been already specified and we can use their specifications. These specifications also contain relations between the values measured in different units. Now we are going to specify the electrical phenomena according to a textbook.

Coulomb's law   A force between two electric charges is proportional to any of the charges and inversely proportional to the square of the distance between these charges. (It is assumed that the charges occupy a space considerably smaller than the distance between them.)

We shall need a constant $8.85 \times 10^{-12}\,C/N\,m^2$ here and further on. Its specification is

    eps0: (*value*: **numeric**;
            value = 8.85 E − 12;);

Now we can represent Coulomb's law precisely:

    let *Coulomb's_law*:
        (*q1, q2*: *charge*;
         F: *force*;
         epsilon: *electrical_conductivity*;
         r: *distance*:
    * *r* is distance between the electric charges *q1* and *q2*

        $F = q1 * q2/(4 * pi * epsilon * eps0 * r \wedge 2)$;);

Homogeneous electric field   We specify a force *F* which acts on a charge *q* in a homogeneous electric field *E*, work *A* needed to shift the charge and the voltage *U* as a difference of potentials between two points of the field.

In this specification we also show units in which the variables must be represented. As before, we could omit these units and write, for instance,

    $F = E * q$;

instead of

    $F.[N] = E.[V/m] * q.[C]$;

but we think that showing the units can sometimes help a user to avoid mistakes.

> *el_field*: (*F*: *force*;
>   *E*: *field_strength*;
>   *q*: *charge*;
>   *A*: *work*;
>   *U*: *voltage*;
>   *s*: *distance*;

* force acting on a charge:

$F.[N] = E.[V/m] * q.[C]$;

* voltage between two points of the field:

$U.[V] = E.[V/m] * s.[m]$;

* work for shifting a charge:

$A.[J] = U.[V] * q.[C]$;);

Planar capacitor

> **let** *capacitor*:
>   (*C*: *capacity*;
>   *q*: *charge*;
>   *U*: *voltage*;
> $q = C * U$;
>   *S*: *area*;
>   *d*: *distance*;
>   *epsilon*: *electric_conductivity*;

* *S* is the area of the surface of the plates of the capacitor with
* distance between the plates equal to *d*.

> $C = epsilon * S * eps0$;

* energy of a loaded capacitor:

> *A*: *energy*;
> $A = C * U \wedge 2/2$;);

Direct current

> **let** *direct_current*:
>   (*I*: *current*;
>   *q*: *charge*;
>   *t*: *time*;
> $I = q/t$;

* Ohm's law:

   R: *resistance*;
   U: *voltage*;
$I = U/R$;

* resistance of a conductor with length *l* and area of cross
* section *S*:

   ro: *specific_resistance*;
   l: *length*;
   S: *area*;
$R = ro * l/S$;

* power:

   W: *power*;
$W = U * I$;);

To complete the section on electricity, we include the specifications presented here in the knowledge base. First of all, we describe an empty concept *electricity*, include it as a part into *physics*, and then add all electrical concepts.

> **program** *electricity*
> **let** *electricity*: ( );
> **insert** *electricity* **into** *physics*;
> **insert** *Coulomb's_law* **into** *physics.electricity*;
> **insert** *el_field* **into** *physics.electricity*;
> **insert** *capacitor* **into** *physics.electricity*;
> **insert** *direct_current* **into** *physics.electricity*;
> **end**;

4.4.4 IDEAL GAS

We are going to demonstrate a direct way of formalizing physical knowledge – translating a text, taken from a handbook, immediately into UTOPIST. For this purpose we have chosen to use a handbook as our source of knowledge rather than using a students' textbook, because handbooks contain knowledge in more concentrated form, which is closer to our representation than any textbook material.

We assume that the following basic physical entities needed for representing properties of ideal gas have been already specified: *pressure, volume, temperature, molar_mass, density, specific_volume*. For example, the concept of temperature can be defined as follows:

> **let** *temperature*:
> (*K*: **numeric**;

virtual

celsius, fahrenheit: **numeric**;

$celsius/100 = (fahrenheit - 32)/180$;

$celsius = K - 273.15$;);

We define Avogadro's number as follows:

A: (*value*: **numeric**;

$value = 6.022 \text{ E}23$;);

Pressure, volume, molar_mass, specific_volume, and *density* can be used as state variables which characterize a state of ideal gas. Let us agree that we can indicate a state with a digit added to the identifier of a variable. So, for instance, *p1, V1* will belong to one state and *p2, V2* to another. Let us open a handbook (Yavorski and Detlaf, 1977; p. 150), where a description of ideal gas begins and let us translate the description into UTOPIST.

Ideal gas

1. An ideal gas is a gas which does not have forces of interaction between its molecules. A gas can be considered as an ideal gas in the cases when its states are significantly different from the states of phase conversion.

2. The following laws hold for an ideal gas:

    (a) *Boyle–Mariotte's law*: if the temperature and the mass of gas are constant then the product of its pressure and volume is also constant:

    $$pV = \text{const}$$

    let *Boyle_Mariotte*:
    (*p1, p2*: *pressure*;
    V1, V2: *volume*;

    * the mass and the temperature are constant for the states
    * 1 and 2.

    $$p1 * V1 = p2 * V2;);$$

    (b) *Gay–Lussac's law*: at a constant pressure, the volume of a given mass of gas is proportional to its temperature:

    $$V = aV_0T = V_0\frac{T}{T_0}$$

    where V_0 = volume of gas at the temperature, $T_0 = 273.15$ K, $a = 1/T_0$ = coefficient of volumetric expansion.

let *Gay_Lussac*:

> (*V, V0*: *volume*;
> *T, T0*: *temperature*;

∗ pressure is constant.

> *T0* = 273.15;
> *a*: **numeric**;
> *a* = 1/*T0*;

∗ *a* is coefficient of volumetric expansion,

> $V = a * V0 * T$;
> $V = V0 * T/T0$;);

(c)   *Charles' law*: at a constant volume, the pressure of a given mass of gas is proportional to its temperature:

$$p = p_0 T/T_0,$$

where p_0 = pressure at the temperature T_0 = 273.15 K.

let *Charles*:

> (*p, p0*: *pressure*;
> *T, T0*: *temperature*;

∗ volume is constant.

> *T0* = 273.15;
> $p = p0 * T/T0$;);

(d)   *Avogadro's law*: at the same pressures and the same temperatures, equal volumes of different ideal gases contain equal numbers of molecules, or, equivalently, at the same pressures and the same temperatures gram-molecules of different ideal gases occupy equal volumes. So, for instance, at the normal conditions ($t = 0°C$ and $p = 101\,325\,N/m^2 = 1\,atm = 760\,mm\,Hg$), a gram-molecule of any ideal gas occupies the volume $V = 22.414$ litres. The number of molecules in $1\,cm^3$ at the normal conditions is called *Loschmidt's number* and it is $2.687 \times 10^{19}\,1/cm^3$.

let *Avogadro*:

> (*t*: *temperature*;
> *p*: *pressure*;
> *V*: *volume*;
> *M*: *molar_mass*;
> *normal*: **boolean**;
> **if** t.[celsius] = 0 **and** $p = 101\,325$ **then**
>   *normal* = **true**;
> **if** *normal* **then**
> V.[*l*]/M.[*g/mol*] = 22.414;

*let us add here Avogadro's number

> A: **numeric**;
> $A = 6.022 \text{ E}23;$);

3.   The state equation for ideal gas is

$$pV\mu = RT,$$

where p, $V\mu$ and T are pressure, molar volume and temperature and R is the general gas constant equal to work done by one kilomole of ideal gas if its temperature is isobarically raised by one degree:

$$R = 8.31 \; 10^3 \, \text{J/kmol.K} = 0.0821 \, \text{l atm/mol.K} =$$
$$0.848 \, \text{kg/mol.K} = 8.31 \; 10^7 \, \text{erg/mol.K} =$$
$$1.987 \, \text{cal/mol.K}.$$

For an arbitrary mass M of gas its volume is

$$V = \frac{M}{\mu} V\mu,$$

and the state equation is

$$pV = \frac{M}{\mu} RT.$$

This equation is called the Mendelejev–Clapeyron equation. Because the specific volume of gas is

$$v = V/M,$$

we have

$$pv = \frac{R}{\mu} T = BT,$$

where $B = \dfrac{R}{\mu}$ is a specific gas constant which depends on molar weight of a gas.

> **let** *state*:
>
> (p: *pressure*;
> V: *volume*;
> T: *temperature*;
> R: ($[J/kmol * K]$: **numeric**;
>   **virtual**
> $[l * atm/mol * K]$: **numeric**;
> $[kgm/mol * K]$: **numeric**;
> $[erg/mol * K]$: **numeric**;
> $[cal/mol * K]$: **numeric**;
> $[J/kmol * K] = 8.31 \text{ E}3;$

$[l * atm/mol * K] = 0.821;$
$[kgm/mol * K] = 0.848;$
$[erg/mol * K] = 8.31\ E7;$
$[cal/mol * K] = 1.987;);$

* R is the general gas constant.

$p * V = 0.001 * R * T;);$

let *Mendelejev_Clapeyron*:

(*p*: *pressure*;
V: *volume*;
M: *mass*;
m: *molar mass*;
R: *state.R*;
T: *temperature*;
$p * V = M * R * T / 1000 * m);$

4.   From the Mendelejev–Clapeyron equation it follows that the number of molecules of one unit of volume of ideal gas is

$$n_0 = \frac{N_A}{V\mu} = \frac{pN_A}{RT} = \frac{p}{kT}.$$

where $k = R/N_A = 1.38 \times 10^{-23}$ J/K $= 1.38 \times 10^{-6}$ erg/K = Boltzmann's constant, N_A = Avogadro's number.

let *Boltzmann_const*:

($[J/K]$: **numeric**;
virtual
$[erg/K]$: **numeric**;
$[J/K] = 1.38\ E - 23;$
$[erg/K] = 1.38\ E - 16;);$

let *number_of_molecules*:

(*n0*: **numeric**;
p: *pressure*;
k: *Boltzmann const*;
T: *temperature*;
$n0 = p/k * T;);$

Here the section about ideal gas ends in the handbook. Analysing the translation, we can observe that the part of knowledge which we could not translate is a verbal definition of the ideal gas. All other parts were translated with the restriction that nothing was said about the applicability of the concepts. To estimate the applicability remains the duty of a user.

We could continue the translation for the next parts of the handbook where mixtures of ideal gases are considered. There we see new concepts:

mixture, component, concentration. New laws are presented – the laws of Dalton, Amaga and the generalized Mendelejev–Clapeyron law. Further on, in the following sections, thermodynamic processes are described for the ideal gases. These processes can be easily represented by means of computational frames. In particular, computational frames can be built for the following processes: isochoric, isobaric, isothermal, adiabatic, polythropic. Building concepts representing physical phenomena can be a good exercise for the reader.

Chapter 5
Knowledge-Based Programming Techniques

This chapter includes subject matter of two kinds. The first two sections are devoted to problems that arise in conventional programming – organization of input–output and the specification of programmer's data types. These sections show us how to introduce the facilities of contemporary programming languages into UTOPIST. The rest of this chapter contains examples of knowledge-based programming which are useful for building various problem-oriented systems and expert systems.

Computer programming itself can be regarded as a problem domain where conceptual programming can be applied. Building tools for computer programming can be considered simply as a particular case of building a program package. The purpose of this package is to facilitate a programmer's work by supplying him with useful input–output functions and data structures, i.e. with general-purpose programming tools. We start this chapter with a discussion of the implementation of such tools in UTOPIST.

5.1 Input–output

There are two different points of view to data input and output: an old programmer's view and a user's view. The difference can be explained with reference to an example of copying a file. A programmer who is accustomed to writing programs on an old mainframe is presumably inclined to consider the task of copying a file as a sequence of input and output operations. The user of a personal computer seldom looks at such tasks as input–output tasks, especially when the files are kept on an internal hard disk. From the user's standpoint, there are three kinds of data transfer:

1. input from a keyboard or magnetic medium;
2. output on a screen or paper;
3. data transfer inside the system.

We shall consider here only the exchange of data between the user and

the computer, i.e. the first two cases. An ideal case would be if a computer could accept data in any form and could output data exactly in the form a user is awaiting it, but obviously this is impossible. At most we can count on an input presented in more or less convenient data language and on an output formatted automatically. Besides that, an interactive system can help a user by means of prompting.

5.1.1 OUTPUT OF PRIMITIVE VALUES

A careful reader may have observed that in the examples of UTOPIST programs we have not used output statements. Indeed, there are no standard input or output statements in UTOPIST, although any implementation of this language has its own input–output facilities. The simplest means are supplied by the macro $PRINT(x)$ where x is the name of an object of type **text**, **numeric** or **boolean**.

This macro has the following definitions:

```
macro
PRINT(&x);
mbegin
call PRINT(&x);
mend;
```

where $PRINT(\ )$ is a program with type-checking facilities for its parameters that accepts a varying number of parameters of **boolean**, **numeric** or **text** type.

Using this program we can also extend the macro $FIND$ specified in Section 3.8.2. The new definition contains an output statement, and the programs containing the new $FIND$ will also print their results:

```
macro
&FIND& &P;
mbegin
actions
FIRST ⊢ &P;
call PRINT(&P);
mend;
```

5.1.2 AUTOMATIC FORMATTING

A user-friendly system must relieve its user from the tasks of detailed specification of input–output formats, and must find convenient formats automatically. To some extent, this objective can be achieved in UTOPIST due to the presence of data specifications.

First of all, we must decide what is a convenient format. Having no information about a problem domain we can make only some general

observations. Input format must be 'natural' and flexible: no special positioning must be needed.

The form

$$\langle name \rangle = \langle value \rangle,$$

which has been used in amendments of inheritance specifications, can be used. We can expect some prompting from the system. If the system knows the name of an input, it must show the name. An output must be easy to understand. The usual rules of pretty-printing can be applied.

All these goals can be achieved using two functions, *name*(x) and *type*(x), which are the system functions of PRIZ. These functions can be used in programs which represent the relations of UTOPIST. The parameter x must be one of the parameters of such a program. The first function returns the name of x and the second the type of x (more precisely, the equivalence class of strong structural equivalence of x). Briefly, the functions *name*(x) and *type*(x) have access to the specifications written in UTOPIST and make available the information contained in these specifications to the program where they are used.

Let us specify some concepts which contain input and output programs with automatic formatting.

> *input*:
>> (**virtual**
>> *value*: **undefined**;
>> *prog*: $\rightarrow$ *value* (INPUT);););
> *output*:
>> (*result*: **boolean**;
>> **virtual**
>> *value*: **undefined**;
>> *prog*: *value* $\rightarrow$ *result*($OUTPUT$);););

A variable *output.result* is used to signal the successful completion of the output operation. It is needed also for automatic planning of output operations, because it is the only output variable of the relation *output.prog*.

These concepts can be used also in **apply** statements: for example,

> **program** *aa*;
>> **let** *a*: *object1*;
>>> *b*: *object2*;
>>> . . .
>> *P1*: *input a*;
>> *P2*: *output b*;
>> **actions**
>>> **apply** *P1.prog*;

```
        aa ⊢ a → b;
        apply P2.prog;
    end;
```

But the input–output programs can be called automatically: for example,

```
    program bb;
        let
            a: object1;
            b: object2;
            ...
            P1: input a;
            P2: output b;
        actions
            bb ⊢ P2;
        end;
```

If several objects have one and the same type, these objects can be handled by one and the same output relation:

```
    program cc;
        let...
                x1,x2,x3:object;
                P: output value is object;
                ...
        actions
            cc ⊢ x1, x2, x3;
            apply P.prog (x1);
            apply P.prog (x2);
            apply P.prog (x3);
        end;
```

Input relations can be used analogously.

5.1.3 PROBLEM-ORIENTED INPUT–OUTPUT SPECIFICATIONS

UTOPIST is intended for building software systems for various problem domains. When using a system of that kind, actual programming is almost abolished, but a considerable amount of work is needed for data input and output. Therefore, the nature of a problem-oriented system is determined, to a great extent, by its input–output facilities. How intelligent a system is seems to depend on the degree of its 'understanding' of input data. The same is applicable to output which must be expressive and easy to read.

Naturally, general input and output concepts which we have described in the previous section must be replaced by specialized concepts in a problem-

oriented system. Every problem domain has its specific objects appearing as input and output. These objects must be represented according to the traditions of the problem domain. For instance, if we design maching parts, then the result of the design must be presented in the form of drawings and, perhaps, in the form of numerical-control programs for automatic manufacturing purposes.

We can take one of two approaches in designing a problem-oriented input–output:

- specifying one concept containing all input-output facilities;
- specifying a separate concept for every type of object.

We shall consider both these ways here. Let $X1, \ldots, Xk$ be the types of object which can appear as input or output. (More precisely, $X1, \ldots, Xk$ represent equivalence classes of weak structural equivalence of types of input–output data.) A general input–output concept is the following:

> *input_output*:
>   (*result*: **boolean**;
>   **virtual**
> $a1: X1; \ldots; ak: Xk$;
> $in1: \rightarrow a1 \, (M1)$;
>   . . .
> $ink: \rightarrow ak \, (Mk)$;
> $out1: a1 \rightarrow result \, (N1)$;
>   . . .
> $outk: ak \rightarrow result \, (Nk)$;);

In a UTOPIST program it is sufficient to use this concept once in the specification part for creating an abstract object and then to apply relations of this object in **apply** statements:

> **program** *aaa*;
>   **let** *io*: *input_output*;
> $x: \ldots$
> $y: \ldots$
>   . . .
>   **actions**
>   . . .
>   **apply** *io. inj*(*x*);
> ∗ a value of *x* that has type Xj is read by this statement.
>   . . .
>   **apply** *io.outj*(*y*);
> ∗ a value of *y* that has type Xj is printed.
>   . . .
>   **end**;

The question may arise why we cannot use input–output programs directly in a **call** statement, writing

> **call** $Mi(x)$;
> **call** $Nj(y)$;

The reason is that programs Mi, Nj must use the system functions *name*(x) and *type*(x) which can be called only from preprogrammed relations. (They must have access to specifications through bound variables of the relation.)

Let us consider now the second way of building specialized input–output concepts where a separate concept is built for every type Xi. Let us assume that the problem domain is linear algebra and we have to read and print vectors and matrices.

The simplest concepts for input are:

> *invector*:
>   (*value*: *vector*;
>   *prog*: $\rightarrow$ *value* (q1););
> *inmatrix*:
>   *value*: *matrix*;
>   *prog*: $\rightarrow$ *value* (q2););

Every object of a problem specification, which must be read, can be supplied with its own input specification:

> **let** $V1,V2,V3$: *vector*;
> $M1,M2,M3,M4$: *matrix*;
> $L1$: *invector* $V1$;
> $L2$: *inmatrix* $M1$;
> $L3$: *invector* $V2$;
>   . . .

Note that in this case there is no need for input operations in the action part of the program. As soon as any vectors or matrix is needed it will be read in by the synthesized program. But automatic sequencing of input operators also causes some problems. We do not know beforehand in which order input data of different objects must be given.

A specialized input can be controlled by a parameter which determines input mode, device and format:

> *inmatrix1*:
>   (*value*: *matrix*;
>   **virtual**
>   *parameter*: **text**;
>   *prog*: *parameter* $\rightarrow$ *value* (q3););

Now a matrix can be read only after the parameter has been evaluated. This permits us to incorporate such an input relation into the specification of *matrix* itself. Let us assume that a specification of *matrix* has a component that represents the data of a matrix. Then we can specify a new concept of matrix as follows:

```
matrix1:
  (copy matrix;
   virtual
   source: text;
   input: source → value (q4););
```

The parameter which controls input is called *source* here.

An example program which computes matrix *M3* from matrices *M1* and *M2* is as follows:

```
program matrices;
  let M1,M2,M3: matrix1;
    M1.source = 'terminal1';
      ...
  actions
    apply M2.input ('disk A');
    matrices ⊢ M2 → M3;
      ...
  end;
```

We had to indicate explicitly in the problem statement that matrix *M2* was evaluated, and we did it by writing *M2* into the input of the problem statement. On the other hand, matrix *M1* can be read automatically from the terminal, if needed, and we did not need to show it in the problem statement as an input of the problem.

Output concepts for vectors and matrices are built analogously.

```
outvector:
  (value: vector;
   virtual
   result: boolean;
   prog: value → result (r1););
outmatrix:
  (value: matrix;
   virtual
   result: boolean;
   prog: value → result (r2););
```

Both of these concepts have a virtual component *result* of **boolean** type.

Programs r1 and r2 assign **true** to the component result if the output operation terminates successfully. But the actual purpose of this component is not signalling the successful termination of output but enabling automatic program synthesis. Output is activated automatically in the following way:

```
program bbb;
    let M: matrix;
        L: outmatrix;
            . . .
    actions
        bbb ⊢ L.result;
    end;
```

Output programs can also have control parameters, and an output concept can contain several output programs. Here we present an output concept with several programs for matrices:

```
outmatrix2:
    (value: matrix;
    virtual
    screen: boolean;
    compact: boolean;
    extended: boolean;
    screen: value → screen (p1);
    compact: value → compact (p2);
    extended: value → extended (p3););
```

The program p1 displays a matrix on a screen, p2 prints the matrix in a compact form and p3 prints it in an extended form.
    After specifying

```
M: matrix;
L: outmatrix2;
```

we can write in the action part of the program

```
apply L.screen(M);
apply L.compact(M);
apply L.extended(M);
```

as well as

```
... ⊢ L.screen,L.compact,L.extended;
```

There are other interesting possibilities for building output concepts.

Let us consider one of them. Our objective will be to display graphically the results of designing shafts, i.e. to draw a shaft initially represented parametrically.

A shaft can be represented as a tuple of necks (cylindric or conic surfaces) which can have individual features such as keys and grooves. Its specification in UTOPIST looks like

> *shaft*:
>   (*S1*: *neck L* = ..., *d* = ...,...;
>   *S2*: *neck L* = ..., *d* = ...;
>
>   ...
>   );

Each step has geometric characteristics – length L, diameter d and perhaps some others. The same applies to keys, grooves etc. These geometric characteristics contain sufficient information to put together a drawing of the shaft. But this information is scattered all over the specification of the shaft and the problem is how to collect it and give it as an input to a program for drawing shafts. We can do this by using name patterns **all**.L and **all**.d which collect together all lengths and diameters. But we apply a slightly more general technique – we introduce a high-level graphic description directly into every part of the specification of a shaft if the part is to be displayed in a drawing. Let us agree to call these objects *draw* and bind their parameters with the parameters of a shaft so that they can be evaluated automatically. For example, the concept of neck can be specified as follows:

> *neck*:
>   (*L*,*d*: **numeric**;
>   *t*: *moment*
>
>   ...
>   *draw*: (*type*: **text**;
>   *type* = '*neck*';
>   *L*,*d*: **numeric**;
>   *draw*.L = L;
>   *draw*.d = d;);

Now we can specify an output concept drawshaft as follows:

> *drawshaft*:
>   (*shaft*: **undefined**;
>   *param*: **space**;
>   *result*: **boolean**;
>   *constr*: *shaft*.**all**.*draw* → *param*(C);
>   *draw*: *param* → *result* (DRAWSHAFT););

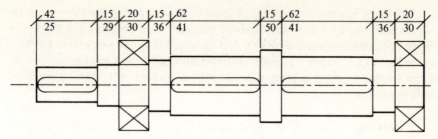

Figure 5.1   An automatically designed shaft.

and use it for drawing shafts:

> **program** *shafts*;
>   **let** *S*: *shaft*;

> * shaft must have descriptions of drawings of
> * its components, and the components must be
> * specified in the order which corresponds to
> * the order of necks of the shaft from left to right.

>   . . .
>   *out*: *drawshaft S*;
>   **actions**
>   *shafts* ⊢ *out.result*;
>   **end**;

Figure 5.1 shows us an example of a shaft constructed automatically and drawn in this way on a screen.

5.2 Programmer's data types

UTOPIST contains only primitive data types. The types needed for a system programmer – stack, queue, reference, table etc. – are absent. Even arrays are absent in pure UTOPIST. But all these data types can be easily added as extensions of the language. Naturally, the efficiency of implementation of arrays as extensions is less than that of their direct implementation. But knowing that the bulk of computations can be always programmed in programs which represent relations, we shall achieve good performance even in computations with arrays.

5.2.1 STACK AND QUEUE

Stack and queue are the data types whose specifications seem to be obligatory to demonstrate the full potential of a new language. We have mentioned these data types in Sections 2.1.3 and 3.5.4. Here we give their full specifications.

A stack is a store of objects of some kind, into which the objects can be pushed and out of which they can be popped. The objects of a stack are popped out in the reverse order to that in which they are put in (i.e. LIFO – last in first out strategy – is used). We specify a stack as a generic data type. When a concrete stack is used, then the type of its elements must be specified explicitly.

> **let** *stack*:
>   (*state*: **space**;
>   **virtual**
>   *element*: **undefined**;
>   *create*: → *state* (ST1);
>   *push*: *element, state* → *state* (ST2);
>   *pop*: *state* → *element, state* (ST3););

The only nonvirtual component of a stack is *stack.state*, which contains all objects put into the stack. A specification

> *N*: **numeric**;
> *M*: *stack element* = *N*;

gives us a particular stack called *M* with elements of type **numeric**. Its current element can be called *M.element* as well as *N*.

Relations of the stack are used in **apply** statements. The first executable statement for the stack must be

> **apply***M.create*;

This initializes pointers.

The statement

> **apply***M.push*(*x*);

checks whether there is memory space available for a new object *x*, and writes the object into the stack if the space is available. *M.state* is changed so that it will point again to the free memory.

The statement

> **apply***M.pop*(*x*);

assigns the last object written into the stack *M* to *x*. Memory is freed and pointers are corrected.

In another version of stack the memory size is specified explicitly. This

stack is represented by the following macro definition:

```
    macro
&P1: &stack& of &P2 size &P3;
    mbegin
&P1:
        (state: space;
        virtual
        element: &P2;
        size: numeric;
        size = &P3;
        create: size → state (ST4));
        push: element, state → state (ST5);
        pop: state → element, state (ST6););
    mend;
```

Parameter *&P2* is to represent the type of elements of the stack and parameter *&P3* is to represent the amount of memory needed for the stack. Now we can specify concrete stacks for elements of primitive type directly:

M1: *stack of* **numeric** *size 55;*

Using this macro we can specify any type of elements directly in a stack specification as shown in the following specification of the stack of triplets of complex numbers:

M2: *stack of* (1 .. 3: (*re,im*: **numeric**;);) *size 500;*

Using the second version of stack we can postpone the specification of memory size until we create a stack:

let *M3*: *stack of* (*name*: **text**; *age*: **numeric**);
actions apply *M3.create* (400);

A data type *queue* is a collection of objects of some type from where the objects can be taken away in the same order as they were inserted. (It uses FIFO – first in first out – strategy.)

The specification of a queue is quite similar to the specification of a stack – the differences are hidden in the programs Q1, Q2, Q3 which represent the relations:

let *queue*:
    (*state*: **space**;
    virtual
    element: **undefined**;

$create: \rightarrow state$ (Q1);
$put: element, state \rightarrow state$ (Q2);
$take: state \rightarrow element, state$ (Q3););

Note   In specifications of *queue* and *stack* the component *state* can be defined not as **space** but more precisely – for instance, in the following way:

state:
 (*from*: **numeric**;
  free: **numeric**;
  to: **numeric**;);

where *from* and *to* are the first and the last addresses of memory for a stack (or a queue) and *free* is the address of the first free location. But to do so would be a deplorable decision, because the usage of the components of state is an internal affair of programs ST1,ST2,...,ST6,Q1,Q2,Q3 which realize the relations of stack and queue. The data type **space** is exactly suitable for encapsulating data and protecting them from incorrect access, because data of this type can be accessed only from preprogrammed realizations of relations.

5.2.2 ARRAYS

We define *array* as an abstract data type with operations *create*, *write*, *read*.

array:
 (*value*: **space**;
  virtual
  element: **undefined**;
  length: **numeric**;
  index: **numeric**
   create: *length*, *element* $\rightarrow$ *value* (M1);
   read: *index*, *value* $\rightarrow$ *element* (M2);
   write: *index*, *element*, *value* $\rightarrow$ *value* (M3););

In the statement

   apply *array. create* (*n*);

n is the number of elements of the array. The program M1 uses besides the number of elements also another input parameter – the element of the array. *Element* is used only for finding the amount of memory required for an element. This can be found by means of the function *type*(*x*) mentioned in Section 5.1.2.

Arrays of higher dimensions are specified analogously. The specification of a two-dimensional array goes as follows:

```
array2: (
   (value: space;
   virtual
   element: undefined;
      I1,I2: numeric;
```

* *I1,I2* are indexes.

```
   length1, length2: numeric;
   create: length1,length2,element → value (M4);
   read: I1,I2, value → element (M5);
   write: I1,I2, element, value → value (M6););
```

Arrays of this type can be accessed in UTOPIST programs by means of functions *read* and *write*. But the main purpose of these arrays is using them as parameters of programs which represent relations. If an array *M* is the output of a relation, then this array need not be created by means of the statement

apply *M.create*( );

because the array is created in a program of the relation. Moreover, even the size of the array can be left open in the specification part of the UTOPIST program.

For example:

```
program arrays;
let x,y,z: numeric;
   M: array element = x;
          → M (Q11);
      M → y (Q21);
actions
   arrays⊢ y;
   z := fun M.read (1);
   PRINT(y, z);
end;
```

According to this specification the program Q11 creates an array *M* and the program Q21 uses it to compute *y*. In the action part, the first element of *M* is assigned to *z*.

There are also other possibilities for defining multidimensional arrays. For instance:

```
array_two: array element = array;
```

Arrays of this type can be used in specifications like

> *compl*: (...);
> *MM*: *array_two element.element* = *compl*

or

> *MATRIX*: (...);
> *MMM*: *array_two element.element* = *MATRIX*,
>   *element.length* = 15
>   *length* = 10;

These examples demonstrate that the first specification of an array is general enough for creating multidimensional arrays. However, to improve performance it may be reasonable to use *array2*, where special programs M4, M5, M6 can be used more efficiently than the general-purpose programs M1, M2, M3.

5.2.3 FILES

We consider here sequential files. A file is a collection of data items processed sequentially. We distinguish input files for reading data from, output files for writing data into and input–output files for combining the two operations.

> *input_file*:
>   (*FCB*: **space**;
>
> * *FCB* is a file control block that contains all the
> * essential data about the file.
>
>   **virtual**
>   *element*: **undefined**;
>   *name*: **text**;
>   *pointer*: **numeric**;
>   *name* → *FCB* (FD);
>
> * the program FD supports an interface
> * with the file system of the computational environment.
> * It allows us to use arbitrary names for identifying files.
>
>   *EOF*: **boolean**;
>
> * *EOF* – end of file.
>
>   *open*: *FCB* → *element*, *FCB*, *pointer*, *EOF* (F1);
>
> * the program F1 opens a file and reads the
> * first element from it.

get: *FCB*, *pointer* → *element*, *EOF*, *pointer* (F2);

∗ the program F2 gets the next element of a file.

next: *FCB*, *pointer* → *EOF*, *pointer* (F3);

∗ the program F3 moves the pointer to the next element and does not
∗ change the current element.

close: *FCB* → *FCB* (F4);

∗ the program F4 closes the file and does not influence the current
∗ element.

);

In every program F1,F2, F3,F4, end of file (*EOF*) takes the value **true** if the pointer is pointing at the last element of file, and **false** otherwise.

We specify an output file without comment, because its specification is quite similar to that of the input file.

output_file:
   (*FCB*: **space**;
   virtual
   name: **text**;
   element: **undefined**;
   pointer: **numeric**;
   name → *FCB* (F1D);
   open: *FCB* → *FCB*, *pointer* (F11);
   put: *element*, *FCB*, *pointer* → *pointer* (F12);
   close: *FCB* → *FCB* (F13););

It is possible to specify a different concept of file where an operation *next* is performed in such a way that the current element is stored in the current place in the file and the next element is selected and read. As before, *EOF* signals the end of a file, but it is allowed to use the relation *next* and to write new elements even if *EOF* is **true** – then the file becomes longer. One more difference is that the pointer is not specified explicitly, but is included into *FCB*. This is a good decision, because now the pointer cannot be accessed wrongly.

file:
   (*FCB*: **space**;
   virtual
   element: **undefined**;
   name: **text**;
   EOF: **boolean**;
   name → *FCB* (F2D);

> open: *FCB* → *element, EOF,FCB* (F21);
> next: *element, FCB* → *element, FCB,EOF* (F31);
> close: *FCB* → *FCB* (F41););

As an example, we present a program for copying into file F2 elements of file F1 that satisfy a given condition.

```
program files;
  let
      record1, record2:
        (name: text;
         data: space);
      F1: file element = record1,
         name = 'people';
      F2: file element = record2,
         name = 'Smiths';
  actions
      apply F1.open;
      apply F2.open;
      while not F1.EOF
        do
        (if record1.name = 'Smith'
         then
            record2: = record1;
            apply F2.next;fi;);
         apply F1.next;);
         od;
      end;
```

5.2.4 SCALAR TYPES

UTOPIST contains no types other than boolean with finite domain. But such types are very useful for some applications. We present here a macro definition of a generic scalar type. This type can be used to specify concrete scalar types.

```
    macro
  &L: &scalar& &N values = (&P);
    mbegin
  &L:
      (values: (1 .. &N: text);
       number: numeric;
       value: text;
       is: boolean;
       values = (&P);
```

> *is: value,values* → *is*(SC1);
> *value: number, values* → *value* (SC2);
> *number: value, values* → *number*(SC3););

The program SC1 tests if a given value belongs to the scalar type. The programs SC2 and SC3 represent a one-to-one mapping between the values of the scalar type and their numbers.

5.2.5 REFERENCES

Reference is a programmer's data type whose reckless use can cause a lot of trouble. Nevertheless, references are extremely useful for handling dynamic data structures some of whose elements are generated during computation. If such an element has a name then its address can be computed from this name. But it can happen that an element of a data structure does not have a name. Then the only way to gain access to the element is to give its address. This is expressed by the following specification:

> *reference*:
> (*address*:
>   (*loc, length*: **numeric**;);
>   **virtual**
>   *name*: **text**;
>   *value*: **undefined**;
>   *name* → *address* (R1);
>   *read*: *address* → *value* (R2);
>   *write*: *address, value* → (R3););

5.3 System design

Let us stop discussing technical tricks now and move on to the general style of knowledge-based programming with a consideration of system architecture. A problem-oriented system can be built in either a top-down or a bottom-up style. Both ways are applicable in conceptual programming. In the first case, the highest priority is given to system design and overall architecture, and the details of implementation are handled in later stages of the project. The second approach is suitable for building a system on a good basis with all details specified systematically.

It is reasonable to start building a completely new system in a top-down way, starting the design from an overall shape of the system. Conceptual programming can be used for representing very general specifications and it enables a designer to begin using a computer at an early stage of a system design.

UTOPIST can be used in top-down design in the following way. The first

version of a system can be sketched very briefly:

> **let** *version1*: (...);

then it can be extended as soon as it is needed:

> **let** *version 2*: (**copy** *version1*;...);

And this process can be repeated. Besides this, any component of the system can initially be specified as **undefined**. In this way an overall structure of the system is represented without detailed specifications of its components:

> *system*:
>   (*subsystem1*: **undefined**;
>   *subsystem2*: **undefined**;
>   ...
>   );

Thus the components of subsystems of undefined type can be used in relations – for example, one can add the following relation into the specification given above:

> *subsystem1.output* = *subsystem2.input*;

The fact that knowledge about a project is already handled automatically by the computer at early stages of the project cannot be overestimated. A computer is used from the start to check the formal correctness of specifications, and the structure of a system is checked and tested in various ways. However, in this section we shall not repeat the facilities given by UTOPIST, but concentrate on an example of the top-down design of an expert system. The concept of an expert system is used here in a wide sense – as a knowledge-based problem solver for a well-defined problem domain. Briefly, we can divide an expert system into three functional parts:

1. kernel – a 'clever program' that contains know-how for using knowledge for problem solving;
2. knowledge base – a container of knowledge;
3. a support system for maintaining the knowledge base and performing various routine tasks connected with problem solving.

The kernel of the expert systems considered here is constituted by the PRIZ system that works with specifications given in UTOPIST. Also the support systems are taken from PRIZ. The knowledge base is formed from the computational frames of concepts specified in UTOPIST, and from programs of the relations specified in the frames. We can look at separate programs as at

small pieces of procedural knowledge. Then the computational frames are larger building blocks. An expert system built in UTOPIST can be looked at as a functional knowledge module of considerable size which can be used in combinations with other expert systems for solving large problems. PRIZ supports compatibility of expert systems built in UTOPIST on the physical and system level. We have only to take care of data compatibility and functional compatibility, and even here we can count on some support by the automatic program synthesizer. For example, let us recall how physical entities measured in various units were made compatible by specifying relations for automatic transformation of units ($length.[cm] = 100 * length.[m]$etc.).

5.3.1 ANALYSIS OF A PROBLEM DOMAIN

The top-down design proceeds according to the following scheme:

problem domain $\rightarrow$ language $\rightarrow$ specifications $\rightarrow$ programs.

We start analysing a problem domain from the classification of problems to be solved. As an example, we take the problems concerning the analysis of electric circuits. We restrict the class of circuits to circuits without distributed parameters and reactive elements. The problems are the calculation of stationary processes – finding the parameters of circuits which give the processes needed – and also mixed calculations concerning parameters of processes and circuits.

Simply speaking, we shall consider electric circuits built of resistors, diodes, sources of voltage and current, etc. The processes in these schemes are described by Ohm's and Kirchhoff's laws. All parameters can be represented as numeric values. The simplest technique for calculating these schemes is taught in physics textbooks. This is a technique for analysing circuits of a restricted class – schemes built as series or parallel connection of elements and fragments of schemes. We shall call them parallel–series circuits. There are also general methods of analysis applicable for any electric circuit.

Performing the analysis of the problem domain, we should like to get the following results:

1. All problems constitute a well-defined set.

2. A probability distribution is defined on the set of problems, specifying for each problem the probability that the need to solve that problem will arise.

3. A function is defined which for any subset of the set of problems gives the cost of implementation of automatic problem-solving facilities for this subset of problems.

4. Some measure of usefulness of solving various problems would also be beneficial. We should like to have this measure also as a function of subsets of the set of problems.

Table 5.1   Classification of electrical circuits.

	Class of schemas			
	General	Planar	Series–parallel and bridges	Series–parallel
Frequency of occurrence	0.05	0.15	0.2	0.6
Implementation costs	6	6	1.5	1

Having this information, we could try to select an optimal set of problems which can be solved by the system designed. Unfortunately, such accurate information can never be obtained. Therefore, we try to construct an approximation of the problem domain by representing it as a set consisting of a small number of classes of problems. We find estimates for the implementation costs, usefulness and frequency of occurrence of the problems of any class. In our example we divide problems into the following classes:

- series–parallel circuits;
- series–parallel circuits and bridges;
- planar circuits;
- general circuits.

These classes of problems are included in each other as follows:

general $\supset$ planar $\supset$ bridge & series–parallel $\supset$ series–parallel.

The expert assessments by users of non-electrical specialities for these classes are represented in Table 5.1. The table shows that using only 25% of implementation costs of the general case we can solve 80% of problems. Using only 17% of costs allows us to solve as much as 60% of problems. The conclusion is that we can start building an expert system with limited resources provided it can be extended later.

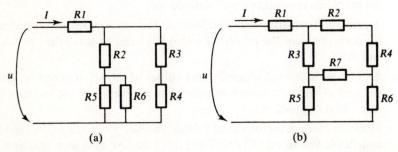

(a)   (b)

Figure 5.2   Electric circuits for analysis.

We complete our analysis of the problem domain by presenting examples of problems which must be solvable by the first version of the expert system. Figure 5.2 shows us series–parallel (5.2(a)) and bridge (5.2(b)) circuits. Besides the current I and voltage U of the whole circuit also currents $I1, I2,\ldots$ and voltages $U1, U2,\ldots$ of their branches can be used in calculations.

5.3.2 SELECTING BASIC CONCEPTS

Designing a language for specifying problems is essentially a process of selecting useful concepts. This can be done only by people who know the problem domain. In general, we do not possess the methods for formalization of this process. Fortunately, in our particular case, the circuits we are considering are quite simple, and we can easily act as specialists.

In our example we have to introduce concepts for specifying components of electrical circuits. Let us select the following components: a resistor, a source of voltage, a source of current. In the development process of the expert system we can extend this set of components. Let us note that all elements and fragments of circuits we are going to build will be ports which can be externally described by voltage, current and resistance (Figure 5.3(a)).

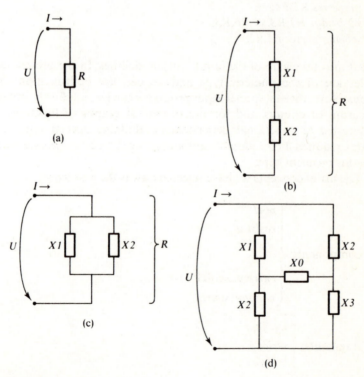

Figure 5.3   The basic parts of circuits.

We therefore also introduce the concept of a port. Remembering what we have been taught at school about electrical circuits, we can introduce concepts of series and parallel connection of ports (Figures 5.3(b, c)).

Now we have concepts for the primitive components of circuits as well as for combining components into more complicated schemes. Let us try to specify the circuit shown in Figure 5.1(a) using the concepts of port, series and parallel connection. At this stage we can ignore details of the specification, and write

> *R1,R2,R3,R4,R5,R6: port;*
> *x1: parallel R5, R6;*
> *x2: series R2,x2;*
> *x3: series R3, R4;*
> *x4: parallel x2,x3;*
> *schema: series R1,x4;*

Now we can extend the set of concepts adding there a concept for a bridge (Figure 5.3(d)). The specification of the circuit shown in Figure 5.2(b) will contain a bridge:

> *R1,R2,R3,R4,R5,R6,R7: port;*
> *x1: series R2,R4;*
> *x2: bridge R7,R3,x1,R6,R5;*
> *schema: series R1,x2;*

We must also take care of the input–output facilities. In the present case all variables are of the numeric type and we can use built-in input–output functions. Nevertheless, special input programs can be built for the interactive specification of circuits and for the output of graphs of functions, if we are interested in functional dependencies. Building special input–output programs requires a considerable amount of work to be done, and we won't discuss this problem here.

The list of concepts we have selected now is the following:

$$\text{components:} \begin{cases} port \\ resistor \\ \\ current\_source \\ voltage\_source \end{cases}$$

$$\text{fragments:} \begin{cases} parallel \\ series \\ bridge \end{cases}$$

input–output: standard facilities.

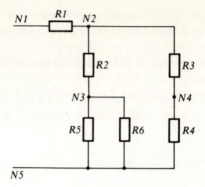

Figure 5.4   Another representation of an electric circuit.

This is not the only possible set of concepts for representing circuits. Existing programs for circuit analysis often use another formalism where the primitive concepts are nodes and components. To encode a circuit, for example, the circuit represented in Figure 5.2(a) we have to assign a symbol to every node of the circuit. The new schema is represented in Figure 5.4. Its specification in the new formalism is

N1,N2,N3,N4,N5: node;
R1: resistor N1,N2;
R2: resistor N2,N3;
R3: resistor N2,N4;
R4: resistor N4,N5;
R5: resistor N3,N5;
N6: resistor N3, N5;

This specification can be translated into a set of equations which must be solved by some numeric method.

As we have decided to implement our expert system as simply as possible, we choose the first way of presenting circuits, because

1.   it is better suited to the direct usage of UTOPIST;

2.   it does not need special software to solve systems of equations;

3.   it can be easily used for nonlinear components of circuits (the same is not true for the second form of presentation).

5.3.3 SPECIFYING CONCEPTS

Some preliminary work for specifying concepts has been done already – we have chosen concepts and have decided how to use them to represent the topology of schemas. Now we must develop detailed specifications of the concepts. In practice, these specifications of concepts are developed gradually, most of the specifications being rewritten several times with modifications.

We present here the final versions of the specifications, supplied with comments. Some general considerations for developing the specifications are:

- analogous components of different concepts must be denoted by the same names;
- the external view of similar concepts must be as uniform as possible – for instance, sets of analogous components must appear in the same order.

In our case we use the following notation:

I – current,
U – voltage,
R – resistance,
G – conductivity.

The knowledge base of our expert system is called *CIRCUITS*.

let *CIRCUITS*: (

* components of circuits are: *port, resistor, current_source,*
* *voltage_source.*

port:
   $(I,U,R,G$: **numeric**;
   if $R \neq 0$ **then** $R * G = 1$
   if $G * R \neq 0$ **then** $R * G = 1$;);
resistor:
   (**copy** *port*;
       $U = I * R$;);
current_source:
   (**copy** *port*;
       $U = 0$;
       $G = 0$;);
voltage_source:
   (**copy** *port*;
       $I = 0$;
       $R = 0$;);

* fragments of circuits are: parallel and series connection of branches
* which are denoted by $X1$ and $X2$.

parallel:
   $(X1, X2$: **undefined**;
      copy *port*;
      $U = X1.U$;
      $U = X2.U$;

$$I = X1.I + X2.I;$$
$$G = X1.G + X2.G;$$
$$1/R = 1/X1.R + 1/X2.R;);$$

series:
   $(X1,X2$: **undefined**;
    copy *port*;
     $I = X1.I;$
     $I = X2.I;$
     $U = X1.U + X2.U;$
     $R = X1.R + X2.R;$
     $1/G = 1/X1.G + 1/X2.G;);$

* the bridge contains branches $X0,X1,X2,X3,X4$.
* $X0$ is the diagonal of the bridge, $X1$ and $X3$ have no common nodes.

bridge:
   $(X0,X1,X2,X3,X4$: **undefined**;
    copy *port*;
  rank12 $X0.I,X0.U,X0.R,$
        $X1.I,X1.U,X1.R,$
        $X2.I,X2.U,X2.R,$
        $X3.I,X3.U,X3.R,$
        $X4.I,X4.U,X4.R,$
        I,U,R (BRIDGE););

The last relation is represented by a program called **BRIDGE**. This program must use a system function *out(x)* for determining for each of its parameters x whether x is an input or output variable for a particular application of the relation.

The semantics of the expert-system language can be tested before any program is actually written. This is done by specifying various problems and testing their solvability by using the program synthesizer. We give here complete specifications of the example problems of the circuits shown in Figure 5.2.

  program *schema1*;
   let $R1,R2,R3,R4,R5,R6$: *resistor*;
    $X1$: *parallel* $R5,R6$;
    $X2$: *series* $R2,X1$;
    $X3$: *series* $R3,R4$;
    $X4$: *parallel* $X2,X3$;
    sch: *series* $R1,X4$;
  actions
   $sch \vdash R1.R,R2.R,R3.R,R4.R,R5.R,R6.R,U \rightarrow I;$

* many other problems can be tested for the same schema. For
* example:

$$sch \vdash R1.I,R1.R,R2.R,R3.R,R4.R,R5.R,R6.R \rightarrow I,U;$$
end;
program *schema2*;
   let *R1,R2,R3,R4,R5,R6,R7: resistor R* = 1;
     X1: series R2,R4;
     X2: bridge R7,R3,X1,R6,R5;
     sch: series R1,X2;
   actions
     $schema2 \vdash U \rightarrow I;$
   end;

In the first program we used only *sch* to represent problem conditions in problem statements, but in the second program we use the specification part of the whole program *schema2*. This is more reliable, but loads the synthesizer more heavily, because the problem model is larger.

5.3.4 THE PROGRAMMING OF RELATIONS

All programs that are referred to in the specifications of concepts must, finally, be programmed. In our expert system we have only one such program, BRIDGE, which realizes all computations for bridge-structured fragments of schemas. The programming of relations is a conventional programming task which we are not going to discuss in detail here. It can be performed using any well-known programming technology. It is facilitated by the information present in specifications of concepts. From a programmer's point of view these specifications can be considered as assembly schemes of some kind which show us how to use separately programmed modules properly.

5.4 Bottom-up specification of a problem domain

In the last section of this chapter we present a systematic bottom-up specification of a knowledge base for the analysis of linear alternating electric current circuits. The problem domain of alternating current circuits differs from that of direct current circuits only in one detail – the values of electric parameters are complex numbers instead of real numbers. Fortunately, we can now use the experience obtained in constructing a program package for the analysis of direct current circuits. We shall use the knowledge base *CIRCUITS* as a prototype. Because of this, we need not be concerned with the general structure of the problem-oriented language and we can concentrate on the semantics of concepts, which is more complicated in the case of alternating current.

A bottom-up specification of a problem domain is usually the result of some longer specification development process which can be carried out as discussed in Section 5.3.2. But, once written, it can be read and understood easily.

To understand this specification, we must bear in mind that it contains an essential part of electrotechniques – physical laws for alternating current circuits which bind frequency, capacity, inductivity and active resistance of parts of circuits with amplitudes and phases of current and voltage in every branch of a circuit.

Now we will define all concepts one by one with brief comments.

cmpl:
  (*re, im*: **numeric**;
  virtual
  mod, arg: **numeric**;
  re, im $\rightarrow$ *mod, arg* (C1);
  mod, arg $\rightarrow$ *re, im* (C2););

This is a concept of complex number containing components for the real and imaginary parts and virtual components for the modulus and argument. The relations

$$re \wedge 2 + im \wedge 2 = mod \wedge 2$$
$$\cos(arg) = re/mod$$

are replaced by preprogrammed relations which are more reliable and can also be used when the equations are not applicable – for instance, when

$$re = 0, \cos(arg) = 0.$$

The following concept represents Ohm's law for alternating current:

Ohm:
  (*i,u,Z:cmpl*;
  u.mod = i.mod $*$ *Z.mod*;
  u.arg = i.arg + Z.arg;);

Series connection of branches *x1* and *x2* gives us:

ser:
  (**copy** *Ohm*;
  virtual
  x1,x2: Ohm;
  Z.re = x1.Z.re + x2.Z.re;
  Z.im = x1.Z.im + x2.Z.im;
  u.re = x1.u.re + x2.u.re;
  u.im = x1.u.im + x2.u.im;
  i = x1.i;
  i = x2.i;);

While parallel connection of branches *x1* and *x2* gives us:

> *par*:
>> (**copy** *Ohm*;
>>> **virtual**
>>> *x1,x2*: *Ohm*;
>>> *g,g1,g2*: *compl*;

$*$ *g,g1* and *g2* are the conductivities of the parallel connection and its
$*$ branches. They are bound with impedances by the following relations:

$g.mod * Z.mod = 1;$
$g.arg + Z.arg = 0;$
$g1.mod * x1.Z.mod = 1;$
$g1.arg + x1.Z.arg = 0;$
$g2.mod * x2.Z.mod = 1;$
$g2.arg + x2.Z.arg = 0;$

$*$ basic relations of parallel connection are the following:

$g.re = g1.re + g2.re;$
$g.im = g1.im + g2.im;$
$u = x1.u;$
$u = x2.u;$
$i.re = x1.i.re + x2.i.re;$
$i.im = x1.i.im + x2.i.im;);$

The components of circuits are *inductor, capacitor* and *resistor*. They are
specified as follows:

> *ind*:
>> (**copy** *Ohm*;
>>> **virtual**
>>> *f* : **numeric**;
>>> *L*: **numeric**;
>>> $re = 0;$
>>> $im = 6.28 * f * L;);$
>
> *cap*:
>> (**copy** Ohm;
>>> **virtual**
>>> *f* : **numeric**;
>>> *c*: **numeric**;
>>> $re = 0;$
>>> $im = - f * c/6.28;);$
>
> *res*:
>> (**copy** *Ohm*;
>>> **virtual**
>>> *r*: **numeric**;

$$re = r;$$
$$im = 0;);$$

Let us specify an example. The circuit we are interested in is the oscillator shown in Figure 5.5.

let f: **numeric**;
 R: *res* $r = 10$;
 L: *ind* $L = 303$, $f = f$;
 C: *cap* $c = 0.00001$, $f = f$;
 $X4$: *ser* $x1 = R$, $x2 = L$;
 sch: *par* $x1 = X4$, $x2 = C$;
 sch.u.re $= 100$;
 sch.u.im $= 0$;
 A: $f = 100$;
actions
 oscillator $\vdash$ *sch.i.mod*;

* let us also compute impedance – frequency characteristics
* for the oscillator:

delete A;
actions
 $f = 8.5$;
 while $f < 10$ **do**
  (*oscillator* $\vdash f \rightarrow$ *sch.Z.mod*;
  print (f,*sch.Z.mod*);
  $f := F + 0.125$;);
   od;
end;

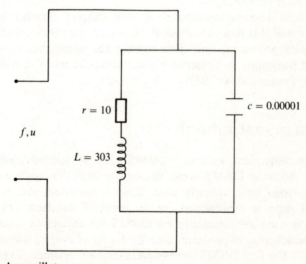

Figure 5.5 An oscillator.

Chapter 6
Applications

In this chapter we consider applications of knowledge-based programming for building software systems in various problem domains where real applications of knowledge-based programming are known to us, and we give references to papers where these applications are described in more detail.

Concepts for data management are introduced in the first section. A database management system DABU has been built as an extension of the PRIZ system (Kalja, 1982) using these concepts.

The second section is dedicated to simulation problems. There are several simulation packages developed on the basis of conceptual programming, the largest of them being a system for modelling the dynamics of hydraulic systems (Pahapill, 1985). The concepts of process and feedback are essentially used in this package.

Stochastic modelling and optimization problems are being solved by means of conceptual programming in the domain of power semiconductor design (Tyugu *et al.*, 1982).

The last domain considered in this chapter belongs to compiler construction and it is more theoretical. However, the results obtained in this field are quite promising and demonstrate the applicability of structural synthesis of programs in constructing the semantic parts of compilers and interpreters (Penjam, 1980, 1983).

6.1 Data management

Database management systems (DBMS) are of special interest to AI researchers, because DBMS were the first practically applicable systems where knowledge was explicitly used. Knowledge about the structure and meaning of data is represented in the form of database schemas. This knowledge is used automatically by DBMS for answering queries, i.e. for planning the solution of problems like 'find a set of objects which satisfy the condition...'. The first DBMS were implementation oriented. They were built

196

bearing in mind physical data structures and physical access to data. But the situation has changed, and now there are several layers of data models used in a DBMS. User views of data and conceptual schemas can be quite independent of physical implementation. In fact, they are semantic models of the domain described by the data in a database.

It has become clear that data contained in a database must be accessible from various systems. This raises the problem of integration of databases with various schemas. Borders between databases and intelligent software packages are diminishing. A package must have good access to data, and sometimes it must also maintain large amounts of data belonging to the problem domain. Hence, an intelligent software package must also perform data management functions.

In the present section we introduce and specify in UTOPIST data management concepts that constitute the basis of the data management system DABU. We also sketch the possibilities of integration of databases with various data models (hierarchical, network and relational models) using computational models to represent data schemas on a conceptual level.

6.1.1 DATABASE MANAGEMENT SYSTEMS

Section 6.1 can be considered as one more example of building an intelligent software package – a package for the data management domain. In this context, the present section is a very brief analysis of the problem domain and of the class of problems to be solved.

A database management system is a set of programs intended for data management, i.e. for creating databases (DB), manipulating data and answering queries to the DB. A DBMS uses knowledge about data for data management. This knowledge is represented in the form of a database schema which is, in some sense, a semantic model of the domain covered by the data, as well as a description of the form in which the data is stored in the database.

A DBMS is applied according to the following schemas. First, knowledge about data, i.e. the database schema, is specified. At a later stage, using the database schema, a DBMS can perform the following functions:

- loading a DB (i.e. data input);
- answering queries (i.e. problem solving);
- manipulating data and housekeeping.

According to functions performed by a DBMS its language is divided into several sublanguages:

- data definition language (DDL);
- query language (QL);
- data manipulation language (DML).

Also the data representation language (or data language – DL) can be regarded as an independent sublanguage of a DBMS.

The principal problem that must be solved when a DB is being built is how to combine the efficient processing of a large amount of data with the flexibility of query language. If we do not require efficiency of data processing, i.e if we ignore the processing time and memory requirements, then the problem of data management can be solved easily – any knowledge representation system could be used as a database management system.

In a real database, data items are grouped into sets. These sets are represented in a computer in the form of logical data sets (files etc.) which have a definite internal structure. This structure is needed for a small number of low-level data handling programs. The internal structure of logical data sets restricts access to data, allowing us to perform some data manipulation tasks efficiently and making a number of other tasks extremely inefficient. For example, the average time for finding an element in data sets of various structures may vary by a factor of hundreds or thousands. (Compare selecting an element by key in a hashed file and in a file ordered by another key.) Therefore, efficient computability is an essential concept applied in data management, and this is a proper case for applying ideas of the structural synthesis.

We are going to solve the problem of data management in the following way. We build a DBMS as a collection of concepts specified in UTOPIST. We assume that a small number of low-level programs exist for manipulating sets of objects. These programs will be used for representing relations which are contained in concepts of the DBMS.

6.1.2 SETS AND SUBSETS

Let us define the concept of *set* with the following features:

1. Any set can be handled as an integral object. Its value is represented by the component *value* of the set concept.

2. A set can consist of elements of any type. The component *element* of the set concept is of the type **undefined**. When a particular set is specified, the type of its components must be determined precisely.

3. If a set is non-empty, then it is possible to select an element from the set. Selecting an element from the empty set gives the result **nil**.

4. Having selected some elements from the set, it is possible to select an element which is different from all selected elements, as soon as such an element exists. This property, together with property (3) enables us to select all elements of a finite set one by one.

5. Knowing a property which uniquely determines any element of a set, it is possible to represent the property as the *key* for selecting elements of the *set*.

The following specification represents the concept of set with the described features:

> **let** *set*:
>   (*value*: **space**;
>   **virtual**
>   *element*: **undefined**;
>   *key*: **text**;
>   *selector*: **numeric**;
>   *r1*: *value, selector* $\rightarrow$ *element* (M1);
>   *r2*: *value, key* $\rightarrow$ *element* (M2);
>   *r3*: $\rightarrow$ *value* (M3);
>   *r4*: *element, value* $\rightarrow$ *value* (M4););

The component *selector* is used for modelling properties (3) and (4) of the set concept. We assume that elements can be selected by their numbers $1, 2, \ldots,$. But this facility can be used only for sequential access to elements of a set, i.e. the numbers of elements must be given in the right order. The relation *r1* is for selecting elements of the set sequentially and the relation *r2* for selecting elements by key.

The relations *r3* and *r4* are added into the set concept for creating a new set and for adding elements into the set.

Examples of usage of the set are

> *points*: *set element* = *point*;
> *department*: *set element* = *employee*;
> *staff*: *set element* = *department*;

In this way we can define various finite sets, even sets of sets, but we cannot give a value to a set because *set.value* has the type **space**.

Let us say some words about the implementation of the set. The programs M1, M2, M3 and M4 depend on the data representation. Actually, these are the only programs which depend on it. All the other programs can use the relations *r1, r2, r3, r4* to build sets and to retrieve elements from the sets.

An important concept for handling sets is the concept of subset. It represents the relation

$$B = \{x \mid x \in A \ \& \ p(x)\}$$

between two sets A and B. The relation is specified by a predicate p which must be a computable predicate. Specification of the subset is as follows:

> **let** *subset*:
>   (**virtual**
>   *of, is*: *set*;
>   *cond*: **boolean**;

$$r: (of .selector \rightarrow is.element, cond),$$
$$of .value \rightarrow is.value \ (M5););$$

This concept has only virtual components, because it represents a relation between the sets A and B that are represented here by virtual components *of* and *is* respectively. The predicate p is represented as a program for computing *cond* in the subproblem

$$of .selector \rightarrow is.element, cond.$$

Some examples are:

$Q: (people,children: set element = person;$
$R: subset of = people, is = children;$
$R.cond = children. element.age < 16;);$

This specification of Q is sufficient to solve the following problem:

$$Q \vdash people.value \rightarrow children.value;$$

If the sets bound by a subset relation are specified independently by separate specifications, then it is necessary to show a way for computing elements of the subset. Often, it can be done by specifying the equality between the elements of both sets:

$Q1: (a: (x,y:$ **numeric**$;);$
$\quad b: (u,r:$ **numeric**$;);$
$\quad A: set \ a;$
$\quad B: set \ b;$

* the equality needed for computations:

$\quad a = b;$

* specification of a condition:

$\quad p:$ **boolean**;
$\quad p = a.x < a.y;$

* and of the subset relation:

$\quad R: subset of = A, is = B, cond = p;);$

It is obvious that the problem

$$Q1 \vdash A.value \rightarrow B.value;$$

is solvable, but if we take away the equality $a = b$, then the problem cannot be solved.

Quite a number of problem specifications contain only a set and a subset specification. It is therefore useful to build a macro for representing such problem conditions:

> **macro**
> *&A is &subset& of &B with the condition &C*;
>   **mbegin**
> *&A: set element = &B.element*;
> *SUB&sysind: subset &B, &A*;
> *SUB&sysind.cond = &C*;
>   **mend**

Now, having an object

> *p*: (*x,y*: **numeric**;);

and a set

> *S*: *set p*;

we can immediately specify new sets which are subsets of the set *S* for instance:

> *S1 is the subset of S with the condition p.x* $\wedge$ *2 + p.y* $\wedge$ *2 < r* $\wedge$ *2*;

6.1.3 MANIPULATING SETS

It is natural to assume that, having two sets *A* and *B*, we can build a new set *C* using *A.value* and *B.value* as input for this operation. The usual operations of this kind are union, intersection, difference and direct product of sets. More complicated is the join operation of sets used in relational databases.

Before specifying these operations we must decide how to handle types of elements of sets. In particular, we shall be in trouble if we decide to make a union of sets which have elements of different types. To avoid this trouble we define the union of sets as a partial operation which is applicable only to sets with identical types of elements. We can even introduce a special program for checking types of elements. This program assigns **true** to the variable *typematch* if the types match and **false** if they do not. (This program can be easily built using the function *type* (*x*) described in Section 5.1.2.)

The union of sets is represented by the following concept:

> *union*:
>   (*result*: *set*;
>   **virtual**
>   *A,B*: *set*;
>   *typematch*: **boolean**;

r0: *A.element,B.element* → *typematch* (M6);
r: **if** *typematch* **then** *A.value, B.value* → *result.value* (M7););

The intersection and difference of sets have even simpler specifications:

intersection:
   (*result: set*;
   virtual
   A,B: *set*;
   r: *A.value, B.value* → *result.value* (M8););
difference:
   (*result: set*;
   virtual
   A,B: *set*;
   r: *A.value,B.value* → *result.value* (M9););

We could continue the list of such specifications, adding a new program for every new concept. These programs are independent from data representation because they use the relations *set.r1,set.r2,set.r3*, for handling values of sets. We also need two operations for binding sets with a file system (with computational environment):

take:
   (**virtual**
   set: *set*;
   from: **text**;
   r: *from* → *set* (M10););
keep:
   (**virtual**
   set: *set*;
   filename: **text**;
   result: **boolean**;
   r: *set, filename* → *result* (M11););

The concept *take* allows us to take the value of a set from a file whose name is given as a value of *take. from*. The concept *keep* is for storing the value of a set in a file. It assigns **true** to *keep.result* if the operation is completed successfully and **false** otherwise.

Even the few concepts introduced so far enable us to specify quite interesting problems. Let us assume, for instance, that we have a file of employees called EMPLFILE. Let us make a program for finding all employees who have salaries more than 200 and are aged less than 25.

program *DB1*;
   let *employee*: *person*;

```
        empls, wanted: set employee;
        X: take empls from = 'EMPLFILE';
        X1: subset empls,wanted;
        X1.cond = empls.element.salary > 200
            and empls.element.age < 25;
        X2: keep set = wanted, filename = 'PRINTOUT';
    actions
        DB1 ⊢ X2.result;
    end;
```

Assuming that the objects *employee, empls, wanted, X1* will be useful for various problems, we can specify a database schema that contains these objects:

```
    let database:
        (employee: person;
        employees, wanted: set employee;
        X: take employees from = 'EMPLFILE';
        X1: subset employees, wanted;);
    insert database;
```

Sometimes we want to specify conditions such as

'the set *S* contains an element with the property *p*'

or

'all elements of the set *S* have the property *p*'.

Quantifiers are needed to represent these statements, and we represent the restricted universal quantifier

$$\forall x(x \in S \ \& \ p(x))$$

and the restricted existence quantifier

$$\exists x(x \in S \ \& \ p(x))$$

by means of the following concepts (where *in* and *cond* represent *S* and *p* respectively):

```
    all:
        (result: boolean;
        virtual
        in: set;
```

    cond: **boolean**;
    r: (*in.selector* → *cond*), *in.value* → *result* (M12););
  exist:
    (*result*: **boolean**;
    virtual
    in: *set*;
    cond: **boolean**;
    r: (*in.selector* → *cond*), *in.value* → *result* (M13););

The value of the component *result* can be computed in these specifications as soon as *in.value* is known and value of the virtual component *cond* is computable for elements of the sets.

As an example of using of quantifiers, we specify the property 'to be an unmarried mother of small children.' For an adult with the specification

  adult:
    (**copy** *person*;
    married: **boolean**;
    children: *set person*;);

the property is the following:

  married ≡ **false** & *sex* ≡ *'female'* & *small_children*;

where

  small_children: *exist children, children.element.age* < 6;

Due to the fact that the concept *exist* contains only one nonvirtual component (*result*) we could use *small_children* instead of *small_children.result* in the expression above.

6.1.4 DEFINING VARIOUS DATA MODELS

By using the concept of set we can now represent basic concepts of three data models – relational, hierarchical and network models. First of all, notice that the set concept can be used directly to represent relationships in a relational model. Indeed, any flat table can be represented as a set of its rows. All operations of relational algebra can be specified in the way we have specified operations over sets. Finally, using the automatic synthesis of programs we can handle all queries to a database which are correct in the relational algebra. In fact, a database management system called DABU (Kalja, 1982) is built in exactly this way.

Let us consider a database of students, professors and courses as an

example:

> **(let** *DB2*: **(**
>
> ∗ the database contains objects
> ∗ of the following three types: *student, professor, course.*
>
>> *student*: (*number*: **text**;
>>   *address*: **text**;
>>   *rating*: **numeric**;));
>> *professor*: (*name*: **text**;
>>   *data*: **space**;));
>> *course*: (*name*: **text**;
>>   *data*: **space**;));
>
> ∗ the objects constitute the following sets:
>
>> *students*: set *student*;
>> *professors*: set *professor*;
>> *courses*: set *course*;
>
> ∗ they are bound by the relations
>
>> *course_taken*: (*who*: *student*;
>> *what*: *course*;);
>> *courses_taken*: set *course_taken*;
>> *delivered*: (*who*: *professor*;
>>   *what*: *course*;);
>> *courses_delivered*: set *course_delivered*;
>> *consultation*: (*who*: *professor*;
>>   *whom*: *student*;);
>> *consultations*: set *consultation*;));

This database schema can be slightly changed in order to economize on space in the database. The objects *course_delivered*, and *course_taken* need not contain *professor, course* and *student*. It is sufficient if they contain the keys of these objects:

> *course_taken*: (*who*: *student.number*;
>   *what*: *course.name*;);
> *course_delivered*: (*who*: *professor.name*;
>   *what*: *course.name*;);
> *consultation*: (*who*: *professor.name*;
>   *whom*: *student.number*;);

Another well-known data model is the network model. The basic concept of the network model is represented in Figure 6.1. This is a relation between

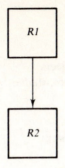

Figure 6.1   The set relation.

objects of two types: *R1*, called owners, and *R2*, called members. The relation itself is called *set*, and it is a one-to-many correspondence between the objects of type *R1* and the objects of type *R2*. It is applicable for finding an object of type *R1* for any given object of type *R2*, and for finding a set of objects of type *R2* for any object of type *R1*. These computational facilities are represented in the following specification:

> *codaset*:
>> (*value*: **space**;
>> **virtual**
>> *owner*, *member*: **undefined**;
>> *currentset*: *set*;
>> *r1*: *owner*, *value* → *currentset* (M14);
>> *r2*: *member*, *value* → *owner* (M15););

This concept is sufficient for specifying network data models. The example database of students, professors and courses has the network schema in Figure 6.2, and this schema has the following specification:

> *student*: (*number*: **text**;
>>   *address*: **text**;
>>   *rating*: **numeric**;);
> *professor*: (*name*: **text**;
>>   *data*: **space**;);
> *course*: (*name*: **text**;
>>   *data*: **space**;);
> *consultations*: *codaset owner = professor*,
>>   *member = student*;
> *courses_taken*: *codaset owner = student*,
>>   *member = course*;
> *courses_delivered*: *codaset owner = professor*,
>>   *member = course*;);

Naturally, this is a simplified representation of a network schema for the database. It does not contain attributes for data manipulation – for instance,

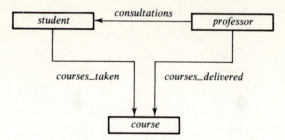

Figure 6.2   Network schema of a DB.

membership attributes etc. These features can be presented by additional components of the concept *codaset*.

The third well-known data model is a hierarchical data model where elements of sets can contain sets. In a pure hierarchical model the hierarchical set relation is the only type of relation. But actually hierarchical databases contain references, i.e. functional relations between arbitrary sets. All these relations are easily representable in our language, because our concept of set has elements of undefined type which can be specified again as sets. Here we present an example of a hierarchical schema of our database:

> **let**
>> *course*: (*name*: **text**;
>>> *data*: **space**;);
>> *professor*: (*name*: **text**;
>>> *data*: **space**;
>>> *courses_delivered*: *set course*;);
>> *student*: (*name*: **text**;
>>> *data*: **space**;
>>> *courses_taken*: *set course.name*;);
>> *DB*: (*professors*: *set professor*;
>>> *students*: *sets student*;);

Only the object *course* remains unchanged in this database compared to the relational and network databases. The object *professor* includes the set of the courses given by the professor. The object *student* includes only the set of names of the courses taken by the student. This avoids redundancy of data stored about courses. A schema of this database is represented graphically as a tree shown in Figure 6.3.

6.2 Simulation problems

6.2.1 REPRESENTING STRUCTURED SYSTEMS AND FEEDBACK

Many systems can be represented as collections of typical building blocks connected with each other in some way. It is convenient to represent the structure of such a system as a schema where each block is represented as a

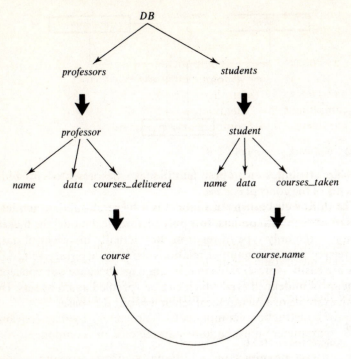

Figure 6.3   A hierarchical schema of a DB.

box and connections between the blocks are represented as lines connecting the boxes. There are many different graphical notations for structural schemas in various problem domains. We ignore the differences in detail and propose here a general technique for specifying structured systems in the UTOPIST language.

First of all, a list of typical blocks must be made and every block on the list must be specified as a concept. In general, a block B has the following specification:

$$B: (x_1: t_1; \ldots; x_m; t_m;$$
$$w_1: s_1; \ldots; w_n: s_n;$$
$$\langle \text{relations} \rangle);$$

where B is name of the block, $x_1, \ldots, x_m$ are parameters of the block, i.e. the variables that are accessible externally, $w_1, \ldots, w_n$ are internal variables of the block. (Some of the parameters and internal variables may be specified as virtual components of the block.)

Specifications of all kinds of blocks represent a problem-oriented language for specifying systems of the particular problem domain. The syntax of the language is the following:

$$\langle \text{system specification} \rangle ::=$$
$$\langle \text{identifier} \rangle : (\langle \text{component specification} \rangle \ldots)$$

⟨component specification⟩ ::=
⟨identifier⟩: ⟨type⟩

$$[\langle \text{parameter} \rangle = \left\{ \begin{array}{l} \langle \text{value} \rangle \\ \langle \text{component} \rangle \\ \langle \text{parameter1} \rangle \end{array} \right\}], \ldots ;$$

⟨parameter⟩ ::= ⟨identifier⟩
⟨component⟩ ::= ⟨identifier⟩
⟨parameter1⟩ ::= ⟨component⟩.⟨parameter⟩
⟨type⟩ ::= $\{A \mid B \mid \ldots \mid C\}$

where $A, B, \ldots, C$ are the names of all possible types of blocks for building a system.

The following constraints are context conditions which must be satisfied for any system specification:

1.   ⟨parameter⟩ in a component specification which has the type B must be a name of some parameter $x_i, i = 1, 2, \ldots, m$ of the block B.

2.   ⟨component⟩ must occur as an ⟨identifier⟩ in a ⟨component specification⟩ before the occurrence of the ⟨component⟩.

3.   In the construction ⟨component⟩.⟨parameter⟩ used as ⟨parameter1⟩ the ⟨parameter⟩ must be some parameter x_i of ⟨component⟩.

Actually, UTOPIST permits some additional syntactic freedom – positional binding of parameters. It can be considered as an acceptable abbreviation.

In addition to this general part of syntax, a description of blocks of a particular language (blocks $A, B, \ldots, C$ in our syntactic rules) must be given. It can be represented in a tabular form – for instance, Table 6.1 represents

Table 6.1   Concepts for the language DIF.

Name	Graphical representation	Parameters	Functions
sum		input1 input2 output	$output = input1 + input2$
mult		input1 input2 output	$output = input1 \times input2$
inv		input output	$output = -\,input$
integrator		input output T init	$output = init + 1/T \displaystyle\int_0^{\tau} input \, d\tau$

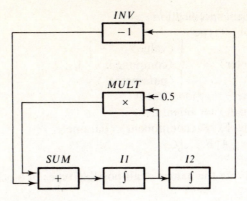

Figure 6.4 An integration problem.

concepts of a language for structural models of ordinary differential equations. Let us call this language DIF.

Implementation of the DIF language is so simple that we present its full specification here.

> **let** DIF:
>> (*sum*: (**virtual** *input1,input2,output*: **numeric**;
>>> *output = input1 + input2*;);
>>
>> *mult*: (**virtual** *input1,input2,output*: **numeric**;
>>> *output = input1 * input2*;);
>>
>> *inv*: (**virtual** *input,output*: **numeric**;
>>> *output = − input*;);
>>
>> *integrator*: (*state*: **numeric**;
>>>> **virtual**
>>>> *input, output, T,*
>>>> *initstate,nextstate*: **numeric**;
>>>> *output = state*;
>>>> *nextstate = state + input/T*;);)

We must bear in mind that the DIF language allows us to specify only the structure of systems of differential equations. We still have to specify the integration process itself, and we shall do this in the next section.

Here we represent the specification of a system whose structure is shown in Figure 6.4.

> **from** DIF;
> **let**
>> *S*: (*I1*: *integrator T = 1*;
>>> *I2*: *integrator T = 0.1, input = I1.output*;
>>> *INV*: *inv input = I2.output*;

$MULT$: $multi$ $input1 = I1.output, input2 = 0.5$;
SUM: sum $input1 = INV.output$,
$\quad input2 = MULT.output$,
$\quad output = I1.input$;);

It is easy to see that blocks *inv*, *mult* and *sum* are superfluous in the DIF language; equations can be used instead of them. A specification of the same problem using equations is even shorter:

SS: ($I1$: $integrator$ $T = 1$;
$\quad I2$: $integrator$ $T = 0.1$, $input = I1.output$;
$\quad I1.input = 0.5 * I1.output - I2.output$;);

However, we can use the blocks *sum, mult, inv* etc. simply because they belong to the language of the domain specialists.

Large systems are sometimes divided, for convenience, into a number of smaller subsystems. For this purpose only the definition of ⟨component specification⟩ needs to be changed:

⟨component specification⟩ ::=

$$\langle identifier \rangle : \begin{cases} \langle type \rangle \\ \langle subsystem \rangle \end{cases} [\langle parameter \rangle = \begin{cases} \langle value \rangle \\ \langle component \rangle \\ \langle parameter\ 1 \rangle \end{cases}], \dots ;$$

A subsystem is specified in exactly the same way as a system, i.e.

⟨subsystem⟩ ::= ⟨system⟩.

Context conditions must now be extended to parameters of subsystems. A new context condition is added: subsystems must be specified before the specification of the system.

Figure 6.5 shows us an example of a subsystem *C1* included into a system *C*. The subsystem is connected with components *K1* and *K2* of the system. These components have types *A* and *B* respectively. Specification of

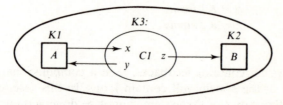

Figure 6.5   The subsystem of a system.

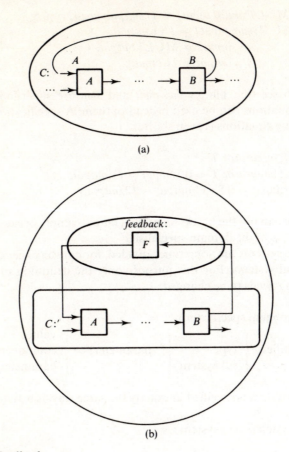

(a)

(b)

Figure 6.6   Feedback.

the system is

let $C1$: $(\ldots x{:}\ldots y{:}\ldots z{:}\ldots)$;
$\quad C$: $(\ldots$
$\qquad K1$: A;
$\qquad K2$: B;
$\qquad K3$: $C1\ x = K1.output$,
$\qquad\qquad\quad y = K1.input$,
$\qquad\qquad\quad z = K2.input$;
$\qquad \ldots)$;

If a system contains feedbacks, then a computational model of the specification of the system will contain loops. In this case, even the computation of the statics of the system cannot be done without simultaneous solution of a system of several equations. In order to simplify this task, we can

specify the feedback explicitly. Let us have a feedback from the block B to the block A in the system C shown in Figure 6.6(a). We transform the system C by adding a new block which explicitly represents the feedback, as shown in Figure 6.6(b).

Now we must introduce a type for the feedback block. Let us regard the whole system C as a system comprising two parts:

F – the block of the feedback,

C' – the remaining part of the system C (C without the feedback).

If the behaviour of the system C is determined by its complete model with feedback, then, obviously, the problem

$A.input \rightarrow B.output$

is solvable on the computational model of the system C'. Let us denote this functional dependency by f, i.e.

$B.output = f(A.input)$.

The feedback block must guarantee the equality $A.input = B.output$, which holds in the original system C. Consequently, the feedback block must solve the equation

$input = f(output)$

where *input* and *output* are input and output parameters of the feedback block:

feedback: (*input,output*: **undefined**;
$\qquad (output \rightarrow input) \rightarrow input, output, (A););$

The program A solves the equation

$input = f(output)$

and assigns the result to its two output variables: *input, output*. The function f is determined by the computational model of the system.

The syntax of the feedback specification is

$\langle$identifier$\rangle$: *feedback*

$$input = \left\{ \begin{array}{l} \langle\text{component}\rangle \\ \langle\text{parameter}\rangle \end{array} \right\}$$

$$output = \begin{cases} \langle component \rangle \\ \langle parameter \rangle \end{cases};$$

If the program A is designed properly, then the concept specified here can be used even for representing multiple feedbacks, because *feedback.input* and *feedback.output* have **undefined** type, and hence can be specified as vectors.

6.2.2 THE CONCEPT OF THE PROCESS

We have discussed the specification of systems without considering the processes which go on in the systems. Processes which go on in blocks can be specified inside the blocks. But besides this, we must specify a concept of the process for the system as a whole, and this process depends explicitly on time.

Let us consider the general equations of dynamics of a system:

$$X' = F(X,U,t),$$
$$V = G(X,U,t),$$

where X is the state of the system at the moment t, X' is the state of the system at the next observable moment of time. U,V are the values of input and output of the system at the moment t. For discrete-time moments $t_1, t_2, t_3, \ldots$ we can rewrite the equations as follows:

$$X_{i+1} = (X_i, U_i, t_i),$$
$$V_i = (X_i, U_i, t_i).$$

We shall also include in the concept of the process the initial time moment $T1$, the final moment of observation of the process $T2$, and time step $DT = T_{i+1} - T_i$ for any two successive moments of observation between $T1$ and $T2$. Let *initstate* be the initial state of the system, *state* – the current state and *nextstate* – the next state, i.e. the state following the current state.

The concept of *process* is

process:
   (*model*: **undefined**;
    T1,T2,DT: **numeric**;
    initstate,state,nextstate: **space**;
    result: **space**;

  ∗ value of the result is a representation of the process, for instance,
  ∗ a table or a graph etc.

    model.**all**.*initstate* → *initstate* (CONSTR);
    model.**all**.*nextstate* → *nextstate* (CONSTR);

$state \rightarrow model.\textbf{all}.state$ (DISTR);
$procrel: (state \rightarrow nextstate), T1, T2, DT, initstate \rightarrow result$
      (PROCESS););

The first two relations of this concept are needed to construct state vectors for the initial state and for the next state from the components distributed between the blocks of the model. The third relation works in the opposite way and distributes the components of the current state vector among the blocks of the model.

A significant assumption is that the states of all building blocks of systems are denoted in one and the same way. The names of initial state, current state and the state computed must be *initstate*, *state* and *nextstate* respectively. We have already used this agreement in the specification of *integrator* in Section 6.2.1.

The concept of *process* specified above is applicable for modelling processes with a constant time step. In the simplest case the program PROCESS only performs one assignment

$state := nextstate;$

Such a program is suitable for modelling stationary systems with independent behaviour of components, i.e. those systems where the next state of any component depends only on the variables of this component.

But the program PROCESS can also contain more specific computations. For instance, it may take into account some balance of resources hidden in the state vector. Such programs are needed for the modelling of demographic and ecological systems.

Structural models of systems of ordinary differential equations are of the type with independent behaviour of components. Hence we can immediately use our concept of process for solving systems of differential equations. Indeed, the integrator is a block the output of which at time t must be

$$output = initstate + 1/T \int_{T_1}^{t} input(t) \, \mathrm{d}t.$$

Euler's integration method with $Dt = 1$ gives us immediately, for $t = T1 + n$,

$$output_n = state_n$$

$$state_{n+1} = nextstate_n = initstate + \frac{1}{T} \sum_{i=T_1}^{n} input_i$$

$$= initstate + \frac{1}{T} \sum_{i=T_1}^{n-1} input_i + \frac{1}{T} input_n$$

$$= state_n + \frac{1}{T} input_n.$$

These are exactly the equations we have specified in the concept *integrator* in Section 6.2.1. Now we can write a complete program for modelling processes in the system shown in Figure 6.4. Let us have the following time parameters $T1 = 0, T2 = 50, DT = 1$ and the initial states of integration $I1.initstate = 1$, $I2.initstate = 0$. Then the program is

> **program** *integration*;
> **let** S: ($I1$: *integrator* $T = 1, initstate = 1$;
> $I2$: *integrator* $T = 0.1, initstate = 0$;
> $I1$: *input* $= 0.5 * I1.output - I2.output$;);
> R: *process model* $= S, T1 = 0, T2 = 50, DT = 1$;
> **actions**
> $R \vdash result$;
> **end**;

In practice it is useful to specify more types of blocks to simulate dynamic systems. The blocks with various transfer functions can be specified completely in UTOPIST using the concept *integrator* as a basic part of the specifications.

6.3 Stochastic modelling

Stochastic modelling can be considered as a particular kind of simulation. It is a multistep process. At every step of this process realizations (values) of a number of stochastic variables are generated and, using these values, the computations are performed on a model. The results of a computation constitute an observation. A set of observations constitutes a selection which is handled using statistical methods. The concept of process that we have described could be directly used in stochastic modelling. Nevertheless, we specify a new concept called *experiment*, and demonstrate some new simulation facilities on it.

> *experiment*:
>   *selection*: **space**;
>   **virtual**
>   *observation*: **space**;
>   *step_number*: **numeric**;
>   *number_of_steps*: **numeric**;
>   *model*: **undefined**;
>   *step_number* $\rightarrow$ *model.**all**. step_number* (DISTR1);
>   *modelling*: (*step_number* $\rightarrow$ *observation*),
>   *number_of_steps* $\rightarrow$ *selection* (MC););

The relation *modelling* fills in a table that becomes the value of *selection*.

Every row of the table is a value of *observation* together with the *step_number* when the observation is made. The value of *step_number* is distributed among the components of the model and it is used in the model to generate new values of stochastic variables. These values are generated using random-number generators. Let us specify generators for several distributions.

> *Gauss*:
>> (*value*: **numeric**;
>>> **virtual**
>>>> *mean, dispersion*: **numeric**;
>>>> *step_number*: **numeric**;
>>>> *step_number, mean, dispersion* $\rightarrow$ *value* (GAUSS););

The program GAUSS generates a random number at its every call. The values generated have normal distribution with given mean value and dispersion. There is no dependence of value on *step_number*, the latter is used only for triggering the random-number generator.

> *even*:
>> (*value*: **numeric**;
>>> **virtual**
>>> *step_number*: **numeric**;
>>> *from, to*: **numeric**;
>>> *mean, density*: **numeric**;
>>> *mean* = (*from* + *to*)/2;
>>> *density* * (*to* − *from*) = 1;
>>> *step_number, from,to* $\rightarrow$ *value* (EVEN););

This concept differs from the previous one only in the shape of the distribution. The program EVEN generates random numbers evenly distributed in the interval (*from,to*). This interval can be given also by the mean value and density of the distribution.

Other distributions, including multidimensional distributions, can be defined analogously.

It is convenient to have a special concept for describing statistical methods:

> *statistics*:
>> (*selection*: **space**;
>> *hystogram*: **space**;
>> *linear_regression*: **space**;
>> *standard_analysis*: **space**;
>> *mean, dispersion*: **numeric**;
>>> *r1*: *selection* $\rightarrow$ *hystogram* (STAT1);

r2: *selection* → *linear_regression* (STAT2);
r3: *_selection* → *standard_analysis* (STAT3);
r4: *selection* → *mean, dispersion* (STAT4););

The relations here represent common statistical subroutines. We can also include output procedures in the programs STAT1,...,STAT4, and this concept can be used then as an output concept in programs of statistical modelling.

Let us apply the concept *statistics* to computing the mean value of current in the parallel connection of branches with randomly varying resistances. The distributions of resistances are normal distributions.

```
program montecarlo;
let S: (R1,R2: res;
    X: par R1,R2,U = 10;
    G1: Gauss mean = 16, dispersion = 0.1;
    G2: Gauss mean = 5, dispersion = 0.5;
    R1.r = G1;
    R2.r = G2;);
    E: experiment model = S, observation = S.X.i,
        number_of_steps = 50;
    E1: statistics E.selection;
actions
    montecarlo⊢ E1.mean;
end;
```

6.4 Optimization

We shall consider a fairly general problem of optimization here and define a general concept of optimization, which will be specified later in more detail. Let us have a set G in some space and real function F which is defined at least on G. The goal is to find an element of G where the function F has minimal (or maximal) value. Let us assume that the set G is determined by a predicate P:

$$G = \{X \mid P(X)\}.$$

We are interested in the situation where F and P are computable on a model of some object (or system). We shall therefore include in the concept of optimization the component *model*. We also assume that the model, in its turn, contains components F,P and X. The latter denotes the variable that must be varied and represents a point of the space containing the set G. In this way we get the most general definition of optimization with constraints:

optimization:
   (virtual
   model: **undefined**;

XM: **undefined**;
$(model.X \rightarrow model.F, model.P) \rightarrow XM(\text{OPT1});)$;

In practice, there are several problems connected with finding the optimal value of a function. First of all, the initial approximation must be found. We shall denote by $X0$ the element of the set G from which the search can be started. Besides this, a number of parameters describing acceptable accuracy, search strategies etc. are needed. We shall denote by e the tuple of these parameters and assign the type **space** to this tuple. Types of F and P are also known, therefore we can specify F and P as components of the concept of optimization. This facilitates typechecking when problems are specified. We include also a component for maximal value of the function into the new concept and denote it by FM.

$optimization1$:
   (**virtual**
     $model$: **undefined**;
      e: **space**;
     $X0, XM$: **undefined**;
     FMF: **numeric**;
      P: **boolean**;
      $F = model.F$;
      $P = model.P$;
   $(X \rightarrow F,P), X0, e \rightarrow XM, FM \ (\text{OPT2});)$;

Even this concept of optimization is far from being complete. First, the parameter e can be specified more precisely. Second, sometimes it is useful to use an external program in the optimization algorithm to compute the gradient of the function F at the point X. We represent the gradient by the component

   $grad$: **space**;

assuming that the program of optimization is able to use it according to the following axiom:

   $(X \rightarrow P, F, grad), X0, e \rightarrow XM, FM \ (\text{OPT3})$;

In practice, different optimization programs are needed for solving different optimization problems. They can be specified in separate concepts. But we can also put them together into one concept as shown below, adding a component $problem\_type$ for choosing the right program.

$optimization2$:
   ($model$: **undefined**;
    $problem\_type$: **text**;
    $X0, X$: **undefined**;

F,FM: **numeric**;
P: **boolean**;
parameters: **space**;
grad: **space**;
$P = model.P$;
$F = model.F$;
model $\rightarrow$ *problem_type* (Se);
if *problem_type* = 'type1' **then**
$(X \rightarrow F,P,grad), X0, parameters \rightarrow XM,FM$ (OPT4)
elif *problem_type* = 'type2' **then**
$(X \rightarrow F,P,grad),X0,parameters \rightarrow XM,FM$ (OPT5)
...

else
$(X \rightarrow F,P),X0,parameters \rightarrow XM,FM$ (OPTM););

This concept contains a relation for finding *problem_type* for a given model, and it contains relations for various optimization techniques.

6.5 Compiler construction

The designing of a new language (either a programming language or a problem-oriented and nonprocedural language) always begins with the definition of the semantics of the language. We presented examples of designs for a specification language of electric circuits, for a system simulation language and also for a language of databases. In these cases the semantics of the languages was represented almost completely in UTOPIST. But the syntax of these languages was predefined – it was an extension of the syntax of the UTOPIST language. It could be adapted to the requirements of a domain specialist only by means of macro techniques.

When a classical approach to the language design is taken, then the semantics of a language is only roughly designed before syntactic design. Precise specification of the syntax of the language is usually the first clearly written document about the language. As a rule, syntax is presented by means of some kind of context-free grammar with definite restrictions on the grammar applied for efficiency of parsing. Contextual conditions for expressing context-dependent properties of the language are also used. Not until this has been done is the semantics designed precisely. As a result, the semantics is bound to syntax and becomes dependent on it.

Let us assume that the semantics of a text written in a language we are interested in can be represented as a single semantic value. For example, for a program written in a programming language such a value may be object code compiled from the source text. Compilation of the semantic value of a text is a difficult task, because this value must be built from 'pieces of semantics' belonging to syntactic structures of the syntactic (parsing) tree of the text.

Despite the difficulty of this classical approach to language design, it is widely used, and a class of grammars (attribute grammars) is developed for representing and implementing the semantics of programming languages within the framework of this approach. The method of attribute grammars enables us to implement a significant part of semantics automatically. This method can be easily applied for automatic compiler construction by means of the structural synthesis of programs.

Depending on the implementation schema, i.e. whether dynamic or static planning of attribute calculations is applied, the UTOPIST compiler is used either as the semantic part of the compiler of the language implemented, or as a semantic constructor, i.e. as a part of a compiler-writing system.

6.5.1 ATTRIBUTE MODELS OF PRODUCTIONS

Let us recall the definition of the context-free (CF) grammar. CF grammar is a quadruple $(V_N,\ V_T, P, S_0)$, where V_N is a finite set of symbols, called nonterminal symbols, denoting syntactic constructions; V_T is a set of symbols, called terminal symbols, for building texts of the language; S_0 is a nonterminal symbol called the initial symbol, which denotes a complete text of the language; P is a set of productions of the form

$$s \leftarrow x,$$

where $s \in V_N, x \in V \cup (V \times V) \cup (V \times V \times V) \cup \cdots, V = V_N \cup V_T.$

Now we can define the attribute grammar. Let A be a set of abstract objects called attribute types. Values of these objects will be semantic values of constructions of the language. Let us have a mapping

$$attr: V \rightarrow A$$

which associates an abstract object with every symbol from V.

Let us consider an arbitrary production $p \in P$. It has the form $p: s \leftarrow x_1 x_2 \ldots x_k$, where $k \geqslant 1$, $s \in V_N$, $x_i \in V$, $i = 1, 2, \ldots, k$. We build the following object for the production p:

> *mp*:
>   (*res*: s';
>   **virtual**
>   *C1*: x'_1;
>   *C2*: x'_2;
>   ...
>   *Ck*: x'_k;
>   ⟨relations⟩);

where relations express the semantics associated with the production p and

$s', x'_1, \ldots, x'_k$ are the following abstract objects:

$$s' = attr(s), x'_1 = attr(x_1), \ldots, x'_k = attr(x_k).$$

The object mp is called the **attribute model** of the production p. Selecting properly attribute types and associating with every production $p \in P$ its attribute model mp we can represent the computability of semantic values of every production.

An **attribute grammar** is a quintuple (V_N, V_T, A, M, S_0), where V_N, V_T, S_0 and P are defined as above, A is a set of attribute types, M is a set of pairs (p, mp) where $p \in P$ and mp is the attribute model of p.

It is said that an attribute grammar is correct if for any syntactically correct text it is possible to compute the semantic value of the text.

6.5.2 THE ATTRIBUTE MODEL OF A TEXT

Let us consider a parsing tree of a text defined by a CF grammar. There are terminal symbols in terminal nodes of the tree, and a production is in every other node. The shape of the tree is determined by the productions, as shown in Figure 6.7 for the node with the production

$$s \leftarrow x_1, x_2 \ldots x_k.$$

This node has k descendants, each one corresponding to a symbol x_j, $i = 1, 2, \ldots, k$, and if the symbol x_j is a nonterminal, then the descendant node has a production rule with the left-hand side x_j.

We start building the attribute model of a text by associating an attribute model with every incidence of a production in the parsing tree and denoting the models by mutually different names. Thereafter we bind attribute models of all incidences of productions occurring in the parsing tree into one semantic model. Let us consider a pair of symbols s, x_i such that

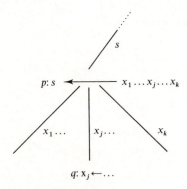

Figure 6.7   A representation of a production.

$p: s \leftarrow x_1 \ldots x_i \ldots x_k$, and $q: x_i \leftarrow y_1 \ldots y_m$ and q belongs to a descendant of the node of the production p. The attribute model mp' of the node p contains a component c_i which corresponds to the symbol x_i in p. The attribute model mq' of the node q has a component res that belongs to the same symbol x_i in q. Consequently, the types of $mp'.c_i$ and $mq'.res$ are identical. From the parsing tree we can conclude that both objects $mp'.c_i$ and $mq'.res$ represent one and the same incidence of the symbol x_i; hence these objects represent one and the same semantic value, and we can write $mp'.c_i = mq'.res$. Such an equation must be written for every descendant of the tree. We finish building the attribute model of the text by adding these equations to attribute models of incidences of productions of the parsing tree.

A problem

$$sem \vdash prog.res;$$

is solvable for any syntactically correct text in any correct attribute grammar, where sem is the attribute model of the text and $prog$ is the name of the attribute model of the incidence of the production

$$s_0 \leftarrow x_1, x_2 \ldots x_m$$

associated with the root of the parsing tree.

The attribute model of a text can be built automatically from the given parsing tree of the text and attribute models of productions. This is done in the following three steps:

1. label the nodes of the parsing tree with numbers in such a way that the label of any node is greater than those of its descendants;

2. specify terminal nodes of the tree in the order of labelling of the nodes, writing for a node with the label l and with the terminal symbol x the specification

$$n_l: x';$$

where $x' = attr(x)$;

3. specify nonterminal nodes of the tree in the order of labelling of the nodes, writing for a node with the label l and with the production $p: s \leftarrow x_1, x_2 \ldots x_k$ the specification

$$n_l: mp \; c_1 = n_{i1}, \ldots, c_k = n_{ik};$$

where $n_{i1}, \ldots, n_{ik}$ are names of the models of the descendant nodes of the node i, corresponding to the symbols $x_1, x_2, \ldots, x_k$ of the production p. For the root of the tree (which is the node with the greatest label) use the name $prog$ instead of n_l.

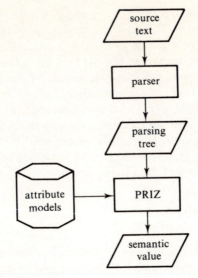

Figure 6.8   A semantic processor.

If the name of the whole model is *sem*, then the problem statement

  sem ⊢ *prog.res*;

gives the result of compilation. This is the technique for using the PRIZ system as a semantic processor of a language represented by an attribute grammar. Figure 6.8 shows the place of the PRIZ system in a compiler where this technique is used.

Let us consider another way of implementing the attribute grammar, using an example. In this case we shall build an interpreter for a specification language of electrical circuits. The semantic value of a complete text is the resistance of the circuit specified by the text.

The syntax of the language is

  p1: ⟨schema⟩ ← *par* (⟨schema⟩, ⟨schema⟩)
  p2: ⟨schema⟩ ← *ser* (⟨schema⟩, ⟨schema⟩)
  p3: ⟨schema⟩ ← *resistor* (⟨number⟩).

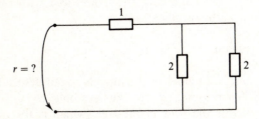

Figure 6.9   An example of a circuit.

We drop the definition of ⟨number⟩, and assume that its semantic value is the value of the number.

The attribute models of the production rules are

> *mp1*: (*res*: **numeric**;
>   **virtual**
>   *c1*: **numeric**;
>   *c2*: **numeric**;
> $1/res = 1/c1 + 1/c2$;);
> *mp2*: (*res*: **numeric**;
>   **virtual**
>   *c1*: **numeric**;
>   *c2*: **numeric**;
> $res = c1 + c2$;);
> *mp3*: (*res*: **numeric**;
>   **virtual**
>   *c1*: **numeric**;
> $res = c1$;);

The schema shown in Figure 6.9 has the following specifications in this language:

> *ser (resistor*(1), *par(resistor*(2), *resistor* (2))).

The parsing tree of this text is represented in Figure 6.10. Using the algorithm given above for building attribute models of texts we can build the following attribute model:

> *sem*: (*n1*: *mp3 res = 1*;
>   *n2*: *mp3 res = 2*;

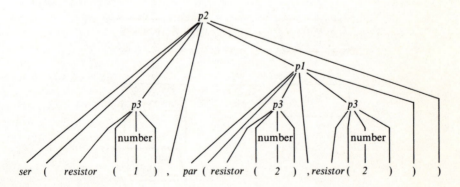

Figure 6.10   A parsing tree.

$n3: mp3\ res = 2;$
$n4: mp1\ c1 = n2, c2 = n3;$
$prog\ mp2\ c1 = n1, c2 = n4;);$

We have omitted, for brevity, specifications of terminal nodes here and have inserted numeric values of resistors directly into the amendments.

The program

```
program attr;
  let sem: (...);
  actions
  sem ⊢ prog.res;
  end;
```

gives the correct result $prog.res = 2$.

6.5.3 THE ATTRIBUTE MODEL OF A LANGUAGE

In this section our goal is to develop an attribute model of a language, which can be used for automatic synthesis of the semantic part of a compiler or interpreter for the language. The synthesized program must have a parsing tree as an input, and it must build the semantic value of any syntactically correct program written in the language. In this case the PRIZ system is used

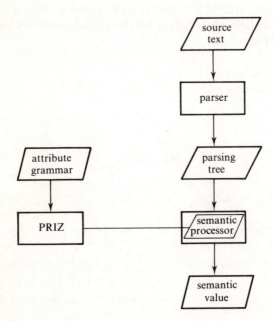

Figure 6.11 A compiler-writing system.

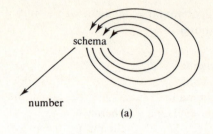

(a)

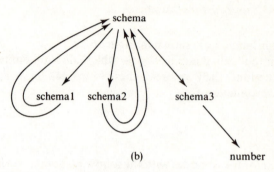

(b)   number

Figure 6.12   Syntactic graphs of a language.

as a constructor of semantic parts of compilers or interpreters as shown in Figure 6.11.

Let us consider the language of electric circuits again. We present the syntax of the language in the form of a (multi)graph shown in Figure 6.12(a). Nodes of the graph correspond to nonterminal symbols of the language. For any occurrence of a nonterminal symbol x_i in the right-hand part of a production

$$p: s \leftarrow x_1 \ldots x_i \ldots x_k$$

there is an arc (x_i, s) from x_i to s in the graph. Let us call a production primitive if it has the form $s \leftarrow x$, where x is a single symbol, and nonprimitive otherwise.

If there are several nonprimitive productions with one and the same symbol s in the left-hand part, then we split the symbol into several symbols so that no symbol will occur more than once in left-hand parts of nonprimitive productions. For our language we must split the symbol ⟨schema⟩ into three symbols – let us call them ⟨schema1⟩, ⟨schema2⟩ and ⟨schema3⟩. At the same time we add new primitive productions

⟨schema⟩ ← ⟨schema1⟩
⟨schema⟩ ← ⟨schema2⟩
⟨schema⟩ ← ⟨schema3⟩

making the transformed grammar equivalent to the initial grammar. As a result we obtain the grammar

$$\langle schema \rangle \leftarrow \langle schema1 \rangle$$
$$\langle schema \rangle \leftarrow \langle schema2 \rangle$$
$$\langle schema \rangle \leftarrow \langle schema3 \rangle$$
$$\langle schema1 \rangle \leftarrow par\,(\langle schema \rangle, \langle schema \rangle)$$
$$\langle schema2 \rangle \leftarrow ser\,(\langle schema \rangle, \langle schema \rangle)$$
$$\langle schema3 \rangle \leftarrow resistor\,(\langle number \rangle).$$

The graph of this language is shown in Figure 6.12(b).

If the graph still contains loops which do not contain nodes for primitive productions, then we break these loops, taking away any node of the loop with a production

$$p\colon s \leftarrow x_1 \ldots x_k$$

and substituting for it two nodes with the following two productions:

$$p'\colon s' \leftarrow x_1 \ldots x_k$$
$$p''\colon s \leftarrow s'.$$

Obviously, this transformation of the grammar does not influence the language specified by the grammar.

We must also transform attribute models of production rules. For every rule $p\colon s \leftarrow x_1 \ldots x_m$ we rewrite its attribute model

$$mp\colon (res\colon s'$$
$$\quad c_1\colon x';$$
$$\quad c_m\colon x'_m;$$
$$\quad \langle relations \rangle);$$

as follows:

$$mp_0\colon (synt\colon (res\colon s'; \ldots);$$
$$\quad\quad inh\colon (\ldots););$$

where inh contains those components c_i which, for any parsing tree, can be computed from the models of the nodes which are higher in the tree than the node for p; $synt$ contains, besides res, those components c_i which, for any parsing tree, can be computed lower than the node p or in the attribute model of p itself. The question remains whether this restructuring is possible at all. This question is answered for various classes of attribute grammar in Penjam

(1983). In our case the restructuring gives us

$mp1_0$: ($synt$: ($res,c1,c2$: **numeric**;);
      inh: **space**;
      $1/synt.res = 1/c1 + 1/c2$;);
$mp2_0$: ($synt$: $res,c1,c2$: **numeric**;);
      inh: **space**;
      $synt.res = synt.c1 + synt.c2$;);
$mp3_0$: ($synt$: ($res,c1$: **numeric**;);
      inh: **space**;
      $synt.res = synt.c1$;);

For any symbol s that appears in the left-hand part of several primitive productions

$s \leftarrow s_1$;
$s \leftarrow s_2$;
$\vdots$
$s \leftarrow s_m$;

we build an additional attribute model:

mp_s: ($synt$: res: s';);
    c_1: s'_1;
    $\ldots$
    c_m: s'_m;
    inh: **space**;
    $(c_1.inh \rightarrow c_1.synt), \ldots, (c_m.inh \rightarrow c_m.synt), inh \rightarrow$
        $synt.res$ (A););

Depending on the value of the variable inh the program A selects one of the subproblems ($c_i.inh \rightarrow c_i.synt$) and, solving it, finds the value of $synt.res$ which is equal to the value of $c_i.synt$. The value of the variable inh is taken from the parsing tree. It shows which syntactic alternative is actually used. In this case all programs, including the program A, must be re-enterable, because in the process of solving a subproblem the program A (and some other programs) may be called several times.

Union of the attribute models of all productions of the grammar now gives us the semantic model of the language. If we call this model sem, then the execution of the problem statement

$sem \vdash m. inh \rightarrow m. res$

gives us the compiler or interpreter for the language, where m is the attribute model of the production for s_0.

Actually, there are quite interesting new results in the field of automatic compiler construction, obtained by means of this technique. These results are represented in Penjam (1980, 1983).

Appendix A
Proof of SSR Completeness

Intuitionistic logic in general does not allow the transformation of formulae into disjunctive normal form, but it still allows simplification by the introduction of new variables. We use this to reduce arbitrary propositional formulae to the equivalent LL-form. We denote by $F_X[G]$ (or $F[G]$) the result of substituting G for X in F. For any sequents S and T, the notation $S \underset{\text{ded}}{=} T$ means that S and T are deductively equivalent, i.e. the derivability of S implies the derivability of T and vice versa.

LEMMA 1

(a) $\Gamma \vdash F[E] \underset{\text{ded}}{=} (X \longleftrightarrow E), \Gamma \vdash F[X]$.

(&) $\Gamma \vdash F[G \mathbin{\&} H] \underset{\text{ded}}{=} (X \to G), (X \to H), (G \to (H \to X))$,
  $\Gamma \vdash F[X]$.

($\to$) $\Gamma \vdash F[G \to H] \underset{\text{ded}}{=} (X \to (G \to H)), ((G \to H) \to X)$,
  $\Gamma \vdash F[X]$.

($\vee$) $\Gamma \vdash F[G \vee H] \underset{\text{ded}}{=} (X \to (G \vee H)), (G \to X), (H \to X)$,
  $\Gamma \vdash F[X]$.

($\longleftrightarrow$) $\Gamma \vdash F[G \longleftrightarrow H] \underset{\text{ded}}{=}$
  $(X \to (G \to H)), (X \to (H \to G)), ((G \to H) \to$
  $((H \to G) \to X)), \Gamma \vdash F[X]$,

where E is any formula and X is a new variable occurring only to the right of $\underset{\text{ded}}{=}$.

Proof

(a) The left-to-right implication follows from the equivalence replacement theorem $(X \longleftrightarrow E) \to (F[X] \longleftrightarrow F[E])$.

230

The inverse implication follows by the substitution of E for X on the right-hand side.

The remaining clauses of the lemma are obtained from clause (a) after the replacement of E by $G \& H, G \to H$, etc. using the fact that the formula $X \longleftrightarrow E$ becomes equivalent to the conjunction of formulae to the right of $\underset{\text{ded}}{=}$.

The following lemma is suggested by the second-order equivalences

$$(p \vee q) \longleftrightarrow \forall x((p \to x) \to ((q \to x) \to x))$$

and

$$\bot \longleftrightarrow \forall xx,$$

where the constant $\bot$ denotes falsity.

LEMMA 2

(a) $F[\bot] \underset{\text{ded}}{=} L \longleftrightarrow (K \& Z) \vdash F(L),$

where K is the conjunction of all propositional variables on the left-hand side, and L, Z are new variables.

(b) $\Gamma, (X \to B \vee C) \vdash F \underset{\text{ded}}{=} \Gamma, (X \to K) \vdash F,$

where K is the conjunction

$$\underset{Z}{\&}((B \to Z) \to ((C \to Z) \to Z))$$

over all variables Z on the left-hand side, provided L does not occur there and $\vee$ occurs only to the left of $\vdash$ in formulae of the form $W \to U \vee V$; U, V, W being variables.

The proof of Lemma 2 is presented in Appendix B, where the normal form theorem is considered.

Note The transformations described in Lemmas 1 and 2 expand the size of sequents quadratically at most. If the transformations 2(b) are not applied, then the increase is linear at most, and the general structure of the derivation is preserved.

THEOREM 1

Any propositional formula A is deductively equivalent to the sequent $A_1, A_2, \ldots, A_k \vdash V$, where V is a variable and each A_i is a variable or a formula of LL.

Proof

Use Lemmas 1 and 2.

THEOREM 2

Any intuitionistically derivable formula of LL is derivable by the structural synthesis rules.

A proof of the theorem, using a long normal form theorem, is presented in Mints and Tyugu (1982) – see also Appendix B.

Now we have established the completeness of the structural synthesis theories. The LL language enables us to encode any intuitionistic propositional formula, and the set of SSR rules is sufficient to derive any intuitionistically derivable LL formula.

Appendix B

Natural Deduction and Normal Form of Derivations

NATURAL DEDUCTION

Propositional formulae are constructed from propositional variables and a constant $\perp$ (falsity) by means of $\rightarrow, \&, \vee$. Negation $\neg$ and equivalence $\longleftrightarrow$ are defined by

$$\neg A \equiv (A \rightarrow \perp), (A \longleftrightarrow B) \equiv ((A \rightarrow B) \& (B \rightarrow A)).$$

The derivable objects are sequents $\Gamma \vdash A$. The axioms have the form $\Gamma, X \vdash X$. There are seven inference rules: one rule for $\perp$ and two rules (introduction and elimination, marked $+$ and $-$, respectively) for each connective:

$$\frac{\Gamma \vdash \perp}{\Gamma \vdash A}(\perp);$$

$$\frac{\Gamma \vdash A_1 \& A_2}{\Gamma \vdash A_i}(\&^-), \quad i = 1, 2; \qquad \frac{\Gamma \vdash A; \Sigma \vdash B}{\Gamma, \Sigma \vdash (A \& B)}(\&^+);$$

$$\frac{\Gamma \vdash A \rightarrow B; \Sigma \vdash A}{\Gamma, \Sigma \vdash B}(\rightarrow^-); \qquad \frac{\Gamma, A \vdash B}{\Gamma \vdash (A \rightarrow B)}(\rightarrow^+);$$

$$\frac{\Gamma \vdash A_i}{\Gamma \vdash A_1 \vee A_2}(\vee^+), \quad i = 1, 2; \qquad \frac{\Gamma \vdash A \vee B; A, \Sigma \vdash C; B, \Pi \vdash C}{\Gamma, \Sigma, \Pi \vdash C}(\vee^-).$$

The sequents over the horizontal line are premises, the sequent under the line is a conclusion.

A deduction is a tree of sequents constructed according to the rules and having axioms as leaves.

A deduction is normal if the leftmost premise of any elimination rule either is an axiom or is obtained by ($\rightarrow^-$) or ($\&^-$). The following proposition is known from proof theory.

NORMAL FORM THEOREM

(a)   Any deduction can be transformed into the normal deduction of the same end sequent.

(b)   A normal deduction contains only subformulae of its end sequent. The rules are applied only for the connectives (and constant $\perp$) occurring in the end sequent and they respect the signs of occurrences: introduction rules for positive ones, and elimination rules for negative ones.

A simple additional transformation yields the following extension.

LONG NORMAL FORM THEOREM

Any deduction can be transformed into a normal deduction of the same end sequent when the conclusion of any elimination rule having a form ($A \rightarrow B$) or ($A \& B$) is itself a leftmost premise of an elimination rule.

Proof

Replace in the following way the topmost sequents $\Gamma \vdash A \rightarrow B$ or $\Gamma \rightarrow A \& B$ violating the additional requirements:

$$\frac{\dfrac{\Gamma \vdash A \rightarrow B; A \vdash A}{\Gamma, A \vdash B}}{\Gamma \vdash A \rightarrow B} , \quad \frac{\Gamma \vdash A \& B \quad \Gamma \vdash A \& B}{\Gamma \vdash A \qquad \Gamma \vdash B}{\Gamma \vdash A \& B}.$$

Proof of Lemma 2

(a) If a derivation of $F[\perp]$ is given, assume it contains only variables from $F[\perp]$ (otherwise replace them by $\perp$). Now replace $\perp$ by $K \& Z$.

All applications of the rules except the rule

$$\frac{\Gamma \vdash \perp}{\Gamma \vdash A} \quad \text{for } \perp$$

remain valid. Applications of the rule for $\perp$ can be restored using the implication $K \& Z \rightarrow G$, derivable for any formula G which contains only variables from K. This gives us the derivation of the sequent $F[K \& Z]$. From Lemma 1 we obtain the derivation of $L \longleftrightarrow (K \& Z) \vdash F[L]$.

$F[\bot]$ can be obtained from $L \longleftrightarrow (K \& Z) \vdash F[L]$ by substituting $\bot$ for Z, L, and using the derivability of equivalence $\bot \longleftrightarrow (K \& \bot)$.

(b) Let us note that, from the normal form theorem, for any derivable sequent $\Gamma, (X \to B \vee C) \vdash F$ satisfying the assumptions of the lemma being proved here, a derivation exists where any formula derived by means of the rule $(\vee^-)$ is a variable, and where the rule $(\vee^+)$ is not applied at all. We can change all occurrences of $B \vee C$ in such a proof to K defined above. Only applications of the rule $(\vee^-)$ with the left assumption $\Gamma \vdash B \vee C$ may become invalid in this case. Actually they take the form

$$\frac{\Gamma' \vdash K; \qquad \Sigma', B \vdash Z; \qquad \Pi', C \vdash Z}{\Gamma', \Sigma', \Pi' \vdash Z}$$

which can be easily turned into the required derivation using the monotone replacement theorem. The transition from $\Gamma, (X \to K) \vdash F$ to $\Gamma, (X \to B \vee C) \vdash F$ is done using the same theorem.

Proof of Theorem 2

Consider a deduction in the long normal form of a sequent

$$C_1, \ldots, C_n \vdash (A_1, \ldots, A_k \to A)$$

where C_i are computability statements or variables, and A_j, A are variables. By the normal form theorem the only rules applied are $(\to^-), (\&^-)$ and $(\to^+)$.

It is sufficient to prove the theorem for $k = 0$ since we can replace (1) by $C_1, \ldots, C_n, A_1, \ldots, A_k \vdash A$. Note that the only antecedent members of the sequents in the deduction are C_i and variables, since otherwise the subformula property would be violated. Consider now some uppermost application of an elimination rule in the deduction. Its left premise is an axiom $X \vdash X$, and X should be one of C_i. If this is an unconditional computability statement $B_1, \ldots, B_q \to B$, then (in view of long normality) the part of the deduction down the considered rule is of the form

$$\frac{C_i \vdash B_1 \to (\ldots \to (B_q \to B)\ldots); \qquad \Gamma_1 \vdash B_1}{C_i, \Gamma_1 \vdash B_2 \to (\ldots \to (B_q \to B)\ldots)}, \tag{1}$$

$$\vdots$$

$$\frac{C_i, \Gamma_1, \ldots, \Gamma_{q-1} \vdash B_q \to B; \qquad \Gamma_q \vdash B_q}{C_i, \Gamma_1, \ldots, \Gamma_q \vdash B} \tag{2}$$

and, after deletion of C_i from the antecedent, it is easily transformed into the SSR-form of $(\to^-)$.

If C_i is a conditional computability statement $(\underline{A} \to B) \to (\underline{C} \to D)$,

then the part of the deduction we are interested in is of the form

$$C_i \vdash (\underline{A} \to B) \to (\underline{C} \to D); \qquad \Gamma \vdash (\underline{A} \to B) \tag{3}$$
$$\frac{}{C_i, \underline{\Gamma} \vdash \underline{C} \to D; \qquad \Sigma \vdash C}$$
$$\frac{}{C_i, \Gamma, \Sigma \vdash D}$$

where two lower levels have the same form as (2). Replacing $\underline{A} \to B$ by each $\underline{A} \to B$ in turn, we obtain the derivations of $\Gamma \vdash \underline{A} \to B$. Moving $\underline{A}$ into the antecedent, we obtain the derivations of Γ, $\underline{A} \vdash B$. So (3) can be turned into $(\to^{--})$. Since the applications of introduction rules are possible only inside figures of the form (3), we have established our theorem.

Bibliography

Apresian, Yu. (1978). *Linguistic support of automatic translation system of the third generation*. Moscow: Academy of Sciences of the USSR (Russian)

Babajew, I., Novikov, F. and Petrushina, T. (1981). 'DEKART – input language of the SPORA system.' *Applied Informatics*, **1**. Moscow: Finansy i statistika (Russian)

Bobrow, D. and Winograd, T. (1970). 'An overview of KRL, a knowledge representation language.' *Cognitive Science*, **1** (1), 3–45

Bratko, I. (1986). *Prolog programming for artificial intelligence*. Wokingham: Addison-Wesley

Briabrin, V. (1978). 'The dialogue information logical system.' (Eds. Hayes, J., Michie, D. and Mikulich, L.) *Machine Intelligence*, **9**, 427–442. New York: John Wiley

Chang, C. and Lee, R.C. (1973). *Symbolic logic and mechanical theorem proving*. New York: Academic Press

Clocksin, W. Mellish, C. (1981). *Programming in Prolog*. Berlin: Springer-Verlag

Codd, E.F. (1970). 'A relational model of data for large shared data banks.' *Comm. ACM*, **13** (6), 377–387

Constable, R.L. (1972). Constructive mathematics and automatic program writers.' *Information Processing*, **71**, 733–738. Amsterdam: North-Holland

Dikovski, A. (1985). 'Solving algorithmic problems about synthesis of programs without loops in linear time.' *System Programming and Computer Software*, **3**, 38–49

Fillmore, Ch. (1965). 'Entailment rules in a semantic theory.' *Project on Linguistic Analysis*, **10**, 60–82

Gentzen, G. '1965). 'Untersuchungen über das logische Schliessen I, II.' *Mathematica*, **39**, 176–210

Gödel, K. (1958). 'Über eine bischer noch nicht benützte Erweiteung des finit en Standpunktes.' *Dialectica*, **12** (3/4), 280–287

Goto, S. (1978). 'Program synthesis through Gödel's interpretation.' *Proc. International Conference on Mathematical Studies of Information Processing.* Kyoto, 287–306

Heyting, A. (1934). 'Mathematische Grundlagenforschung, Intuitionismus, Beweistheorie.' *Ergebnisse der Mathematica etc.* **III**, (4). Berlin: Springer-Verlag

Kalja, A. (1982). 'Data base management system DABU.' *Estonian Management Planning Institute.* Tallinn, p. 56 (Russian)

Karzanov, A. and Faradjev, I. (1975). 'Solution planning for problem solving on computational models.' *System Programming and Computer Software,* **4**

Kleene, S. (1952). *Introduction to metamathematics.* Amsterdam: North-Holland

Kolmogorov, A (1932). 'Zur Deutung der Intuitionistischen Logik.' *Mathematica,* **25**, 58–65

Kypp, M. (1986). 'MicroPRIZ – A user friendly problem solver.' *Personal Computers and their Applications,* 29–30. Tallinn: Valgus

Lyndon, R. (1966). *Notes on logic.* Princeton: Van Nostrand

Manna, Z. and Waldinger, R. (1971). 'Towards automatic program synthesis.' *Comm. ACM,* **3**, 151–165

Martin-Löf, P. (1979). 'Constructive mathematics and computer programming.' *Proc. 6th International Congress of Logic, Methodology and Philosophy of Science,* Hanover

Maslov, S. (1964). 'Reverse method of deduction in classical predicate calculus.' *Soviet Math. Dokl.,* **159**, 17–20

Mikulich, L. (1982). 'Natural language dialogue systems: a pragmatic approach.' (Eds. Hayes, J., Michie, D. and Pao, Y.-H.) *Machine Intelligence,* **10**, 383–396. New York: John Wiley

Minsky, M. (Ed.). (1968). *Semantic information processing.* Cambridge: MIT Press

Minsky, M. (1975). 'A framework for representing knowledge.' (Ed. Winston, P.) *The psychology of computer vision.* New York: McGraw-Hill

Mints, G. (1977). 'E-theorems.' *Journal of Soviet Mathematics,* **8**, 323–329. New York

Mints, G. and Tyugu, E. (1982). 'Justification of the structural synthesis of programs.' *Science of Computer Programming,* **2** (3), 215–240

Mints, G. and Tyugu, E. (1987). 'The programming system PRIZ.' *Journal of Symbolic Computation,* (4)

Nariniani, A. (Ed.) (1978). *Man–machine natural language interface.* Novosibirsk: Computing Center of the Acad. Sci. (Russian)

Nepeivoda, N. (1978). 'Correspondence between natural deduction rules and statements of algorithmic languages.' *Soviet Math. Dokl.,* **239** (4), 526–529

Nepeivoda, N. (1981). 'The logical approach to programming.' *Algorithms in Modern Mathematics and Computer Science, Lecture Notes in Computer Science,* **122**, 261–289. Berlin: Springer-Verlag

Pahapill, J. (1985). 'Programmpaket zur Modellierung der hydromachinen Systeme.' *6. Fachtagung Hydraulik und Pneumatik*, Magdeburg, 609–617

Penjam, J. (1980). 'Realization of attributive semantics.' *Cybernetics*, **16** (2), 199–206

Penjam, J. (1983), 'Synthesis of semantic processors from an attribute grammar.' *System Programming and Computer Software*, **9** (1), 29–39

Polya, G. (1946). *How to solve it. A new aspect of mathematical method.* Princeton, NJ: University Press

Popov, E. (1982). *Man–machine interface on a restricted natural language.* Moscow: Nauka Publishers (Russian)

Pospelov, D. (1974). *Large systems (situational control).* Moscow: Nauka Publishers (Russian)

Raphael, B. (1964). 'A computer program which "understands".' *Proc. Fall ICC AFIPS*, 577–590

Roberts, R.B. and Goldstein, I. (1978). *FRL manual*, Report no. 409, AI Lab. Cambridge: MIT Press

Robinson, J. (1965). 'A machine-oriented logic based on the resolution principle.' *Journal of the ACM*, **12**, 23–41

Sato, M. (1979). 'Towards a mathematical theory of program synthesis.' *Proc. IJCAI*, **6**, 757–762

Tyugu, E. (1970). 'Problem solving on computational models.' *Journal Applied Math. and Mathematical Physics*, **10** (Russian)

Tyugu, E. (1972). 'A data base and problem solver for computer-aided design.' *Information Processing*, **71**. 1046–1049 Amsterdam: North-Holland

Tyugu, E. (1977). 'A programming system with automatic program synthesis.' (Eds. Ershov, A. and Koster, C.H.A.) *Methods of Algorithmic Language Implementation, Lecture Notes in Computer Science*, **47**, 251–267. Berlin: Springer-Verlag

Tyugu, E. (1979). 'A computational problem solver.' (Eds. Hayes, J., Michie, D. and Mikulich, L.) *Machine Intelligence*, **9**, 211–224. New York: John Wiley

Tyugu, E. (1980). 'Towards practical synthesis of programs.' *Information Processing*, **80**, 207–219. Amsterdam: North-Holland

Tyugu, E. (1981). 'The structural synthesis of programs.' *Algorithms in Modern Mathematics and Computer Science, Lecture Notes in Computer Science*, **122**, 261–289. Berlin: Springer-Verlag

Tyugu, E. (1986). *Logic programming beyond PROLOG.* Turing Institute Rep.

Tyugu, E., Grigorenko, V. and Sotnikova, N. (1982). 'Optimal design of power semiconductor devices.' *Computers in Industry*, **3** (4), 261–270

Tyugu, E. and Harf, M. (1981). 'Algorithms of structural synthesis of programs.' *System Programming and Computer Software*, **4**, 3–13

Volozh, B., Matskin, M., Mints, G. and Tyugu, E. (1982). 'Theorem proving with the aid of a program synthesizer.' *Cybernetics*, **6**, 63–70

Yavorski, B. and Detlaf, A. (1977). *Physics handbook.* Moscow: Nauka Publishers (Russian)

Index

DATE DUE

NOV 03 1988			
Danen			

DEMCO 38-297